Postcolonial Encounters

The series debates the making of contemporary culture and politics in a postcolonial world.

Volumes explore the impact of colonial legacies, precolonial traditions and current global and imperial forces on the everyday lives of citizens. Reaching beyond postcolonial countries to the formation of external ethnic and migrant diasporas, the series critically theorises

- the active engagement of people themselves in the creation of their own political and cultural agendas
- the emerging predicaments of local, national and transnational identities and subjectivities
- the indigenous roots of nationalism, communalism, state violence and political terror
- the cultural and religious counter-movements for or against emancipation and modernity
- the contradictions in the argumentative imagination of post-colonialism
- the social struggles over the imperatives of human and citizenship rights within the moral and political economy.

Arising from the analysis of decolonization and recolonization, the series opens out a significant space in a growing inter-disciplinary literature. The convergence of interest is very broad, from anthropology, cultural studies, social history, comparative literature, development, sociology, law, and political theory. No single theoretical orientation provides the dominant thrust. Instead, the series responds to the challenge of a commitment to empirical, in-depth research as the motivation for critical theory.

The series is published in association with the International Centre for Contemporary Cultural Research (ICCCR).

Postcolonial Identities in Africa

edited by

RICHARD WERBNER AND
TERENCE RANGER

Zed Books Ltd
LONDON & NEW JERSEY

Postcolonial Identities in Africa was first published by
Zed Books Ltd, 7 Cynthia Street, London N1 9JF, UK,
and 165 First Avenue, Atlantic Highlands, New Jersey
07716, USA in 1996.

Cover designed by Andrew Corbett
Set in Monotype Garamond by Ewan Smith
Printed and bound in the United Kingdom
by Biddles Ltd, Guildford and King's Lynn

A catalogue record for this book is available from the
British Library

US CIP data is available from the Library of Congress

ISBN 1 85649 415 2 cased
ISBN 1 85649 416 0 limp

Contents

Acknowledgements

This book grew from the second Inter-University Colloquium hosted by the International Centre for Contemporary Cultural Research, Manchester, on behalf of the Standing Committee of University Studies of Africa. The Colloquium was held at Holly Royde House, the University of Manchester, from 13 to 16 May 1994 in co-operation with the Netherlands African Studies Association and the African Studies Centre of Leiden University. Chapters, 1, 2, 5, 7 and 9 were presented in earlier versions at the Colloquium, and the rest were specially commissioned for this volume. Among the participants were Bawa Yamba, Wim van Binsbergen, Mthuli Ncube, Cheryl-Ann Michael, Christopher Davis, Robert Young, Jocelyn Alexander, John McCracken, Arthur Mutambara and Richard Fardon. We wish to thank them and the Fellows of the Centre, David Maxwell, John Hutnyk and Bobby Sayyid, for their efforts in making the Colloquium a forum for constructive debate. We are very grateful also to Philip Gillon and Laura Turney for their help in the preparation of the manuscript.

Contributors

Patrick Chabal is Professor of Lusophone African Studies at King's College London, University of London. He has lived, worked and conducted research in several West and East African countries and has written extensively on the contemporary history, politics and literature of Africa. His books include *Amilcar Cabral* (1983), *Power in Africa* (1992), *The Postcolonial Literature of Lusophone Africa* and the edited volume *Political Domination in Africa* (1986). He is a member of the editorial board of *Politique Africaine* and *Portuguese Studies*.

Donal B. Cruise O'Brien is Professor of Political Studies at the School of Oriental and African Studies, University of London. He is the author of *Saints and Politicians* (1975), (with C. Coulon) *Charisma and Brotherhood in African Islam* (1988), (with J. Dunn and R. Rathbone) *Contemporary West African States* (1989). With his theoretical interest in youth, he recently took a leading part in a major multidisciplinary project on Islam in Modern Africa. He was writer in residence, Rockefeller Foundation, in 1994.

Filip De Boeck is Assistant Professor of Anthropology at the University of Leuven, Belgium. He has conducted extensive field research among the aLuund of south-western Zaire, and is currently studying the impact of diamond trading on rural and urban Zairean life. He has written numerous articles in academic journals and co-edited *Alimentations, traditions et développements en Afrique intertropicale* (1995).

Harri Englund is Honorary Research Fellow at the International Centre for Contemporary Cultural Research, University of Manchester. His initial research has been in the Malawi–Mozambique borderlands, on the basis of which he wrote his PhD thesis, *Brother Against Brother: the Moral Economy of War and Displacement in the Malawi–Mozambique Border* (1995). His present theoretical interests are in popular culture and political consciousness, with a special focus on Malawian youth. He is a member of the international research group, Postcolonial Moralities in the Making – Local and Translocal Innovations in Southcentral Africa.

Cyprian Fisiy holds a post at the World Bank as a social scientist working on social impact assessment and migration planning. Trained as a legal anthropologist at the University of Leiden, he is the author of *Power and Privilege in the Administration of Law: Land Law Reforms and Social Differentiation in Cameroon,* and numerous papers. His research interests include tenure systems, natural resource management, witchcraft and state law, legal and institutional pluralism.

Peter Geschiere is Professor of African Anthropology, University of Leiden. His main theoretical interests are in state formation, anthropology and history, economic anthropology and local politics. He has carried out fieldwork in Tunisia, Cameroon and Senegal. His books include *Village Communities and the State* (1982) and *Old Modes of Production and Capitalist Encroachment* (1985). He is currently directing a multisite and large-scale project on globalisation and the construction of communal identities.

Adeline Masquelier is Assistant Professor of Anthropology at Tulane University. She did her doctoral research in Niger on *bori* spirit possession and the politics of healing. Her interests include medicine, gender, commoditisation and ritual processes in the postcolonial world. She is currently doing research on Islamic fundamentalism, veiling, and discourses of truth and power in Niger and France. She has published articles on spirit possession and is preparing a book about *bori*.

Jessica A. Ogden is Research Fellow in Social Science, ODA Tuberculosis Programme, London School of Hygiene and Tropical Medicine. Her academic distinctions include the Peters Prize (University of Manchester 1991), Hull University Award, Royal Anthropological Institute Sutasoma Award. Among her publications are (with S. Wallman) *Six Approaches to Sex in Context* (1992), and contributions to S. Wallman and others, *Kampala Women Getting By* (1996). Her main research interests are the relationship of identity to health, and socio-cultural approaches to relevant interventions for health and public welfare.

Peter Pels lectures at the Research Centre Religion and Society, University of Amsterdam. His publications include *The Microphysics of Crisis: Contacts between Missionaries and Waluguru in Late Colonial Tanganyika* (1996), *Constructing Knowledge* (edited with L. Noneel, 1991) and *Colonial Ethnographies* (edited with O. Salemink, 1994). He is currently carrying out research on political discourse in colonial Africa and occultism in nineteenth-century Britain.

Terence Ranger is Professor of Race Relations and African Studies, University of Oxford. His most recent books are *Peasant Consciousness and Guerrilla War in Zimbabwe* (1985), *Are We not also Men?* (1995) and the edited volumes, *The Invention of Tradition* (with Eric Hobsbawm, 1983), *Soldiers in Zimbabwe's Liberation War* (with Ngwabi Bhebe, 1995), *Society in Zimbabwe's Liberation War* (with Ngwabi Bhebe, 1995). He is on the board of several academic journals including *Journal of Southern African Studies*, of which he was Chair for fifteen years.

Robert Thornton is Associate Professor of Anthropology at the University of Witwatersrand. His current research includes the transformation of South Africa after Apartheid, cultural difference and the history of anthropology. His most recent book is *The Early Writings of Bronislaw Malinowski* (with Peter Skalink).

Rijk van Dijk is affiliated to the Africa Studies Centre, Leiden, as a member of the project on Globalisation and the Construction of Communal Identities. His curent focus is on Christian fundamentalists in Accra and Kumasi and their relations with diasporic communities in Amsterdam and The Hague. *From Camp to Diplomacy: Metaphors in the Ghanaian Political Economy of Desire* (1995) is his first report on this research. His earlier research in Malawi was on young Puritan preachers, youth movements, social criticism and the opposition to gerontocratic power. A recent publication is 'Fundamentalism and its Moral Geography in Malawi: The Representation of the Diasporic and the Diabolical', *Critique of Anthropology* (1995).

Richard Werbner is Professor of African Anthropology and Director of the International Centre for Contemporary Cultural Research at the University of Manchester. Among his books are *Ritual Passage, Sacred Journey* (1989), and *Tears of the Dead* (1991), for which he received the Amaury Talbot Prize of the Royal Anthropological Institute. He has carried out long-term research in Zimbabwe and Botswana. He is co-editor-in-chief of *Social Analysis* and a member of the editorial board of *Journal of Southern African Studies*, *Cultural Dynamics*, *Journal of Legal Pluralism*, and *Journal of Religion in Africa*.

Multiple identities, plural arenas

Richard Werbner

The story of ethnic difference in Africa threatens to overwhelm the larger debate about postcolonial identity politics across the continent. It is as if an old narrative, once told in terms of tribe and now in terms of ethnicity and ethnogenesis, is still spell-binding. Yet ethnic identities are merely a small fraction of the many identities mobilized in the postcolonial politics of everyday life. This is a simple point, but it leads to a major challenge which our contributions confront. It is the analysis of how, over time, and in a plurality of contested arenas, postcolonial strategies improvise multiple shifting identities.

The convergence of our arguments on the postcolony with those of Achille Mbembe is important, as the following suggests:

> the postcolony is made up not of one coherent 'public space', nor is it determined by any single organizing principle. It is rather a plurality of 'spheres' and arenas, each having its own separate logic yet nonetheless liable to be entangled with other logics when operating in certain specific contexts: hence the postcolonial 'subject' has had to learn to continuously bargain [*marchander*] and improvise. Faced with this ... the postcolonial 'subject' mobilizes not just a single 'identity', but several fluid identities which, by their very nature, must be constantly 'revised' in order to achieve maximum instrumentality and efficacy as and when required. (Mbembe 1992a: 5; on connivance and zombification, see also Stoller 1995)

According to Mbembe, the postcolonial dynamic comes, on the one hand, from the characteristic style of political improvisation. This fits 'a tendency to excess and a lack of proportion' and it also fits 'distinctive ways in which identities are multiplied, transformed and put into circulation' (Mbembe 1992b: 3). On the other hand, that style materialises within 'a series of corporate institutions and a political machinery which, once they are in place, constitute a distinctive regime of violence' (ibid.).

Mbembe carries his argument a step further by taking seriously the obscene laughter *with* and not merely *against* the regime (on postcolonial derision and hollow laughter, see also Bayart 1993: 293). He makes us recognise a link between domination and the grotesque in what he calls the banality of power in the postcolony. He moves our understanding of playfulness in the face of tyranny – be it bureaucratic, charismatic, domestic, nationalist or otherwise close to home – from an overemphasis, in socio-political theory, on resistance to a perception of connivance: 'Precisely because the postcolonial mode of domination is as much a regime of constraints as *a practice of conviviality and a stylistic of connivance* ... the analyst must be attentive to the myriad ways in which ordinary people bridle, trick, and actually *toy* with power instead of confronting it directly' (italics in original; Mbembe 1992a: 22). The smile on the face of the tyrant makes a ubiquitous postcolonial icon standing midway between consensus and coercion.

Anthropologists might find some resonance with Max Gluckman's argument on 'Rituals of Rebellion' (1963). But Gluckman's theoretical interest was in what he regarded as 'an instituted *protest* demanded by sacred tradition, which is seemingly against the established order, yet which aims to bless that order to achieve prosperity' (my italics; 1963: 114). Identities were persuasively formed in support of established value, in Gluckman's view, by open yet highly formalised expression of conflict under specific ritualised conditions.

It is the *toying* with power that takes the postcolony beyond familiar formulations for precolonial or colonial conditions. Mbembe, who himself calls upon Bakhtin, does so only to stand Bakhtin on his head. For Bakhtin, especially when writing at the height of the Stalin era, unofficial humour scoffs at the deity, opposes the official world, unmasks its pretence of reality and opens 'a second world and a second life outside officialdom' (Bakhtin 1984: 6). For Mbembe, however, the divide between official and unofficial collapses into the baroque style of political improvisation in which everyone indulges. To bend Clifford Geertz's colonial *bon mot* (1973) to Mbembe's postcolonial purposes, the wink, and the thick description of the wink, is the postcolonial work, *par excellence*. Connivance reigns.

Building upon Mbembe's insights, the arguments in this book open postcolonial studies to a major field of social analysis: the cultural politics of identities in transition within postcolonial Africa. We recognise that the postcolonies are radically unalike. Hence we aim to illuminate the disparate identity strategies emerging in everyday life. More or less deliberate, 'rational' or 'irrational', such varying identity strategies put their distinctive imprint upon postcoloniality through local languages, through the cultural richness of specific idioms, images, metaphors and metonyms. Hence interpretations of these languages in their historic specificity are, and have to be, an important part of our own debate.

Because we locate utterances in changing socio-political contexts, we are able to trace the rise of different arguments in a new politics of identity and belonging, one which centres within the postcolony on who represents whom, and to/for whom. In turn, our accounts lead us to

reflexive issues, to the deconstruction of perception, to our own authority
for speaking, to the consequences for postcolonial theory of each analyst's
own language and claim to use universal concepts in representing African
realities.

We address a wide range of postcolonial identity strategies. Of these,
some defend moral agency, respect and respectability, in the face of
catastrophe, such as the AIDS pandemic (Ogden), or argue for novel
Christian or Muslim identities in redefining the boundaries of humanity
and morality (Masquelier; van Dijk and Pels). Others call upon the 'identity-
giving power of the land' and landscape (Thornton), emancipate the
'sovereign subject' (Fisiy and Geschiere) or make social subjectivities
powerfully felt as occult realities (De Boeck; Fisiy and Geschiere;
Masquelier; Ogden). Still others disrupt the very grounds of perception,
identity and subjectivity (van Dijk and Pels), and even threaten the existence
of moral agency (Chabal; De Boeck; Fisiy and Geschiere; O'Brien;
Thornton).

A further problem, at once theoretical and empirical, is thus the way
the postcolonial imagination as a highly specific and locally created force
reconfigures personal knowledge in everyday life. What the book discloses
is how that reconfiguration shapes the subjective, moral and religious
realities around the uses and abuses of postcolonial power.

Not all of that transition is peaceful, of course. 'Culture-as-political
struggle' is waged by violence, also. The postcolonies we discuss are, after
all, 'societies recently emerging from the experience of colonisation and
the violence which the colonial relationship, *par excellence*, involves'
(Mbembe 1992b: 3). Hence our essays address both crisis and confrontation
in order to understand the making of culturally specific personal knowledge. The accounts show, for different postcolonies, how traumatic
identities are formed in intergenerational struggles and how other personal
transformations are made in and through political violence or human
violation (Chabal; Englund; Fisiy and Geschiere; O'Brien).

To follow that in theory and in substantial accounts we need first to
get into perspective how we understand the notion of the postcolonial
itself, what its currency is in mainstream postcolonial studies, and how
that mainstream makes its object of study. Upon that basis, we can put
the case for our own arguments about cultural politics, identity strategies
and plural arenas within postcolonial states.

The colonial, the *post* and the palimpsest

No simple narrative, periodising from the precolonial to the colonial to
the postcolonial, underwrites our arguments. History as linear progress
has nothing to do with our usage of the postcolonial. Instead, we take the
colonial legacy, its nature and its impact, to be problematic, for it is

contested, sometimes with nostalgia for an imaginary past of colonial or precolonial sociality, in the face of deepening social inequality across the continent.

In the postcolonial, as Linda Hutcheon reminds us: 'On the one hand, *post* [sic] is taken to mean "after," "because of," and even unavoidably "inclusive of" the colonial; on the other, it signifies more explicit resistance and opposition, the anticolonial' (1995: 10). The *post* in postcolonial is a marker of dynamic complexity: posted with both hands, not one.

Obvious enough, perhaps, but in need of some qualification none the less. Achille Mbembe challenges us to understand that postcolonial, taking *post* in all its senses, is not merely resistance or collaboration or the refusal to be captured, but a promiscuous relationship: 'a convivial tension between the *commandement* and its "targets"' (1992: 5). And by the *commandement*, Mbembe means the successor to the colonial authority in its widest sense, or more specifically for his own example of Cameroon, the postcolonial regime of authoritarian domination.

The fact that the postcolonial is a postponement, at once a presence and an absence, the now in tension with the not-now, is a politicised reality. That is all the more so, because, as Homi Bhabha and other postcolonial literary critics are fond of reminding us, the colonial, too, is reinscription – by analogy to the palimpsest. Bhabha writes of 'the perverse palimpsest of colonial identity' (1986: xxv, cited in Gates 1991: 461). But that is an ambiguous analogy; perhaps deliberately so, given Bhabha's postmodern penchant for the deferral of meaning, contingency and ambivalence. The palimpsest can be either a slate – in which case it is for writing on and wiping out, for possible effacement without trace (can colonialism ever wipe the slate clean?) – or it can be, according to the OED, 'a monumental brass turned and re-engraved on the reverse side' (on the model of 'palimpsestual inscription and reinscription' and the politicised 'imbrication' of cultural layers over time; see also, Young 1995: 173).

The cultural politics of identity plays dynamically upon that palimpsestual tension. It uses the not-now imaginary to negate, renegotiate, or playfully compromise present authority. In turn, it also reaffirms authority, or its possibility, by counteracting the traces of colonial and precolonial sociality within the postcolonial. In its multiple shifting realities, the postcolonial encompasses contradictory complexity and times out of time. In the postcolonial struggles for authority in public life arises a daunting challenge for analysis, which we take up: to show how and why the present reconstructions of personal and collective identity, of social subjectivity and of moral agency draw on the culturally nuanced resources of social memory for negation, for affirmation and for playful fun.

Pitfalls of the postcolonial

From the very start, as Patrick Chabal's opening essay illuminates through a critical overview, the pitfalls of the postcolonial as a theoretical object command our attention (McClintock 1992; Hutcheon 1995; Jacoby 1995). Chabal raises our awareness of the pitfalls in Western perceptions by building on his landmark account of postcolonial power in Africa (1994, see especially his engagement with Bayart's work). Perhaps the most obvious argument is that to speak of the postcolonial for Africa is to mark the end of an epoch falsely by placing a break where none exists. Terence Ranger returns to this question of continuity in his Postscript in order to underscore a recognition that runs throughout the book. We look to the *longue durée* in periodising the postcolonial.

With political independence in Africa has come no freedom from the imperial grip, though often, but importantly not always, a change of the alien hands in effective, if mediated, command. The ever more pervasive condition is late capitalist domination by Western metropolitan powers, including the transnational corporations and global agencies which are metropolitan based.

Worse still, many African countries appear to be states in name only. Their sovereignty is virtually a political fiction; their control over economic flows across their boundaries, effectively minimal; their lapses from public security into political violence, fostered by foreign arms dumping; their retreat in practice from the populist promises of the early nationalist period after independence, often externally enforced; their impoverishing withdrawal from public welfare institutions, internationally sanctioned; their proliferation of the state salariat, frequently foreign-aid driven. Africa's debt crisis, its increasing economic dependence, its kleptocracies in collusion with extractive transnationals, the suborning of its postcolonial elites by global consumerism, all these complex realities across different parts of the continent invite the simplistic formulations of neo-colonialism. Everything comes down to the passage from territorial imperialism to neo-colonialism, or Global Americana.

Here the temptation is to fall back on 'dependency' theory, on the sociology of underdevelopment as the key to contemporary marginalised Africa. With that comes the addictive desire for all-purpose explanation: Western hegemony, whether met in practice by resistance or collusion, serves as cultural machine; it is as if Western hegemony manufactures the stuff of local sociality, even the contentious stuff, as its own invention. Be it a struggle vital for identity or agency or subjectivity, it all collapses into the reactive response to Western imperialism. But to yield to such temptation – the global fix for the superabundance of local contradictions – is to end the postcolonial analytic engagement virtually at the start, well before the urgent questions are asked, never mind answered.

Postcoloniality and diasporic literary critics

Such engagement in social, political and cultural analysis is important as a fresh departure from the way that mainstream postcolonial studies makes its object as a new discovery of literary theory. Recent as postcolonial studies may seem to be, it already carries the constraints of conventional wisdom and canonical works. The conventional wisdom, as Robert Young puts it somewhat ironically, is that, as in the colonial heyday of the British Empire, so in postcolonial studies: today India 'is the jewel in the crown of colonial-discourse analysis' (Young 1995: 166).

But who speaks for the jewel, a mute object? Not Indians in India, at least not as the foremost spokespersons the mainstream audience hears. In postcolonial studies as a whole, so far, the arguments are most forcefully driven by diasporic intellectuals as literary critics. But their inspiration comes perhaps more from nicely subtle readings of fashionable European theorists, Foucault or de Man and Derrida or Bakhtin and Lacan, than it does from the jewel in the crown, or current local knowledge of the cultural politics of everyday life in postcolonial hinterlands. As for their inspired understanding of the metropolis or the capital in the postcolony: that may be a very different thing, indeed.

On the one side, heavily influenced by Foucault, focused on hegemonic representation and perhaps past the heyday of his own influence, is Edward Said (1978). Somewhat on the other side, and acutely critical of Foucault and the notion of hegemony itself, are Gayatri Spivak (1988; 1990) and Homi Bhabha (1994). A 'First World Indian diasporic', in her own ironic terms (1990: 78), Spivak acknowledges the immediately fruitful influence of de Man and Derrida and, of course, her reading of Marx, 'against the grain'. For Bhabha, more attentive to Lacan and Bakhtin, to Freudian psychoanalysis and dialogics, the key word is 'negotiation rather than negation' (1994: 25) – or counter-hegemony. Said, Spivak and Bhabha are together Young's Holy Trinity. Their diasporic approaches, perhaps because of their basic disagreements, are still setting the pace for postcolonial studies (Young 1995: 160–3). In a critical reflection, Chabal argues: 'used in current cultural and ideological parlance, [postcolonial] refers to the implications of the postcolonial or postimperial condition for the definition of our own identity in the West today. It is, therefore, more a concern about ourselves than about those who do live in actual postcolonial societies.' For this reason, Chabal devotes much of his essay to the echo in discourse about Africa of Western discourse about itself; he examines the context within which Africanists create their concepts of the 'other' in contemporary Africa, so as to challenge us critically to adopt a more reflexive approach to our own imagination and its contribution to the postcolonial world.

But is postcoloniality to be distanced from the postcolony? Is it a condition of the diasporic imagination? Is it mainly for migrants and displaced persons, or a colonial space in metropolitan space, as Bhabha (1994) would have it?

For Africa, the answer is clear: from colony to postcolony, more marginalising, hence of secondary importance in the theoretical arguments on what postcoloniality is. This, despite 'the long shadow of Conrad's *Heart of Darkness* ... on so many texts of the postcolonial pedagogy' (Bhabha 1994: 212), despite the critical ferment around Fanon's paradoxical vision of decolonisation and the New Man (1952; 1961; see the brilliant meta-commentary on the commentaries by Gates 1991; and also the interventions by Parry 1987; Said 1989; Amuta 1989; Bhabha 1994: 35, 40–65; Pieterse and Parekh 1995) and despite the recent salience of contributions by Kwame Appiah (1992), Achille Mbembe (1992a; 1992b) and Valentin Mudimbe (1988), arguably an African Trinity in the emerging canon, but a lesser Trinity.

Radical objections to that conventional wisdom and its canon are already well registered, of course, particularly in Aijaz Ahmad's telling critique (1992, 1995; see also, Parry 1987). Ahmad exposes the self-serving amnesia by which mainstream postcolonial studies makes its object in disregard of earlier, comparative debate about the postcolonial state in Asia and Africa (1995: 5–6; and see also, Alavi 1972; Saul 1979; Martin 1982; Shaw 1982; and the most recent review in Bayart 1993). The point is not to revive a dogma, as it were, back to the state as an Ultimate Ground for materialist explanation in political theory. Instead, it is a recognition of a problematic that is still formidable, still in need of critical analysis, and not to be swept under the carpet.

The state of the postcolony

There are four main reasons why, for the analysis of the cultural politics of identity and everyday life in Africa, postcolonial studies must foreground the state and state-created domains. Much of the rest of this introduction considers these reasons, in turn. As an overview, a list follows, but presented briefly in advance of the discussion it is necessarily condensed, perhaps too much so. The reasons are these:

— the 'retreat of the state' or its transformation;
— the importance of political violence and state genocide;
— the reappropriation of the state, reciprocal assimilation, and political hybridity; and
— the change in identity degradation, stereotyping and the occult imaginary of the postcolony.

A caution is in order. Our interest in the state is primarily in relations with and to the cultural politics of everyday life, in what is sometimes roughly called 'low politics' and, with that in mind, only secondarily do we pursue the 'high politics' of states, rulers and parties.

Admittedly, with regard to the overall problematic, the conclusion Ahmad reaches is contentious, too myopic on labour history, and too generalised in class terms to be convincing for the very different post-colonies of Africa, never mind the globe: 'the nation-state remains, globally, the horizon for any form of politics that adopts the life-processes of the working classes as its point of departure' (1995: 11). Ahmad's conclusion is an intended counter-statement to Bhabha, for whom 'the cultural and historical hybridity of the postcolonial world is taken as the paradigmatic place of departure' (1994: 21).

Whatever may be the reality of 'the retreat of the state' as a global phenomenon, in Africa the extremes are great. So too must our points of departure be variable, not necessarily privileging hybridity or the working class, if we are to locate the changing horizons of identity politics across the continent. Conventional class analysis all too readily leads to the dubious thesis of the single dominant class for the postcolony, the state bourgeoisie, which, as a unity, is effectively in command of state power (for a powerful critique, see Bayart 1993: 176–9 and passim; and for a Gramscian alternative for the postcolony, see Chabal 1994: 217–32).

Against that, our arguments about cultural politics in diverse post-colonies start from the distinctive postcolonial realities of multiple arenas, fluid identities and positional relations of power, all of which are at once within and also negotiably constitutive of the state. As postcolonies, some African nation-states, marked among other things by their swelling state salariat, are still on the march, even if they do withdraw from, in Ahmad's terms, 'the realm of welfare and social entitlements'. In many, the government is still the largest single employer in the national economy. Africa is yet to see the end of oppressive regimes like Banda's in Malawi which, throughout its long era, coerced its subjects through terror, intimidation by the security services, and everyday controls, including the carrying of Malawi Congress Party membership cards, attendance at political rallies and required proof of tax payment (Englund). Other postcolonies are distressingly in ever more rapid decay or virtual collapse; and here our present concern, recognising the greater potential for self-alienation, leads us to a series of problems where the state fails: the modes of local resiliency, the cultural assertion of social identities for survival, the re-cuperation of moral and political agency.

In that vein, Donal Cruise O'Brien asks what identity choices youth have in a context of state decay, given the decline in opportunities for education and employment, and also the rapid demographic expansion. The cases he analyses, from Senegal, Mali and Liberia, illustrate a range of possibilities: membership in a warband, a religious grouping, a criminal gang, a riot, a clientele. In all that, youth remain manipulable by elders with greater financial or organisational resources. As students, themselves aspiring to privilege while leading local protest, they form transient oppositional coalitions, sometimes with unionised workers or junior military officers. Revolutionary change is yet to be an option in actuality. Even when they riot for democracy, they bring about the downfall of 'semi-democratic' regimes. What young become, in these cases, is the agency for institutional disruption. However, as Harri Englund shows for Malawi, they may also be at the forefront of the effective transition to multiparty politics. This, despite the fact that at first the very vanguard position of the youth was proof for the elders of their view that '*matipati* [multi-party politics was] a force prepared to tear the nation apart'.

Shifting identities, plural arenas

For Banda's oppressive era in Malawi and its immediate aftermath, Harri Englund qualifies Mbembe's argument, first, by reviewing the importance of the official/unofficial divide in the literature on popular theatre, song, ritual and poetry. Coded allusions conveyed officially inadmissible messages cryptically; it was a protection for unofficial voices to keep on speaking publicly yet in dissent, and they could not be held responsible for subversive utterances.

From actual narration and his own observation in Southern Dedza, however, Englund goes on to delineate the interplay between the official and the unofficial. For this, he turns to the alternative biographies of Banda, official and unofficial, as the 'father and founder' of Malawi as a nation. With Banda's identity was created one image or another of Malawi as a nation. In the official version, a man of both ancient Chewa wisdom and Western education, working hard for the public good, takes up the call to lead the nation to victory in its struggle for independence. Cunning, ambitious and of uncertain, ambiguous or mixed origins, the stranger in the unofficial version is acquisitive; a trickster, he invents the nation and makes it his own. These alternatives are complementary, one narrative does not necessarily subvert the other, Englund suggests, but only a fool would take the official version at face value. On the flip side of the tyrant's smiling icon is the trickster figure of popular scepticism. 'For many non-members,' Englund observes, '*nyau* [the secret society of masked initiates] was a striking instrument of state coercion and oppression', and yet for them, too, the masquerade *is* a masquerade.

No doubt, more than naked force supported Banda's authoritarian regime. The reception of Banda's father-image and personality cult, like the appeal to nationality, was not at all straightforward, however. The popular imagination was not dominated, in any simple or humourless sense. Here, more in accord with Mbembe's argument, Englund finds that even the local supporters of Banda's Malawi Congress Party were party to the trick; they too toyed with the image of Banda as the greatest trickster of them all, as if the authoritarian joke were of the people, for the people, by the people – and on them, too.

But would the nation dissolve with the overthrow of the Ngwazi, Kamuzu Banda, and his regime? Yes, was the answer for many villagers in central Malawi, uneasy and unwelcome as that answer was, for all their being in a 'power base' of Banda's or Tembo's; and yes, even when they decided to defy the risk, protest and openly take a moral stand against the overweening insolence of the Banda regime. They knew the state to be personalised and presidentialised as Banda's own; Southern Dedza itself was the constituency of John Tembo, the Minister of State in the Banda regime. Moreover, the biographical narration of the nation, both versions of which identified the nation with its 'father and founder', left such villagers fearful of the end of both, and of a civil war like that, recently, in neighbouring Mozambique, about which they knew all too well from the flood of refugees in their midst. But asserting their identity as Christians gave village elders a public authority for an appeal against the regime's arrogance. It is in Christian rhetoric that they found the moral ground for an oppositional stand, transcending the regime's *commandement*: 'God alone will lead us' (see also, van Dijk, n.d.).

Englund contends that authoritarian as the founding postcolonial regime was, it did not manage fully to colonise the imagination of its subjects. 'The illusions and traumas of the Banda regime were filtered through an array of quite disparate experiences, images and influences', he observes. The Southern Dedza villagers Englund studied were aware of northerners' grievances and acknowledged their justified dissent. If connivance in simulacra is real and far-reaching in the postcolony, Englund's argument suggests, it may well not be complete, unqualified or fully at ease; and it is liable in moments of crisis to be challenged with persuasive appeals to locally axiomatic morality and by people strategically using already available identities.

It might be thought that Englund's argument leads down the same slippery slope taken by some, both academic analysts and elite activists alike, who now formulate the plot of politics in Banda's era as if it were a tribal conspiracy. After all, even the outstanding social historians of the invention of colonial tribalism in Malawi, Leroy Vail and Landeg White, label Banda 'a culture broker for the Chewâ' (Vail and White 1989: 181), and represent his reach for a Chewâ political base as part of 'alliance-building' on the basis of tribe or ethnic group.

On empirical and theoretical grounds, Englund insists that such representations mistake political language for political organisation and grossly inflate the significance for political mobilisation of postcolonial ethnic difference. It is a conflation which is itself now becoming 'usable history', obviously despite the best intentions of such critically aware historians as

Vail and White. The simulacra for the art of ethnic politics, like the means for the Sorcerer's Apprentice, have a volatile way of taking on a real life of their own. Activists' efforts to create political roles as ethnic representatives by valorizing ethnic identity are constitutive of postcolonial tribalism. Putting that in critical perspective, Englund's conclusion is that 'Christianity, *nyau* [the secret associations of masked dancers] and activism in the MCP [Malawi Congress Party] have been more critical parameters of identity politics. None of these has coincided with one ethnic category only.' If, as Chabal suggests, 'the "tribal" imperative is now often represented as the *ultima ratio* of African politics', then its exposure as a false representation – or rather, a manipulated fiction – is plain in Englund's essay and, indeed, throughout this book.

Post-Apartheid, postmodern, postcolonial

Robert Thornton pursues Mbembe's insights further by asking the question, 'Is "post-Apartheid" postcolonial?' Thornton urges us to recognise a transitional condition. At present, in the immediate moments after the end of the old regime, South Africa seems more postmodern than postcolonial. To make the point, Thornton follows Mbembe's suggestion that the postcolony, which fragments into a plurality of political arenas, has a distinctive play of political style and *commandement*. Thornton observes:

> South Africa is a country still [mid-1995] without a permanent constitution, a temporary 'government of national unity' enduring uncertainty about the ownership or access to land and housing, continuing debate about who qualifies as *bona fide* political actors ... uncertainty about virtually all levels of geographic boundary demarcation from Provincial to neighbourhood and household, and in which almost all identities – previously legislated and believed to be immutable – are suddenly open to threat and negotiation.

Most striking at the moment, according to Thornton, is a decentred, distinctively postmodern predicament. It is yet to be named, even 'unspeakable', and prefuture in that it 'treats the future as if it were already history'. Its postmodern hallmarks include: the superabundance of whimsical hybridity and globalised pastiche ('the stagy pastiche of colonial and anti-colonial' with television apocalyptic in the uniforms of the Afrikaner Weerstandbeweging); the playful juxtaposition of grotesque incongruities; the radical fragmentation of subjectivity; the social field as a heterogeneous, partially connected ensemble; the plurality, contingency and indeterminacy of social boundaries; the constant innovation; the collapse of an authoritarian bureaucratic master plan with the end of a master narrative for the total order of a modern nation-state.

If, for Thornton, all of that is distinctively postmodern, much of it is distinctively postcolonial for Mbembe (on the baroque style in the postcolonial politics of the belly, see also, Bayart 1993: 248). Their disagreement is not total, however. Like Mbembe, Thornton finds that the standard binary categories for domination, including hegemony/counter-hegemony or resistance/accommodation, are inadequate for postcolonial relations of power in general and thus specifically for negotiated identities in South Africa (for a similar critique in reflection on subaltern studies of colonial India, see Spivak 1987: 197–221). In part, Thornton and Mbembe disagree because of the historic, structural differences in the cases they have in mind; Cameroon and South Africa are in many obvious respects extremes in postcolonial transformation. But their disagreement goes beyond that: it is theoretical. Thornton's perspective looks to 'the hollowness of the State' in the postcolony (Bayart 1993: 258). It represents postcolonial states as countries but little more, their sovereignty so precarious they are seemingly in fragments, not one but, as it were, many sovereign zones. From this perspective, South Africa, too, is a loosely organised, semi-autonomous yet complicated congeries of centres and their hinterlands. From a different starting point, Mbembe theorises the institutionalisation of *commandement*; he conceptualises an authoritarian yet grotesquely playful mode of effective domination by a violent regime, and for him the state looms large in the postcolony, increasingly so.

State violence, the genocidal state and quasi-nationalism

The force in the postcolony both of state violence against ethnic groups (van den Berghe 1990; Wilmsen et al. 1994) and of the genocidal state (Lemarchand 1990, 1994; De Waal 1994) is a second reason why postcolonial studies, in illuminating identity politics, needs to foreground the problematic of the state and state-created domains. Nationalism as a liberation struggle against colonial domination brought with it the identification of nation and state. Nationalism also brought with it, in many parts of Africa, what I have called 'quasi-nationalism':

> Quasi-nationalism, like the nationalism with which it breeds, is a movement of ideas and practices that wins its often cruelly violent moments within the formation of the nation-state in the twentieth century. If energised by a myth of being prior to the nation-state, of revenging old scores left as unsettled from ancient hostilities, quasi-nationalism is none the less made in and by the struggle for power and moral authority in the nation-state. Nor should quasi-nationalism be confused with ethnicity, which operates differently in different situations, irrespective of any dominant cleavage dividing the nation. (Werbner 1991: 159)

Writing before the recent waves of 'ethnic cleansing' in Europe, I continued:

The catastrophe of quasi-nationalism is that it can capture the might of the nation-state and bring authorised violence down ruthlessly against the people who seem to stand in the way of the nation being united and pure as one body. In such times, agents of the state, acting with its full authority, carry out the violation of the person. It is as if quasi-nationalism's victims, by being of an opposed quasi-nation, put themselves outside the nation, indeed beyond the pale of humanity. They are dealt with ferociously not merely for the sake of political dominance by one part of the nation over another, but importantly also for the sake of moral renewal of the nation as a whole. The attack by the state on the victims' own bodies, in the present instance [in western Zimbabwe by the Fifth Brigade in the 1980s] by starvation and torture, even to death, seems to fulfil the objective of purifying and cleansing the body of the nation. (Ibid.: 159–60)

I found that the catastrophe in postcolonial Zimbabwe left many survivors alienated from their nation-state, some deeply convinced it proved that the war for Zimbabwe had failed to make it one nation. As I was told by a member of the family I knew best in western Zimbabwe: 'Mugabe says he fought and won the country. But has he got a country? No, he has no country.'

Silence is complicity, mainstream postcolonial studies often remind us in rightly speaking out against the living force of our heritage of colonial racism. But what about the impact of and responsibility for state violence against internal 'enemies', genocide and quasi-nationalism? Who, among the diasporic spokespersons for postcolonial studies, puts that on the critical agenda? (For Said's critique of *Western* perceptions of 'terrorism' and stigmatised identity, see Said 1995: 341–59.) Like the colonial legacy of which it is a reinscription, the quasi-national legacy lives as an unfinished moral narrative, and it motivates survivors to call again and again for political debts to be met and moral violations to be put right, especially by the state and its agents (Werbner 1995: 102, 106).

The reappropriation of the state, reciprocal assimilation and political hybridity

This brings us to the third reason for moving into the foreground of postcolonial studies what are the cultural politics of everyday life within or against state-created domains. Jean-François Bayart writes of 'the reciprocal assimilation of elites' and derives the notion from Gramsci: 'In the case of Caesar and Napoleon I, it could be said that A and B, whilst being distinct and opposed entities, could after a molecular process, still end up in an "absolute" fusion and reciprocal assimilation' (Gramsci 1983: 503, cited in Bayart 1994: 322–3, note 78).

A current illustration, from a *Guardian* obituary, is the Oba of Benin's appointment of Benin's first British-trained doctor, a former Minister of

Health and retired high court judge, to the post and 'title of Iyase of Benin, regarded by traditionalists believing in a divine kingship as "the highest rank to which a mortal can aspire"' (Ighodaro 1996: 11).

In Bayart's usage, the notion covers relations between new and traditional or established elites and their encompassing identities. It extends to their social inclusion or even political fusion, the elites being typically distinct in identity if historically related, sometimes being of the same familial or local origins. As Bayart makes explicit, it is a notion which is meant to foreground the importance of the *longue durée* for hybridity in political culture. In other words, reciprocal assimilation is a notion of continuity *and* change; and applied to the postcolony, it problematises agency – that of the unlike political actors in the selective co-optation and alliance of disparate postcolonial elites – and it also problematises hybridity: in postcolonial political culture, the active and changeable synthesis/antisynthesis involving the manipulation of precolonial and colonial legacies (on the parallel of syncretism/antisyncretism, see Stewart and Shaw 1994; Werbner 1994). With such assimilation and hybridity may come acquiescence and/or resistance to state power; there is potential for either or both according to specific socio-political contexts.

Given Bayart's stress on the *longue durée*, it would be a mistake to read his argument as if it implied that political hybridity, as such, is distinctively postcolonial. Or to say, in that choice image of postcolonial literary criticism, that the reinscription of the palimpsest begins in postcoloniality. That makes a false contrast between the colonial and the postcolonial, one that all our essays reject, in terms of our shared problematic. What Bayart challenges us to follow is the reworking of the traces of colonial political hybridity in the postcolonial (on colonial political hybridity, see Werbner 1969).

Part of the continuity and change Bayart brings in view has had a bad press in the West. As Chabal notes, caustically: 'Africans appear to outside observers to have "gone back" to some of their "age-old traditions" … and much nonsense has been published in the media about Africa's "backward" civilisation.' The stereotypes, revealing more about Western perceptions than about African 'phenomena', are themselves a blatant yet still dangerous fallout from the past of Western colonialism and racism. Nevertheless, Chabal contends that for understanding present shifts in identity strategies, we do need to ask what 'retraditionalisation' means in contemporary Africa (on 'political Africanisation', see Chabal 1994: 200–16; and on elite 'retribalisation' in Botswana, where 'tribe', an accepted, often highly valorized part of both local and national discourse, is recognised in the national constitution, see Werbner 1993: 103–5). Even more broadly, what is the distinctive imprint of African political cultures in the present crisis of the postcolony?

Filip De Boeck's answer addresses the crisis by accounting for resiliency in the face of the virtual collapse of the state in Zaire. De Boeck enables us to understand better the historicity of the reciprocal assimilation of elites, because he shows the shift to a radically new phase of identity politics. This carries the argument about political hybridity a stage further.

In an earlier phase of decline in the state, elites of Zaire, like Mobutu himself, operated with, among other things, a model of politics derived from the precolonial, via the colonial, big man (Schatzberg 1988: 80–1, after an argument of Vansina's). They opportunistically manipulated a precolonial, and eventually colonial, gift logic for purposes of postcolonial power, authority and economic exchange. The biggest big man of them all, the ruler, was the political entrepreneur who mixed public resources and private wealth in ever more extractive transactions. With power came wealth, in the usual ways of neo-patrimonialism (see Werbner 1993). But not encompassed by the precolonial patron–client model and its entrepreneurial manipulation were sovereign–subject relations.

Also in terms of political hybridity, what Mobutu's regime did, De Boeck describes, was to appropriate political assumptions and images of the invisibility of kingship: 'nocturnal power' and other 'traditional elements in order to back up and touch up the violent realities of naked power'. None of this implies a Golden Era in the past; the 'nocturnal power' of kingship is not some image of Arcadia, and in no way does De Boeck's account assume that the prior colonial state was stable or unmarked by violent disruption. Some anthropologists still find it hard to shake off the romantic idyll of culture, culture being a seamless whole in a social equilibrium. Against that, De Boeck recognises a very different understanding which the people he studies, the aLuund, have of their past and of what it means to be Luunda:

> For centuries the lives of the aLuund have involved contacts, sometimes brutal, with neighbouring groups, such as the Chokwe, or with total outsiders, such as slavers during the time of the Congo Independent State, or Belgian, British and Portuguese colonising forces. In that historical context, their dealings with UNITA rebels and the Zairean regime, or their role in the diamond trade, are in some respects contemporary prolongations of older cultural patterns of trade and political contacts. As in so many precolonial states throughout Central Africa, an outsider is at the base of the Luunda political culture … The romantic idealisation of an untouched cultural whole is, therefore, alien to their own conception of what it means to be Luunda.

Claiming 'authenticity' for itself, Mobutu's postcolonial regime subverted the chiefship of less powerful rulers, ostensibly for the sake of reform, unified local administration and greater incorporation within the state on a more centralised basis. Relatively unregulated, however, were what we might loosely call – after Hyden's dubious notion of the 'uncaptured peasantry' – 'the uncaptured kings', the *grand chefs coutumiers*, formerly the sovereign paramounts from the great 'states' of colonial indirect rule, such as the Kuba, Luba and Luunda.

In the current phase of 'crumbling autocratic control' and 'dysfunctional economy', De Boeck finds an even greater 'hiatus between local political structures and the state'. Seen from a hinterland, there is a perceived danger not only in decreasing access to state power but also in displacement from relations of political authority. Who belongs to the state? And to whom does it belong? In a new crisis of identity, what becomes questionable is not merely who represents whom, or even who belongs, but beyond that, what can representation and belonging *mean*?

One strategy in response, De Boeck suggests, is to open up 'more or less separate worlds to construct encompassing social identities'. Instead of the precolonial gift logic of the big man, what is brought to bear more prominently by elites and subalterns is an alternative from precolonial political culture: 'the longstanding notions of a ritualised tributary political economy'. This alternative is imaged morally and aesthetically with great cultural force, persuasive richness of metaphor and metonym, and highly memorable material transactions. It is the embodiment of authoritative subject–sovereign relations in all their complex ambivalence.

Ambivalence – the stress is here not a product of postmodern chic but of a human predicament which is double-edged, one might say Janus-faced, threateningly tense, contradictory and volatile. In this situation, the same identity strategy – tributary encompassment – means very different, indeed, contradictory things from opposed perspectives. It is one thing from the perspective of uncaptured kings; while they aim to get beyond local encapsulation to regional and national integration, they strive to reappropriate the state on their own terms, which are not terms of subordination. It is quite another thing from the perspective of the president, his officials and party henchmen; they seek to counteract the retreat of the state by incorporating ancient, autonomous authority and local power structures on terms that legitimise their own domination.

That meaningful disparity holds all the more so, perhaps paradoxically, because the engaged elites, whether from the capital or, at a remove, from 'major traditional political power centres', do agree on the historic political game they are playing: 'the political arena draws upon a plurality of "time-spaces" to which all political actors subscribe' (Bayart 1993: 255). They agree not merely on the underlying assumptions of received/invented political culture, but also on the actual gestures of deference, the material transactions of fealty, the homage-making moments with leopard bonnets, beaded crowns, royal raffia-cloth, togas and, in abundant largesse, cash. What they disagree about is the reference of the tributary logic, who is actually paying tribute to whom in such gestures, transactions and moments. What does it mean politically when the king becomes a knight in the National Order of the Leopard, the highest distinction of the

Second Republic, is *ipso facto* placed above the law and enjoys the personal protection of the president? Who has captured whom?

The emergent political hybridity, like the reciprocal assimilation of elites, is a two-way process in the postcolony. If the would-be capturers from the regime become wolves in sheep's clothing, the local sheep wear the wolfskins – admittedly, a somewhat misleading conceit, given the fact that all the ruling elites are wolves, or rather lions (or leopards), according to the received cultural axioms for governance, and not only popular scepticism. But the point is that the cross-dressing is mutual: for the kings, spectacles like the president's and for the president, the regal leopard bonnet. Also mutual is the intervention in the political space of the other. On one side, the kings are flown to the presidential palace, invited to party congresses and rallies, and given cars and residences at the capital. People's representatives, party functionaries and high officials of state attend upon the kings' shrines, their enthronements and other meetings at court, on the other side. Neither side can or does any longer monopolise access to the space of the state or of the kingdom; each side is on the move, not settled down for the convenience or stability of the other.

As De Boeck discloses: 'In this way, both sides have actively collaborated with one another, in an association that, at times, has taken the form of a *contest of representation*, each conforming – both consciously and unconsciously – to the other's style, creating an image of self that can be used and negotiated in the ongoing dialogue with the other.' Here De Boeck himself speaks in dialogue with Bayart (1993) and the contributors to the influential journal *Politique Africaine*, including Mbembe. In Cameroon, there is a saying, 'The goat eats where it is tethered'. Bayart interprets it throughout his classic text, subtitled 'The Politics of the Belly' (1993). The force of the saying, along with the subtitle of Bayart's book, grasps the reach for power and wealth, the accomplishments of political entrepreneurship. For the English edition of his classic, however, Bayart adds the other side, the popular meaning expressed in criticism of corruption: the goat should not eat beyond its own area (Bayart 1993: ix). He also reiterates that he poses his *fragestellung* in response to Foucault's notion of 'governmentality'. Carrying this dialogue forward, De Boeck goes beyond Bayart and comes perhaps closer to the late Foucault by clarifying the importance for 'governmentality' of the active cultural negotiation or *arrangement* of subjectivity and sovereignty (on subjectivity and differences between the late and early Foucault, see Norris 1993: 69–99; and on governmentality in African political discourse, see Gulbrandsen 1995). De Boeck advances a theoretical vision of political actors deliberately engaged in manoeuvre, not merely for patronage–clientage but for more encompassing tributary exchange in the face of state decay.

Identity degradation, stereotypes, occult imaginary

An underlying problem, which takes us to our fourth and final reason for rethinking the emphasis in mainstream postcolonial studies, is the role of the state when the postcolonial imagination reconfigures personal knowledge in crisis. What effects the management of stereotypes, of the degradation of identity? And how and what does the imaginary of the occult represent in the changing postcolony?

Drawing on historical semantics for a case study on the AIDS crisis in Kampala, Jessica Ogden perceives postcolonial intimacy and domesticity as a politicised terrain that is undergoing an uneasy transformation. Much contested are assertions about *omukyala omutufu*, the 'Proper Woman' in Kampala. Stereotypes stigmatising town women and giving them spoilt identities are a colonial legacy. Ogden shows that identity strategies which formerly were empowering, in colonial usage, give rise to disempowering contradictions in postcolonial contexts. Ogden's theoretical approach, starting from the historicity of identity politics, enables her to clarify what has been the changing impact for town women not merely of negative stereotypes but of their own strategies, their own personal and moral defences against stereotyping. Once reinscribed out of context, identity strategy as positive self-defence threatens to turn into its destructive nemesis, the degradation of identity.

Fisiy and Geschiere, who also address the changing configuration of personal knowledge, focus on the forms, especially the directly aggressive or violent forms, which attacks on moral identity take in different parts of Cameroon. Important in their discussion is the general resurgence of witchcraft, both as a topic of academic discourse and, more openly than ever within African postcolonies, as a public discourse in itself, the highly ambiguous discourse about damage to others by occult means (on the resurgence of academic interest in witchcraft, see Englund n.d.).

In earlier work, Fisiy and Geschiere have themselves made major contributions to redirecting the theoretical interest in witchcraft discourse from ahistorical questions of social control, responsibility or micropolitics in interpersonal relations to historical questions of moral and political economy within the state under changing conditions of capitalism. *Pace* Fisiy and Geschiere, it must be said, however, that even the earlier anthropology analysed how the colonial state criminalised and dealt with witchcraft. An outstanding, though admittedly now much neglected, analysis is Isaac Schapera's account, 'Witchcraft Beyond Reasonable Doubt', in which he traces through the courts the introduction and impact of demands for 'tangible proof' of witchcraft under the indirect rule of strong chiefs in colonial Botswana (Schapera 1955; and see also 1969).

Beyond that, Fisiy and Geschiere follow a line of enquiry that relates the imaginary world of occult aggression to perceptions of realities of capitalism, of accumulation and consumption, and of modernity. The 'magic aeroplane' lands for the dangerous delivery of modern goods so that some feed and consume at the secret expense of intimate others. Or, in another 'modern' imaginary, witches transform their victims into zombies, carry them in 'lorries' to a mysterious mountain, and there enslave them on 'invisible plantations'.

The very ambiguities of witchcraft discourse, Fisiy and Geschiere suggest, facilitate perceptions of contemporary socio-political realities in their contradictory complexity. The witchcraft discourse is not one-sided, they argue; it is not merely for or against either the entrepreneurial winners or the impoverished losers emerging under postcolonial capitalism. The rich and the poor, the accumulators and the levellers, the weak and the powerful, all are accessible to being stigmatised or regarded as able to use the weapons of occult aggression for antisocial purposes. The same discourse which upholds kinship amity and intimate trust in the face of familial jealousy, aggression and ambivalence also reinforces 'personal ambition and a quest for individual autonomy, which in these societies are in themselves certainly not wrong'.

In their present chapter, Fisiy and Geschiere say more about the varying role of the state in response to popular pressure for the state to be a party, in significantly different ways, to the making or contesting of spoilt identities through witchcraft discourse. They extend their account of the regional differentiation in the witchcraft discourse developing within post-colonial Cameroon.

Two regions are most salient, the forest areas and the Grassfields. Since the 1970s, only in one region, the forest areas, has the state through its courts frequently condemned witches on the opinion mainly of diviners or witchfinders and sometimes without supporting evidence from dis-covered 'evil objects' (*maléfiques*), 'fetishes' (*fétiches*), or other 'tangible proof' (*preuves tangibles*) (cf. Schapera 1955). This postcolonial break in judicial practice has come where the colonial state, in incorporating segmentary societies, did not produce or amplify strong political authority, *com-mandement*, under the indirect rule of chiefs. Here, in the forest areas, the postcolonial state has been mobilised directly by local people against the morally stigmatised, though effectively not against the rich and powerful who never emerge from court as the state's condemned witches.

Elsewhere in the Grassfields, in the presence of colonially enhanced chiefdoms, where chiefs have consolidated their positions even in post-colonial times (the reciprocal assimilation of elites is thriving 'ruthlessly' here) the courts hear cases of assault or slander involving witchcraft accusations but they condemn no one as a witch. The state does not do the dirty work of identity degradation for local political communities in the Grassfields. The management of much of the aggression or violence around new forms of witchcraft is largely regulated by chiefs and their disciplinary associations, as it was in precolonial and colonial political communities. It is around the chiefs and their disciplinary associations, and more or less under their command, that social exchange takes place which assimilates within the socially acceptable what are otherwise suspicious riches, identities and capacities. What is derived here from precolonial/colonial political culture is a means of legitimising new forms of wealth, ambition and power as rightful, a means the incorporated segmentary societies lack, according to Fisiy and Geschiere. Hence, in their view, a tragic paradox: segmentary societies which, perhaps even more than chiefdoms, strongly and continuously resisted the imposition of the colonial state and its new forms of domination and violence now reach out, in the postcolony, for state intervention in their politics of identity degradation, in their political violence and in the intimacies of their moral economies.

With an eye to even more rapid change in postcolonial identity representations, Adeline Masquelier takes up a crisis in southern Niger in which 'yan izala, Muslim fundamentalists and their religious adversaries are being pitted against each other. Pursuing her theoretical interest in identity strategies in storytelling and rumour-mongering, Masquelier interprets and contextualises villagers' degrading utterances which animalise the Other in their midst. On that basis, she explains how and why their postcolonial discourse is becoming ever more bitter, confrontational and dispossessing: 'Rumours of inhumanity, and in particular fundamentalist inhumanity, constitute a form of social consciousness that is revealing of the ways rural Nigeriens objectify and assess their own situation in a swiftly changing and increasingly unstable postcolonial world.'

Ogden, Geschiere and Fisiy, and Masquelier advance their arguments by tackling the problem of the construction of the Other *within* the postcolony. From the politics of everyday life in the city or the hinterland, each of them illuminates the internal identity degradation, the stigmatisation of the intimate by the intimate. Not the distanced Othering of the Rest by the West: their accounts take us well beyond mainstream postcolonial studies and the hegemonic, Eurocentric obsession with Orientalist discourse. The 'intimate enemy' *is* an intimate, in their ethnography.

What about the cultural politics of ethnography itself? Are they the same, with the same implications for identity, knowledge, subjectivity and authority in the postcolony, as they were in the colony? For Rijk van Dijk and Peter Pels, asking this question is not an invitation to rehearse the routines of anthropology's crisis of representation, or the academic textual criticism in the life work of 'The Anthropologist as Author' (Geertz 1988). Instead, the challenge for van Dijk and Pels is the power-play over perception historically situated *within* the postcolony, and they seek to make us understand the sensory tactics by which postcolonial subjects of study assert themselves and their authority over the ethnographer as fieldworker.

In their chapter van Dijk and Pels document this with a case from van Dijk's own fieldwork, which he carried out in the commercial capital of postcolonial Malawi among Christian fundamentalists, 'Born-Agains'. It is a rare case recording the reception of an ethnographer's text as a moment in postcolonial cultural politics. Van Dijk published his article in a local Catholic magazine, a fact taken as a breach of confidence, since Born-Agains distrusted the Catholics as part of the establishment in Banda's oppressive regime: it provoked the Born-Agains' demand for his humbling in public penance. This he contritely offered in an apology at a large revival meeting. The immediate response and later events also drove home to him that there was a basic conflict, grounded in incompatible modes of perception, which remained unresolved and was perhaps unresolvable.

There is in all this a far-reaching power struggle over whose perception, or even mode of perception, must prevail. The situation in which religion counters postcolonial *commandement* gives the politics of perception a distinctive importance. If, for postcolonial subalterns secretively in tension with an oppressive regime, 'the real source of power and authority' is speaking and hearing the Word of God, having the sense of divine inspiration, then an ethnographer's mode, apparently agnostic, may become threatening. It is all the more so when the ethnographer makes an account public, available to the subalterns' enemies, which seems to valorize 'book-knowledge' or hierarchy over spontaneous revelation. To disrupt the ethnographer's mode, attacking both identity and perception, is a forceful counter-tactic in self-defence: hence in subaltern performance, the de-constructed ethnographer.

Religious apprenticeship and identity through initiation come to the fore in van Dijk and Pels's argument. It may be that becoming an apprentice or undergoing fieldwork as an initiation has always been the mode of situated learning for some fieldworkers, whether colonial or postcolonial. But what is distinctively postcolonial, though often labelled postmodern, is the efflorescence of apprenticeships, and apprenticeships in religion in particular, as first a mode of interactive encounter during fieldwork and then as a retrospective mode for the organisation of ethno-graphy in the memoir genre.

If the colonial anthropologist, say an Edward Evans-Pritchard, a Marcel Griaule, a Max Gluckman or even an Audrey Richards, sometimes postured as the Great Man of the kingdom, among their postcolonial successors the more acceptable posture is being the Little Man/Little Woman under the religious and sensory tutelage of a hinterland master (dominantly male, very rarely female). From the Great Man in the colonial to the Little Man/Little Woman in the postcolonial, it is a reversal of roles, from dominance/manipulation to subordination/touching and feeling, in keeping with the changed opportunity for and disciplinary expectation of the contemporary subject's power-play.

With that role-reversal comes a further significant shift, important for accounts of postcolonial identity strategies. It was everyday personal knowledge, common sense and the matter-of-fact that motivated witchcraft, from the viewpoint Evans-Pritchard adopted. That fitted his taking enough of a participant's role in everyday life and in seances to claim to be an objective observer of witchcraft. An example of a postcolonial reaction, reversing that approach and viewpoint, is Paul Stoller's richly evocative and quite searingly personal memoir of being a sorcerer's apprentice among the Songhay of Niger (Stoller and Olkes 1987). Stoller has been criticised, as van Dijk and Pels report approvingly: '[His] rhetoric of the experiencing "I" tends to downplay the banality and matter-of-factness of Songhay magic and religion in favour of a rarefied idea of the occult.' Yet van Dijk and Pels go on to defend the heuristic force of putting one's body at the disposal of a postcolonial religious master, as Stoller courageously risks doing. In this way, having access to an 'inner' experience of conversion, the postcolonial anthropologist can or perhaps must dare to merge the magical authority with the ethnographic. The ethnographer becomes directly and personally implicated in 'the profound contradictions and tactical *bricolage* of the "contact" zone'. Getting in touch, feeling it on and below one's skin, marks that postcolonial anthropologist who – body-tattooed as it were – emerges as the postmodern tribal, the hybrid in perception. Here, in a word, *complicity* is the postcolonial tactic *par excellence*. We are reminded of Mbembe's postcolony, the banality of power and the political culture of complicity: as in political culture, so in perception.

The arguments in this book go well beyond the grasp of the present introduction. There are fresh implications for the revision of postcolonial scholarship on colonial discourse. Elsewhere Ranger has argued for a general view of a major shift in sociality from the precolonial period to the colonial:

> Almost all recent studies of nineteenth-century pre-colonial Africa have emphasized that far from there being a single tribal identity, most Africans moved in and out of multiple identities, defining themselves at one moment as subject to this chief, at another moment as a member of that cult, at another moment as part of this clan, and at yet another moment as an initiate in that professional guild. These overlapping networks of association and exchange extended over wide areas. (Ranger 1983: 248)

With the colonial period came a 'conscious determination on the part of colonial authorities' (ibid.) and missionaries to combat what they saw as 'untraditional chaos' by tidying up the complexity. The main thrust of their efforts was towards new social rigidities, the creation of stabilised, well-defined tribes, the reifying of custom in inflexible codes, the tightening of control over subjects less able to negotiate their own identities. Our present arguments highlighting the strategic negotiation of multiple identities in the postcolonial period raise questions about the actual force of that thrust. How far did the colonially imagined 'custom-bounded, microcosmic local society' actually become an everyday reality? (On the vision of the society without frontier and the crossing of strangers in colonial movements, see Werbner 1989: 223–44). It is to such questions that Ranger returns in his Postscript.

Throughout this book, we give accounts of the constructive and the destructive force that identity strategies have in contemporary Africa. We redirect postcolonial studies away from diasporic concerns back to the multiple arenas within the postcolonial states themselves. We reflect upon our own participation in the making of Africa's postcoloniality. Our debate is critically with the postcolonial subjects themselves, and not only with other Africanists or, more broadly, with anthropologists, political scientists, sociologists, social historians and literary critics. But our focus on Africa never becomes an exclusive one. Each chapter engaging analytically with the historic distinctiveness of identity strategies discloses another facet of a wide field for general comparison even beyond Africa. Through these specifically informed contributions, the book paves the way for understanding on a broad theoretical basis the disparate trajectories of identity politics in postcolonial transformations.

References

Ahmad, Aijaz. 1992. *In Theory: Classes, Nations, Literatures.* London: Verso.
— 1995. 'The Politics of Literary Postcoloniality,' *Race and Class* 36 (3): 1–20.
Alavi, Hamza. 1972. 'The State in Postcolonial Societies: Pakistan and Bangladesh', *New Left Review* 74. Reprinted in Kathleen Gough and Hari P. Sharma (eds), *Imperialism and South Asia.* New York: Monthly Review Press.
Amuta, Chidi. 1989. *The Theory of African Literature: Categories and Springboards.* London and New Jersey: Zed Books.
Appiah, Kwame. 1992. *In My Father's House: Africa in the Philosophy of Culture.* London: Methuen.
Bakhtin, Mikhail. 1984. *Rabelais and His World.* Translated by H. Iswolksy. Bloomington: Indiana University Press.
Bayart, Jean-François. 1993. *The State in Africa: the Politics of the Belly.* Translated by Mary Harper, Christopher Harrison and Elizabeth Harrison. London: Longman.
Bhabha, Homi. 1986. 'Remembering Fanon: Self, Psyche and the Colonial Condition', Foreword to Frantz Fanon, *Black Skin, White Masks.*
— 1994. *The Location of Culture.* London and New York: Routledge.
Chabal, Patrick. 1994. *Power in Africa.* London: Macmillan.
De Waal, Alex. 1994. 'Genocide in Rwanda', *Anthropology Today* 10 (3): 1–2.
Englund, Harri. n.d. *The Morality of Accumulation: Money and Witchcraft in Central Malawi.* Unpublished manuscript, Peters Prize Essay, University of Manchester.

Fanon, Frantz. 1952. *Black Skins, White Masks*. Translated by Charles Lam Markmann. Reprinted London: Pluto, 1986.
— 1961. *The Wretched of the Earth*. Translated by Haakon Chevalier. Reprinted Harmondsworth: Penguin, 1967.
Gates, Henry Louis, Jr. 1991. 'Critical Fanonism', *Critical Inquiry* 17: 457–70.
Geertz, Clifford. 1973. 'Thick Description: Toward an Interpretive Theory of Culture', in his *The Interpretation of Cultures*. New York: Basic Books.
— 1988. *Works and Lives – The Anthropologist as Author*. Stanford, CA: Stanford University Press.
Gluckman, Max. 1963. 'Rituals of Rebellion in South-East Africa', in his *Order and Rebellion in Tribal Africa*. London: Cohen and West.
Gramsci, Antonio. 1983. *Cahiers de prison*. Vol. II. Paris: Gallimard.
Gulbrandsen, Ornulf. 1995. 'The King is King by the Grace of the People: the Exercise and Control of Power in Subject–Ruler Relations', *Comparative Studies in Society and History* 37 (3): 415–44.
Hutcheon, Linda. 1995. 'Introduction: Complexities Abounding', *PMLA* January: 7–16.
Ighodaro, Anthony. 1996. 'A Woman's Place in Africa', *Guardian* 3 January: 11.
Jacoby, Rusell. 1995. 'Colonial Writers Lost in the Post', *The Times Higher Education Supplement* 29 December: 17
Lemarchand, Rene. 1990. 'Burundi: Ethnicity and the Genocidal State', in van den Berghe (ed.), *State Violence and Ethnicity*.
— 1994. *Burundi: Ethnocide as Discourse and Practice*. Cambridge: Woodrow Wilson Center Press and Cambridge University Press
McClintock, Anne. 1992. 'The Angel of Progress: Pitfalls of the Term "Postcolonial-ism"', *Social Text* 31/32: 84–98. Reprinted in Francis Barker, Peter Hulme and Margaret Iversen (eds), 1994, *Colonial Discourse/Postcolonial Theory*. Manchester: Manchester University Press.
Martin, Guy. 1982. 'Africa and the Ideology of Eurafrica: Neo-Colonialism or Pan-Africanism', *Journal of Modern African Studies* 20 (2): 221–38.
Mbembe, Achille. 1992a. 'Provisional Notes on the Postcolony', *Africa* 62 (1): 3–37.
— 1992b. 'The Banality of Power and the Aesthetics of Vulgarity in the Postcolony', *Public Culture* 4 (2): 1–30.
Mudimbe, Valentin. 1988. *The Invention of Africa*. Chicago: University of Chicago Press.
Norris, Christopher. 1993. *The Truth about Postmodernism*. Cambridge: Blackwell.
Parry, Benita. 1987. 'Problems in Current Theories of Colonial Discourse', *Oxford Literary Review* 9: 27–58. Reprinted in Bill Ashcroft, Gareth Griffiths and Helen Tiffin (eds), *The Postcolonial Studies Reader*. London: Routledge, 1995.
Pieterse, Jan Nederveen and Parekh, Bhikhu. 1995. *The Decolonization of Imagination*. London: Zed Books.
Ranger, Terence. 1983. 'The Invention of Tradition in Colonial Africa', in Eric Hobsbawm and Terence Ranger (eds). *The Invention of Tradition*. Cambridge: Cambridge University Press.
Said, Edward. 1978. *Orientalism: Western Representations of the Orient*. London: Routledge and Kegan Paul.
— 1989. 'Representing the Colonized: Anthropology's Interlocutors', *Critical Inquiry* 15 (2): 205–25.

— 1995. 'Identity, Negation and Violence', in his *The Politics of Dispossession*. London: Vintage.

Saul, J. 1979. *The State and Revolution in East Africa*. New York: Monthly Review Press.

Schatzberg, Michael, 1988. *The Dialectics of Oppression in Zaire*. Bloomington: Indiana University Press.

Schapera, Isaac. 1955. 'Witchcraft Beyond Reasonable Doubt', *Man* 55: 72.

— 1969. 'The Crime of Sorcery', *Proceedings of the Royal Anthropological Institute*: 15–23.

Shaw, Timothy. 1982. 'Beyond Neo-Colonialism: Varieties of Corporatism in Africa', *Journal of Modern African Studies* 20 (2): 239–61.

Spivak, Gayatri. 1987. *In Other Worlds: Essays in Cultural Politics*. New York and London: Methuen.

— 1988. 'Can the Subaltern Speak?', in Cary Nelson and Lawrence Grossberg (eds), *Marxism and the Interpretation of Culture*. London: Macmillan.

— 1990. *The Post-Colonial Critic: Interviews, Strategies, Dialogues*. Edited by Sarah Harasym. New York: Routledge.

Stewart, Charles and Shaw, Rosalind (eds), 1994. *Syncretism/Antisyncretism*. New York and London: Routledge.

Stoller, Paul. 1995. *Embodying Colonial Memories: Spirit Possession, Power and the Hauka in West Africa*. London. Routledge.

— and Olkes, C. 1987. *In Sorcery's Shadow. A Memoir of Apprenticeship among the Songhay of Niger*. Chicago: University of Chicago Press.

Vail, Leroy and White, Landeg. 1989. 'Tribalism and the Political History of Malawi', in Leroy Vail (ed.), *The Creation of Tribalism in Southern Africa*. London: James Currey.

van den Berghe, Pierre. 1990. *State Violence and Ethnicity*. Niwot, CO: University of Colorado Press.

van Dijk, Rijk n.d. *Fundamentalism, Gerotoncratic Rule and Democratisation in Malawi: the Changing Position of the Young in Political Culture*. Unpublished manuscript.

Werbner, Richard. 1969. 'Constitutional Ambiguities and the British Administration of Royal Careers among the Bemba of Zambia', in Laura Nader (ed.), *Law in Culture and Society*. Chicago: Aldine.

— 1989. *Ritual Passage, Sacred Journey*. Washington, DC: Smithsonian Institution Press.

— 1991. *Tears of the Dead: The Social Biography of an African Family*. Edinburgh and Washington, DC: Edinburgh University Press and Smithsonian Institution Press.

— 1993. 'From Heartland to Hinterland: Elites and the Geopolitics of Land in Botswana', in Thomas J. Basset and Donald E. Crummey (eds), *Land in African Agrarian Systems*. Madison: University of Wisconsin Press.

— 1994. Afterword, in Charles Stewart and Rosalind Shaw (eds), *Syncretism/Antisyncretism*.

— 1995. 'Human Rights and Moral Knowledge: Arguments of Accountability in Zimbabwe', in Marilyn Strathern (ed.), *Shifting Contexts*. London: Routledge.

Wilmsen, Edwin, Dubow, Saul and Sharp, John. 1994. 'Ethnicity, Identity and Nationalism in Southern Africa', *Journal of Southern African Studies* 20 (3): 347–53.

Young, R. 1995. *Colonial Desire: Hybridity in Theory, Culture and Race*. London and New York: Routledge.

PART ONE

Crisis, state decay and transitional identities

CHAPTER I

The African crisis: context and interpretation

Patrick Chabal

The notion that it is difficult to understand the politics of postcolonial Black Africa is hard to escape. Indeed, the accounts given of events taking place there point to a situation in which journalists and academics alike seem at a loss to interpret what is happening. Optimism is followed by despair. Explanations are offered only to be discarded or retracted. Forecasts are quickly invalidated or overtaken by events which were not anticipated. Of course, events in Africa are not the only ones which we (Western Europeans) find difficult to explain. Much that is happening today in Eastern Europe also appears largely to escape our understanding. Indeed, the parallel with Eastern Europe is instructive; for it helps us recognise why explaining the politics of the 'other' is such an eminently subjective activity and why we so often fail to see that it is.

This chapter is in four parts. First, I examine the nature of the present African 'crisis'. Second, I look at the current historical, intellectual and ideological context within which we, Africanists, are trying to understand what is happening in contemporary Africa. Third, I discuss the question of the interpretation of postcolonial African politics. Finally and briefly, I suggest some possible lines of enquiry for future research. Throughout, my focus is on what we (Western Africanists) do when we try to understand contemporary Africa.[1]

The African crisis

I begin with a summary of what most observers think is the crisis in Africa today, bearing in mind that any generalisation about the whole of Black Africa is bound to be both overly sweeping and overly limiting. Africa's current predicament is seen as a combination of four distinct (though obviously interrelated) factors: an acute economic crisis, political instability, the so-called 're-traditionalisation' of African societies, and the marginalisation of Africa on the international scene. I discuss each in turn.

Economic crisis This seems to be the easiest and most straightforward aspect of Africa's problems to grasp. Indeed, there is scarcely any disagreement about the depth of Africa's economic crisis since, whatever indicators are used, it is patently obvious that, taken as a whole (and with few exceptions), Africa's economies today are in a worse state than they were at the time of independence. It is not just that there has been no growth or development, but that in absolute terms both the economies of African countries and the economic prospects of the majority of Africans have been steadily eroded over the last decade.

In the cold light of statistics, Africa's present crisis is grave indeed. Economic growth has failed to keep up with population increases. Exports have declined in relative and absolute terms. Food production has declined. Imports of food and other necessities have risen greatly. Import-substitution industries have not lived up to expectations. Industrialisation has, with some exceptions, failed to materialise. Borrowing and debt have soared. Currencies (including the almighty CFA franc) have weakened or collapsed. State revenues have plummeted. State-controlled economic activities (whether parastatals or state retail systems) have foundered. State-funded services have declined or disintegrated. Official economies have shrunk and parallel economies have grown.

Whatever the causes of this economic crisis – about which there is (quite legitimately) debate – we cannot ignore or deny the magnitude of the continent's economic predicament. Nevertheless, taking stock of Africa's economic breakdown is no substitute for analysis and any interpretation of this crisis must attempt to unravel what is cause and what is effect. And it is precisely at the level of interpretation that the (implicit or explicit) use of simplistic causalities often reduces Africa's economic predicament to a series of casuistic or tautological clichés, some of which, such as the 'innate economic inability' of Africans, carry distinct racist connotations.

I do not propose to review here the various explanations offered for Africa's current economic crisis; instead I want to focus attention on the extent to which, in the case of Africa, there is such readiness to resort to specific, *sui generis* and personalised assumptions about the possible causes of economic failure. Above and beyond the general tendency to ascribe to others motives and characteristics which we would repudiate for ourselves, in the inclination to interpret the African economic predicament from the perspective of its 'Africanness' there is a bias which requires attention.

It is this bias which makes it possible both to satisfy ourselves with facile explanations for economic failure and with equally facile remedies for economic recovery. Indeed, the successive World Bank reports on the state of Africa's economies provide both text and subtext on the extent to which outside 'experts' are prepared to simplify and revise their diagnoses of Africa's economic ailments. The justification for the present structural adjustment programmes – whatever their technical merits – is a case in point. It is not just that African countries are rarely in the position to resist the conditionalities imposed by the World Bank, but also that it is taken for granted that it is entirely appropriate to impose such conditions on Africa, whereas it is debatable whether such conditionalities should be imposed on the former Soviet Union or other Eastern European countries.

Political instability   In this area too, the failures of Africa are well-known and need hardly be rehearsed. Africa is not just a continent of great political instability, it is also a continent where incompetence, greed and the lust for power have unleashed untold violence on ordinary men and women. Following the latest atrocities in Rwanda, hard on the heels of recent events in Burundi, Liberia, Mozambique, Angola, Sudan, Somalia and Zaire, it seems difficult to avoid the conclusion that postcolonial Africa has been afflicted by an extraordinarily high degree of wilful political violence. This is undoubtedly true, although, unfortunately, there has been equally savage political brutality outside Africa.

Again, I do not want to chronicle here the political instability of postcolonial Africa, nor even to detail the acute degree of human suffering endured by Africans because of the dereliction of political morality. I want rather to highlight our perception of these events and the interpretations we give of them. It is true that we are (rightly) repelled by the atrocities currently perpetrated in Africa in the name of politics. Nevertheless, there is today a distinct feeling in the West that what is happening in Africa is special, 'beyond the pale', a kind of barbarity which represents some form of typically 'African' violence.

It is perhaps easiest to illustrate what I mean by comparing what has been said in the recent past about violence in South Africa, Burundi and Rwanda. For quite some time, the cause of violence in South Africa between the ANC and Inkatha was readily ascribed to 'tribal' hostility between Xhosas and Zulus, widely seen as incapable of overcoming age-old 'tribal' violence for the sake of a democratic order. A confirmation, as it were, that the hostility between Zulus and Xhosas was akin to that between the Tutsis and Hutus in Rwanda and Burundi. Yet, while the account of South African politics given above will have struck most informed observers as absurdly reductionist, a very similar account of events in Rwanda and Burundi was much more readily accepted and indeed acceptable. Why? Is it only because we know so much less about Rwanda and Burundi? (For a most useful recent volume, see Lemarchand 1994.) Or is it because we know that there were good political grounds for violence in South Africa, grounds which have now been removed by the democratic elections?

I do not want to underline here simply the slovenly, hypocritical or even racist basis for such simplistic explanations of political violence in Africa. I want to emphasise the very process by which we think we can satisfy ourselves with such reductionist causalities when it comes to Black Africa. And I want to ask how our political interpretation of postcolonial Africa would change if we made the effort not to resort to the excesses of analytical simplifications in which we have indulged for too long.

What is happening in the former Republic of Yugoslavia today is proof, if proof were required, that when it comes to analysing the political violence of the 'other', we quickly resort to simplistic explanations. However, for the Africanist, it has the merit of exposing the vacuousness of causalities which reduce violence in Africa to 'tribal' hostility, political greed or incompetence. These attributes are shared equally throughout the world. What is happening in Africa is in this respect no different from what has happened elsewhere, even if the scale of instability and especially the depth of incompetence do, obviously, require explanation.

The point here, therefore, is not in any way to minimise the acuteness of Africa's political frailties and the importance of its failures, but to argue for the right level of political analysis: an analysis based on the degree of conceptual clarity and the range of historical knowledge which we would deem suitable for the understanding of the politics of our own societies. An analysis, that is, which respects rather than demeans Africans. In this respect, we outsiders could do worse than listen to Africans when they press us to think more carefully about the implications of our political interpretations for the well-being of the continent: supporting dictators or justifying structural adjustment all have immediate consequences for the lives of ordinary men and women.

The 're-traditionalisation' of Africa I refer here to the accounts given recently of the ways in which Africans appear to outside observers to have 'gone back' to some of their 'age-old traditions' and the consequences of such 'regression' for African politics. Although much nonsense has been published in the media about Africa's 'backward' civilisation, it would be unwise to dismiss all the accounts of what I call 're-traditionalisation' simply because of these crass and gross simplifications. There is undoubtedly something going on in Africa but, here again, we (outsiders) are uncertain what it is and, especially, what it means.

Of course, the notion that a group of people – let alone a whole number of nations – could be regressing is one which rests on an assumption (however subterranean) about the linearity of 'progress'. Not surprisingly, it is an assumption held most comfortably by those who see themselves as being at the leading edge of such a process. The whole debate about what it means to be 'civilised' goes on endlessly and evolves according to the circumstances in which we find ourselves. It is tied to the question of identity, an important issue of debate today. But I want here to focus on those things which specifically suggest the 're-traditionalisation' of contemporary Africa.

There are essentially two aspects to this question. The first is the extent to which individuals in Africa increasingly are, or are perceived to be, behaving according to norms, criteria, values and so on, more readily associated with what passes for 'traditional' Africa than with the Africa which the colonial masters thought they had constructed. The second is the degree to which it seems that politics in Africa is conducted in ways (both overt and covert) that are either incomprehensible to the West or appear to be reminiscent of what precolonial politics is supposed to have been. Obviously, these are matters of perception and we are talking here about the Western perception of Africa; but perceptions matter and they should be discussed.

Examples of 're-traditionalisation' abound. There is the abiding strength of what is called sorcery or witchcraft and the apparent revival of African religion. There is too the ostensible 'traditionalisation' of the Christian churches in Africa. Similarly, and contrary to some expectations, there is in Africa greater use of local and national languages, even by those who speak the official European language. The publication of books in African languages has increased rather than decreased over time. Finally, to give only one more example, there is every indication that urban Africans are behaving in their family lives in ways which are seen as 'traditional' rather than 'modern': witness, for example, the enduring force of bridewealth and polygamy.

Above all, and inevitably, there is the whole issue of what is quaintly called 'tribalism'. Whatever one's view of ethnicity, it seems difficult at first sight to resist the conclusion that ethnic considerations are (again?) becoming increasingly salient in contemporary Africa. It is not just that ethnicity is important to the conduct of politics, it is also that violence appears more and more to be channelled along ethnic lines. Thus, the conclusion is easily drawn that Africans are peculiarly ethnic in their sense of identity and, more to the point, that ethnicity is (once more?) the political *ultima ratio* in African countries.

Although the question of identity is the most visible, it is by no means the only one in which evidence is found of 're-traditionalisation'. In the economy, too, there is apparent 'regression'. It is now widely accepted that, in agriculture, many of the changes which were believed to have taken place during the colonial period and after independence masked the continued importance of the so-called 'traditional' African mode of production. As the economic situation deteriorated in postcolonial Africa, so it appears that many producers returned to 'subsistence' farming. Today, agricultural production is lower than it was at independence and many farmers now trade solely on the parallel market, as they did in precolonial times.

Furthermore, there is debate about the failure of Africa to 'take off' economically. Why are African countries not developing like many Asian countries? Why is it that the preferred option of most African entrepreneurs is exchange and trade rather than the kind of productive economic activity which can provide the foundations for a country's economic development? Here too hints of the 're-traditionalisation' of Africa are circulating. Is African 'culture' inimical to productive investment? Are African entrepreneurs still prey to the 'traditional' demands of the (excessive) display of wealth, for which consuming is more important than investing?

Finally, there is the perennial question of the apparent failure of 'modern' (liberal or socialist) politics in Africa – a question which must be asked again today when democratisation is firmly on the agenda. Why have African politics 'degenerated' or 'regressed' from what were seen as the relatively auspicious political circumstances of their birth at independence? Is what is happening in contemporary Africa rightly interpreted as the degeneration of a 'modern' model of politics? The undeniable failures of the state and of good government on the continent make it inevitable that many will read this process as the 're-traditionalisation' of the African political order. Here too one must ask how appropriate it is to think in those terms.

The marginalisation of Africa   The final aspect of Africa's current predicament is the undoubted growing marginalisation of the continent on the international scene (see Adedeji 1993). Partly as the result of the general perception of the causes of the problems discussed above and partly for reasons which have little to do with Africa, there is a sense today that the continent has become irrelevant in the world perspective. This appears to be true both objectively and subjectively, and it also appears to be true in the two key areas of international affairs: the economic and the political.

In economic terms, Africa is becoming marginal to world industrial development and to global commerce. Its contribution to world trade is increasingly confined to primary products and its share of the world market is reducing over time. Furthermore, with some exceptions (like South Africa), there is declining foreign investment in African countries and whatever investment is made is confined to those areas related to the extraction and export of primary products. The continent is becoming more dependent on foreign aid and food imports. A crushing debt burden and the conditionalities of structural adjustment are slowly reducing the economic options for Black Africa.

This objective situation is generating a subjective frame of mind in which the outside world looks at Africa not just as an economic failure but also as an area in which it is fruitless to invest and with which it is better not to trade. Because of political instability, foreign investors feel it unwise to become involved in any long-term productive activities. Short-term profit considerations prevail. This reinforces a situation in which Africans themselves are reluctant to invest in their own countries, and seek quick profits, often to be hoarded abroad.

Although the former colonial countries do have an economic stake in some parts of Africa, this constitutes a declining proportion of their overall economic activities. Equally, imports from Africa are also a dwindling proportion of the 'advanced' world's total imports. Finally, in the wake of the collapse of communism in the former Soviet Union and Eastern Europe, there is greater concern in the West, particularly in Europe, to support financially, to invest in and to trade with the countries of the former Eastern bloc. This can only lead to the greater economic marginalisation of Africa.

In political terms too, Africa's international situation has deteriorated. True, historic ties with traditional European or other partners survive. The French still have a military presence in Africa and continue to be influential in some of their former colonies. Similarly, the British have close links with Nigeria, Kenya and Zimbabwe. The Americans have some lingering interests in countries such as Liberia or Zaire. On the whole, however, Africa has become much less central to the foreign policy of even the most Africa-oriented country. Sporadic European involvement takes place, mostly in response to crises (as in Chad, Rwanda, Burundi, Somalia), but the industrialised G7 countries do not see Africa as an area of priority.

That this is so is not due, of course, only to Africa's economic decline. It is also the outcome of the collapse of communism in the Eastern bloc, the break-up of the Soviet Union and the end of the Cold War rivalry, particularly in Africa. The avowed failure of 'socialism' in Africa and the decline in the influence of the former Soviet Union (and its allies) have left African countries to face the growing influence of the West and Western-dominated international and financial institutions.

This has had positive effects in that conflicts (like those in Namibia, Angola, Ethiopia, Mozambique) which were sustained by the Cold War became more liable to end in peaceful resolution. Nevertheless, it also means that African countries are now no longer in a position to use superpower rivalry to get foreign aid and political or military support. No one in the West today fears growing communist influence in Africa. And no former Eastern bloc country has spare cash to buttress its position in Africa.

Equally, non-alignment now means very little and it brings little kudos. All African countries, like the countries of the former Eastern bloc, want to join the diplomatic and financial institutions of the Western world. Even in the United Nations, where African countries' votes were long courted by the West, there is now little need for the West to 'buy off' voting support. At a time when an increasing number of African countries need UN assistance in one form or another, they are scarcely in a position to dictate the agenda or even to pressurise the West on issues which matter to them. The present international context is undoubtedly one in which Africa's voice is weak and Africa's concerns are rarely perceived as deserving of priority.

Context

It has always been true that the West's vision of Africa has been the product of its own imagination rather than that of a serious interest in what actually happens on the continent. Nevertheless, the context within which we, Africanists, are today trying to understand Africa is one which is in particularly rapid mutation. What is different today is that Africa's crisis impinges on the consciousness of the West at a time when the West itself is doing battle with its own sense of identity. And, of course, it is because there is uncertainty about our own identity that we are so taken with the possible fate of Africa today.

If the most obvious new factor in the international context is the collapse of communism, it may not be the most significant to the interpretation of contemporary African politics. Our interpretation of the failure of communism is coloured by the search for meaning and identity which is the hallmark of the Western world today. As such, it could well be that the most significant aspect of the 'end' of communism is not so much the collapse of regimes which had long outlasted whatever usefulness they may have had, but the impact it is having on the West's sense of its own direction.

Our attempt to understand contemporary Africa is driven (in part at least) by a need to make sense of what the manifest 'failure' of a whole continent can mean for our 'civilisation'. The expectation that postcolonial Africa would make good progress has been confounded and we are grappling with the consequences of such failure at a time when we are beginning to doubt the notion of identity which has underpinned our own (over)confident march into modernity and comfort.

We are disturbed by the atrocities currently being committed in Rwanda (or Liberia, or Burundi, or Angola, and so on) not simply because we feel guilty about our colonial past or because of our concern for the loss of African life, but also, and perhaps primarily, because it makes us wonder about the potential barbarity present in us all. The parallel with events in Bosnia is obvious and is one from which it is difficult to distract our attention.

For this reason, it is useful to pause and ask ourselves why it is that we think as we do at this juncture in our history. There are obviously many possible approaches to this question but I thought a good starting-point here might be the simple observation that we seem intent on defining ourselves in terms of what we no longer are. We see ourselves as the 'post-something' generation and for better or worse it is the context within which we seem to be operating. I now look briefly at four aspects of this 'post-mania': the notions of the postcolonial (or postimperial), the post-national, the postmodernist and the postideological.

Postcolonial The present debate about our postcolonial identity is not one primarily concerned with the historical fact of the end of colonial rule (broadly from 1947 to 1964). There is indeed more talk today about the postcolonial than there was at the time of the end of empire. Nor is the notion of postcolonial here meant to reflect the condition of African countries after independence. In the sense in which it is used in current cultural and ideological parlance, it refers to the implications of the postcolonial or postimperial condition for the definition of our own identity in the West today. It is, therefore, more a concern about ourselves than about those who do live in actual postcolonial societies.

Although ostensibly the concept of postcolonial has become a code-word for saying that we are part of multicultural, multiracial societies, its import is actually deeper. In Europe, and in particular in the former imperial countries, the term has arisen to reflect the necessary coming to terms with the legacy of our colonial past in the midst of our contemporary society. We are indeed multiracial and multicultural societies in which the descendants of our colonial subjects have become neighbours, friends, foes or simply competitors. Nevertheless, the fact that we are now acknowledging explicitly the presence of so many who were either ignored or rejected for so long is not coincidental.

First, it takes at least a generation before a colonial country can fully come to terms with the loss of empire and begin to debate the consequences of decolonisation; see for example, the recent spate of books and films in France about Algeria. In this respect, Portugal is not yet at the stage where it can confront openly its own colonial past. Second, it is usually the second generation of colonial immigrants who assert fully and forcefully their right to be part of the postcolonial society and who, in so doing, question some of the assumptions on which the identities of the former mother country have been constructed. African British or Algerian French are not just *Gastarbeiter*, they are fully-fledged citizens of Europe.

Third, there has been for the past decade or so a backlash against both our colonial guilt and the gradual acceptance in our midst of immigrants from the former colonies. This has, of course, been part of a more general reaction against the perceived liberal values of the 1960s. More significantly, it has also been the result of a specifically revisionist outlook on our colonial history and its heritage. Broadly, the revisionist view has been that (1) on balance the colonial world benefited from colonial rule; (2) former colonies have been worse off since independence; (3) we should thus be proud of our colonial achievements; and (4) our identity today must be built on the recognition of our achievements as imperial countries rather than on the attempt to expiate a colonial 'crime' we did not commit.

Fourth, there is in Europe an increasingly strong and vocal right-wing xenophobic movement. Although in sociological terms, this movement is in part explained by the consequences of economic crisis and rising unemployment, there is clearly a correlation here between xenophobic stridency and the uncertainties of our contemporary (postcolonial) identity. Indeed, the common feature of all the European right-wing movements is the need to redefine identity in terms of a single racial and cultural 'national' type. Accordingly, the form that racism takes today is one which focuses with singular vehemence on the necessity to return to our 'real' (that is, in fact, imaginary) preimperial roots.

The debate about the meaning of the postcolonial in our societies is thus at heart a debate about the nature of our contemporary identity. Pitted against each other are those who argue that our present identity is not just multiracial and multicultural but quite simply part of a complex, multiple and fluid 'world culture', and those who seek to redefine the fundamentals of our contemporary societies in essentialist and national(ist) terms. This debate touches on the most deeply-felt difference of perception about the nature of the present-day nation-state. Given this context, in which ways can we in the West say that are we living in 'nation'-states?

Given our doubts about the nature of our own postcolonial 'national' identity, we are naturally sensitive to those aspects of contemporary African politics which impinge on our consciousness of the uncertain meaning of the African postcolonial identity. In the face of a formerly colonised world in which there is often a violent 'fundamentalist' backlash against westernisation and modernism – which is mirrored by the xenophobic movement in Europe – our ability to understand contemporary African societies is necessarily influenced by the extent to which we accept or reject the argument about our postcolonial identity. This in turn affects our view of the nature and relevance of nationalism in today's politics.

Postnational   Concurrently with the debate on the postcolonial, there is today a view that we have entered the postnational age, by which is usually meant that the nation-state is being superseded or at the very least that it is becoming increasingly irrelevant to the 'modern' world in which we live. The argument that nationalism and the nation-state are anachronisms in contemporary Western societies is not, of course, new. There are long traditions, particularly on the left, with an anti-nationalist pedigree. What is new, however, is the more general notion that the very development of modern society makes the nation-state redundant.

The argument is usually in two parts: one about the consolidation of a global economy, the other about the contemporary technological and communications revolution. As the international economy spreads more and more worldwide, it is argued, countries are becoming increasingly interdependent. Business, finance and banking operate across the globe with little respect for national boundaries. Poorer countries which are integrated into this world economy can quickly make giant strides forward, as is evident among the Pacific Rim countries. And it is this new international economic status, rather than old-fashioned nationalism, which, it is claimed, determines the success of individual countries today.

Similarly, it is argued that Western countries are both increasingly dependent on and vulnerable to the emerging economies of the former Third World countries now launched on their own economic revolutions. According to this view, the recent GATT agreement will open up national borders, increase international trade and benefit the successful emerging economic countries at least as much as the Western world. Economically, therefore, we are moving in the direction of a much more highly integrated and more mutually interdependent world in which outdated considerations of international diplomacy and politics will become secondary to the economic imperative.

Furthermore, the current technological revolution in telecommunications is creating conditions in which news, information, visual and documentary material will become available simultaneously in all parts of the world, thus invalidating national boundaries concretely and symbolically. As power is linked to information, it is argued, this revolution will both diffuse and internationalise the basis on which politics is conducted, in this way making narrow national issues less compelling. The globalisation of information will also force the political focus away from the more parochial nation-centred issues.

Finally, the growing importance of regional economic and political groupings will, it is believed, further remove everyday issues from the strict purview of the nation-state. The evolution of the European Union is, in this respect, seen as a logical response to the demands of the modern world, both in economic terms and in terms of the political parameters relevant to the increasing interdependence of neighbouring nation-states. We in Western Europe cannot fail to be influenced by our view of the extent to which we believe the European Union to be a model of things to come.

In respect of Africa too, there are now more and more voices expressing both the limitations of the existing system of nation-states and the need for new forms of co-operation. The present economic crisis and the apparent non-viability of a number of smaller or resource-less African countries have led many, in and outside Africa, to propose radical (regional or pan-African) supra-national solutions. Here the argument is that, given how recent and artificial African nation-states are, it is both realistic and feasible to set in train new forms of association which would in time make the present national divisions of Africa redundant. The notion that the nation-state in Africa is no longer appropriate for its future well-being has been strengthened by the view that the African state is both predatory and impotent: an obstacle to the resolution of the African crisis.

Whether or not such supra-national solutions are realistic depends on the view taken of the historical decline of the nation-state. In particular, it depends on one's interpretation of the changing pattern of individual and social identity. The argument here is that contemporary forms of identity are increasingly at odds with the narrow constraints of the nation-state. People today think and act less and less in terms of the local *terroir* and increasingly according to cross-national values and outlooks. The internationalisation of the economy goes hand in hand with the globalisation of culture.

However, in view of the events currently taking place in the former Soviet Union and Eastern Europe as well as of the countless incidents of 'tribal' violence in Africa, it may be well to ask whether the failures of the nation-states are not likely to result in more, rather than less, 'nationalist' politics. Or at the very least whether the weakness of the state is not likely to release the pent-up frustration of infra- rather than supra-national energy. Certainly in Africa the signs all point in that direction. In any event, our notion of whether the debate about the 'postnational' points to a real lessening of the nationalist imperative or whether it merely reflects a desire for less parochial politics in the West depends in part on the view we take of the current debate about postmodernism.

Postmodernist   It is not possible here to discuss the many-splendoured meanings of the considerable (and continually growing) postmodernist discourse. Suffice it to paint in broad strokes the main arguments which may impinge on our understanding of contemporary Africa. Of course, the whole notion of postmodernism is one rooted in Western cultural and sociological self-examination and it could at first be argued that it is utterly irrelevant to the condition of the Third World. But the point here is to examine the political, intellectual and ideological context within which we, Africanists, conceptualise the 'other' in contemporary Africa. For this reason, therefore, and also because Western discourse has a habit of finding an echo in Africa, we ought to give some thought to the possible import of postmodernism to African studies.

The two aspects of postmodernism which we might like to consider are those which are said to reflect the interconnection between identity and values. The thrust of the postmodernist argument is that the contemporary world is one in which individual identities are increasingly cross-cultural and values increasingly relative; the former because technological change and the globalisation of culture have created conditions in which societies experience progressively diverse cultural influences; the latter because the modern world is one in which the force of absolute collective moral or religious imperatives is in decline and the creativity of individualisms is seen increasingly to nourish artistic and scientific achievement.

This is perhaps best illustrated in literature. Salman Rushdie's *Satanic Verses* might in this respect represent both the promise and the ambiguities of (one form at least of) postmodernist literature, combining successfully the art of the West and the inspiration from a non-Western culture. One could also argue that Wole Soyinka's work points in the same direction, at once utterly modern in the Western sense but also fundamentally African in both inspiration and artistic sensibilities. Similarly, Ben Okri's recent novels may be seen as instances of the postmodern in a new literature of Africa. The point being here that, regardless of the present condition of Africa, a genuinely creative African literature would be as resolutely post-modern as its Western counterpart. Or rather, that the two are no longer separate but part of one universal literary creation which can speak to us all.

Even in the circumscribed realm of literature, however, the postmodern argument is contested in the West itself. There is indeed acute debate between the proponents of postmodern relativism and those who argue that it is both possible and necessary to identify a literary canon. Furthermore, critics of postmodernism readily point to the confusion which exists between the necessity to understand the multiplicity of cultural meanings present in modern society and the need to retain a sense of the culturally significant. They deny that changes in perceptions and values amount either to a loss of cultural identity or to the abandonment of specific cultural models.

Other than in literature (and music, for example), it is rather more difficult to see the relevance of postmodernism to African studies or to the realities of contemporary African politics. For the mass of ordinary men and women in African villages, the influence of postmodernism is unlikely to be significant. Yet there are at least two ways in which, above and beyond the influence postmodernism exercises on our minds, it could concretely affect African societies. The first lies in the rapid development of the means of communications, which can now bring satellite television to the most remote corners of the globe. The second has to do with the reaction in Africa to the discourse of postmodernism in the West.

Of course, satellite television may not be considered to be the most edifyingly representative example of our so-called postmodern culture, but it may well be deemed to be so by the African viewers who will 'consume' its product. And in so far as such television offers a diet of 'entertainment' which does reflect a very 'relative' level of cultural and moral values, as it does, it will (rightly or wrongly) be perceived as exemplary of what Western culture is all about. The question here is not that African viewers are less sophisticated than their Western counterparts, but that they are viewing from a culture which is some distance from the West. What they view will create or confirm an image of the (postmodern) Western culture which is not, and cannot be, politically neutral.

This notion of westernisation, however corrupt, will easily be seen by those for whom it is convenient to do so as evidence of the nefarious or even evil influence of the West. It is, of course, no surprise that it is in fundamentalist and 'socialist' states such as Iran or China that Western culture is perceived as the emanation of morally corrupt and politically dangerous Western societies. In those countries, the state seeks to prevent access to Western culture and to peddle a sanitised interpretation of the local (political or religious) orthodoxy. The process is not new, of course, but the context is. It is infinitely more difficult for China to keep Western culture at bay than it was for Japan during the period of the Meiji Restoration.

The paradox, however, is that the postmodern culture which is seen partly to be the result of the increasingly cross-cultural influences experienced in the West may have serious, if unintended, consequences in non-Western countries. At best, of course, it will show that contemporary Western culture has been meaningfully influenced by non-Western culture. Most likely, however, the revolution in information technology will merchandise a form of 'entertainment culture' which will attract and offend in equal measures but will in any case mislead. And as we know from Iran and now Algeria, fundamentalist backlashes can be very nasty indeed.

What, then, of postmodernism and Africa? The notion that modern culture, in the West as in Africa, is moving in a postmodern direction could blind us to what is really happening in Africa today. It could also distract attention from the other, perhaps more subtle and meaningful, ways in which Western culture is indeed affecting Africans. More significantly, the postmodern discourse could influence the manner of our conceptualising postcolonial African politics, not primarily because we think that Africans are now suddenly postmodern (whatever that might mean) but because we might be beginning to think of the notion of the individual, and the relationship between individual and society, in ways which are influenced by the postmodern discourse.

Indeed, any notion of the individual as being increasingly multicultural and universal in outlook – whether such is an accurate description of what is happening to Western societies or not – would make it more difficult for us to understand the ways in which Africans behave as individuals. It would also be in contradiction with what in other contexts we tend to view as the 're-traditionalisation' of African societies. And, in so far as this apparent 're-traditionalisation' is obviously at odds with the causalities implied in the notion of the postmodern, instead of working to understand Africans as they are, we might yet again look at them holding a mirror to ourselves.

Postideological   The argument here is simple even if it has tended to be too neatly encapsulated within the debate popularised by Fukuyama about 'the end of history' (first published in Fukuyama 1989). The grounds on which we are said now to live in a postideological world are essentially two. The first is that, with the end of the Cold War and the apparent collapse of communism, there is now no longer any ideological battle to be fought. Socialism is dead and there is no worthwhile political ideology to challenge the liberal democratic ideal. The second, therefore, is that the political agenda is now firmly one of democratisation or, more broadly, the improvement in democratic political accountability.

To take the first point first, it is true that the end of the Cold War has created a new political context for Africa. The end of superpower rivalry and the *de facto* supremacy of the West in international affairs have certainly restricted the diplomatic options of African states and narrowed the scope of their agenda to what might be called 'structural adjustment plus democratisation'. African socialism is long dead and all former 'socialist' countries officially favour economic and political liberalisation. There is no longer any prospect of foreign aid coming from the former Soviet Union or Eastern Europe. All this is true as far as it goes, but in the case of Africa it does not go very far.

Leaving aside Fukuyama's spurious neo-Hegelian simplifications and narrowing our focus here to considerations which matter to Africa, it is not difficult to see that the consequences of the end of the Cold War are practical rather than ideological. Africans rulers 'become' democrats because the World Bank says they should, not because they suddenly accept either that democratisation is a 'better' political way forward or that their rule should be subject to democratic political accountability. Indeed, where there are other paymasters, other ideologies are easily adopted. For example, there is in some African countries a distinct move towards Islamic fundamentalism which is not unrelated to the (financial and ideological) influence of countries such as Iran or Saudi Arabia.

The assumption, therefore, that the end of the Cold War is *ipso facto* likely to strengthen democratisation in Africa is an illusion, and a dangerous illusion at that. The much heralded death of socialism cannot in any way seriously be taken as the advent of a postideological world. First, so long as China remains a communist country it is a trifle premature to disregard communism as an ideology (whatever it may in practice mean). Second, there are other non- (or even anti-) socialist 'ideologies' currently challenging the liberal democratic ethos, of which two of the most powerful are clearly the religious and the nationalist, which have combined in countries such as Iran. Third, the belief that the ruin of one ideology implies the advent of a less ideological world is a belief which rests on the naive assumption that there is an ascending political evolution by which man eventually leaves ideology behind.

The evidence in postcolonial Africa does not point to a great battle between the two Cold War ideological perspectives; rather it shows that underneath the rhetoric of their rulers Africans have sought to reinterpret the ideological superstructure on which the postcolonial state claims to rest according to the moral, cultural, political and religious values which determine and make sense of their everyday life. How they have done so, how this has influenced the conduct of politics and whether it has increased accountability are all questions which can be answered only in the specific study of individual countries.

The current belief in a postideological world could, of course, have a liberating influence on the ways in which we approach the study of contemporary African politics. If the end of the Cold War means that we pay less attention to the high politics of ideological pronouncements and more to the multilayered meanings of what the French have called '*politique par le bas*', then we might begin to understand better what is happening in Africa. If, on the other hand, we interpret recent events as the triumph of liberal democratic ideology over its competitors, then we might seek to find in Africa confirmation for our (very ideological) assumption of Western democratic supremacy.

In this respect, the present debate about democratisation in Africa is not overly encouraging. That the World Bank should impose (democratic) political conditionalities on African countries is not startling. Nor is it surprising that the Western media have greeted the 'conversion' of the continent to democracy with unabashed enthusiasm. It is, however, a little worrying when Africanists interpret the recent events in Africa as firm evidence that (1) there is a simple causal relation between 'the end of ideology' and democratisation, and (2) that there is indeed in Africa a move towards greater political accountability. The process is far more complex, and unless that complexity is understood we run the risk of comforting ourselves once more with what will turn out to be only the latest delusion about Africa.

Interpretation

Having set the context within which Western Africanists work today, I now want to look at the question of the interpretation of African post-colonial politics. One thing which is clear is that, when it comes to analysing contemporary politics, there is no overall consensus on what 'understanding' might mean. At the very least, therefore, it is important to make explicit the purpose of understanding. I suggest that there are here three broad frameworks for the interpretation of postcolonial African politics: the historical, the analytical and the prescriptive (or policy-oriented). The three are obviously interrelated and obviously impinge on each other. I separate them here for the sake of conceptual clarity precisely because I believe that the failure to make explicit the perspective from which one writes about Africa has been one of the main causes of the weakness of interpretation in respect of what is actually happening in Africa today.

The general handicap under which we, Western Africanists, labour is our heritage – by which I mean the accumulated weight of what our culture says about Africa. To us in the West, Africa is that part of the world which remains most deeply endowed with the two central facets of the 'other': that is, the mysterious and the exotic. Mysterious not just in the sense that we do not understand its reality well but also in that its reality is not really amenable to our understanding. Exotic in that it fulfils in us that most enduring need to find in some (suitably distant) 'other' that quality of inexplicability which is both frightening in its apparent irrationality and reassuring in that it highlights our own rationality.

Leaving aside these general considerations, which, however trivially obvious they may appear to be, have in my opinion much more influence on our present understanding of Africa than we realise or are prepared to accept, I now turn to some of the more specific analytical difficulties which we, Africanists, face. The three I have chosen to highlight are: (1) the politics of the mirror; (2) the tyranny of causalities, and (3) the implications of enunciation. I discuss each briefly in turn.

The politics of the mirror   I refer here to the way in which Africanists have approached Africa, nowadays as in the past. Partly because Africa has been seen as both mysterious and exotic, Africanists have been prone to seek in Africa a counterpoint to their own history. Although this is perhaps most obvious in respect of the anthropologist, looking for the 'primitive' societies from which we are supposed to have evolved, it is also visible in the work of almost all other Africanists.

Explorers, missionaries, colonial officials, settlers, economists, experts and political scientists, have all at some point looked at Africa from the perspective of the evolution of their own Western societies. This is particularly noticeable and consequential when it comes to the work of postcolonial (economic or political) developmentalists. Indeed, the assumptions they have made on the trajectory of contemporary Africa have in large part issued from their notion of the 'backwardness' of the continent in relation to the development of the West.

'Politics of the mirror', therefore, in that the main effect of such a teleological perspective has been to search in Africa for an image of the

African that would confirm our developmentalist assumptions about ourselves. The consequences have been as inevitable as they were predictable. First, we have perennially been disappointed in that the reality of Africa has never matched our expectations. Second, and more ominously, we have failed to look at Africa as it is (in its local and historical context) rather than as we imagine it to be. Third, and as a result, we have confined Africa to the dustbin of history; that is, as a continent the history of which we cannot be expected to understand and on which we eventually 'give up'.

The other aspect of the politics of the mirror which it is worth considering is what I call the Caliban syndrome. This takes two forms: (1) the fact that when Africans speak we only hear what comforts the notion of Africa we hold; and (2) the extent to which Africans have learned to speak the language we want or need to hear. This has been a problem throughout the history of Western–African relations and I would argue it is still very much a problem today. Perhaps the most revealing illustration of this syndrome is the whole question of 'tribalism'. Historians of Africa now readily accept that the notion of ethnicity, like that of the nation, is largely an invention, that our original assessment of the continent's ethnicity was essentially a figment of our historical imagination and that Africans were not slow in exploiting the ethnic language devised by the colonial mind.

Less clear, but maybe more consequential, is the extent to which the Caliban syndrome continues to dictate our perception of the condition and needs of contemporary Africa. I will mention here only two examples. The first has to do with the area of project aid, the second concerns the debate about democratisation.

The controversy over project aid has arisen because of the realisation that aid could in fact be detrimental to the development of Africa. The argument here is that (1) projects are defined in the terms that are congenial to the donor, not to those for whom the projects are intended; (2) that those African officials who press for such project aid do so because they know that this is the language they must currently use to extract resources from the West; and (3) those resources will be used primarily by those who claim them rather than by those in whose name they are claimed. The donors give because this is part of a congenial image they have of themselves (and also because they will directly benefit). The recipients ask to be given to because they know that this is the language best suited to elicit aid today.

As for democratisation, the case is even clearer. The West demands a democracy in which it can recognise itself: party plurality, party competition, regular multiparty elections and parliamentary politics. Africans oblige by setting in motion a process of democratisation which meets these conditionalities. Whether this advances the cause of democracy is

another matter. I am not saying that the current process of democratisation
in Africa is meaningless; rather that its agenda is largely set by the West,
with the (more or less enthusiastic) acquiescence of those Africans who
have learned to speak the new language of democracy, regardless of
whether the circumstances of individual countries are propitious to the
creation or strengthening of political accountability by way of the Western
recipe of multiparty elections.

The same could be argued of structural adjustment. It is not that there
is no need for the financial and economic management which adjustment
entails, as there obviously is. The question is whether structural adjustment is the most appropriate package of economic reforms for all African
countries or whether it is merely the latest in a long line of 'development'
blueprints for Africa. The fact that some Africans are now prepared to
support structural adjustment is not in itself an indication of its desirability.
It is, rather, the proof that those Africans are adept at learning the language
which will deliver the most financial aid from the West.

The paradoxical effect of the politics of the mirror is that in the
failure to find an image of Africa which is congruent with our vision of
ourselves, we have tended to explain away what happens in Africa by way
of its 'Africanness'. That is, in so far as the reality of Africa continually
frustrates our understanding of the continent in terms of an account of
ourselves, we all too easily resort to the other extreme: that is, saying that
Africa is special, unique, *sui generis*. And because of this we slide into the
tautological interpretative trap which consists of saying that what happens
in Africa, such as 'tribalist' violence, is due to the 'Africanness' of African
politics.

The tyranny of causalities   The point I want to make here is simple and
it follows in part from the previous one: in trying to interpret events in
contemporary Africa we have all too willingly resorted to simple causalities
in at least two ways. The first is the widespread (ab)use of theories of
historical causation. The second is the quite extraordinary tendency to
explain complex processes in Africa by way of simple causalities which
we would never accept in respect of our own societies.

A review of the main paradigms for the analysis of postcolonial African
politics shows the hold which causal explanations have had on our various
interpretative frameworks (see Chabal 1992). From the succession of
Marxist or dependency theories to the various developmental schools, by
way of a myriad of supposedly causally significant cultural interpretations,
our view of contemporary African politics has been singularly obsessed
by the search for an all-conquering theory of causal explanation.

This, of course, is nothing new. The 'exploration' and the subsequent
annexation of Africa occurred in the heyday of the great theories of
evolution and historical causation. From the beginning, Africa fitted neatly

into the vision of the development of the human race which took hold of the European mind in the nineteenth century. In social and cultural terms, the Africans were deemed to be near the bottom of the evolutionary scale. In terms of economic development, they were thought to occupy a slot a shade above hunting and gathering societies but well below feudal ones.

For this reason, the colonial 'mission' was justified and underpinned by a belief in the simple causality of development which European imperial rule would undoubtedly create and sustain. The postcolonial disillusion at the lack of 'progress' in Africa is thus not just a matter of disabused colonial pride but also the process of coming to terms with the end of the great colonial developmental dreams – itself part of the realisation in the last third of this century of the limitation of the (Marxist as well as anti-Marxist) theories of historical causation.

Paradoxically, however, African nationalists and the rulers of post-colonial Africa have continued to reason in terms of the causalities which seemed to explain both the advent and the end of colonial rule. Flush with the experience of the 'inevitable' collapse of colonialism and well tutored in the theories of development which both left and right proposed in the 1960s, it was also in their political interest to interpret independence as the great causal trigger to economic and political development. In this they were comforted by West and East which, at the height of the Cold War, peddled their own theories of causality.

The gradual realisation that all such theories, whether economic, political or cultural, failed to explain what was going on in Africa has not, unfortunately, marked the end of the age of teleology in relation to Africa. Instead of deducing from the interpretative failure of such theoretical schemes the need to forgo simple causality in the analysis of contemporary Africa, there has for some time been a tendency to look for the African (as opposed to universal) causality of events in Africa. So it is, for example, that the 'tribal' imperative is now often represented as the *ultima ratio* of African politics. Of course, this too has been made worse by the fact that African rulers have themselves readily indulged in 'tribal' rhetoric and have in this way helped to create a climate in which political competition and hostility are readily channelled along ethnic lines.

In this respect, we seem generally to be no nearer to understanding 'tribalism' in Africa today than we were a hundred years ago. The primary reason why we continue to be baffled by ethnicity in Africa is largely because we come to it from a preconceived perspective both on the notion of human 'evolution' and on the place of ethnicity within such a scheme of 'evolution'. Ethnicity, therefore, is a condition which afflicts the 'other' at an early stage in evolution. Stated in this way, this reasoning is immediately seen as crude and would now no longer be acceptable to many. But in the more tortuous language used by journalists and 'experts', it

sometimes seems difficult to get away from the notion that ethnicity is
either a 'left-over' from a previous age or the false consciousness which
afflicts peoples easily misled by ruthless leaders.

Yet, as Lonsdale has demonstrated in his recent work, the problem we
have with the notions of ethnicity and tribalism in Africa issues largely
from the way we approach them. He writes:

> Western students of Africa have, until recently, felt defensive about the
> continent's political ethnicity, anxious to disarm the racist prejudice of our
> readers. We used to make excuses for Africans: tribalism was not their fault.
> Now that some European tribes have proved to be more savage than most of
> Africa's, that timidity is disappearing. But the issue will always be complex.
> Ethnicity is a world-wide social fact; all human beings make their cultures within
> communities that define themselves against 'others'. But we do not always
> politicise culture; and when we do, it may not necessarily be to pursue a
> reactionary xenophobia. To imagine the existence of a new 'tribe' may be the
> best way to look outward, to embrace social progress. Students of Africa are
> now beginning to understand such ambiguity – that while some aspects of
> ethnicity are indeed inherited and conservative, its meanings are also reinvented
> every day, to meet new needs. Cultural identity is what people make it rather
> than what they historically and ineluctably are. And 'moral ethnicity' – what I
> call that contested internal standard of civic virtue against which we measure
> our personal esteem – is very different from the unprincipled 'political tribalism'
> with which groups compete for public resources. (Lonsdale, n.d.; for a more
> general treatment of his argument as applied to the Kikuyu, see Lonsdale 1992)

It follows from this that the complexities of ethnicity and the political
usages to which it may be put are to be explained historically. Once we
accept this, we can see that ethnicity, like nationalism, can become
politically salient under certain circumstances and that whether its political
impact is constructive or destructive depends on the specific historical
context.

The example of ethnicity illustrates the more general proposition that
an analysis of contemporary African politics demands that we move away
from the curse of causalities which has obscured our understanding of
the continent for so long. To do so, of course, we shall have to know its
history better. We shall also have to be mindful of what we say.

The implications of enunciation   Beyond the need to resist the temptation to indulge in the vocabulary of causalities, I want to discuss the
particular difficulties which Africanists face in the choice of words they
use to 'explain' Africa. I do not here just mean the sensitivity to use a
language that does not demean the people about whom we write – which
I take for granted – nor do I mean to recommend the use of a politically
correct language, for political correctness is one of the most stultifying
and limiting discourses extant today.

I refer rather to the difficult issue of the relationship between the analysis of reality and its enunciation. Once we move away from the coded language of simple or at least well understood causal explanations, we enter the territory of greater subtlety but also greater ambiguity. Nothing is plain, nothing is entirely clear. What we see, or what we think we see, is not objectively identifiable but depends in part on how we apprehend and enunciate it. To return to the perennial African example, how the colonial mind perceived and enunciated the 'fact' of ethnicity had a direct bearing both on the perception and reality of that 'phenomenon'.

Mercifully, most of us are now aware of the importance of enunciation. But we are still too close to a situation where we know what we should not say but are not so sure of how to express ourselves in order to account for contemporary African politics – still a defensive rather than positive attitude. We need now to search for the concepts and the vocabulary which will make it possible to advance insight into the realities of contemporary Africa.

In this respect, there is no doubt that the work of those French political scientists associated with *Politique Africaine* has pointed us in the right direction.[2] The focus on *le* rather than *la politique* and the injunction to take on board 'politique par le bas' – low rather than high politics – have been useful.[3] Much good work has issued from this approach which, taken in conjunction with the advance in African historiography, has enabled us to move away from simplistic causal explanations. Similarly, works on the politics of areas which hitherto had not received much attention (such as literature, slang, music, religion, sport) have greatly helped us better understand what is sometimes called the politics of civil society.

Perhaps the most widely cited, if undoubtedly the least read, of the French volumes is Bayart's *L'Etat en Afrique: la politique du ventre* (1989; 1993). This is an important book for many reasons, not the least of which is that it synthesises much of the work done in France over the decade before its publication. But I want to discuss here one particular aspect of the book: the way in which its author attempts to enunciate what he believes to be the realities of postcolonial African politics. By definition, a book which seeks to enunciate rather than merely to explain African politics is one which is not amenable to simple summary. Its interpretative virtues and analytical insights lie in the creative ambiguity of its vocabulary and in the tone of the language used.[4] At the heart of Bayart's account of the role of the state in Africa is the search for the appropriate African metaphor for the business of politics: in the event he chose '*la politique du ventre*'.

Bayart justifies his choice on the grounds that what he renders in French as 'la politique du ventre' is a common and widely-used concept of political analysis in Africa. This is important in that it shows that the author's starting-point is the very language in which Africans themselves express their understanding of politics rather than some extraneous notion which is deemed by Africanists 'to explain' African politics. The contents of the book make good the promise to analyse African politics in a language congruent with the way in which Africans perceive and express 'their' politics. This is as it should be and no more than we would expect of a similar book on 'our' politics. To understand the local context of the political language of Africans is the first step towards relating the specifics of the case at hand with the more universal analytical concepts which are needed to explain political processes in comparative perspective.

The book thus brings home the importance of enunciation in political analysis, which we know instinctively to be true of our own societies but which we have failed, for too long, to realise in respect of Africa. Nevertheless, *L'Etat en Afrique* also demonstrates the limits, and even the pitfalls, of this (necessary) approach. Indeed, the use of the metaphor of '*la politique du ventre*' is both insightful and mischievous. It is insightful in that it expresses one of the fundamental aspects of African politics and certainly an aspect of which there has been far too little understanding. Equating '*la politique du ventre*' with corruption, for example, is a typically reductionist form of analysis.

It is mischievous, however, in that it cannot have escaped Bayart (as it will not escape his readers) that the implications of the metaphor are double-edged. It may well reflect accurately one of the principal ways in which Africans (and others, for that matter) perceive and conceptualise politics but it certainly does not encompass the full range of the African political experience. Furthermore, the use of the word '*ventre*' is not neutral and it could easily comfort us into thinking, again, that Africans are fundamentally different. In that way, the metaphor is limiting and, as Bayart himself surely must know, a trifle patronising. It occurs to me that Bayart would have been slightly more cautious in his choice of metaphor had he been writing of Frenchmen rather than Cameroonians. But perhaps not!

Future research

I conclude by referring briefly to the two central arguments of my book, *Power in Africa* (1992). They are simple. The first is that we need to study the particular – that is, what is 'African' in African politics – by means of universal concepts: by which I mean general concepts of political analysis which we would be happy to apply to our own societies. The second is that we must ground our political analysis of contemporary events in the deep history of Africa – that is, the history which reconnects the present with the colonial and precolonial past. Readers of *Power in Africa* will know why I argue for a political analysis grounded in the notions of power and accountability.

The five concepts which I discuss extensively in the book are: the political community, political accountability, the state, civil society and production. But I would stress what I believe are the three most fundamental notions of political analysis: identity, political community and political accountability. These are universal in the sense that they are self-evidently relevant to the political analysis of any part of the world. Yet, they are broad enough to make possible the analysis of specific case studies, in Africa as elsewhere. Furthermore, they provide a focus for the study of politics at different levels: local and regional as well as national.

Simple as these concepts may appear to be, it will be immediately apparent to the political analyst of Africa that we are still a long way from being able to use them profitably. This is because we lack knowledge of both the actual realities of postcolonial Africa and of the long history of Africans. The truth about much current analysis of postcolonial African politics is that it is singularly ill-informed about anything other than the overt, explicit discourse of high politics. And it seems to have escaped the notice of many who write on Africa that the discourse of high politics is, always and everywhere, the smoke-screen behind which the real business of politics is conducted. As for the focus on high politics, it is necessarily at the expense of an examination of 'low' politics, the politics of everyday life.

My argument is that the concepts of identity, community and accountability form the foundations of political analysis. It is in the multifarious ways in which individuals define themselves and others that the political community takes shape and evolves. Political accountability – the manifold and complex practice through which the ruled seek to hold the rulers to account – in turn, provides the principle by which political communities keep together. Without some form of mutually acceptable political accountability, the political community cannot survive for long without recourse to force or violence. While the threat of force is part of the calculus of power, its actual (and especially repeated) use is evidence of the manifest failure of accountability.

An analysis based on these concepts makes it possible to ask fundamental questions about the make-up and functioning of any polity. But it is particularly appropriate to the study of the postcolonial politics of African nation-states for at least four reasons. First, it focuses attention on the realities, as opposed to the discourse, of politics in Africa. Second, it enables us to link the study of high and low politics. Third, it forces consideration of the deep history (from precolonial to the present) of what lies behind these three notions. Finally, and perhaps most importantly, it makes it clear that political analysis is all about understanding processes over time – that is, the opposite of edifying 'snapshot' explanations.

I believe there are three important lines of further enquiry for the analysis of politics in contemporary Africa. First, the relationship between identity and politics, and in particular the systematic study of what Lonsdale calls 'moral ethnicity and political tribalism'. Some important issues here would concern the notion of individual, the meaning of political community, political language, the foundations of political legitimacy and the components of political accountability.

Second, the nature of the relationship between nation and state. Among the key issues here are: the apparent deliquescence of the state in Africa, the debate as to whether Africa needs a stronger state or a more decentralised one and, finally, the plausible paths for more politically accountable politics in Africa, the changing complexion (or possible demise) of the postnationalist nation-state in Africa, the break-up of some independent countries, the debate about pan-Africanism and regionalism, the possibilities of a federal Africa.

Third, the connection between culture and economic development, that is, looking essentially at the question raised, among others, by the Cameroonian Axel Kabou in his provocative book entitled *Et si l'Afrique refusait le développement* (What if Africa refused to develop) (1992). The arguments here are complex but they boil down to an investigation into whether the causes of Africa's lack of economic development, that is productive investment, are to be found in its cultural make-up. Important issues include the nature of Africa's economic dependence, the relationship between mentalities and technological development, the primacy of 'display' over investment and the role of political leadership in economic development.

Notes

1. In this chapter I draw on the arguments of my book (Chabal 1992).
2. *Politique Africaine* was launched in 1980 by the members of the Association des Chercheurs de Politique Africaine and is now on its fifty-fifth issue. Each volume focuses on one specific theme or country.
3. The distinction between *le politique* and *la politique* is as follows: the former refers to all that which is 'politic' in society while the latter concerns politics in its usual and practical meaning.
4. Much of which seems to have defeated those charged with translating the book.

References

Adedeji, Adebayo. (ed.). 1993. *Africa within the World: Beyond Dispossession and Dependence.* London: Zed Books.

Bayart, Jean-François. 1989. *L'état en Afrique. La politique du ventre.* Paris: Fayard.

— 1993. *The State in Africa: The Politics of the Belly.* Translated by Mary Harper, Christopher Harrison and Elizabeth Harrison. London: Longman.

Chabal, Patrick. 1992. *Power in Africa*. London: Macmillan, 2nd edn, 1994.

Fukuyama, Francis. 1989. 'The End of History', *National Interest* 16: 3–18.

Kabou, Alex. 1992. *Et si l'Afrique refusait le développement*. Paris: L'Harmattan.

Lemarchand, Rene. 1994. *Burundi: Ethnocide as Discourse and Practice*. Cambridge: Woodrow Wilson Center Press and Cambridge University Press.

Lonsdale, John. 1992. 'The Moral Economy of Mau Mau', in B. Berman and J. Lonsdale (eds), *Unhappy Valley: Conflict in Kenya and Africa*. London: James Currey, 265–504.

— n.d. *Moral Ethnicity and Political Tribalism*. Unpublished manuscript.

CHAPTER 2

A lost generation? Youth identity and state decay in West Africa

Donal B. Cruise O'Brien

It has been convincingly argued that the marginalised youth of postcolonial
Africa in general have an unpromising political role. On the one hand,
they are a natural opposition, having so little to lose and being so resentful
of a situation in which they are left to get by as best they may. On the
other hand, however, these young people are very poorly equipped to
make their opposition effective: with their limited resources, they are easily
manipulated by their elders. A youth revolution, therefore, is not around
the corner. This is the realistic conclusion of Bayart, Mbembe and
Toulabor, the co-authors of *Le Politique par le bas en Afrique Noire* (Bayart
et al. 1992). For these authors, the emergence of a counter-hegemony will
depend upon the emergence of a counter-elite, which is in general a
possibility rather than an actuality.[1]

One may ask then how young people in West Africa see their political
identity, how far they see their generation as one with a distinct predicament. Answers to such questions will have to be nuanced, will vary from
one situation to another, although in overall terms one may see the
problem in something like the terms used by Sunil Khilnani for the Indian
demos: 'free to engage in the creation of collective identities, an activity
which in a democracy will always partly escape the powers of the state to
define and coerce' (Dunn 1992: 205). West Africa does not of course
offer any example of a democracy as rooted as that of India, but the
limited powers of the state in matters of identity are comparable. In West
Africa the formation of political identity is an area of possibility for the
young, one thing that young people can do in an otherwise prevailing
powerlessness.

To study youth politics is to study politics 'from below', very clearly so
if one follows Bayart in defining 'youth' in political rather than biological
terms, studying the politics of the powerless. This is a challenging research
agenda: when the explicitly political, in parties or associations, is controlled
by the dominant elders, the implicit politics of those without power must
proceed by 'mobility, by ambivalence, by what isn't said' (Bayart 1992b:

40). Dissimulation is also of course among such weapons of the weak, but it is the ambivalence which is most strongly emphasised in Comi Toulabor's studies of the Togolese crowd under the Eyadema regime (Toulabor 1986; Bayart et al. 1992). Thus the crowd is seen as participating in Eyadema's domination over them: they do ridicule the General in obscene terms, but there is also a furtive collusion in popular attitudes to the extravagances of power.

Violence is a recurrent feature of youth politics. Riot and looting, crime, the 'daily deconstruction of the state' (Bayart 1992a: 17), are popular under 'democratic' regimes (such as Senegal and Mali) as well as under authoritarian ones. And the Togolese example helps to make the general point that the people may be opposed to democracy. The theme of the ambivalence of popular attitudes to power returns in Achille Mbembe's postcolony, where the 'laughter' of the subject at the extravagances of power is heard as an ambiguous sound: 'the obscenity of power … is also fed by a desire for majesty on the part of the people' (Mbembe 1992a: 25). This postcolony, Cameroonian in most of its details, is characterised above all by scarcity, the backdrop for the extravagant official processions. The plebeians are happy to cheer at the imperial parade, or so at least it would appear. That's entertainment, perhaps, but there is derision also in those cheers, indicating a disposition not to obey.

This ambivalence in popular attitudes to the state has been noted by other observers of African politics, as for example by Michael Bratton, who remarks that while citizens 'resent the intrusion of the state into family life' they 'remain drawn to the state because, even in diminished circumstances it remains a major source of spoils and one of the only available channels for getting what little there is to get' (Bratton 1989: 414–15). Young people's attitudes toward 'le pouvoir' in Mali are seen in similarly dichotomous terms by Louis Brenner (1994: 2, 4). Access to the state is the most valued of prizes, while the exactions and impositions of the state are resented and feared, coming as they often do in brutal or incomprehensible forms.

The particular situation of the youth of the 1980s in Africa has led more than one observer to use the phrase 'a lost generation': in Kenya, where Kalenjin repossession of previously Kikuyu land has involved the violent displacement of large numbers of people who were made homeless around the time of the 1992 elections (Human Rights Watch/Africa Watch 1993: 80); in Liberia, where civil war has similarly led to massive population displacement, a social upheaval seen by Paul Richards as a crisis of youth (Richards 1994); in South Africa, where the 'political' youth generation of the 1980s ('liberation now, education later') has had to come to terms with unemployment and social marginalisation in the 1990s. Thus in his East London study Lungisile Ntsebeza puts the question, 'What happens to the out of school out of work youth who were involved in politics?'

(in the 1980s) and answers that 'today excessive liquor consumption seems
to be their alternative ... since the late 1980s and early 1990s, terms like
the "Lost Generation", and "marginalised youth" have gained wide
currency' (Ntsebeza 1993: 163–6).[2]

The common denominator for these different youth situations is that
the young people have finished schooling, are without employment in the
formal sector, and are not in a position to set up an independent household. This is the common material predicament of the young people
studied in Mali, Senegal and northern Nigeria, in an interdisciplinary
research project focused on youth in modern Africa (co-principals: Brenner,
Cruise O'Brien, Last, Parkin).[3] Together with the evidence from East Africa
(Kenya) and South Africa, it would seem clear that the situation is of
continental proportions.

The 'lost generation' label may thus mark a rupture from the relatively
comfortable socialisation procedures of the period from 1960 to the late
1970s – boom years, at least as seen in retrospect.[4] Yet it must immediately
be recognised that some of the young are more lost than others, even if
the shared backdrop is one of marginalisation. There are predators among
the young as well as heroes and victims, criminals in the shanty-towns and
military entrepreneurs in the warzones. Thus the *casseurs* (breakers) have
emerged in urban Senegal since 1988, taking advantage of political crises
to go on looting sprees: 'undesirable and long marginalised actors are
destroying, or taking by force, property to which they had long been
denied access' (Diop and Diop 1993: 30). The young *tsotsis* in South Africa,
out of work and out of school, have taken similar private advantage on
the margins of political action in the 1980s: their actions are remembered
by one ex-comrade, 'M': 'in times of action, whilst we hold meetings and
articulate positions, they attend such meetings and listen. The minute a
decision is taken to boycott buses, for example, they will leave the meeting
and disappear. By the time the meeting is over, a few buses will have been
stoned. That is how they operate. They like anything that tends to be
disruptive, that is what they enjoy' (Ntsebeza 1993: 145). In Senegal, as in
South Africa, political meetings and parties have been the prerogative of
the educated, including those in revolt against their education; 'politics' in
a sense is for the already privileged.

To return to the question of a generational consciousness, an awareness
of a common situation in relation to preceding generations, there is often
to be heard a contrast of today's hard times with the relatively prosperous
circumstances in which one's parents grew to adulthood – and set up
their independent households. A tendency to the breakdown of the family
in more recent times has been remarked by some observers and in some
circumstances, although many young people can still call on their parents
for material support well past the years of adolescence. With a shrinking
number of viable new independent households, however, anchored in

some sort of secure employment for the head of household, one must see the future as dark enough. This would appear to be a liminal generation, on the edge of what can become a social collapse, as in Liberia and a number of other state situations where violence tears at the fabric of social relations.[5]

A generational contrast can thus be made between those who grew to adulthood in the first two decades of African independence (1960–80), and their successors who see their 'youth' as something which is at risk of becoming indefinitely prolonged. This contrast has its material definition: economic independence, to have enough resources to marry and set up one's own family, is the fundamental aspiration of youth, in West Africa as elsewhere in the world. In contemporary West Africa, however, for most young people the realisation of this aspiration (which many in their parents' generation could take for granted) seems to be a near impossibility. Youth continues to aspire to adulthood, to an escape from the dependence of a junior status: one youth in Dakar, interviewed for a local newspaper in the period leading up to the presidential election of 1993, put his electoral choice bluntly in this perspective: 'If you start from the principle that youth has no perspectives and no future, what we want from the next president is simple: to work, provide for the future, to become somebody' (Wigram 1994: 20).[6] Becoming somebody can no longer be taken for granted.

Demographic considerations are relevant here, and the case of Senegal is taken to illustrate the apparent perils in the medium- to long-term trends. Youth accounts for an increasing proportion of total population, with a recent rapid fall in infant and child mortality: while the country's total population grew at the rate of nearly 3 per cent per annum, over the period 1976–88, those of 'school' age (six to fifteen) grew at the rate of 4 per cent p.a. And those below eighteen years of age accounted for a very clear majority, 57.7 per cent. Senegal's population is thus in proportional terms increasingly young, and it is also increasingly urban: the growth rate for the capital city over this same period was 3.9 per cent p.a. These are not exceptional statistics in African terms, but they amount to a warning for future political stability and civic peace, particularly when taken together with national statistics in the fields of education and of employment. The tendency to urbanisation is on the increase, and is unlikely to be reversed in the near future (Senegal 1993).

One government response to this urbanising tendency is to look to the provision of mass education, which at least in the short term can shore up regime legitimacy even in extreme circumstances, as for example in Zaire (Young and Turner 1985: 135–7).[7] Educational provision responds to a real popular demand, it has had the support of international donor agencies, it helps to avert the sort of chaos which has descended, for example, on Liberia. But besides being of low quality, mass education creates problems for the future, as the partially educated young people have new expectations in terms of jobs, of income, of lifestyle. Understandably, the Senegalese government has chosen the short-run solution of increasing educational provision. Under the Diouf regime, over the period 1980–89, numbers in primary schools have increased 5.8 per cent per annum; in middle schools 6.7 per cent p.a.; in secondary schools 9.1 per cent p.a.; in higher education, 5.7 per cent p.a. By the end of this decade (1989) a clear majority of the eligible population attended primary school (59 per cent), while a substantial minority (16 per cent) attended secondary school. Such educational statistics, when taken together with those for Senegal's continuing economic stagnation, amount to a recipe for future disaster: in one expert's opinion, it would take an economic growth rate of 7–10 per cent p.a. to absorb this educated population, a rate far beyond realistic expectation in this context.

So what happens to all these partially educated young people, an increasing proportion of them in towns? Very few of them can hope to find employment in the 'modern' sector: the public sector (in Senegal as in many other West African states) has been under structural adjustment for more than a decade, with very tight constraints on new hiring, and the industrial sector has been shedding labour since the mid-1980s. Roughly 40,000 young people each year in towns came to working age in Senegal; of them, perhaps 5 per cent find jobs in the formal or modern sector. The rest are either unemployed or are absorbed by the informal sector, in petty trade, hustling, getting by, with a significant residue in crime. A criminal life may look like a rational choice in this setting, more promising than political activity.

Comparison with the youth of Bamako, Mali, as studied by Brenner and Bagayogo (Brenner 1994), helps to put the case of Dakar in perspective. In Bamako even more than Dakar the route to economic independence is blocked for the younger generation, with the consequence of 'increasing tensions between families and between the sexes' (ibid.: 1). Tensions within families, together with a breakdown in intergenerational communication, were also observable in Dakar in 1989, following two years which had been marked by periods of near-uncontrollable rioting in that city. In October 1989, six months after the mass killing of Mauritanians in the towns and cities of Senegal, some forty-to-fifty-year-old interviewees expressed what amounted to a fear of the younger generation. The young had learned how to kill, and an unspoken question sometimes seemed to lurk: were any of my children among those killers? A student interviewed at this time confided that 'young people are storing their knives'.[8] Students too can be predators, as in Mali, where traders have taken to forming self-defence groups to meet the threat of students in marauding bands (Wigram 1994: 36).

The older generation have also called on traditional procedures for the maintenance of social control, as in Bamako through 'the manipulation of shame ... reinforced by the position the family occupies within various clientelist networks' (Brenner 1994: 1–2). As much could be said of Dakar, where the clientelist networks furthermore appear to be in a good deal more robust condition. In the Senegalese case these networks are embedded within what it is not absurd to call a (religiously based) civil society, an associational life with a degree of independence of the state. Intergenerational tensions are to be remarked within and through these religious associations, a point which is developed below.

The substance of statehood in Senegal, the linkages between state and society, have been above all in interactions with the country's Sufi brotherhoods. The brotherhoods provide a framework for negotiation with the state, through which society can exert pressure on those in power by the threat of a withdrawal of co-operation. Those in power have learned, from long experience, to respect such threats, so that there is more democracy in Senegal than is obvious from national election returns. Youth identity within those brotherhoods has long been subsumed within a corporate allegiance to a brotherhood, an allegiance embracing all generations: but times are changing here, and over the last ten years a distinct political identity of youth has emerged.

Youth politics within Senegal's religious brotherhoods has been focused in recent years around the Parti Démocratique Sénégalais (PDS), with its slogan and rallying cry of change (*sopi*). The 1988 election, in particular, marked a high point of enthusiasm and then of disappointment for a younger generation which had been mobilised around the PDS electoral slogan (Young and Kanté 1992). The anger and violence of young PDS supporters were most conspicuous in the capital city, after the official declaration of the governing Socialist Party's victory, but the hope for change had been widespread in the country at this time. Younger disciples in the Mouride brotherhood, and also a younger segment of the brotherhood's leadership in Touba, were voting PDS in 1988 despite the instructions (the *ndiggel*) of the brotherhood's Khalifa-General to vote for the governing party.[9]

The fact that the governing Socialist Party won the 1988 election, according to the officially declared results and also in the opinion of the best-qualified independent observers, would appear to have endorsed the Khalifa-General's political judgement. But the consequence within the brotherhood was that the supreme leader had seriously compromised his own position, having given 'binding' electoral instructions that were widely disobeyed. At the same time the Khalifa-General had also revealed to the Senegalese government that the effectiveness of his role as an electoral broker was diminishing (Villalon 1994: 332). There are democratic pressures at work within the Mouride brotherhood, pressures on the part of a younger generation which has grown impatient with the view of Senegal's changeless political horizons. Senegal is a quasi-democracy, in which multiparty elections are held every five years; the same party, under different names, has always won these elections since national independence (indeed, since 1952).

Younger disciples within the Sufi brotherhoods, interviewed in 1989 and 1992,[10] frequently expressed their intention to make their electoral choices independent in future, without regard to the brotherhood leaders. In heated discussions the younger urban disciples (ages roughly eighteen to twenty-five) defended what amounted to a secular position: *marabouts* should keep out of politics. The religious leaders appear to have heeded such opinions: at the next round of the national elections, in 1993, Senegal's Muslim brotherhood leaders for the first time since national independence abstained from giving orders or advice to the disciples to vote for the governing party. Such reticence in the religious leadership may be seen as marking another manifestation of democracy, a recognition by the leaders that they risked losing disciples if they persisted in the traditional political engagement.

The mobilisation of youth in Senegal in recent years has not only been occasioned by electoral politics. The ethnic violence of April–May 1989, when hundreds of Mauritanians were killed in angry retaliation for the reported killing of Senegalese in Mauritania, was at the hands of marauding mobs. Spontaneous rage would appear to have predominated in the first stage of this outburst, a response to the news of mutilated corpses found on a train coming from Mauritania. This was the time when Senegal's young people were getting a reputation for violence, following the 1988 electoral riots and looting. Looting was involved in 1989 also, and some degree of shadowy organisation, notably in a second stage: the sacking of Moorish shops. Possible religious solidarities – as the protagonists on both sides were Muslim – appear to have weighed little against ethnic or racial antagonism. Senegal's Sufi brotherhood leaders in general made little attempt to restrain their disciples from involvement in this inter-Muslim slaughter, no doubt because they feared that their advice would be ignored and that they would lose popular esteem. Maraboutic abstention in this context looks like another indicator of the limits of their authority over the young.

Of course, it may be misleading to emphasise the moments of mass youth violence, as in Senegal in March 1988 or April 1989. Victoria Ebin's study of the survival strategies of young people in Dakar (Ebin 1993)[11] draws attention to the significance of another kind of pivotal moment in the lives of the young, in the movement of Set Setal (Be clean, make clean). This was a movement in 1990, when young people took over the streets, directed traffic, decorated the walls with paintings of their heroes, and took to the cleaning of their long neglected neighbourhoods. In the opinion of one local observer, the philosopher Aminata Ndaw, Set Setal could have been the portent of a new, 'organic', democracy, a refreshing change from artificial multiparty activity, the monopoly of the well-educated (Ndaw 1992: 326). Set Setal began as an initiative 'from below', although it is worth noting that even at the movement's euphoric origins the buckets and brushes were advanced by the municipality. Organisation soon got the better of spontaneity in this instance, as NGOs and the state captured Set Setal, but the moment is remembered by the Dakarois rather in the way that Parisians remember May 1968.

The cleaning movement has had its counterparts elsewhere in Africa, in more or less spontaneous responses to the collapse of municipal services, but it remains the case that responses to state decay in terms of violence may be more portentous for the political future. Paul Richards thus discusses the rebel armies of the Liberia/Sierra Leone borderland in this way, suggesting that in the study of African politics 'the youth factor ... may take over from ethnicity'. Military entrepreneurs in this case can 'provide employment and hope for significant numbers of potentially dissident, part-educated rural youths mobilised by international media [Rambo and Bruce Lee films on video, notably] and alienated from the state by the collapse of educational and formal sector employment opportunities' (Richards 1994: 1, 16).

A critical question remains: are these young soldiers, whose ages range down to eleven and twelve, to be seen as acting on their own behalf, playing out the potentially subversive role of Bayart's social juniors (*cadets sociaux*)? Such a possibility is suggested by Paul Richards with reference to the Revolutionary United Front (RUF): 'The culture of youth violence which the RUF has espoused may now have a life of its own. The youth army may be a force beyond the control of its leaders' (Richards 1994: 9). While such a possibility should, of course, be considered, another assessment would be that these youths are easily manipulated victims, without independent resources or organisational skills. The Liberian warlord Charles Taylor talks of his Small Boys Unit, an unpaid personal security force, as orphans of war: 'We keep them armed as a means of keeping them out of trouble. It's a means of control' (Berkeley 1992: 52). Women soldiers have also been preferred as bodyguards by superior officers within Taylor's NPFL – a role for the *cadets sociaux*, perhaps because they are considered to be less likely to turn their guns on those whom they guard. There may of course be unwelcome surprises in the future for Taylor or his officers, but for the present their assessment of the social juniors seems a good deal less than apprehensive.

A closely studied example of youth social promotion through civil war, taken from outside the West African region, is that of Renamo in Mozambique. Christian Geffray sees the relevant background here as lying in 'the deep crisis of the country's youth'. As the Frelimo government drove young 'parasites' and 'potential delinquents' from the towns, to return to their districts of origin and productive agricultural activity, the young returnees in many cases enlisted with Renamo instead of accepting a dependent junior status in their home communities. And a Renamo soldier was a man of respect: 'the free and uncontested head of a household, far from the elders ... spared any matrimonial obligation' (Geffray 1990: 108–11). All that, 'little servants' and a woman, the life of the Renamo soldier must have had its attractions to young men being driven from urban unemployment to rural subordination. While youth social promotion was the result of initiatives taken from below, the decision to break with the home community and defy the government, and the viability of such initiatives, have depended also on favourable international alignments – youth liberation courtesy of the Rhodesian and South African security services. While some young men did achieve emancipation of a sort, women would appear to have been subjugated as part of the same process.

Mass violence tends to be accompanied by a sharpening of ethnic definition, tribalism as the 'descent of politics toward the masses' (Bayart 1992a: 20). An observation of the Kenyan dispossessions of 1992 is pertinent to many West African situations: 'the violence has deeply affected the children. Many of the children have witnessed their family members being killed or their houses burned down. The children have acquired a keen awareness of their ethnicity and that of their attackers.' The international observers put this trauma in context: 'prior to these clashes, children of all ethnic groups would play with each other' (Human Rights Watch/Africa Watch 1993: 80). Ethnic identification should in general be seen in contextual terms, and the effect of violence on the young could be seen in similar terms in the case of the secessionist war in southern Senegal (the Casamance), or of the Mali army's attempts to contain the Tuareg revolt in the north of that country.

Ethnic identification does not in general take on a sharp adversarial quality, however, in most of Senegal or in most of Mali. Senegal's religious brotherhoods (or orders) have long held the field in matters of identity in the country north of the Gambia river, interacting with ethnic identities, blurring the boundary lines. Thus, Leonardo Villalon observes:

> depending on the situation, sometimes religion, sometimes ethnicity may prove to be the determining factor in an individual's identity and behaviour. The organisational versatility of the orders that has made them the primary modes of organisation vis à vis the state lies in their capacity to adapt to this ambiguity, and even capitalise on it ... today a social group under pressure (even at times ... an ethnic group) finds that the most readily available model for organising a claim to the attention of the state is the maraboutic one. (Villalon 1995: 75, 247)[12]

The case of one ethnic group under (mild enough) pressure, that of the Serer in Fatick, eloquently demonstrates this latter point: the Serer turn to a *marabout*, M. A. Niang, who makes their case for them by keeping his distance both from the government and from the country's major Islamic brotherhoods. The government has taken the hint: if he won't come to them, with the usual requests for patronage, they must go to him, and deliver.

Senegal's bureaucrats are impatient about this sort of situation, impatient in general about their dependence on maraboutic intermediaries in this 'cohabitation without affection'. 'State officials consider their form of "indirect rule" a distinctly suboptimal situation and maintain the long term goal of relegating maraboutic authority exclusively to the personal and spiritual domain' (Villalon 1995: 357–8). Yet maraboutic intermediation in Senegal has provided state–society linkages more effectively than in any other state in West Africa. The holy men may be an irritant, but they have also been indispensable: without the (ambiguous) support of religious brokerage, the wheels of bureaucracy would turn in empty air.

Religious commitment also has offered many young people a way of escape from social marginalisation, as for example in Uganda in the case of the born-again Christians. 'In Museveni's Uganda, to an extent not possible in much of Africa, Pentecostalism need not be an opting out, it can be an opting in' (Gifford 1994b: 18), offering a way in from a life of drugs and aimlessness. Paul Gifford in his study of Christianity in Uganda remarks how 'these churches particularly help women, students, young men with skills or ambitions to leadership and responsibility' (ibid.: 18). The negative counterpart to this tale of uplift is an 'appalling' strife between these churches, with pressure to 'show that you are still necessary because the others were all deficient' (ibid.: 25). Satan and demons are much invoked in this competition, which, one might note, has had an Islamic counterpart in discord between candidates to Sufi sainthood. The Christian context in Africa is seen by Gifford as one where 'Christian missions are ... the biggest single industry in Africa today', as in Uganda where the central government has 'withdrawn' and churches are 'increasingly tied up with the survival, jobs, health, schooling, prospects, travel, advancement of ordinary Ugandans' (ibid.: 2).[13]

Some young people see a solution in the life of the warband, others turn to God, the identities of soldier or religious believer. Educational institutions must also be considered in this context, a context of widely remarked failure. The role of the college or university student in particular has been emphasised in the literature on African politics, as for example in A. Mbembe's *Les Jeunes et l'Ordre Politique en Afrique Noire* (Mbembe 1985), more a general affirmation than a detailed case study. A comparison between Senegalese and Malian student politics, as undertaken by Sophie Wigram, shows variant forms of politics of student identity ('vanguards' or 'vandals') (Wigram 1994). In Senegal as in Mali, students in recent years have been to the fore in leading riots in the cause of democracy, helped by the more radical pupils from secondary school (the *lycées*). Such riots in the aftermath of the 1988 elections in Senegal entailed a severe crisis for the regime, the most threatening since 1968 (another year of student riot, in Dakar as in Paris). In Mali, students, together with the *lycéens* and the unemployed, were involved in the demonstrations which led to the downfall of the Traoré regime in 1991. Students in such instances can be seen as leading defenders of liberty, Mbembe style, heroes of democracy, 'vanguards', but in general terms their role should be seen as ambivalent. The students' aspiration is to gain government employment, membership in the ruling elite, privilege. And students will riot for their privileges too, as when they burned the National Assembly and the Ministry of Education in 'democratic' Mali in 1993, defending their 'right' to better scholarships (Brenner 1994: 3).

Education produces inequality and privilege, as Louis Brenner remarks, but it has in recent years failed to deliver enough in terms of privilege, leaving students, who have reached the peak of the educational process, at an impasse in terms of employment. Today's students compare themselves with preceding generations, those who could count on getting government jobs because of their degrees; they see themselves as an abandoned generation. It is to be remarked that they do retain some significant advantages: subsidised accommodation in a common location in the capital city (Bamako and Dakar), subsidised meals, lots of time. In the Cheikh Anta Diop University of Dakar the students organise strike action on an annual basis, with an elected strike committee, and they also take a leading role in demonstrations – as recently in protest against the devaluation of the CFA franc (January–February 1994).[14]

The University of Dakar leads in what Aminata Ndaw (1992) has termed the 'confiscation' of democracy in Senegal, in 'the Democracy of the Literati'. In Senegal's multiparty politics, an impressive number of party leaders are university professors; this points to a weakness in the democracy, political parties with elaborate ideological definition and very little popular audience, even among university students. There is a partial exception in the Parti Démocratique Sénégalais, led it is true by a professor, Maître Abdoulaye Wade, but a party prudently short on ideology and campaigning more effectively than any other party in opposition. The PDS slogan, *sopi*, has in recent years been the cry of the streets in times of crisis. City dwellers in general have defected to the PDS in the most recent Senegalese national elections (1993), although the ruling Parti Socialiste still won overall, thanks to the rural vote. Leonardo Villalon stresses the extent of voter apathy even in the cities, the low rate of electoral participation; this electoral apathy extends to university students (Villalon 1994). The students yearn for the downfall of the Diouf regime, but they have lost confidence in Professor Wade, indeed they have lost belief in the possibility of the government losing an election. They also appear to be unable or unwilling to mount any revolutionary project, seeing themselves to be still blocked by the *marabout* state – blocked, if you will, by the democracy of the unlettered.

Students thus might not look like a formidable political force in Senegal today, although they have in the past (1968, 1988) led demonstrations which focused an oppositional coalition together with striking trade unions, and came close to bringing about the downfall of the national government. Fear may thus explain in part the extent to which students still command the attention of the government. Fear, and also pride: comparison with Mali suggests the priority of education in governmental self-legitimation in African states. Louis Brenner thus writes of 'the virtually sacred role attributed to education in the process of "development" by successive Malian governments as well as by international donor agencies' (Brenner 1994: 3). The World Bank of late has been critical of the disproportionate amount of Senegal's education budget which is consumed by the University of Dakar, but the government works to extend university education, with a new university at St Louis. In Mali the students brought about the resignation of a 'democratic' government in February 1994, when the government hesitated to use any significant force against the destructively rioting students. For a recently installed democratic government to invoke military force would be to run the risk of a return to military rule, democracy's deposition by *coup d'état*.

Thus students can inspire fear that they may perhaps indirectly provoke the overthrow of democratic government. Together with unionised workers, they, rather than soldiers in uniform, may represent the best organised elements of society. In Senegal in 1968 and 1988 the student–worker alliance threatened a breakdown of civic order severe enough to compel military intervention. That sort of intervention, with many other African examples in mind, could easily take on an enduring status, could be the introduction of military rule. The Diouf government in 1988 appears to have convinced leaders of the Senegalese opposition that they would be unwise to press their case on the streets, as disorder might lead to the downfall of (semi-)democracy rather than the mere defeat of an incumbent government (Diop and Paye 1994: 32). Semi-democracy in Senegal results in the power of a ruling class, which includes leaders of opposition parties; one may always lose in elections but one can also always hope for (individual or collective) co-optation into the governing party, for a share in the privileges of state. Co-optation along these lines has been a feature of Senegalese politics ever since independence, recent individual examples including Abdoulaye Wade for a time (1991–92) and then the leftist Abdoulaye Bathily (a government minister since 1993).[15] Even the unrewarded can keep their dreams, which means that actual or potential membership of Senegal's ruling class includes all of those with party office, and no doubt many more besides.

There is a subtlety in the way that Senegal's rulers have dealt with political opposition over the years, to be contrasted with more or less brutal procedures in neighbouring states under single-party or military government. Momar Coumba Diop and Moussa Paye thus write of a 'culture for the management of social conflict ... allowing the ruling class to capture the leftist leaders who are most attracted by a share in the spoils of a bankrupt state' (Diop and Paye 1994: 32). Diop and Paye see the Diouf government's handling of the 1988 crisis as illustrating official subtlety, in particular through the manipulation of rumours of an impending military coup to scare the opposition party leaders. There may have been substance, however, behind those (useful) rumours. Senegal's immunity from military coups since independence may be explained by the continuing presence of a French army base in Dakar, and in recent years by the strong international preference for the maintenance of democracy in Senegal. But international preference might prove insubstantial in a crisis, and the French might stand aside: the rumour of a planned *coup d'état* in 1988 would be unlikely to have been regarded as a bluff in opposition circles or elsewhere.

Thus rioting students may be seen in West African states as part of a potential or episodic oppositional coalition, together with striking workers (many of them civil servants) and junior army officers. This is a model to be set beside that of a ruling coalition, as explored by Catherine Boone in the Senegalese instance (Boone 1992: 251–72): state employees, religious notables, those engaged in the paralegal networks which ultimately depend upon the state. A notable absentee from the oppositional coalition, either in Senegal or in Mali, is that of militant Islam (both states have preponderantly Muslim societies). There was the case of the young *marabout* Moustapha Sy, with his religious youth organisation known as the Dahiratoul Moustarchidina wal Moustarchidaty, who a week before the 1993 elections in Senegal 'delivered a scathing critique, complete with allegations of sex scandal and more, against Abdou Diouf' (Villalon 1994: 180). Sy's supporters did participate in post-electoral rioting, but without threatening to be the nucleus of any mass movement. Where the Dakar students are concerned, finally, Islamist movements have been unable to take over from variants of Marxism.

It would be very misleading, however, to portray the students of West Africa characteristically either as rioters or as Marxists. They may riot on occasion, and the fear that they are about to do so is frequently enough to become an official preoccupation. They may use elements of a Marxist vocabulary, or even be members of movements of a broadly Leninist inspiration. An oppositional stance is commonly adopted on campus. But none of these presentational considerations should deflect attention from the fact that the fundamental preoccupation of these students is with securing state employment. That objective may appear increasingly remote, but discreet clientelism and unpublicised membership of the governing party can still be seen as potentially rewarding strategies in that connection (Ebin 1993: 15–19).

The student role has been considered at some length here because students in West Africa can be seen to occupy a politically significant space, in which they play a role of inherent ambiguity. On the one hand, they are popularly seen as candidates for elite status, as idle and unproductive: they may even be held in a sort of contempt. On the other hand, these same students emerge in times of political crisis as leaders of the crowd: they are then held in a sort of temporary respect. Temporary subversives, aspirant elitists, these students are indicators of the likely direction of political change in contemporary West African states.

Students, of course, constitute only a small minority of West African youth; in Mali even schoolchildren are few in number; 'most young people have either left school without receiving any diploma or, especially in the rural areas, have never attended school at all' (Brenner 1994: 5). Senegalese education is much more widely diffused, and there is some contact between the *lycéens* and the students, but, in normal circumstances, in between riots, there is little enough contact between student and non-student youth. A residential university campus, as in Dakar, favours student isolation, and in general it may be said that the geographical concentration of the student population in colleges and universities, as well as the predictable organisation of student time according to the teaching calendar, offer advantages to the incumbent government in the exercise of political control.

Education remains a political subject, a matter of access to political power (or of closure from that power) at all levels, from the university to the primary school: 'it is in school that one acquires the tools of political domination, literacy in the French language, which in turn also determines the position one might occupy in the clientelist system which is rooted in the state' (Brenner 1994: 37). Thus of Mali, as in Senegal: and the language of power in the postcolony is the ex-colonial language, the medium of state education, the route to the resources of the state. In Mali the failure of the state (economic and political) leaves room for instruction in the Arabic language to compete quite effectively with French, in the expanding Madrasa system. The postcolony has greater resources in Senegal, where furthermore it is parental preference which has maintained the dominance of the French language in the educational process, to the exclusion of the Wolof language (although Wolof is spoken as the first or second language by some four-fifths of the country's population, and is written by an intellectual minority) (Cruise O'Brien 1979). A Francophone identity still makes quite good career sense, for the urban young as well as for their parents, in the Senegalese postcolonial context.

In Senegal too, however, there are the signs of institutional decay, falling living standards, rising crime: 'a monopoly of violence is beyond the state's resources ... with self-defence incidents in town, lynching of thieves or in some cases of those who cause traffic accidents' (Diop and Paye 1994: 34). And in one part of the countryside, the Casamance, a 'razzia culture' has developed on both sides of the secessionist struggle, with atrocities and summary executions, on the fringe of which are flourishing criminal activities, smuggling of drugs or arms. State decay in Senegal also affects the educational process, 'although the state has protected educational spending, particularly so at the university, to the detriment of other sectors' (Diop and Diop 1993: 29).[16] There is a school crisis at primary and secondary levels, with overcrowded classes and an increasing proportion of repeat years: with shrinking means and demographic growth, 'educational quality is in constant regression' (ibid.: 29). It looks dismal to a Senegalese eye, although it might be quite impressive to a Malian one.

For those who don't go to school at all, or who drop out, the struggle to acquire the resources necessary for independent adulthood can be all the more difficult. Some youths who are integrated into a well-established trading network, as with the Mouride second-hand clothes merchants of Dakar, can do well enough in superb disregard of educational qualifications (Ebin 1993: 38–42, and Boone 1992: 211–12, 231–4), but these are the adepts of clientelism. Those outside such privileged networks may help to make up the urban crowd, a volatile political force, on the fringes of a life of crime. The political impulses of the crowd are economically motivated above all, as with the 'Rice Uprising' of 1979 in Liberia, which began in protest against a proposed official increase in the price of rice and led to the downfall of civilian ('democratic') government with the Doe coup of April 1980. In this case it was a section of the elite, in the Progressive Alliance of Liberia (founded 1978) which called for a protest demonstration against the 1979 rice price increase: the PAL's populist stratagem 'made echoes among the market women, yenna boys, the unemployed, and school drop-outs – that vast majority of the population which really struggles to survive' (Thomas-Queh 1987: 198).[17] The echoes in this case seem also to have reached the ears of Master-Sergeant Samuel Doe, thus contributing to the demise of civilian government in 1980. The politics of the youthful crowd may not lead to a counter-hegemony, but they can produce a military *coup d'état*.

What, after all, does multiparty parliamentary democracy have to offer to the youthful unemployed? The question is not rhetorical: party democracy works in clientelist networks, of a kind which still appear to have some significance for youth in Dakar, despite the prevalent mood of disenchantment with partisan politics. Democracy may even help in the survival strategies of Senegalese youth, which appear to rest first on family allegiances, then to involve the quest for outside patronage. The authority of family elders often rests on the continuing employment of the head of household, even if such employment is subject to a steady decline in income. For every person employed in the formal sector, there are perhaps ten dependants. Political patronage in Senegal will seldom provide for basic survival, there are very few jobs, but it may help around the margins (those buckets and brushes for the cleaning operation of 1990, Set Setal). And in the case of the more adroit of clients, using religious or other political brokerage, it is still possible to secure access to some of the spoils of state: electoral competition provides a relatively favourable context, from the client's point of view. For the youthful unemployed there are the looting possibilities of electoral rioting to be considered, as well as the occasion to give expression to a voice of protest.

The 'democratisation' observable in recent years in West Africa cannot yet be said to have changed the basics of the political situation. At the high point of democratic enthusiasm, the years from 1988 to 1991, the youthful crowd appears to have placed some very high expectations (with significant international encouragement) in the future downfall of incumbent regimes. Material expectations were certainly included in the hopes of those who cried for *sopi* in Dakar (democracy as a sort of cargo cult). *Plus ça change, plus c'est la même chose?* It is reasonable in Senegal to conclude, with Stephen Ellis, that victorious opposition movements in Africa 'find it hard to locate a new political base other than in the machinery of government itself or by taking over the networks, and the techniques, of the ruling parties they seek to replace' (Rimmer 1993: 140).

If multiparty politics offers limited material possibilities, then, it remains the case that the fundamentals of hardship in West Africa are obstinately in place. Economic hardship is producing increasing strains within families, including strains between the generations. But then the family can adjust, redefine itself, in some cases can profit from adversity, even from internal war. In the case of the youthful soldiers of Liberia, a local journalist deplored the way in which 'parental accomplices ... have been blindfolded by looted materials and money often brought home from the frontline by these kids' (*Liberia Now* I [2]: 24). Did some of those parental accomplices urge their children into the field? Whether or not they did, the case illustrates the point that it may be too soon to write off the family as a social unit in West Africa. It can indeed be argued that the family is the most durable of political institutions in such a context, perhaps with a shifting balance of power between the generations (A. B. Diop 1981).

The older generation retains significant instruments of control, however, sometimes even in matters of identity as in contemporary Sudan, where 'cognizant of the political volatility of the young, a large sector of the political elite has seized upon the impetus for an Islamic "direction" in order to define the terms of Islamicisation so as not to lose (and in many cases so as to maximise) its privileged position' (Simone 1994: 109). The 'freedom' of the young in the choice of their identity may thus be more circumscribed than is immediately apparent: the elders may have doctored the menu. More evident forms of control include an official emphasis on sport, as in Senegal where the governing party funds sporting competition through the Associations Sportives et Communales, since the explosion of youth violence in 1988 and 1989 – keep the violence to the football field? And in Mali the traders form their self-defence groups to hold the marauding students at bay. There may even be a democratic majority behind the maintenance of the authority of age. Some youths would profit from institutional collapse, those with a talent for the use of violence, but the great majority of young or old would be the losers, truly a lost generation.

Notes

1. As Bayart summarises the situation, 'the social element which is most resolute in confronting the system of domination, because it has nothing to lose, that of marginalised young people, getting by under the ragged authority of their elders, is also the least equipped to direct the change which it has helped to provoke' (Bayart et al. 1992: 94).

2. Lungisile Ntsebeza's thesis is an insider's account of youth politics in East London, categorising the youth population in terms of the actors' perceptions and labels, with a sensitive eye to changes in perception and definition over time, from 'red' (traditionalist) and 'school' in the country, to 'bumpkin' and *tsotsi* in town, with 'political' youth in the 1970s and 1980s, and the unemployed in the 1990s. I am very grateful to Ian Edwards for suggesting this MA thesis, and for making it available.

3. 'Islam in Modern Africa', funded by the Leverhulme Foundation through the British Academy 1987–92. This collaborative project was co-ordinated from the School of Oriental and African Studies, and a major theme of the research was the study of Muslim youth in contemporary Africa.

4. The commodity boom of the 1970s, supporting many West African patrimonialisms, was followed by price collapse around 1980 and then steeply rising interest rates (see, for example, Fauré 1990).

5. For a view through a glass darkly, focused in Bamako, Mali, but ranging widely across time, space and subject, see Kaplan 1994.

6. The quotation is from *Sud Hebdo*, 7 January 1993. Sophie Wigram's MSc thesis, comparing student politics in Mali and Senegal, finds governmental corruption to be more 'blatant' in Mali, where students moved from being the 'vanguards' of democracy in 1989 to being 'vandals' by 1993 – with a very telling cartoon from a Malian newspaper of students with cutlasses between their teeth (see Wigram 1994).

7. 'The reality of political closure has by no means effaced the powerful myth of mobility associated with the educational system: an understanding of the myth's power is central to grasping the relative passivity of lower classes in the face of congealing structures of inequality and the deteriorating material conditions' (Young and Turner 1985: 135).

8. This was during an enquiry into Muslim opinion in Senegal, 'Islamic Attitudes

to the West', for the United States Information Agency (Dakar, St Louis, Kaolack, 1989). Those interviewed (in the excellent company of Leonardo Villalon) were from a range of occupational backgrounds, mostly professional. Apart from the students, they were in their middle years (thirty to fifty) for the most part.

9. This movement of electoral dissension in Mouride circles in fact began at the previous general election, in February 1983 (see Cruise O'Brien 1983: 7–12).

10. September–October 1989, research for the USIA on 'Islamic Attitudes to the West'. Dakar visit May 1992, for Overseas Development Agency project 'Getting By: Survival Strategies of Urban Youth in Africa', report produced 1993 (author: Victoria Ebin; project director: D. Cruise O'Brien).

11. Dr Ebin's exemplary research in Dakar (for the calendar year 1992) involved study by participant observation, with the youth population divided into seven distinct categories (street children, university students, the Scouts, Mouride traders in second-hand clothes, Serer women as millet pounders or market traders, the Set Setal movement, the inhabitants of a run-down neighbourhood, Fass). The youth in this sample were often quite impressively organised, although in a context of decay.

12. L. Villalon's PhD thesis, *Islam and the State in West Africa. Disciples and Citizens in Fatick, Senegal,* was completed in 1992 for the University of Texas at Austin. It has been published by Cambridge University Press, a major new statement in the comparative politics of West African Islam (Villalon 1995).

13. These citations are from an unpublished article on Uganda (Gifford 1994b). For an indication of some of the directions of Paul Gifford's research, see Gifford 1994a.

14. An article in *Le Monde* (18 February 1994) reported that five policemen had been killed in these riots, and attributed the violence to the extremism (*jusqu'au boutisme*) of unemployed and abandoned youth: 'hundreds of youths, armed with clubs and iron bars', rioted and looted near the Presidential Palace in Dakar ('Emeutes de la Dévaluation à Dakar').

15. For some relevant background, on A. Bathily's involvement in protests of an earlier time, see Bathily 1992.

16. Warmest thanks to Momar Coumba Diop for forwarding the texts of these important co-authored articles.

17. Thanks to François Prkic, research student at the Centre d'Etudes d'Afrique Noire in the University of Bordeaux for his help with the provision of material on Liberia.

References

Bathily, A. 1992. *Mai 68 à Dakar ou la Révolte Universitaire et la Démocratie.* Paris: Chaka.

Bayart, J.-F. 1992a. 'Introduction', in Bayart et al. *Le Politique par le bas en Afrique Noire.*

— 1992b. 'Le Politique par le bas en Afrique Noire', in Bayart et al., *Le Politique par le bas en Afrique Noire.*

— 1992c. 'La Revanche des Sociétés Africaines', in Bayart et al., *Le Politique par le bas en Afrique Noire.*

— 1992d. 'L'Afropessimisme par le bas', in Bayart et al., *Le Politique par le bas en Afrique Noire.*

Bayart, J.-F., Mbembe, A. and Toulabor, C. 1992. *Le Politique par le bas en Afrique Noire: Contributions à une Problématique de la Démocratie*. Paris: Karthala.

Berkeley, B. 1992. *Between Repression and Slaughter*. Unpublished paper.

Boone, C. 1992. *Merchant Capital and the Roots of State Power in Senegal*. Cambridge: Cambridge University Press.

Bratton, M 1989. 'Beyond the State: Civil Society and Associational Life in Africa'. *World Politics* 41 (3).

Brenner, L. 1994. 'Youth as Political Actors in Mali', paper presented to the SSRC workshop, *Political Transitions in Africa*. Chapel Hill: University of North Carolina, 10–12 March.

Cruise O'Brien, D. 1979. 'L'Enjeu de la Wolofisation', *Année Africaine*: 319–35.

— 1983. 'Les Elections Sénégalaises du 27 fevrier 1983', *Politique Africaine* 11: 7–12.

— 1990. *Islamic Attitudes Towards the West: The Case of Senegal*. Report. Washington, DC: United States Information Agency.

Cruise O'Brien, D., Dunn, J. and Rathbone, R. (eds). 1990. *Contemporary West African States*. Cambridge: Cambridge University Press.

Diop, A. B. 1981. *La Société Wolof*. Paris: Karthala.

Diop, M. C. 1992/3. *Sénégal: Trajectoires d'un Etat*. Dakar and Paris: Codesria and Karthala.

Diop, M. C. and Diop, A. 1993. *Les Villes du Sénégal*. Dakar: Cinergie.

Diop, M. C. and Paye, M. 1994. *Armée et Pouvoir au Sénégal*. Typescript. Dakar.

Dunn, J. (ed.). 1992. *Democracy: The Unfinished Journey, 508 B.C. to A.D. 1993*. Oxford: Oxford University Press.

Ebin, V. 1993. *Getting By: Survival Strategies of Urban Youth in Africa*. Report. London: Overseas Development Administration.

Ellis, S. 1993. 'Democracy in Africa: Achievements and Prospects', in Rimmer (ed.), *Action in Africa*.

Fauré, Y. 1990. 'Côte d'Ivoire', in Cruise O'Brien et al. (eds), *Contemporary West African States*.

Geffray, C. 1990. *La Cause des Armes au Mozambique: Anthropologie d'une Guerre Civile*. Paris: Credu/Karthala.

Gifford, P. 1994a. 'Some Recent Developments in African Christianity', *African Affairs* 93 (373): 513–34.

— 1994b. *Uganda*. Typescript. London.

Human Rights Watch/Africa Watch. 1993. *Divide and Rule: State-Sponsored Ethnic Violence in Kenya*. New York, etc.: Human Rights Watch.

Kaplan, R. 1994. 'The Coming Anarchy', *Atlantic Monthly*, February: 44–76.

Khilnani, S. 1992. 'India's Democratic Career', in Dunn (ed.), *Democracy*.

Mbembe, A. 1985. *Les Jeunes et l'Ordre Politique en Afrique Noire*. Paris: L'Harmattan.

— 1988. *Afriques Indociles: Christianisme, Pouvoir et Etat en Société Postcoloniale*. Paris: Karthala.

— 1992a. 'Provisional Notes on the Postcolony', *Africa* 62 (1): 3–36.

— 1992b. 'Le Palabre de l'Indépendance', in Bayart et al., *Le Politique par le bas en Afrique Noire*.

— 1992c. 'Pouvoir des Morts et Langage des Vivants', in Bayart et al., *Le Politique par le bas en Afrique Noire*.

— 1992d. 'Pouvoir, Violence et Accumulation', in Bayart et al., *Le Politique par le bas en Afrique Noire*.

Ndaw, A. 1992. 'La Démocratie des Lettres', in M. C. Diop, *Sénégal.*

Ntsebeza, L. 1993. 'Youth in Urban African Townships, 1945–1992: a Case Study of the East London Townships', MA thesis, Durban: University of Natal, Department of Economic History.

Richards, P. 1994. 'Rebellion in Liberia and Sierra Leone: a Crisis of Youth', forthcoming in O. W. Furley (ed.), *Conflict in Africa.* Forthcoming.

Rimmer, D. (ed.). 1993. *Action in Africa: the Experience of People involved in Government Business and Aid.* London: James Currey.

Senegal. 1993. *Recensement général de la population et de l'habitat de 1988.* Dakar: Direction de la prévision et de la statistique.

Simone, T. A. M. 1994. *In Whose Image? Political Islam and Urban Practices in Sudan.* Chicago and London: University of Chicago Press.

Thomas-Queh, J. 1987. 'The Liberian Nation in Revolt', *Liberian Studies Journal* 13 (2).

Toulabour, C. 1986. *Le Togo sous Eyadema.* Paris: Karthala.

— 1992a. 'Jeu de Mots, Jeu de Vilains', in Bayart et al., *Le Politique par le bas en Afrique Noire.*

— 1992b. 'L'Enonciation du Pouvoir', in Bayart et al., *Le Politique par le bas en Afrique Noire.*

Villalon, L. 1992. *Islam and the State in West Africa: Disciples and Citizens in Fatick, Senegal.* PhD thesis. Austin: University of Texas.

— 1994. 'The Senegalese Elections of 1993', *African Affairs* 93 (371): 163–94.

— 1995. *Islamic Society and State Power in Senegal: Disciples and Citizens in Fatick.* Cambridge: Cambridge University Press.

Wigram, S. 1994. *Elites, Vanguards and Vandals: The Political Role of Students in Senegal and Mali (1968–1993).* MSc thesis. London: School of Oriental and African Studies.

Young, C. and Kanté, B. 1992. 'Governance, Democracy and the 1988 Elections (Senegal)', in G. Hyden and M. Bratton (eds). *Governance and Politics in Africa.* Boulder, CO: Lynne Rienner.

Young, C. and Turner, T. 1985. *The Rise and Decline of the Zairean State.* Madison: University of Wisconsin Press.

CHAPTER 3

Postcolonialism, power and identity: local and global perspectives from Zaire

Filip De Boeck

After more than a decade in a maelstrom of aggravating political and economic crises, Zaire is in an advanced state of political and administrative collapse, threatening the ultimate break-up of the state (see Young 1994). The 1995 outbreak of Ebola in the town of Kikwit clearly highlighted the absence of a centralised state structure. Two waves of looting across the country in 1991 and 1993 have greatly contributed to the steep decline in the economy, accelerating dramatically over the past five years.

In this chapter, exploring the moral and cultural bedrock for the developing Zairean crisis, I analyse local strategies of survival and resiliency in the face of collapsing national structures. In the first part, I consider the ways of overcoming the hiatus between local political structures and the state, its crumbling autocratic control and dysfunctional economy. My question is: How does (ethnic) self-representation operate as a psychological and cultural strategy for coping with the chaotic and despotic socio-politics and economics in a peripheral 'frontier' situation? Drawing on recent case material, I deal with the ambivalent political, ritual and symbolic exchange between national (Zairean and Angolan) power-brokers and local rural traditional authorities, against the background of Zairean–Angolan diamond-smuggling activities. In particular, I focus on the ambivalence in the ongoing dialogue and dialectics of power between local and national political actors. My analysis covers their dual arguments of identity, their respective politics and poetics of mimesis and alterity; it also discloses their appropriation, representation, interpretation and invention of multiple identities for strategic uses. My ethnography illuminates the rise of new strategies for socio-economic and cultural goals and conflict resolutions, when the focus of economic and social interest is localised and problematised by a particular ethnic and/or informal economic grouping.

My conclusion, extrapolating more broadly from my ethnographic case, theorises the disintegration of overarching political and administrative structures and state institutions and shows its impact on the local in interaction with the global. The interaction between the hinterland and the merchant and political capital is still too often viewed as a one-way process, in which the *villageois* passively experiences the imperative gaze of the metropole. However, I contend that in contemporary Zaire the merchant and political capital no longer fully controls emerging identities, power, authority and (self-)representation. Instead, the hinterland plays most powerfully in social processes that run parallel to national and international processes of political and economic decision-making. This deeply affects and alters the nature of such commonly used concepts as 'state', citizenship and nationhood, or conventional state–society and urban–rural oppositions.

The crisis of the African state, fallen victim to the political instability and the capitalist banditry that it nurtured itself, raises questions about the various sources of resilience mitigating against total chaos or a Hobbesian 'war of all against all'. Are order, morality and social control relegated to local-level village, kinship and co-operative units? Are social co-operation and control limited to small pockets of society in the absence of a generalised, overarching civic and political culture, or are there still wider dynamics at play? Do local ethnic formations form an alternative for or a mobilisation channel against the moribund state? In what ways, and to what extent, are rural realities articulated to modern state processes? Is there a continuity of rural culture(s) or are they eroded by the 'predatory rule' (Fatton 1992) of the dominant and (supra-)national structures? These questions call for a predominantly cultural focus, emphasising the potential of local cultures for incorporating and transforming elements and influences from 'outside'.

Forms of interaction between local and (trans)national power formations

My evidence comes from extensive field research between 1987 and 1994 among the aLuund of the Upper Kwaango (region of Bandundu, zone of Kahemba) and in Kinshasa and Kikwit. The Luunda area of my field research is situated along the Zairean border with Angola, and extends well into the Angolan province of Lunda Norte. Traditionally, the political and ritual authority of the paramount Luunda titleholder, who resides in Zaire, extends over a large territory (*ngaand*) on both sides of the border, including the strategically important diamond-mining town of Cafunfo (Kafunfu), a good two days' walk from the Zairean Luunda royal village.

aLuund from both Angola and Zaire cross the border almost daily, and play a prominent role in the Angolan–Zairean diamond traffic, dating from 1979/80. Throughout the 1980s, diamond traders travelled back and forth between Kinshasa, or diamond centres such as Tshikapa or Mbuji

Mayi, and the border town of Kahemba. From there, they sent goods to Angola in exchange for diamonds from the Angolan Cafunfo mine and its neighbours.[1] Diamonds were thus acquired directly from the mines, from individual diggers, or through middlemen (*cocseurs*). The goods (usually wax cloths, cigarettes, whisky, radios, batteries, soap, sardines and dried salted fish) were carried across the border by groups of *pincheurs*, who worked on their own or in association with financially stronger traders or a *comptoir*. The import into Angola coincided with its severe shortage of consumer goods in the 1980s (Azam et al. 1993). Throughout the 1980s local trade roles were mainly the carrier, guide or scout. Crossing the Zairean–Angolan borderline, which is officially closed, was (and still is) a dangerous venture. Frequently, people were killed by landmines or shot by Angolan government troops, *faapul* (from FAPLA), who controlled Cafunfo and most of the Lunda Norte province throughout the 1980s.[2] Returning to Zaire was equally hazardous, not only because the export of diamonds was declared illegal by the Angolan MPLA, but also because, on the other side, Zairean soldiers patrolled the borderline, officially to defend Zairean territory from MPLA attacks and arrest trespassing 'Angolans' (mostly local aLuund, who attach little importance to the borderline or to an Angolan or Zairean national identity), but basically to loot returning diamond traders.[3]

Since the early 1990s, the diamond trade has changed considerably. In December 1992, rejecting the outcome of the presidential elections, UNITA attacked the town of Cafunfo, which it had been sharing with MPLA during the period of the peace treaty. UNITA thus gained control over the diamond-mines, formerly a main source of income for the MPLA. During the following months, Cafunfo was attacked and bombed extensively by the MPLA. In October of 1994, shortly before the signing of a new peace treaty in Lusaka, the MPLA took control of Cafunfo again, while parallel digging activities along the Kwaango river remained under UNITA supervision.

Under the UNITA occupation of Cafunfo, bartering virtually came to an end. Since late 1992, the diamond trade has been monetised: all diamonds are paid for in dollars, hence creating a monetary economy that functions independently from, or has replaced, the 'official' Zairean and Angolan money markets. The changed nature of the trade also stopped the export of Zairean goods into Angola, making the whole Zairean–Angolan diamond activity more sedentary. Under the UNITA occupation of Cafunfo, Zaireans were allowed to settle in the mining sites along the Kwaango to dig up diamonds. As a consequence the *pincheurs* and diamond traders (*kamangistes*) have been joined by numerous 'children of Lunda' (*bana Lunda*), penniless Zairean youngsters from all over southern Zaire and Kinshasa, who often walk hundreds of miles to try their luck in Angola. In the first half of 1994, an estimated 25,000 to 30,000 Zaireans were permanently living in and around Cafunfo, digging diamonds under the sharp control of UNITA, which saw to it that it received a large percentage of all the diamonds thus produced. In this way, UNITA basically used cheap Zairean labour to help sponsor its war.

How do the local traditional Luunda authorities enter into all this? As we know, MPLA continued to exert control over Lunda Norte till late 1992. Contrary to some of the minor Chokwe, Luunda and Shiinji title-holders in the area under the Luunda paramount's control, however, the latter was never supportive of the MPLA. In the 1970s, the actual Luunda titleholder, not yet enthroned and still living in Angola, openly supported Roberto Holden's FNLA and, after its disappearance from the Angolan political stage, started backing UNITA. When the MPLA killed one of his sons, and the future titleholder himself got into trouble with the MPLA because of his UNITA sympathies, he moved across the border, settled in Zaire, and was enthroned in 1984.[4] Since his enthronement, he has grown into a strong and powerful chief, capable not only of strengthening traditional ties with other subregional titleholders and of assuring the unity of his territory, but also able to create contacts with the administrative and political scene on a regional and (trans)national level.

Event 1   In August 1993, UNITA, recognising the Zairean Luunda paramount titleholder's traditional authority over the Cafunfo area, calls on the latter in order to protect ritually and 'hide' (*-jiinjik*) the mining town from MPLA air attacks. In keeping with traditional Luunda notions that both harm and healing come from outside (see De Boeck 1993), the paramount titleholder calls on three Yansi ritual specialists and one Angolan Shiinji healer and sends them to Angola in order to carry out the protective rituals asked for by UNITA. After the ritual of the performance the Angolan representative of the Luunda paramount titleholder is flown to the UNITA headquarters in Huambo where he is thanked for his services by Savimbi himself.

Savimbi's association with one of the main traditional authorities of the Lunda Norte province is subsequently used for propaganda through extensive coverage on UNITA radio. In the meantime, both the Luunda commoners, the minor Luunda, Shiinji, Chokwe and Suku titleholders as well as members of the Luunda royal lineage continue to be persecuted, arrested, killed, raped, tortured and deported by the local UNITA troops, who suspect them of collaborating with MPLA. At the same time MPLA agents, known as *anti-mutim* (anti-terrorists), hide in Luunda villages bringing the risk of UNITA reprisals on the villagers.[5]

Event 2   In July 1991, Mwakahiiy,[6] a relative of the Luunda titleholder, kills his neighbour with an axe during a drunken fight. The victim's relatives demand restitution. Mwakahiiy, after having served his prison sentence, goes to dig diamonds in Cafunfo. In January 1994, Mwakahiiy digs up a 175-carat stone, a most unusual find. With the help of some relatives, and unknown to the local UNITA officials, the stone is smuggled out of Angola. In Kahemba, the relatives sell the stone for a ridiculously low price to Joseph, a Lebanese diamond trader. The same day Joseph flies to Kinshasa where the diamond is transferred to a Lebanese associate of two men with top functions in the Zairean army and the SNIP, the Zairean security force. These two men in turn are associated with the son (son 1) of a most prominent member of Zaire's political elite.

Soon word reaches the Cafunfo UNITA command that an exceptionally large diamond was sold in Kahemba. Mwakahiiy (who had no knowledge of the sale and never received his share of the profits) is arrested by UNITA troops, who threaten to execute him if he does not share the profits. Since Mwakahiiy is a relative of the Luunda paramount chief, the latter intervenes and promises the UNITA officials that he will pay the sum asked for, on condition that Mwakahiiy is released. The Luunda titleholder is also angered by the fact that Joseph did not pay him 'money of the land' (*nfalaang ja mavw*), as the stone was dug up and the transaction took place in his territory. Two of the titleholder's dignitaries are sent to Joseph to renegotiate the sale and obtain a higher price. Joseph, however, refuses to meet with the titleholder's delegation, reportedly for fear that they might use sorcery on him. The delegation returns to the village empty-handed.

Around that time Donatien, a *pincheur*, arrives in the Luunda royal village. Donatien is an associate of a Kinshasa-based diamond trader who is in turn associated with a highly ranked officer of the Zairean army, himself associated with another son (son 2) of the same prominent politician mentioned above. The Luunda titleholder asks Donatien to contact his partner in Kinshasa and see whether he might be able to exert pressure on Joseph. Donatien's intervention (by means of a radio-call in Kahemba town, 250km from the royal village) proves to be all too efficient: within weeks three land-cruisers arrive in the royal village, transporting son 2, together with a large following of bodyguards and members of the intelligence service. Fearing the titleholder's nocturnal powers, after having spotted a snake in his compound, the visitors refuse to spend the night there. The following morning, the Luunda titleholder is put in one of the land-cruisers and transported to Kinshasa, after a brief stop in Kahemba where Joseph is harassed.

In Kinshasa, the Luunda titleholder is promised an audience with a high-ranked official to discuss Mwakahiiy's problem. Three months later, however, the audience has still not taken place, although he has managed to lobby successfully against one of his long-standing political enemies, the Kahemba *commissaire de zone*, who as a result is switched to another administrative zone. However, the Luunda titleholder's hopes of a financial settlement dwindle. In practice, he is being held hostage, while the two sons and their associates each try to get the most out of the diamond transaction.[7]

As in the UNITA case, the Luunda paramount's presence in Kinshasa was used for propaganda reasons as well: he was taken to meetings of the *mouvance* and his appearance there was broadcast by the OZRT, the Zairean television station. Finally, it may be remarked that some of my informants considered the whole event was used by the regime in order to contact the Luunda leaders and pave the way for the presidential elections in their area.

The two events illustrate how local actors are caught up in wider national and supra-national political and economic events and power games. Local cultures and their representatives seem to be sandwiched between, and made use of in, larger power struggles and interests that transcend the regional level. However, to regard these local groups as passive victims of larger forces imposed on them from outside covers only part of the intricate processes that are actually going on. In reality, a complex dialectics of power is at play, in which both sides take part.

The dialectics of power: the central state apparatus and traditional political symbolism

The neologistic cultural doctrine of the 'return to authenticity' (*recours/retour à l'authenticité*), so characteristic of the Second Republic, was partly structured around a whole reality of more deeply rooted ideological and symbolical referents that drew from a pool of precolonial metaphors and images pertaining to the office of traditional sovereign paramounts. Many of the traditional symbols and values related to sovereign paramount rulers, such as royal paraphernalia (the leopard skin, the staff, the flywhisk, the throne, the praise-name) or notions of kinship, lineage, family, power, authority and legitimacy, have been selectively manipulated and subverted in order to give form to the aims of the Mobutist regime, to legitimise the Guide's status as 'Father of the Nation', and to manifest his right to power as an ancestral right (Callaghy 1984; Young and Turner 1985; and especially Schatzberg 1988)

The inherent ambivalences of the father-image are adroitly used by the regime (Schatzberg 1988: 78ff). By means of a perverted interpretation of the traditional 'gift logic', in which debt becomes positive, offering a source of social cohesion, the notion of 'gift' (gifts from the 'father of the nation' to his children) creates a 'debt' and a dependence of the people upon their leader. In 1991, for example, every university professor in Zaire received a Mitshubishi Galant from the president. By a skilful manipulation of the imagery of the chief as father or maternal uncle –

with its traditional implications of reciprocity and mutual exchange –
theft, corruption, exploitation and abuse of funds are thus constructed
into 'gifts' returned by the children of Zaire to their generous father.[8] By
disconnecting the links between established signifiers and what they stand
for, basic relations and values are emptied of their original meaning and
redefined. In the same way, the element of coercion is covered up by
reference to the sacred or divine nature of the president's rule, adding the
notion of the 'charismatic chief' to the notions of the 'strong chief' and
the 'just chief' (see Balandier 1967: 207–8). The notions of the 'strong
chief' and the 'just chief' are largely covered by the paternal symbolism.
About the first aspect, the 1974 constitution clearly stated that 'the chief
has the plenitude of the exercise of power' by virtue of his being 'the
incarnation of the M.P.R. family' (quoted by Schatzberg 1988: 94). Practices
of political repression are concealed by the same imagery. As a good
father, the chief may use forceful means against his disobedient children,
but always justly, i.e. for their own good. Under the Second Republic, the
aspect of the charismatic chief was clearly present in the attempt to
appear, for example, as Mobutu Moyi, the divine king, an image which
inspired some scholars to compare the nature of his rule to that of Louis
XIV (see Callaghy 1984).

African popular conceptions of traditional rulers commonly relate their
power to a politics of revelation and concealment of nocturnal powers
and forces. For example, the Luunda king is believed to 'eat' some of his
ascendants and descendants during his enthronement, thereby eliminating
his own life-source, and himself as life-source for future generations (De
Boeck 1994). The royal titleholder thus becomes his own origin, and as
such he lies at the origin of the unity of the territory over which he rules:
he illustrates that he is capable of holding the needs of the commoners
above his own personal attachments. Situated outside every form of
physical reciprocity or social exchange, as well as outside the ordinary life-
cycle between origin and end, ascendants and descendants or birth and
death, the Luunda royal body exemplifies the ideologically important
unchanging continuity of the ancestral order, against the transformations
of society as lived in everyday life. Thus rooted in ancestrality and legitimated by the past, the invisible and immobile Luunda king clearly forms
the antithesis of the 'modern' politician, for whom visibility, movement
and a project with a focus on the future are of prior importance. Nevertheless, MPR party ideologists have also stressed the aspect of nocturnal
power in the president's rule (see Young and Turner 1985: 214–15), thereby
striking a cultural chord concerning the nature of political legitimacy that
is deeply embedded in the popular collective imagination.[9] The notion of
ritualised legitimate use of nocturnal power as constitutive act related to
the office of the traditional titleholder is thus subverted and successfully
used to cover up acts of violence and unlawful coercion.

The reinvention and perversion of traditional elements to back up and touch up the violent realities of naked power have thus been (more or less subtly) made use of to instil respect, awe, fear and subservience for a personal coercive regime. At the same time, the incorporation of traditional concepts of authority also served other purposes. The recourse to authenticity as a legitimating myth, and the inclusion of 'traditional' symbolic features borrowed from long-standing precolonial power bases situated outside the core areas of support for the regime (Kongo, Kuba, Luba, Luunda), were attempts to legitimate the regime's position *vis-à-vis* these traditional centres, and to incorporate the rural hinterland into the state domain (Young and Turner 1985: 213).

However, the recycling of the powerful traditional symbolism was not meant to revive or promote traditional power-centres, but constituted an active attempt to abolish these chieftaincies as potential hearths of resistance. A 1973 law for the reform of chieftaincy transferred chiefs to other areas, and abolished customary tribunals and traditional principles of hereditary investiture. In practice, the law amounted to an orchestrated attempt at abolishing traditional power structures. The repression of traditional chieftaincy, so characteristic of the regime's policy in the mid-1970s, was not confined to a strictly political level, but was also accompanied by a repressive attitude towards the precolonial cultural heritage as a possible source of resistance against the regime. Ironically enough, the *recours à l'authenticité* thus inspired a policy that continued the line of conduct of the Belgian authorities.[10]

Actually, the 1973 law for the reform of chieftaincy meant a switch in the regime's policy. Under Belgian colonial rule, most chieftaincies were kept under firm tutelage, with the exception of some traditional 'states' such as Luunda and Kuba, having a policy of indirect rule. The Belgian administration designated chiefs (*chefs medaillés*) and actively intervened in customary criteria of succession. In the early postindependence years, many of these local chiefs, considered collaborators of the Bula Matadi, were chased from their office, or became targets of revolutionary violence during the rebellion period in 1964. At the same time, many chiefs *de facto* consolidated their prestige or authority in the institutional and administrative chaos that followed independence. In an attempt to depoliticise the country after the 1965 coup, Mobutu returned to office all the chiefs who had been deposed. The 1973 law put an end to this favourable attitude, in an attempt to incorporate the local collectivities into the administrative structure of the central state.

By 1976, the reform had proved a total failure. Most transferred chiefs were allowed to return to their original collectivities, sustaining hereditary principles (de Lannoy 1976). In 1982 the restoration of the chiefdom to its full status led to a situation in which the state apparatus co-exists in various degrees of interdependence with traditional socio-political structures of varying degrees of coherence, power and autonomy. Some of the more powerful rulers, such as the *mwami* chiefs in the Kivu, the Kuba king and the Luunda *mwaant yaav*, in short those chiefs granted a relative degree of autonomy by the Belgian administration, had altogether escaped the reform. In their case, the 1973 reform had only marginal effects, and the regime simply recognised them both as customary chiefs and as administrative zone commissioners, a practice known as *dédoublement* or *cumul* (Callaghy 1984: 379).

From 1982 to 1990, the state attempted to lay its territorial administration down on top of the existing traditional structures without abolishing them, a 'coverover strategy', characterised by a mixture of bargaining, manipulation, co-operation, coercion and domination (Callaghy 1984). Important traditional chiefs (*grands chefs coutumiers*) were flown over to the presidential residence in Gbadolite, were invited to MPR party congresses, or, after 1990, political rallies of the presidential *mouvance*. Some of them were given presents and money, or cars and residences in the capital, and many were knighted in the 'National Order of the Leopard' (*Ordre National du Léopard*). Looked at from the outside, the regime thus managed to give the impression that it had veritably extended its control over these major traditional political power-centres, which were being manoeuvred into the position of signboards of the regime. However, as I show, bargaining is a two-directional process and therefore ambivalent: the regime continues to perceive the traditional authorities as potentially threatening.

The other end of the spectrum: issues of representation and self-representation in the state–society interaction

In comparison with other regional chiefs, such as the Yaka sovereign paramount ruler, recognised by the colonial authorities as the most important traditional ruler and main stabilising factor in the Kwaango, the aLuund of the Upper Kwaango were completely ignored. From a traditional point of view, though, the Luunda paramount titleholder's status is senior to that of the Yaka paramount (see Van Roy 1988). Numerically feeble, the political impact of this Luunda group was, however, less great. Also, the Upper Kwaango was penetrated and administered later than the rest of the Kwaango, and the colonial authorities considered the area of no economic value (see Adriaens 1951).

After independence, this colonial policy was continued. The 1973 administrative reform diminished the importance of the Luunda paramount even further. The reform failed, however, because the government miscalculated the continuing impact of existing traditional power relations in the organisation of the administrative units. This was also the case in the Luunda paramount titleholder's area.

From 1984 onwards, the latter has campaigned for an upgraded administrative status more suitably reflecting his traditional importance. The paramount titleholder explored, hesitantly at first and with more bravado later, the administrative networks on the level of the zone of Kahemba and beyond, through his immediate kinship ties with local government officials, and later, through extended kinship ties, on a regional and national level.[11]

During the 1980s, the Luunda paramount titleholder from Kahemba, actively seeking a close association with the regime, conformed to its style to further his own agenda; for example, to obtain promotion to a higher administrative level, or to settle a fight with some of his opponents. The regime would manipulate traditional symbols of authority to legitimate its rule, and so, throughout the 1970s and 1980s, traditional paramount chiefs like the Luunda titleholder would pursue their own goals by integrating MPR symbols into the existing traditional discourse and practices of power and authority. In this way, for example, the Luunda chief's yearly meetings with all the local chiefs and titleholders of his territory were outwardly transformed into MPR meetings. On these occasions, he would wear a leopard bonnet instead of the traditional beaded crown, as well as spectacles resembling the president's; underneath the traditional royal raffia-cloth, an *abacost*, imprinted with MPR slogans; he would order the Zairean flag raised in his courtyard; and he would address the gathering in Lingala, the military and political *lingua franca* (while all present were aLuund and many had not fully mastered Lingala), and incorporate idioms used by government officials in his speech.

The Zairean authorities, on the other hand, were readily inclined to affirm the association with the Luunda chieftaincy of Kahemba, since, after the débâcle of the 1973 law, they had tried to get the local populations of former chiefdoms used to seeing their chief as an agent of the administration, rather than as a representative of the ancestors and guardian of the land. However, in their attempt to maintain their influence and consolidate their relationship with the chief, government officials also made use of traditional vocabularies, thereby reinforcing rather than undermining the status of the paramount chief as ancestral representative. For example, during the Luunda paramount chief's enthronement in 1984, former *commissaire du peuple* Mwaku Yala, who became vice-governor of Bandundu in 1994, wore a chief's traditional dress while kneeling in front of the Luunda titleholder.

In this way, both sides have actively collaborated with one another, in an association that, at times, has taken on the form of a contest of representation, each conforming – both consciously and unconsciously – to the other's style, creating an image of self that can be used and negotiated in the ongoing dialogue with the other. Underneath the con-tested collaborations lurk sometimes parallel, sometimes different and contradictory, aspirations. The regime stays in close touch with the

Kahemba Luunda aristocracy in an attempt to strengthen its grip on the hinterland, reduce the Luunda chief's role to a purely administrative one (at least till 1991), and also, possibly, to be able to check the recent growing success of some sort of Luunda 'nationalism' and ethnic revival. The promoting, empowering, and, in some cases, (re)inventing of the Luunda traditional heritage and prestige for strategic political reasons in the interaction with the state has not been confined to the aLuund of Kahemba alone, but may also be observed among other groups of Luunda origin in the Kwaango (see Matadiwamba 1988). To the regime, this Luunda revival, although modest, arouses old suspicions, for the CONAKAT, the Luunda political party which was founded after the Second World War and headed by Moïse Tshombe, lay at the basis of the violent Katanga secession, the Kivu invasion in 1967 and the Shaba wars in 1977 and 1978.

In the case of the Kahemba Luunda chief, other elements, of a more strategic and economic nature, also explain the regime's interest in this Luunda chieftaincy. Undoubtedly, a traditional authority widely recognised in a large part of the Angolan province of Lunda Norte holds an important potential for the Zairean regime, which may use and manipulate this traditional network to keep in contact with UNITA forces. The second reason, related to the regime's sympathies for UNITA, concerns the key position of the Luunda chieftaincy in Angolan diamond trading. The commercialisation of diamonds from Angola has gradually become one of the regime's few remaining sources of money: Zaire has become a real 'gemocracy'. Increasingly, one of the problems faced by the regime towards the end of the 1980s and the early 1990s was to ensure the control over the Lebanese, Greek and Indian circuits buying the UNITA diamonds. One can understand easily, therefore, why the regime would choose to keep in touch with a Luunda chief who might, if so desired, facilitate and – directly or indirectly – control this diamond importing.

Only dimly aware of the detailed geo-politico-economic background in which he figures, the Luunda titleholder in Kahemba has knowingly been stressing his cultural Luunda heritage, nevertheless. His aim, primarily, is to promote the cultural and ethnic revaluation of his area, which he thinks is not sufficiently recognised by the central government, but certainly also to attract the regime's attention by playing on the connotations that 'Luunda' has evoked in the capital ever since the days of the CONAKAT. Because of the Kahemba chief's initiative, the Luunda royal village there has become known as 'the second *musuumb*' (royal village), the first *musuumb* being that of the Luunda *mwaant yaav* in Katanga (to whom the regime's administrative coverover strategy had never applied). The association between the Kahemba Luunda titleholder and the *mwaant yaav* was strengthened further when they met for the first time in Kinshasa in 1988. On that occasion, *mwaant yaav* endowed the Kahemba paramount titleholder with the ancestral kaolin and with a royal beaded crown, an event which undoubtedly helped the latter to gain prestige in the eyes of the authorities.

Luunda identity and the process of intercultural exchange

Traditional Luunda culture is marked by its openness and its capacity to absorb outside influences. The Luunda cultural whole is made up of several clusters and, often contradictory, ritual and therapeutic subsystems, some of which have their origin outside the Luunda cultural order. The same capacity to incorporate outside influences has characterised the Luunda political system. Luunda political administration is shaped by a system of positional succession and perpetual kinship, creating a political network of titles which is defined in terms of real, putative or fictive consanguinity. It is the existence of this particular system which also explains the enormous Luunda potential for conquest in the past. All political titles (including non-aLuund) are integrated into a vast genealogy that focuses on the paramount titleholder.

The intricate web of political relations creates interdependencies and guarantees the continuity of the hierarchical political organisation and the tributary network, which reinforces the Luunda identity of political rulers. The tributary dependence links the various layers of the smaller segmentary authority structures into one integrated whole and enables the traditional political authority at the top to draw non-aLuund into the system. In terms of the aLuund's self-definition as political rulers and 'lords' (*amaant*), those non-aLuund are considered to be socially and politically inferior. Situated at the periphery of the Luunda political power, they are nevertheless an essential part of it, for they make possible and confirm the aLuund's auto-definition as 'lords'.

Many aspects of the traditional modes of socio-political and cultural interaction and exchange recur in the aLuund's interaction with the regime and the state. From the point of view of the Luunda lords, the adoption and assimilation of the regime's style, discourse and arguments, as described above, are not interpreted as a loss of identity; nor are they signs of subordination which turns them into a mere administrative extension of a larger national and supra-national system. On the contrary, the adopted symbols and markers referring to the regime are viewed as an alien symbolic surplus added to the traditional symbols of political authority, thereby empowering the titleholder's traditional basis of authority. In the same way, the interest of the Zairean regime or of UNITA in the Luunda chief is interpreted by the latter as an extra external dimension of legitimacy, adding to the importance and stature of his role as *grand chef coutumier*. In this interpretation the centre–periphery relation is inversed.

As Event 3 makes clear, for example, the interaction between the chieftaincy and the state may thus be interpreted in terms of an extension of the tributary network focusing on the paramount titleholder.

Event 3   At the end of 1988, after considerable lobbying, the Luunda paramount titleholder was knighted in the 'National Order of the Leopard' (*Chevalier de l'Ordre National du Léopard*), one of the highest distinctions under the Second Republic which places the recipient *de facto* above the law, for he enjoys the personal protection of the president. The chief's decoration was confirmed when one of the court dignitaries returned from Kinshasa with the official document, caught in a fine wooden frame, and signed by the president himself. The document was handed over to the Luunda ruler, represented for the occasion by his senior wife (*mwaant mwaadi*) and one of his younger brothers, himself holder of the important court-title of *mulopw*, during an elaborate courtyard ceremony that unfolded in front of the royal ancestral shrines. The way in which the ceremony unfolded closely followed the structure of the Luunda ritual for the bringing in of a leopard skin, one of the traditional royal regalia. The leopard skin is a prestigious gift, given as tribute to the paramount ruler by lesser titleholders and vassals. At the same time, the ceremony echoed various aspects typical of enthronement ritual, such as the spatial layout from east to west. During enthronement, the regalia are always carried by a ritual specialist, representing the *mwaant yaav*, from the east (where *kool*, the ancestral origins and the *mwaant yaav*'s court are located) to the west, where they are handed over to the chief-to-be.

Facing east, the *mwaant mwaadi* and the *mulopw* were seated on a raffia mat, the prerogative of important titleholders. Drummers, lined up along the ancestral shrines, started beating the rhythm of the *musaangw*, a royal sword dance which is the performed enactment of the paramount title-holder's conquest of the territory over which he rules. Other court dignitaries fired gunshots in the air with their muzzle-loaders, while onlookers uttered loud ululations of joy. Preceded by a court dignitary, two members of the royal lineage walked westward through the entrance gate into the royal enclosure, while holding the framed 'National Order of the Leopard', metonymically representing the leopard skin. They were followed by the man who would present the gift to the titleholder (and who represented the government and, ultimately, Mobutu himself). The procession approached with the same slow and majestic pace that is adopted by important titleholders or by ritual specialists during enthrone-ment ritual. Then the document was put down at the feet of the *mwaant mwaadi* and subsequently anointed by one of the court's ritual guardians with kaolin and a herbal preparation that would normally have been applied to the leopard skin. The same substances were also applied to the *mulopw*'s chest. Then the person who had transported the document from Kinshasa to the village, and who in that capacity represented the regime, briefly addressed the *mulopw*. The latter responded by returning a gift (a goat or its equivalent in money) to the speaker (usually the hunter of the leopard).

The staging of the ceremony clearly brings out the ambivalences in the contest of representation between the national power-holders and the local Luunda lords. The chief's decoration by the regime – a decoration which he had struggled so hard to get and which had required considerable financial efforts on the part of the court – was reconstructed both in terms of enthronement ritual and in terms of the traditional tributary system.

Restated in terms of the enthronement ritual, the handing over of the document mirrored the handing over of the regalia during enthronement. It was indeed the only time that I have seen the paramount titleholder dance the *musaangw*, a dance he himself performs only during his own enthronement. In his eyes, however, the dancing of the *musaangw* was appropriate, for, in addition to his ritual enthronement according to ancestral practice, the decoration signified his enthronement in the regime's terms (and actually by Mobutu, here equated to the *mwaant yaav*, himself).

Restated in the terms of the tributary gift, however, the decoration became a tribute from the ('subordinate') state to the (paramount) title-holder, thus restructuring the relationship between the latter and the regime as a traditional relationship between paramount titleholder and subaltern. The court indeed considered the decoration to be the expression of the fact that the Luunda chieftaincy was situated 'in the middle of power' (*pakach ka waant*), as it was described triumphantly.

Finally, the ritual entrance of the leopard skin into the royal courtyard symbolically signified the subduing of the dangerous realm of the wild bush to the order of the village and the rule of the Luunda paramount chief. At the same time, the bringing in of the dangerous exterior, metonymically represented by the leopard skin, fortifies and empowers the interior, i.e. the village and by expansion the whole Luunda territory, of which the royal courtyard is the focal point. In this reconstruction, the relationship between the Luunda villages (inside or centre) and the state (outside or periphery) is recast in terms of a relationship between cultural order and wild nature.

Local/global contacts, identity and the question of authenticity

In the contact with broader power networks and in the face of events that transcend the local level, the aLuund, like many other 'traditional' local populations, live multiple differentiated identities. However, these are not experienced as contradictory or mutually exclusive categories. On the contrary, it is the attempt at combining these identities which for the aLuund seems to provide a more or less effective way of overcoming the postmodern disjunctions at play. As such, the issue of Luunda (self-) representation should not be conflated with the discussion on the crisis of representation that has haunted American anthropology in recent years.

The state, the war, the economic world-system (in the Luunda case most clearly in connection to the diamond trade), these are all compelling realities. As such, they have a large impact on the aLuund's lives and impose upon them the necessity to integrate into their own culture something of the institutional forms, symbols, styles, discourses and practices by means of which the dominant power structures define their relation to them and extend their control over them. The successful achievement of such cultural politics seems to be a prerequisite for the aLuund's cultural and political survival. Success in this field is linked apparently to the capacity to objectify one's own culture by creating an appropriate 'ethnic identity' for outward use, in a form that allows collective action in collaboration with or in opposition to broader political and economic networks.

Against the creation of an objectified version of Luunda identity, the aLuund seem to suffer from a severe disadvantage. As described in Events 1 and 2, the Zairean regime and UNITA make ample use of the audiovisual media to create a Luunda identity which conforms to their own goals. Unlike the Brazilian Kaiapo (Turner 1992), for example, the aLuund do not have access to such powerful instruments to achieve the successful objectification and self-representation of their Luunda cultural identity. Nor do they have access to newspapers and other written media, as people in Kinshasa have. However, aLuund engage in the contest of representation by using the means at their disposal. The image of the traditional chief is in itself already so powerful that the central state has used it extensively to legitimise its actions. Consequently, in interaction with the regime, the Luunda titleholder knowingly attempts to play up his persona as *grand chef coutumier* and inflate his regional importance. At the same time, the image of the chief also allows for a counter-objectification, enabling the aLuund to recast their relationship with the state in terms of tributary relations. As shown in Event 3, some of the subtleties of these Luunda strategies are lost on the regime and are therefore not very successful from an outsider's point of view, but to the aLuund themselves they seem appropriate and effective. The outcome of Event 2, for example, may be viewed as a failure: the contact that the Luunda court established with people close to the centre of national politics did not, in the end, lead to an advantageous financial settlement. However, in the margin of this event, the Luunda titleholder was capable of successfully lobbying against one of his political foes.

The complementary aspect of the objectification of one's own culture is 'intercultural adultery' or loss of 'cultural virginity' (Turner 1992). The question is: What is the impact of the incorporation of elements, techniques and perspectives of the dominant culture? Does this incorporation not produce a counter-effect that eventually leads to the destruction of local cultures? This raises again the question of authenticity, a concept that in the Zairean context is loaded with multiple significations. Luunda culture has never been experienced as a seamless whole by the aLuund themselves, I must stress. For centuries the lives of the aLuund have involved contacts, sometimes brutal, with neighbouring groups, such as the Chokwe, or with total outsiders, such as slavers during the time of the Congo Independent State, or Belgian, British and Portuguese colonising forces. In that historical context, their dealings with UNITA rebels and the Zairean regime, or their role in the diamond trade, are in some respects contemporary prolongations of older cultural patterns of trade and political contacts. As in so many precolonial states throughout Central Africa, an outsider is at the base of the Luunda political culture (see de Heusch 1972; Palmeirim 1994). The romantic idealisation of an untouched cultural whole is, therefore, alien to their own conception of what it means to be Luunda.

The borrowing and appropriating of cultural practices and rituals of other groups (most clearly in the case of traditional political symbols and therapeutic and ritual practices) is in itself a characteristic trait of traditional Luunda culture and identity. Event 1, in which the Luunda titleholder calls on outside ritual specialists from neighbouring groups to carry out the protective rituals asked for by UNITA, provides a characteristic illustration of this mechanism. As illustrated in Event 3, the aLuund give form to these borrowed or external elements in terms of tributary relations that are proper to their own social organisation and their own culturally-determined categories and classifications. The Luunda assimilation of political, cultural and socio-economic rituals and practices of the dominant power centres resembles and unfolds according to the same logic of incorporation and assimilation that also characterises the older traditional (political and ritual) relations with other groups. Rather than giving way to a process of acculturation in which one's cultural identity is lost or becomes a 'desubjectivised projection' of the dominant (and passively experienced) gaze of the state, the aLuund thus engage in cultural politics in which external elements are creatively incorporated on their own social and cultural terms, and in which identities imposed upon them are countered by powerful images of self-representation, that also provide the possibility of a counter-objectification.

Issues of identity and the breakdown of dichotomies

The Congo has long fascinated the Western imagination, from Conrad's *Heart of Darkness* (1902) to de Villiers' SAS pulp *Panique au Zaïre* (1978), a spectacularly racist cocktail of exoticism, sex, violence, intrigue and betrayal. In various gradations, 'Zaire' appears in these works of fiction as a powerful negative image of the Western Self, in which the West projects all its fears and fantasies. In the wake of the 1995 Ebola outbreak in Kikwit, for example, a leading Belgian newspaper characterised the virus as symptomatic of a wild and undomesticated country. The great discrepancy between this topos, the Zaire of the imagination, and the topicality of the physical Zaire, which is rendered invisible by the strength of the imagined place, seems to go unnoticed by most.

Related to the Western failure to reach beyond its blurred vision of a largely fictitious Zaire is the development of a second form of cataract, which is becoming increasingly apparent in the incapacity of much of the academic discourse to grasp fully and make visible the changing realities in contemporary Zaire. Faced with worlds and interactions such as those described above, one becomes acutely aware that it is futile to explain some of the processes currently taking place in Zairean society by means of the standard vocabularies usually used by social and political scientists and economists. This observation applies in the local and regional levels as well as the national level. Terms and concepts such as 'state', 'administration', 'government', 'governability', 'opposition', 'democracy', 'army', 'national budget', 'citizenship', 'law', 'justice', or even 'education' and 'health care' no longer seem to apply to the realities usually covered by those terms.

Why is a building called 'national bank', 'university', 'state department', 'hospital' or 'school' when the activities which take place in it cannot be given standard meanings and realities usually covered by those words? In January 1995, for example, Belgian newspapers reported that the Zairean national bank's total stock of foreign currency amounted to US$2,000 and a handful of Swiss francs. Similarly, university professors today earn US$2 a month, and most departments of Kinshasa's national university have not bought books, or produced a single doctoral dissertation, since the Zaireanisation in the early 1970s. Why continue the social convention of referring to a banknote as 'money' when one is confronted daily with the fact that it is just a worthless slip of paper? The withdrawal (November 1993) of the IMF and the World Bank from Zaire attests to the fact that Zaire today no longer partakes in the formal world economy. But what is the use of distinguishing between formal and informal or parallel economies when the informal has become the common and the formal has almost disappeared?

For some years now, Zaire's 'second economy' (MacGaffey 1991) has become the first and virtually only one. The world of modernity with its tempting promises, embedded in a vision of an expansive capitalism in service of the nation-state, has become the fool's paradise in which the Zairean nation is no longer capable of living. This was the feeling recently voiced by the Zairean star Pepe Kalle in one of his songs: 'They went to Europe, but had to land in the desert' (*bakende Poto, bakweyi na désert*). For Zaireans it has become a cliché to say that no economic model can, say, explain how a city like Kinshasa, with its estimated 4 million inhabitants, survives (see Rapoport 1993). For the *pousse-pousseurs*, taxi-drivers, shoe-shiners, night-watchmen and street vendors in the urban *cités* who daily experience in the flesh the continuing deterioration of their standards of living, and whose lives unfold in *avenue misère* (Nlandu 1992), the common discourses of political and economic analysts are therefore totally devoid of sense. To them, *Kinshasa-la-belle* has long since become *Kinshasa-la-poubelle*, referred to as *Koweït City rive gauche* or, more recently, *Sarajevo*.

Applying a linguistic and sociological perspective to the daily scene in Zaire, one could say that the rupture between discourse, action and structure is total. The Zairean reality, deeply marked by a crisis of meaning-fulness or leading sense, has gradually turned into a world in which fact and fiction are interchangeable. In Zaire today, it is no longer possible to forget or deny the Saussurian arbitrariness of the sign, or the facticity of the social fact. What Taussig has termed the 'mimetic faculty' (Taussig 1993), the capacity to pretend that one lives facts, not fictions, has ceased to operate in an adequate way. To put it differently, there is a strong sense of what Baudrillard (1983) has termed the 'precession of simulacra', thereby pointing out the changing relations between the signifying 'real' and the representational 'imaginary', or the liquidation of all referentials. The common links and paths of transfer between signifier and signified, or between predicate and subject, have imploded or are subverted: the *faire croire* and *faire semblant* have often taken over from reality. What poses as true is actually false, the lie becomes truth. As a result, the boundaries between legal and illegal are continuously shifting, by the widespread mechanism of reversibility. For example, to nab the profits made in diamond transactions (see Event 2), the rackets, formed by the high-ranking army personnel and family members of some of the leading politicians, use the vocabulary of law and order. Racketeers thus pose as law-abiding members of government agencies created to investigate 'dubious' diamond deals and fraudulent transactions. In this way, the racketeer becomes the upholder of morality, whereas the owner or buyer of the diamonds – such as Mr Joseph (Event 2), who, all things considered, had acquired the 175-carat stone in a perfectly normal transaction – is reconstructed in terms of a swindler (which, of course, he often is too).

The crisis of meaning that can be observed at all levels of Zairean society has profoundly alienating effects on both macro- and microlevels of societal life, equally affecting, for example, the ways in which decisions at the top are made, and the ways in which relations within such basic social building-blocks as the familial unit take shape. The breaking up of the doxic experience, the taken-for-granted quality of a world that goes without saying for those who experience, live in and belong to it, has indeed far-reaching consequences; it jeopardises cohesive cultural systems and threatens cultural identities and habituses.

Kozanga esika (to be without a place)   Many popular songs bemoan the 'lack of a place to which one fully belongs' (*kozanga esika*), thereby indicating a deeply-felt rupture with one's lived world (see Ngandu 1992). In fact, the dividing line between urban and rural realities, 'modern' and 'traditional' worlds, or the local and the global, can no longer be drawn in a self-evident way. In many ways, 'city' and 'village' have become qualities of mind, rather than spatial realities. Commodity relations, based on monetary transactions, have formed the key metaphor for the structuring of relationships in urban contexts over the past decades. Today, however, the Zairean urban context is undergoing a marked ruralisation or *villagisation* (see also, Devisch 1995). This process goes hand in hand with growing social barriers and an increasing polarisation and segregation of the urban space, between the commercial and 'European' centre of the city, urbanised by the Belgians before 1960, and the endless 'peripheral city', *la cité* (La Fontaine 1970; Nzuzi 1992). Paradoxically, as in the times of the pre-colonial slave and ivory trade in which the aLuund were deeply involved, the 'periphery' has at the same time regained centrality in the economic dynamics. As such, the ruralisation of the city, especially in the *cité*, goes hand in hand with the monetarisation of the traditional gift logic in some of Zaire's rural areas, such as Kahemba; while an increasing number of people – the vast majority of Zaireans who do not have access to diamond dollars – no longer participate in a failing system of commodity market exchange. Dollars, excessive spending and consumerism have become the major marker of success in the world of the diamond trade.

In the face of these changing African realities, our standard frames of analysis, such as the classic dichotomy between rural and urban, no longer fit an increasingly 'exotic', complex and chaotic world that seems to announce the end of social life and the societal fabric as most of us understand it. The same applies to the delineation we commonly make between 'state' and 'society'. What, for example, is the usefulness or adequacy of such concepts as 'state', or 'democracy' for an improved understanding of the manifold processes of collapse and change that have given shape to the Zairean reality as it presents itself today? As I argue in the next sections, I believe that analysis of the central issues foregrounded in the Zairean crisis – issues concerning representation, identity, ethnicity, nationalism, violence, strategies of survival and resilience, the role of the media, the notion of citizenship and civil society – no longer benefits from an explanatory frame that presupposes the 'state'. The need is not for more refined typologies of state-systems in Africa (see Chazan et al. 1992). Rather, we should focus, as I have tried to do above, on the interaction between local and global spheres of socio-political, economic and cultural interaction, and on the hinge-joints between 'traditional' and 'modern' worlds, concepts, beliefs and practices. This implies an explanation of such processes of interaction, through an analysis of cultural entities as forms, not only of hegemony and resistance, but also of adaptation, accommodation and collaboration.

In search of new Zairean identities   An important observation in this ethnography is that much of the cultural and political struggle in Zaire today focuses on control over a politics of identity as self-representation, which implies that it is self-generated and self-constructed. The changing socio-political context seems to give rise to a new politics of identity (see Jewsiewicki 1993). To a large extent the arguments of identity today centre round the question of who represents whom, and to/for whom. Recourse to colonial and postcolonial stereotypes may be inevitable in situations where identities are at play. Who is author, who is subject of representation?

In relation to the national and international contexts, the 1970s and 1980s offered two models of identity to Zaireans. On the one hand, there was the relationship with the West, the world of the former Belgian coloniser, 'our uncle' (*noko ya biso*), viewed in avuncular terms. The relationship between mother's brother and sister's children is one of respect and reciprocity. Hence the *noko* model created an ambivalent spectre of rights, duties and expectations on both sides (Devisch 1994; Ntite-Mukendi 1994), which could lead only to mutual disillusion and disappointment. The MPR, on the other hand, offered an alternative, paternal model, in a movement away from the colonial past, the individualistic 'maternal uncle' and his unfulfilled promises of modernity, towards 'authenticity', solidarity and a new Zairean identity defined by Mobutu, 'the Father of the Nation'.[12] In the early 1990s, both the avuncular and the paternal models of identification broke down. The 1991 looting of supermarkets, Western companies, restaurants and other symbols of luxury in Kinshasa signified the rejection of the uncle's world (Devisch 1994: 76). At the same time, Mobutu's announcement of the end of the Second Republic in N'Sele, April 1990, and the ensuing move towards multipartyism, made official the loss of credibility that had long marked the paternal alternative. The 1991–92 sovereign national conference (CNS), held to 'reconcile the people of Zaire with themselves', as an official slogan had it, therefore coincided with a search for a new identity.

No longer identifying themselves as children in relation to the father, or sister's children in relation to the uncle, a growing number of Zaireans today reject being pictured as mute subjects of a despotic regime, or as peasants and proletarians subject to the rules imposed over and above their heads by the West, represented by the IMF and other international organisations. The current politics of identity, usually stressing one's independence and self-supporting qualities, is evidenced by the proliferation of 'popular' painting, theatre and local newspapers as chronicles and commentaries on the urban context (see Biaya 1989; de Villiers 1992; Jewsiewicki 1989); by the proliferation of spiritual healing in urban, and to a lesser extent also rural, contexts (Ndaywel 1993); by the (re)emerging and (re)inventing of ritual as exemplary enactment of co-operative sociability, whether or not it is actually realised outside the time of the performance itself; by a renewed stress on ethnic identity; by the emergence of new forms of reciprocity in church-connected grassroots organisations that play an increasing role in the promotion of people's self-awareness (see de Dorlodot 1994; Jewsiewicki et al. 1995); by actions such as the *radio tableau* in the *cités* of the city of Kikwit, where international radio-news (RFI, BBC, Canal Afrique, Afrique No. 1) is spelled out and commented upon by the owners of small portable radios on a blackboard in the street while the whole neighbourhood contributes batteries to keep the radio working, as a way of escaping interpretations and representations imposed upon them from elsewhere.

L'arrangement The analysis of the ongoing dialogue between the local and the global, or the rural and the urban, reveals a challenge for arguments of identity and issues of (self-)representation. It is the intricacy of the complexities and contradictions in the interaction between the postcolonial state and the various levels of the civil society. Such complexities and contradictions are far more intricate than is contemplated by the standard conceptualisations which proclaim a dichotomous relationship between political superstructures and local socio-political forms of organisation. This relationship is usually analysed in terms of an antagonism, or a binary opposition in terms of above and below. In the 1970s and 1980s, the more classical focus on the management of regime relations and the conduct of 'high politics', or politics from above, gradually shifted to the 'frog' perspective of a 'politics from below' or 'deep politics' (Bayart 1992; Chazan et al. 1992). Within this perspective, an early, pathbreaking work in the field of African political studies was Weiss's analysis of a movement of rural revolution, executed by a peasantry mobilised by a young political elite, and directed against the rapidly disintegrating Congolese central authority (Weiss 1967). The approach of Hyden (1980), on the other hand, was seminal in that he showed how large parts of the Tanzanian peasantry remained 'uncaptured' by the postcolonial state and market. More recently, a group of scholars including Bayart (1989) and Mbembe (1988; 1992) have written the chronicle of the dynamics of the invention of African processes of democratisation 'from below'. In the same vein, the essays in Jewsiewicki and Moniot (1988) describe popular Zairean responses to institutional power, and show the multilayered connections between the machinations of power and cultural patterns. In their exploration of the multiple socio-political spaces and cultural levels that shape the actual African political field, these authors focus in particular on forms of 'hybridisation', 'fusion' and cultural innovation.

However, in the current context, tropes of the 'above' and the 'below' become increasingly costly, for they seem to conceal more than they reveal. For example, whereas the approach of Bayart and Mbembe has the advantage of dealing with the *praxis* of the postcolonial state and stresses processes of *mediation* (see Bayart 1992: 12) between 'the above' and 'the below', it does not, in my view, sufficiently problematise the concept of the state or the dichotomy between state and society (even though Bayart states that he does not want to be locked in this dichotomy [ibid.: 10]). What, today, is 'above' and what 'below'? As Hyden (1992), referring to recent literature on state–society relations (such as Callaghy 1984; Migdal 1988; Rothchild and Chazan 1988), and Fatton (1992) remark, the use of the state/society dichotomy is problematic because the (African) state is rarely the sole harbinger of power. At the same time, the public realm is weak: 'Individuals see nothing wrong in using public resources for private or communal purposes. This attitude extends to a wider set of institutions than those we officially call the state' (Hyden 1992: 6). This applies to the Zairean context all too well. The shifting boundaries between legality and illegality are susceptible to political pressures (MacGaffey 1992: 247).

One of the problems is, however, what precisely does illegality mean in Zaire. The lines between the illicit, the illegal and the illegitimate are extremely difficult to draw. Secondly, it is no longer clear whether 'illegality' is *still* and *uniquely defined* by the nation-state, as MacGaffey contends (1992). In the current situation, there is illegality initiated by the state – in reality a small political elite of *dinosaurs* (see Braeckman 1992) who form the personal coercive regime's 'domestic structure of repression' (Fatton 1992: 129). This illegality has spread from the centre to broader layers of society, according to a dynamic which increasingly escapes the mechanisms of state control as such, and also involves an international network that surpasses by far the national Zairean 'mafias' that are active in the arms trade, the diamond and petrol traffic, the laundering of narco-dollars and other similar activities (see also, Askin and Collins 1993). On the other hand, one could say that, paradoxically, unlawfulness, arrogant arbitrariness and illegality are the only elements that put an increasingly fictional 'state' in evidence and continue to make it visible. For most people, the state has become the looting soldier's nocturnal knock on the door, 'turning the house upside down' (*soda unatumbula na ndako*), as Kinshasa's *indubil*, a Lingala argot, powerfully puts it. Furthermore, as illustrated by Event 2, the structure of the state is often reduced to competing factions who follow their own 'pathways of accumulation' (Geschiere and Konings 1993).

For two decades, the oppressive state has forced itself into the spaces of survival of the common Zairois by means of corruption and repression (Fatton 1992: 82; Leslie 1993; MacGaffey 1988; Schatzberg 1988; Young and Turner 1985). Today, the increasingly blurred boundaries of the state apparatus provide people on the local urban and rural levels of society with the opportunity to penetrate 'the black hole of power' (Zartman 1995: 7), the spaces previously occupied by the imploding state and the regime. In Zaire today, everybody 'works politics'.[13] This naturally leads to the implosion of the classic hierarchical state–society picture and to the creation of a new dynamic 'model' of interaction, the contour of which is still only vaguely outlined. It is a model of interaction between multiple, dialectically interdependent, socio-political and cultural spaces and groups, linked to one another in constantly shifting hierarchies that are defined by the personalistic strategies of the dinosaurs and of other actors on the local and the global level. These networks, although largely based on personal links, cannot exclusively be defined as political prebendalism and patronage. According to the context, 'patronage may take on very different connotations from those generally associated with self-interested exchanges; it may partake of the quality of "gift-giving" (in the Maussian sense of the term) and summon a level of trust unknown among urban clienteles' (Lemarchand 1988: 151). Lemarchand therefore opts for a clear distinction between patronage, tribute and prebend: 'All three involve certain types of self-interested exchange. Yet they each tend to develop within specific institutional frameworks and are sustained by radically different normative orientations' (ibid.). Yet, in practice, they often interact and interpenetrate each other in more or less complex ways, a fact also acknowledged by Lemarchand.

It is precisely this interaction of conceptual grids and normative orientations that I am interested in here. For example, the fact of being knighted in the 'National Order of the Leopard' provides a protected status to the beneficiary, and allows the regime to supplant a relation of traditional clientelism (the tributary relationship between the subordinate Luunda chief and the paramount Luunda *mwaant yaav*) by a relationship of political patronage in the 'modern' sense between the Luunda chief and the 'state'. On the other hand, receiving the 'National Order of the Leopard' allows the Luunda aristocracy to redefine the transactions with the regime in terms of tributary relations, thereby promoting a shift away from a postcolonial political patron–client relationship to a more familiar form of clientelism which also enables a redefinition of the status differences between the two sides involved.

Tribute has always been one of the most important organisational modes of the Luunda empire's architecture as well as a means of adapting its political organisation to the impact of economic globalisation and expansion (Vansina 1990: 237; Vellut 1972). For the aLuund, the interaction described in Event 3 is understood as a way of introducing and handling tribute, and thus a Luunda morality of exchange, in the space of the state, thereby redefining in totally different terms what appears at first to be a mere patron–client relationship in which the Luunda occupy the subordinate position. Rather than mere patronage, tributary relationships imply a political economy of gift exchange as well as the making of political relations that reinstitutionalise the personalised sphere. In the same way as tribute is sent to the royal village and complementing royal gifts are returned to tributary chiefs (see Bustin 1975a: 4; Miller 1988: 60), so the Luunda royals' and the regime's interaction is based on transmission and exchange (exemplified by the return gift of a goat in the ritual described in Event 3), subject to this difference that respective positions ('king', 'tributary chief') are defined vaguely enough to shift according to the situation and the respective points of view. Within the Zairean context, the concept of the state should consequently be problematised and redefined in terms of a great number of political strategies which cannot simply be described as forms of political 'decay' or pathological dys-functioning, but which aim at the creation of networks and spaces of contact, palaver, (asymmetric) exchange, solidarity and complicity, enabling the circulation of commodities, money and wealth in people.

Such a redefinition of the state, and of politics in general, as an inventive mixture of capitalist, tributary and kin-ordered modes of political and economic production, also problematises another aspect stressed in many contemporary analyses of the (African) political scene: that of conflict and/or opposition. Generally, state–society relations are seen in antagonistic terms, in terms of a 'big brother'-like state on the one hand and a resisting society on the other, struggling against the state (see Callaghy 1984; Osumaka 1994) with the 'weapons of the weak'. Often this antagonistic relation is analysed in currently fashionable Gramscian terms of hegemony and counter-hegemonic practices. In this respect, it is interesting to look at certain paradigms of resilience, such as ethnicity, or the significance of ethnic identity. As the work of Gluckman, Epstein and Mitchell in the 1950s and 1960s, or more recent historical approaches to African ethnicity, such as Amselle (1990), Amselle and M'bokolo (1985) and Vail (1989) have illustrated, the formation of ethnic identities was certainly stimulated by the processes of state-formation, urbanisation and industrialisation in the colony and the postcolony. In today's context, ethnicity, as a form of resilience, cannot unequivocally be understood in simple terms of opposition against an oppressive state, for the regime too exploits ethnicity as an instrument or strategy to accumulate political and economic capital (see Bayart 1993: 342; Biaya 1993). The ongoing dialectics of power between the local and the global is therefore played out in much more dynamic and complex ways, in which notions of interrelation play as important a role as elements of opposition.

For example, the Luunda chiefs discussed above use arguments of identity and policies of presentation and (ethnic) self-representation to create an objectified image of themselves for outward use, namely to deal with regional and national representatives of the administration and the regime. Although there is a subtle critique of the regime embedded in these Luunda cultural politics, their basic attitude is not so much one of contest, resistance or conflict with the state. Rather, they try to use the 'state', collaborate with it and invade its space in order to further, among other things, their own political agenda. These local strategies of resilience are not only directed *against* the state or in opposition to the state, but are also – perhaps even in the first place – inspired by the desire or the necessity to transcend the constraints of the local level and to *participate* in economic and political spheres that are under the influence or control of the merchant and political capital.

Undoubtedly, it is in this sense that one must understand the post-1991 complaints (heard in the Zairean hinterland more often than in the capital) that everything was better before *la démocratie* arrived. Because the collapsing totalitarian Zairean state has failed to extend central control fully over more traditional local power structures, it has shaped an arena in which 'tributary' interdependencies have been created, and in which there is room to manoeuvre.

In the quotidian praxis of governance and politics, conflict and opposition against the state have therefore often been transformed into a specific mode of negotiation and compromise which can be referred to as *l'arrangement*. As Zaireans like to say: *tout finit par s'arranger*. Local actors such as the Luunda aristocracy have access to these spaces of negotiation and mediation; it provides them with a possibility of striving for the existence of their version of *démocratie*, cast in terms of personalised, 'feudal' structures of decision-making, deliberation, sharing of power and distributing of wealth.

Conclusion

In this chapter I endeavour to expand our cultural metalogue in order to capture the ways in which people, individually and collectively, experience, undergo and try to make sense of the profound changes in social, cultural, political, economic and moral patterns that characterise the contemporary Zairean reality. In particular, I deal with strategies of resilience on the level of the socio-political body, in the interaction between local and more global spheres of political and economic interests. I show how, by developing these strategies, local actors seek to overcome the contradictions and ruptures embedded in dichotomies (between open–closed, rural–urban, society and state) which, as I argue, are themselves gradually breaking up and dissolving.

In one way or another, these strategies all focus on issues of identity.

On all levels of society, the existence of a postmodern multiple Zairean identity is evident, but at the same time Zaireans inventively search for ways to overcome the fragmentation inherent in this multiplicity. In that respect, the importance of the ritual context certainly stands out. Undoubtedly, in political, economic and cultural terms, the structural circumstances of the Zairean state and the society at large differ considerably from precolonial polities and realities.

On the one hand, recent Africanist academic discourse has perhaps focused too narrowly on the postcolonial situation. I have argued that both the current Zairean crisis and the various responses to it are to some extent also rooted in a moral, social and symbolic matrix that reaches beyond the fractures inflicted by the postcolonial world and the myth of modernity, and that also draws from precolonial sources. In the fragmentation and multiplicity of 'urban' and 'rural', or 'modern' and 'traditional' worlds, realities and values, people seem to continue to make sense of their world by inventing transitional spaces and interconnecting strategies.

On the other hand, people do deliberately turn their backs on the falseness of the nationalist myths and the various representations that are imposed upon them. They also continue to refer, or have started to refer again, to a cultural, moral, aesthetic and ethical framework informed by and rooted in (reinvented or reimagined) 'tradition'. This move, however, should not be mistaken for escapism into the past. Rather than being crushed under the weight of tradition, or closing themselves off from larger political and economic processes, they aim at opening up more or less separate worlds to construct encompassing social identities. The Luunda example of the construction of wider networks with reference to long-standing notions of a ritualised tributary political economy conveys this point. As such, the Luunda case also illustrates the fact that, in its predictability, the current 'reflexive celebration of hybrid marginality ... as resistance against state hegemony' (Knauft 1994: 406) does not capture the complexities of the empirical realities lived by many in Zaire today.

To capture this dynamic, ritual (whether it be a protective ritual as in Event 1, a political ritual as in Event 3, or, in another context, therapeutic ritual in urban healing churches) presents a privileged dimension, for it not only offers the possibility of resistance, but also the opportunity to create a space-time of negotiation, collaboration and accommodation in which sense can be made of the multilevelled contradictions of the postcolonial universe. As such, ritual and other cultural practices of public performances play a crucial role as local and global vehicles to (re)produce, contest, transform, deconstruct and adapt to varying forms of authority. The ritual reproduction and transformations that can be witnessed in a ritual as described in Event 3 form part of a more encompassing cultural praxis and identity which appears as an ultimate resilient paradigm. As a form of resiliency it not only represents and reflects the crisis in Zaire, but it equally offers the possibility of generating an innovative response to the need for new, mediating identities and forms of governance and of political, moral and social authority.

Acknowledgements

Sustained field research was made possible thanks to grants from a variety of institutions. I would like to thank the Research Fund of the Catholic University of Leuven, the Belgian National Fund for Scientific Research (NFWO) and 'Vlaamse Leergangen' for their financial support. I also thank the African and African-American Research Center of the University of California, San Diego, for inviting me to convene a focus research group on the Zairean crisis (San Diego, May 1994). I especially benefited from discussions with B. Jules-Rosette and T. K. Biaya. Parts of this paper were also presented at the EHESS (Paris, May 1994), the African Studies Centre, Leyden (October 1994) and the Centre d'Etudes et de Recherches Internationales (CERI), Paris (December 1994). I thank J.-F. Bayart, R. Devisch, S. Ellis, P. Geschiere, E. Hopkins, J. Vansina and R. P. Werbner for their comments and remarks.

Notes

1. Another major diamond-mining site, Losambo, is located some 40km from Cafunfo. Before independence, both mines were exploited by the Portuguese DIAMANG company. Together these two mines covered 60 per cent of the actual Angolan diamond production. The other 40 per cent mainly derives from Dundo-Lukapa, towards the east. In recent years numerous 'wild' mining sites have developed along the Kwaango river.

2. In 1981 and 1984 UNITA unsuccessfully tried to take Cafunfo and drive out the MPLA.

3. For a short while, with the introduction of the multiparty system in Zaire, Zaireans entering Angola, especially those suspected of having UDPS sympathies, were also tortured or killed by the fighters of UNITA, who thereby took revenge for the fact that Zaire had turned its back on Mobutu, long-standing friend and ally of Savimbi and UNITA.

4. In this sense, the borderline is not only a cumbersome division between Angolan and Zairean aLuund, it also offers the possibility of refuge from war or escape from state control and repression. Even in colonial times, aLuund crossed the border into Angola whenever the demands of the Belgian colonial administrators conflicted with theirs. In 1957, the Belgians therefore decided to regroup the population, a plan that never materialised. The Luunda royal court has been located in Zaire for the greater part of this century. At least for three generations of paramount titleholders, however, a parallel but subordinate royal court has existed on the Angolan side. In this way, the Luunda paramount titleholder, while residing in Zaire, has always been able to maintain his influence over Lunda Norte. In recent years, the political situation has threatened to create a cleavage between the two royal courts, for the Angolan court had no choice but to co-operate with

MPLA. When UNITA took control of the area, some Angolan members of the royal clan were arrested and beaten on suspicion of collaboration with the MPLA. In May 1994, however, MPLA bombed the Angolan royal village as a reprisal for its links with UNITA.

5. After the 1992 peace treaty signed between MPLA and UNITA in Portugal, the MPLA troops were disarmed, and a short-lived period of UNITA/MPLA cohabitation set in. However, president Dos Santos created the *anti-mutim* forces, who would monitor the pre-election period. In reality, the *anti-mutim*, trained in Spain, were used to report on the activities of UNITA and their Zairean following in places such as Cafunfo. For UNITA, their presence was a violation of the treaty, and this led to a serious conflict between UNITA and MPLA which ended the cohabitation in the diamond-mining area. UNITA reportedly sabotaged the Cafunfo mine and killed the MPLA-appointed Filipino superintendent of the mine.

6. Apart from the names of prominent public figures, I have changed or omitted the names of the people involved.

7. It may be observed that by transporting the Luunda king to Kinshasa and keeping him there, the regime replicated, probably without even realising, traditional patterns of pawnship that were commonly applied at Luunda and other royal courts.

8. Next to the precolonial political heritage which inspired much of the political imagery of the Second Republic, there is an undeniable colonial heritage, for, as Callaghy (1984) notes, the image of the strong personal, patriarchal and patrimonial ruler is also to some extent the product of colonial imagery, reflecting, for example, the patrimonialism of King Leopold II.

9. It is no coincidence, for example, that the regime's death-squads, which operated in the streets of Kinshasa in 1991 and 1992, became known as *les hibous*, the owl being associated with sorcery and witchcraft. When one tunes in to *radio trottoir*, the *cité*'s pulsating heartbeat, it becomes clear to what extent the popular collective imagination views the politician in powerful images of witchcraft and cannibalism (cf. also Geschiere 1995; Warnier 1993). At one point, the regime's close ties with Ceaucescu also gave rise to a popular discourse on vampirism and the vampire state (for a comparative example, see White 1990 on the removal of bodily fluids by the Kenyan colonial state). The blood symbolism was further reinforced by rumours concerning the *Prima Curia* in the early 1990s. The politicians and high-ranking officials said to be members of this mysterious institution which originated in the MPR, were believed to conclude a blood pact during an esoteric ritual.

10. Bustin (1975b: 116), for example, reports that some Luunda and Chokwe cult movements, which germinated from precolonial *mungonge* rituals, had their central beliefs in the resurrection of dead ancestors. These movements promised a subversion of colonial rule following the resurrection and they evoked repression by the colonial administration in Katanga.

11. One of the titleholder's political friends (a Luunda descendant through his mother) had namely been appointed as *commissaire du peuple* (representative of the people) representing the zone of Kahemba, and became president of the regional assembly of Bandundu province in 1990, and secretary of state in the 1991–92 national government of Nguunz a Karl i Bond (a Luunda from Shaba, with close ties to the *mwaant yaav*'s court, and with a predominantly Luunda and Luunda-related power base).

12. It is widely assumed, interestingly enough, that the 'Father of the Nation' has never known his own father. As fatherless Father, he thus becomes both his

own and his country's origin, thereby echoing the traditional symbolism with regard
to the making of the king during the enthronement ritual.

13. 'To do politics' (*kosala politique*) is an activity which is not dishonourable,
even though it is also synonymous with 'scheming' or 'being corrupt'. The more
elitist *kosala politique* has a populist counterpart in the 'fifteenth clause', article 15,
or the *système D* of the common man: *débrouillez-vous*, help yourself. Today, article
15 no longer seems to be adapted to the harsh conditions of life, and people have
started therefore to refer to the article 16: *démerdez-vous*, survive by adapting to the
predatory rule of the street.

References

Adriaens, E.-L. 1951. *Recherches sur l'alimentation des populations au Kwango*. Brussels:
    Ministère des Colonies.
Amselle, J. L. 1990. *Logique métisses. Anthropologie de l'identité en Afrique et ailleurs*.
    Paris: Payot.
Amselle, J. L. and M'bokolo, E. (eds). 1985. *Au coeur de l'ethnie. Ethnies et état en
    Afrique*. Paris: La Découverte.
Askin, S. and Collins, C. 1993. 'External Collusion with Kleptocracy: Can Zaïre
    Recapture its Stolen Wealth?', *Review of African Political Economy* 57: 72–85.
Azam, J. P., Collier, P. and Cravinho, A. 1993. 'Crop Sales, Shortages and Peasant
    Portfolio Behaviour: An Analysis of Angola', *Journal of Development Studies* 30
    (2): 361–79.
Balandier, G. 1967. *Anthropologie Politique*. Paris: Presses Universitaires de France.
Baudrillard, J. 1983. *Simulations*. New York: Semiotext(e).
Bayart, J.-F. 1989. *L'état en Afrique. La politique du ventre*. Paris: Fayard.
— 1992. 'Introduction', in J.-F. Bayart, A. Mbembe and C. Toulabor, *Le Politique
    par le bas en Afrique Noire: Contributions à une Problématique de la Démocratie*. Paris:
    Karthala.
— 1993. 'Conclusion', in Geschiere and Konings (eds), *Pathways to Accumulation in
    Cameroon*.
Biaya, T. K. 1989. 'L'Impasse de Crise Zaïroise dans la Peinture Populaire Urbaine,
    1970–1985', in Jewsiewicki (ed.), *Art and Politics in Black Africa*.
— 1993. 'Ethnicity: The Root of Nationalist Ideology', in Kankwenda Mbaya (ed.),
    Zaire: What Destiny. s.l.: Council for the Development of Social Science Research.
Braeckman, C. 1992. *Le dinosaure. Le Zaïre de Mobutu*. Paris: Fayard.
Bustin, E. 1975a. *Lunda under Belgian Rule. The Politics of Ethnicity*. Cambridge, MA
    and London: Harvard University Press.
— 1975b. 'Government Policy toward African Cult Movements: The Case of
    Katanga', in M. Karp (ed.), *African Dimensions: Essays in Honor of William O.
    Brown*. Boston, MA: African Studies Center Boston University.
Callaghy, T. M. 1984. *The State–Society Struggle: Zaire in Comparative Perspective*. New
    York: Columbia University Press.
Chazan, N., Mortimer, R., Ravenhill, J., and Rothchild, D. (eds). 1992. *Politics and
    Society in Contemporary Africa*. Boulder, CO: Lynne Rienner.
Conrad, J. 1902. *Heart of Darkness*. Harmondsworth: Penguin, 1973.
De Boeck, F. 1993. 'Symbolic and Diachronic Study of Intercultural Therapeutic
    and Divinatory Roles among the aLuund ("Lunda") and Chokwe in the Upper

Kwaango', in W. van Binsbergen and K. Schilder (eds), *Ethnicity in Africa* 9 (1–2): 73–104. (Thematic issue of *Afrika Focus.*)

— 1994. 'Of Trees and Kings: Politics and Metaphor among the Aluund of Southwestern Zaire', *American Ethnologist* 21 (3): 451–73.

de Dorlodot, Ph. 1994. *Marche d'Espoir Kinshasa 16 Février 1992. Non-violence pour la démocratie au Zaïre.* Paris: L'Harmattan.

de Heusch, L. 1972. *Le Roi Livre ou l'Origine de l'Etat.* Paris: Gallimard.

de Lannoy, D. 1976. *Aspects de la réforme administrative au Zaïre. L'administration publique et la politique de 1965 à 1976.* Brussels: Centre d'Etudes Africaines. (*Cahiers du CEDAF*, 4–5.)

de Villiers, G. 1978 *Panique au Zaïre.* Paris: Plon.

— (ed.). 1992. 'Zaïre 1990–1991: Faits et dits de la société d'après le regard de la presse', *Les Cahiers du CEDAF* 1–2.

Devisch, R. 1994. 'Une filiation imaginaire. A propos des images en miroir que Zaïrois et Belges se renvoient', in G. de Villiers (ed.), *Belgique/Zaïre. Une Histoire en Quête d'Avenir.* Brussels and Paris: Institut Africain-CEDAF and L'Harmattan. (*Cahiers Africains* 9–11.)

— 1995. 'Frenzy, Violence and Ethical Renewal in Kinshasa', *Public Culture* 7 (3): 593–629.

Fatton, R. 1992. *Predatory Rule. State and Civil Society in Africa.* Boulder, CO and London: Lynne Rienner.

Geschiere, P. 1995. *Sorcellerie et Politique en Afrique. La Viande des Autres.* Paris: Karthala.

Geschiere, P. and Konings, P. (eds). 1993. *Pathways to Accumulation in Cameroon.* Paris and Leiden: Karthala and Afrika Studiecentrum.

Hyden, G. 1980. *Beyond Ujamaa in Tanzania: Underdevelopment and an Uncaptured Peasantry.* Berkeley: University of California Press.

— 1992. 'Governance and the Study of Politics', in Hyden, G. and Bratton M. (eds), *Governance and Politics in Africa.* Boulder, CO: Lynne Rienner.

Jewsiewicki, B. (ed.). 1989. *Art and Politics in Black Africa.* Quebec: Canadian Association of African Studies and Editions Safi.

— 1993. 'Construction Narrative des Identités', in J. Tshonda Omasombo (ed.), *Le Zaïre à l'Epreuve de l'Histoire Immédiate.* Paris: Karthala.

Jewsiewicki, B. and Moniot, H. (eds). 1988. *Dialoguer Avec le Léopard? Pratiques, Savoirs et Actes du Peuple Face au Politique en Afrique Noire Contemporaine.* Paris and Quebec: L'Harmattan and Editions Safi.

Jewsiewicki, B., Mbuyamba, F.-K. and Mwadi, wa Ngombu, M. D. 1995. 'Du Témoignage à l'Histoire, des Victimes aux Martyrs: La Naissance de la Démocratie à Kinshasa', *Cahiers d'Études Africaines* 35 (1): 209–37.

Knauft, B. M. 1994. 'Foucault Meets South New Guinea: Knowledge, Power, Sexuality', *Ethos* 22 (4): 391–438.

La Fontaine, J. S. 1970. *City Politics. A Study of Léopoldville 1962–1963.* Cambridge: Cambridge University Press.

Lemarchand, R. 1988. 'The State, the Parallel Economy, and the Changing Structure of Patronage Systems', in Rothchild and Chazan (eds), *The Precarious Balance.*

Leslie, W. J. 1993. *Zaire. Continuity and Political Change in an Oppressive State.* Boulder, CO: Westview Press.

MacGaffey, J. 1988. 'Economic Disengagement and Class Formation in Zaire', in Rothchild and Chazan (eds), *The Precarious Balance.*

— 1991. *The Real Economy of Zaire. The Contribution of Smuggling and Other Unofficial Activities to National Health*. London and Philadelphia: James Currey and University of Philadelphia Press.

— 1992. 'Initiatives from Below: Zaire's Other Path to Social and Economic Restructuring', in G. Hyden and M. Bratton (eds), *Governance and Politics in Africa*. Boulder, CO: Lynne Rienner.

Matadiwamba Kamba Mutu. 1988. *Espace Lunda et les Pelende Khobo*. Bandundu: Ceeba Publications.

Mbembe, A. 1988. *Afriques Indociles*. Paris: L'Harmattan.

— 1992. 'Provisional Notes on the Postcolony', *Africa* 62 (1): 3–37.

Migdal, J. 1988. *Strong Societies and Weak States: State–Society Relations and State Capabilities in the Third World*. Princeton: Princeton University Press.

Miller, J. C. 1988. *Way of Death. Merchant Capitalism and the Angolan Slave Trade 1730–1830*. London: James Currey.

Ndaywel è Nziem, I. 1993. 'La Société Zaïroise dans le Miroir de son Discours Religieux (1990–1993)', *Cahiers Africains/Afrika Studies* 6.

Ngandu Kashama, P. 1992. 'La Chanson de la Rupture dans la Musique Zaïroise Moderne', in M. Quaghebeur and E. Van Balberghe (eds), *Papier Blanc, Encre Noire. Cent Ans de Culture Francophone en Afrique Centrale (Zaïre, Rwanda et Burundi)*. Brussels: Labor.

Nlandu Mayamba, T. 1992. *Misère*. Unpublished theatre play.

Ntite-Mukendi, A. K. 1994. 'Le Discours Zaïrois sur les Oncles: Significations et Ambiguïtés', in G. de Villiers (ed.), *Belgique/Zaïre. Une Histoire en Quête d'Avenir*. Brussels and Paris: Institut Africain-CEDAF and L'Harmattan. (*Cahiers Africains* 9–11.)

Nzuzi Lelo, 1992. 'Gestion Foncière et Production de l'Habitat Urbain au Zaïre', *Géokin* 3 (2): 241–63.

Osumaka Likaka. 1994. 'Rural Protest: The Mbole Against Belgian Rule, 1897–1959', *International Journal of African Historical Studies* 27 (3): 589–617.

Palmeirim, M. 1994. *Of Alien Kings and Ancestral Chiefs. An Essay on the Ideology of Kingship among the Aruwund*. Phd Thesis. London: School of Oriental and African Studies.

Rapoport, H. 1993. 'L'Approvisionnement Vivrier de Kinshasa (Zaïre): Stratégies d'Adaptation à la Crise du Système Alimentaire', *Cahiers des Sciences Humaines* 29 (4): 695–711.

Rothchild, D. and Chazan, N. (eds). 1988. *The Precarious Balance: State and Society in Africa*. Boulder, CO: Westview Press.

Schatzberg, M. 1988. *The Dialectics of Oppression in Zaire*. Bloomington: Indiana University Press.

Taussig, M. 1993. *Mimesis and Alterity. A Particular History of the Senses*. London and New York: Routledge.

Turner, T. 1992. 'Defiant Images: The Kayapo Appropriation of Video', *Anthropology Today* 8 (6): 5–16.

Vail, L. (ed.). 1989. *The Creation of Tribalism in Southern Africa*. London: James Currey.

Van Roy, H. 1988. *Les Byaambvu du Moyen-Kwango. Histoire du royaume Luwa-Yaka*. Berlin: Reimer Verlag.

Vansina, J. 1990. *Paths in the Rainforests. Towards a History of Political Tradition in Equatorial Africa*. London: James Currey.

Vellut, J.-L. 1972. 'Notes sur le Lunda et la Frontière Luso-Africaine (1700–1900)', *Etudes d'Histoire Africaine* 3: 61–166.

Warnier, J.-P. 1993. 'L'Economie Politique de la Sorcellerie en Afrique Centrale', in G. Gosselin (ed.), *Les Nouveaux Enjeux de l'Anthropologie. Autour de Georges Balandier*. Paris: L'Harmattan.

Weiss, H. F. 1967. *Political Protest in the Congo. The Parti Solidaire Africain during the Independence Struggle*. Princeton, NY: Princeton University Press.

White, L. 1990. 'Bodily Fluids and Usufruct: Controlling Property in Nairobi, 1917–1939', *Canadian Journal of African Studies* 24 (3): 418–38.

Young, C. 1994. 'Zaïre: The Shattered Illusion of the Integral State', *The Journal of Modern African Studies* 32 (2): 247–63.

Young, C. and Turner, T. 1985. *The Rise and Decline of the Zairean State*. Madison: University of Wisconsin Press.

Zartman, I. W. 1995. 'Introduction: Posing the Problem of State Collapse', in I. W. Zartman (ed.), *Collapsed States. The Disintegration and Restoration of Legitimate Authority*. Boulder, CO: Lynne Riener.

CHAPTER 4

Between God and Kamuzu: the transition to multiparty politics in central Malawi

Harri Englund

In October 1993, a group of men were discussing matters of national interest over a calabash of beer in the Dedza District of Malawi. They had just heard the news that Dr H. Kamuzu Banda, then Life President of Malawi, had been taken to a hospital in South Africa to undergo brain surgery. As they had done many times before, these villagers began to speculate about Banda's imminent death. This time the discussion revolved round the question of where his burial would take place. One man contended that he would be buried in Blantyre, the largest city in Malawi. Others protested and suggested places which, in their view, were more probable sites for Banda's burial; England, Ghana and America were all mentioned in their deliberations. After having listened to the discussion with increasing bewilderment, I ventured to make what seemed to me a very reasonable suggestion. Perhaps, I said, Banda would be buried in his home district of Kasungu in Central Malawi.

I realised very rapidly that my suggestion provided no answer to the problem. It merely transferred my bewilderment to my companions. Some were amused by the apparent innocence of my suggestion, while others, not a little irritated by my ignorance, observed that my stay in Malawi was drawing to a close and I still thought that Banda was from Kasungu District! Reflecting on my previous conversations about Banda with Dedza villagers, I did, indeed, recall numerous occasions when the mention of Kasungu District had produced the solemn revelation that 'it is not his home' (*sikwawo kumeneko*). Nevertheless, given all that I thought I had learned about funerals and the importance of burying the deceased in the graveyard of his or her home, I was perplexed by the ambiguity surrounding Banda's burial-place. What else did this ambiguity indicate?

It did not simply indicate the fact that Banda's days as the head of state were felt to be numbered. Rather, the uncertainty about his burial-place unravelled the uncertainty concerning his home, origins and, indeed, the Malawian national identity among these Chichewa-speaking villagers. Banda's 'official' story is familiar to most villagers. He is a mission-educated

Chewa from Kasungu who walked, as a young boy, all the way to South
Africa to earn enough money to pursue his studies; he became a medical
doctor in America and worked in Britain and Ghana before he returned
to Malawi in 1958 to 'break the stupid Federation' of the Rhodesias and
Nyasaland (Malawi Information Department n.d.; Short 1974). The fact
that Dedza villagers are less than convinced by the details of this story
attests to their active engagement in the contestation and in the production
of images of the nation and its leadership. The aim of this chapter is to
show how these images and discourses informed villagers' participation in
the transition from one-party state to multiparty politics.

Fabrication and manipulation shaped Banda's political career from its
beginning. When Henry Chipembere, one of the young activists responsible
for devising the nationalist campaign, invited Banda to return from Britain,
he had a specific image in mind. In a famous letter to Banda in 1957,
Chipembere explained that the image of a saviour was required; 'human
nature is such that it needs a kind of hero to be hero-worshipped if a
political struggle is to succeed' (quoted in Short 1974: 83). Playing upon
his seniority and Western education, Banda became one of the numerous
charismatic and patriarchal leaders among the first-generation heads of
independent African states (see Chazan et al. 1988: 157–60). Banda, like
Kwame Nkrumah, Julius Nyerere, Kenneth Kaunda, Jomo Kenyatta,
Ahmed Sekou Touré, Felix Houphouet-Boigny, among others, embodied
the nation-building in his person. The 'traditional' imagery of power in
Africa was freely appropriated; Banda's life-presidency and style of government carried allusions to paramountcy and, on occasion, to divine kingship
(see Balandier 1967: 207–8).

The outcome, however, has hardly been a projection of chieftaincy on
the scale of a postcolonial state. From at least the sixteenth century
onwards, the Maravi chieftaincies, which were to give the name to the
Malawi nation, produced many obstacles to centralisation (Langworthy
1972: 29–31). The matrilineal succession of subordinate headmen endowed
villages with some autonomy and made the loyalty to the paramount chief
a matter of constant negotiation. Moreover, the all-male secret society
nyau and the territorial rain-shrines had officials of their own, who also
represented, usually, a power-base distinct from the paramount chief
(Schoffeleers 1992: 44–8). In contrast to the Maravi chieftaincies, Banda's
Malawi was marked by extreme centralisation of both political and
economic power, a small elite having owed its position directly to the
patronage of the Life President (Mhone 1992). Nevertheless, in this chapter
I quote proofs that coercion and oppression failed to confer on Banda
the status of the absolute; in the world of Dedza villagers, divinity
remained distinguished from earthly contrivance. Routinely described by
outside observers as one of the most repressive regimes in postcolonial
Africa (see, e.g., Africa Watch 1990), Banda's Malawi would seem to have

left little space for local counter-images of the nation and its leadership. Fear and oppression were certainly a part of the Dedza villagers' everyday life. Yet accounts of research in Malawi during Banda's era noted that oppression did not secure acquiescence: Banda's authority was reflected on and sometimes vigorously challenged in song (White 1987: 245–6), in ritual (Kaspin 1993: 48–9), in drama (Barber 1986; Kerr 1989) and in poetry (Vail and White 1991: 280–2). Allusions and cryptic codes were deployed to undermine the efforts to pinpoint dissenting voices. On the other hand, an alternative to the official rhetoric on the origins and nature of the nation is not necessarily a sign of conscious dissent. The images and discourses described in this chapter have been acceptable in many cases even to the local supporters of the Malawi Congress Party, the ruling party of Banda's era. Indeed, in spite of his being, in these images, the greatest trickster of all, it is not so much Banda himself as his closest aides who are generally detested.

Whatever traditions of anticolonial struggle the Banda regime tried to invent for its subjects, it did not colonise their imagination (see Ranger 1983, 1993). Certainly, a whole world of postcolonial innovation and experience is eclipsed, if Banda's manipulation of 'tradition' is allowed to explain the apparent submission of Malawians (see Forster 1994). In Africa, just as elsewhere, the so-called national cultures and ideologies are constantly being enlarged, contested and revitalised in particular lived-in worlds (see Coplan 1991). If the nation appeared as a contrivance to Dedza villagers, their participation in the contrivance represented an innovation in its own right. Their world is one in which the illusions and traumas of the Banda regime were filtered through an array of quite disparate experiences, images and influences, the sources of which ranged from Christianity to labour migration, from transistor radios to witchcraft, from the war in Mozambique to the intricacies of village politics and so on. In such a varied and often contradictory world, participation in an oppressive regime should not be taken at face value. In tracing the emergence of an unliveable contradiction in the period of political transition, I do not mean to imply, however, that this chapter highlights the path to multipartyism in Malawi as a whole. On the contrary, there is a great need to understand how this historic moment was conceived and acted upon in other particular lived-in worlds.

An essential background to my analysis is a brief chronology of the events that contributed most directly to Banda's downfall and to the rise of multiparty politics. The new era is commonly assumed to have dawned with the Lenten letter of the Roman Catholic bishops in March 1992.[1] The letter, read in the Catholic churches throughout Malawi, was afterwards declared 'seditious' by the government. In April, the opposition leader Chakufwa Chihana returned to Malawi from exile in Zambia and was promptly arrested at the airport. His subsequent appearances in court in

Lilongwe and Blantyre were accompanied by demonstrations. In May 1992 there were unprecedented strikes and riots in these major towns, where over forty people were shot dead by the police. In the same month, foreign donors suspended all non-humanitarian aid to the Malawi government. In October, Banda announced that a referendum would take place on the question of multiparty government.

The opposition parties, still spoken of as 'pressure groups', were in principle allowed to campaign freely, but in practice encountered considerable obstacles in some areas. Nevertheless, in the referendum of June 1993, 63 per cent voted for the adoption of the multiparty system of government. Banda accepted the result but denied that he had received a vote of no confidence. In the general elections of May 1994, Bakili Muluzi of the United Democratic Front (UDF) was elected as the new president of Malawi, and Banda's Malawi Congress Party (MCP) was driven into opposition. Chihana's Alliance for Democracy (Aford), with its relatively small power-base in the sparsely populated Northern Region, also found itself in opposition at first. But it was later invited to join the UDF in the cabinet, and Chihana was given the position of the second vice-president.

The aim of this chapter is not to dwell on these events at the national level (for more details on the political elite during the transition, see van Donge 1995). Instead, I describe the ways in which the perceptions of Banda, the Malawi nation and multiparty politics intermingled during my fieldwork among the villagers of the southern margin of Dedza district, near the Mozambique border.[2] The focal event in this chapter is the 1993 referendum rather than the 1994 elections. It is particularly interesting to note how, in this area, which in the political landscape of Central Malawi marks the divide between 'Chewa' and 'Ngoni' chiefdoms, religious affiliations rather than ethnicity informed the local discourse on political change. This contrasts sharply with the discourse among some Malawian politicians and intellectuals. As will be discussed in the concluding section of this chapter, a 'tribalist' discourse seems to hold increasing appeal for the critics of Banda's regime.

An unusual founding myth

Two things must be kept in mind when discussing the perceptions that villagers in southern Dedza have of Kamuzu Banda. First, it would be inaccurate to suggest that their alternative view of Banda's biography forms a coherent and uncontested narrative. On the contrary, there are great variations in the extent to which different persons claim to 'know' Banda's story, and few are able, or sufficiently interested, to produce a coherent account that would cover the details of Banda's past before he had arrived in Malawi. The significant point, however, is the fact that most villagers find the official version highly implausible and that there is considerable consensus that Banda is not a Malawian at all.

Secondly, the accounts that contradict the official version are not, in fact, considered as 'alternative' viewpoints, because the official version is seen to be inextricably linked to the reproduction of the artificial 'history' of Banda. The 'alternative' version, therefore, is seen to be telling the 'true' story, whereas the official version is (or was) learned at school and in political rallies and recounted to those who were not trusted. Certainly, the cost of spreading the 'alternative' version has been at least detention for many Malawians. Nevertheless, it is arguable, again, to what extent even the politically correct MCP officials actually *believe* the official story. I learned parts of the 'alternative' from local MCP officials who, however, did not think that they were showing lack of respect for Kamuzu Banda.[3]

Although it is misleading, in a sense, to present the 'alternative' as if it were one coherent story, I reproduce below an account in order to identify salient themes in villagers' perceptions of Banda. The following account was given to me by a man in his early thirties, who worked as a clerk in an office in the town of Dedza. He himself had learned the story from a woman who had worked as a secretary in the same office. The woman, who came from Kasungu District, had disclosed that her sister's husband was one of Banda's 'relatives' in Kasungu. This brother-in-law had fled, however, to Mozambique, because too many of Banda's 'relatives' had died mysteriously. Before his flight, he had revealed Banda's true story to a few members of his wife's family. It should be noted, especially, that only a few Dedza villagers claim to know Banda's 'real' story.

Richard Armstrong was born long time ago in America. His father was an American and his mother a Ghanaian, probably a former slave. Armstrong's father was an affluent man who wanted his son to acquire a secure profession. Hence Armstrong embarked on a study of medicine. During his studies, he became acquainted with an African from Nyasaland whose name was Kamuzu Banda and who was also studying medicine. Armstrong, perhaps because of his own African parentage, was much intrigued to hear about life in Nyasaland and spent many hours in discussion with Banda. However, Banda became seriously ill and died before either of them had completed their studies. Armstrong, on the other hand, wanted to see the world after his studies. He left America and subsequently decided to take up a job in Edinburgh. There for the first time he heard about the emerging nationalist cause in Africa. He sought the company of students from both Nyasaland and the Gold Coast. To the former he presented himself, recalling his deceased friend's name and stories, as Kamuzu Banda; when he was with the latter, he used a name derived from his mother's family. The fact that he also, perhaps even first and foremost, had ambitions concerning the Gold Coast led him to go there first. However, for some reason things did not go as planned in the Gold Coast, and Armstrong decided to concentrate his efforts on Nyasaland.[4] In order to succeed he had to reveal his identity to a small circle of collaborators, and at least Aleke Banda, Gwanda Chakuamba and John Tembo proved to be indispensable aides from early on.[5] With their help he bought relatives in Kasungu District. These 'relatives' have been kept well paid ever since, but every once in a while one of them has been detained in order to deter others from revealing the truth.

This elaborate counter-biography is almost certainly a recent invention, influenced by similar stories which appeared in the new 'independent press' during the transition. However, the counter-biography itself fed upon deep-seated Malawian disbelief: the idea of Banda's non-Malawian origins is not new. Kanyama Chiume (1975: 90–1), one of the early nationalists, recalls the bewilderment Banda aroused among young activists after he had returned to Malawi: he refused to eat *nsima*, the staple food, dismissed the residential segregation that was in force and insisted that he wanted to live in a house that had belonged to a white man. The house which he accepted had belonged, in fact, to a Portuguese. Banda was, Chiume recalls, 'for all intents and purposes, a white man ... No wonder there were rumours growing among the officials of the party that a white man had been brought to lead them' (1975: 91). In 1960, in the Federalist camp, the claim was made in the Federal Parliament that Banda was not a 'Nyasa' at all (Short 1974: 140). The irony, of course, is that his subjects were entertaining similar doubts over three decades later.

Kamuzu Banda was built up by the official rhetoric as a redeemer who, as a young boy, walked from Malawi to South Africa, who single-handedly dissolved the federation and who has been the sole source of 'peace and calm, law and order' in Malawi ever since.[6] The disjunction between Banda's honorary titles and the names by which he is known in the villages attests to the fact that the official rhetoric has often been excessive for villagers in southern Dedza. Such titles as *Nkhoswe* (Number One)[7] and *Mkango Wa Malawi* (the Lion of Malawi) have been little more than jokes, although they were frequently used when referring to and addressing Banda in political rallies. Among southern Dedza villagers, the spontaneously-used titles and names for Banda have been *Ngwazi* (an archaic term meaning approximately a 'heroic warrior' but used solely to refer to Banda), *Pulezidenti* (the President), Kamuzu[8] and, simply, *wamfupi* (the short one). Although of this list of names and titles only *wamfupi* is unacceptable to the official rhetoric, villagers' rejection, and ridicule, of Banda's honorary titles give further evidence of defiance and critical distancing beneath the overt repression.

However, southern Dedza villagers' views of Banda's biography and honorary titles should not be taken to mean an outright dismissal of the official rhetoric. Rather, their versions of Banda's biography appropriate details of the official rhetoric and make them elucidate his obvious otherness. In this sense, the official version and the 'truth' contribute to one another. Banda would never have been accepted as a political leader without a fictitious narrative of his past; on the other hand, that imaginative narrative itself and Banda's curious ways call for a proper elucidation of that past. Hence Banda's official biography sowed the seeds of doubt and, for some, a whole new counter-biography.

Banda's regime did little to clear up his enigma; from the controversy surrounding his date of birth to the public but apparently illegitimate relationship with the 'Official Hostess' C. Tamanda Kadzamira, it was Banda's style to make himself accessible as a person. During the three decades of his rule, he always addressed 'his people' in English with an interpreter translating the message into the vernacular; he never gave up the famous costume of a three-piece suit, black homburg hat, beige raincoat and brown leather gloves; and he always traversed the sky with his helicopter or aeroplane as only a white man can do.[9] Perhaps one should not be surprised, therefore, if southern Dedza villagers find the suggestion of his Chewa origins excessive.

Yet did not the widespread disbelief concerning the official biography undermine Banda's legitimacy as a ruler? The disbelief, as such, was not a source of political discontent, and here it must be understood that neither the official biography nor its alternative narrates a story about Banda as an individual. Both recount the past of the 'father and founder' of the Malawi nation. By the same token, they create an image of Malawi as a nation. The official version depicts a hard-working man, inculcated with ancient Chewa wisdom, who is subsequently called to lead the struggle for independence. The counter-biography depicts a stranger of mixed parentage who, after failing to realise his ambition elsewhere, conquers the country by means of careful planning. In the first account, the nation, however rudimentary, exists before the arrival of its redeemer, whose indigenous wisdom and Western education combine to make the nation a success. In the other account, the redeemer is a fabrication, and the nation is a fulfilment of personal ambitions rather than a natural unit existing apart from the self-appointed redeemer.

There are thus two founding myths of the Malawi nation: the nation as an objective entity and the nation as an invention. Again, the latter does not necessarily subvert the former. As will be seen below, the suspicion that initially characterised many southern Dedza villagers' views of multiparty politics arose precisely from the fear that the subversion of *Ngwazi* would dissolve the nation into many quarrelling factions. It was, in other words, more the perceived origins of the nation than the support for Banda's regime that accounted for the initial suspicion. If Kamuzu Banda were to fall, so would Malawi, not because his wise leadership would be lost, but because the nation was entirely his own creation. The fabricated biography was, therefore, a necessary element in the illusion, but only a fool would take it at face value. However, few villagers viewed themselves first and foremost as Malawians. What were seen as assaults on God during the heated run-up to the 1993 referendum settled the matter for many. The referendum became a very grave event indeed: it posed a choice between God and Kamuzu.

The elusive universe of ethnicity

In practice, Banda's Chewa identity has been as ambiguous as any other aspect of his identity. His apparent interest in the 'traditions' and language of the Chewa (see Banda and Young 1946) and, after independence, his insistence that there are no ethnic divisions in Malawi are two contradictory aspects of that identity. Yet the perception of his Chewa bias has informed analyses of Malawian postindependence politics (see Vail and White 1989; Lwanda 1993). This bias has been seen as a reason for an over-representation of ministers from the Central Region in Banda's cabinets and for various dissatisfactions in the Southern and Northern Regions; the promotion of Chichewa as the sole African national language has perhaps been the most obvious source of discontent. From a historical perspective, it is somewhat surprising that the Central Region should have gained such prominence in Malawian postindependence politics. During the colonial period, superior opportunities for education in the north and the development of markets and communications in the south were probably factors that explain why anticolonial activism took place there earlier than in Central Malawi (see McCracken 1968: 190–7). The first anticolonial protests and risings were led by Elliot Kamwana in the north in 1909–15 and by John Chilembwe in the south in 1915.

Some motivation for the perceived Chewa dominance can, however, be found in the historical observation that various Chewa communities are the autochthonous inhabitants of the area in contrast to such late-comers as the Ngoni and the Yao. As was mentioned at the beginning, these communities formed a complex of chieftaincies known as Maravi, and this was adopted as the name for the Malawi nation (see Schoffeleers 1972). Many observers, including Banda himself (see Banda and Young 1946), have seen *nyau*,[10] a male secret society, as a key institution in Chewa culture. The most striking aspect of *nyau* is its masked characters, known as 'animals' (*zilombo*), who formerly appeared mainly during funerals and girls' initiation ceremonies. *Nyau* became a central source of conflict between early missionaries and the local population, a conflict which Western scholars later came to describe in terms of 'Chewa resistance' (see, e.g., Linden with Linden 1974). Oddly enough, Banda's regime came to parade *zilombo* as entertainers of the general public in political rallies.

Despite this, however, in parts of the Central and Southern Regions *nyau* continues to evoke awe and has a crucial place in the lived-in world. As a concomitant, the essentialisation of *nyau* lingers on even in contemporary ethnography. Kaspin, for instance, has recently described *nyau* as a synonym for 'the signs and symbols that define the substructure of rural Chewa consciousness' (Kaspin 1993: 54).

As mentioned above, southern Dedza is the locus of a divide between Chewa and Ngoni chiefdoms. In the local administrative structure this means that particular villages are considered to be 'Chewa' or 'Ngoni' villages depending on who is their sub-chief or chief.[11] Conventional Ngoni history begins with the dispersion of the original Ngoni complex in present-day South Africa, and depicts a long and eventful march northwards (see Barnes 1954; Read 1956; Rennie 1966; but see also Vail 1972; 1978; 1981). According to this history, wars were waged, autochthonous populations conquered and alien cultural influences adopted. Moreover, different Ngoni factions emerged, and contemporary Ngoni in southern Dedza, together with their neighbours in Ntcheu district, recall Domwe in northern Mozambique as the site from which the final dispersion took place (see Linden 1972). Hence in so far as *nyau* and Chewa identity are synonymous, the distribution of men initiated into *nyau* would appear to be easily determined. They all live in, or are from, the 'Chewa villages' of the area.

In fact, this is not the case. The reason is not simply the frequent intermarriages between 'Chewa' and 'Ngoni' villages which make local ethnic identities somewhat varied and negotiable. *Nyau* has members who identify themselves as Ngoni and take pleasure in relating 'the history of the Ngoni' (*mbiri ya Angoni*). However, when confronted with the question how they can be both Ngoni and members of *nyau*, these men typically resort to Banda's famous dictum 'we are all Malawians'. Conversely, the headmen and elders of those 'Ngoni villages', where supposedly there are no *nyau* members, do not usually evoke ethnic distinctions either. Their villages do not have *nyau*, they say, not because they are Ngoni but because they are *Christian*. In practice, even some of these villages have men who covertly, and in some cases rather inactively, belong to *nyau*. For them, there is no conflict between *nyau* and Christianity in principle, although in practice they are under constant threat of being excommunicated from the Church because of their *nyau* membership. In many cases, these men have had little or no schooling and have, for one reason or another, few prospects of advancement in the local village and Church politics. Yet, as is discussed more fully below, the Christian majority in these villages also saw these men often as staunch supporters of Kamuzu Banda and the Malawi Congress Party.

The Christians in the area are predominantly Roman Catholics. An independent church by the name of the African Church has a small congregation scattered over several villages, whereas the Church of the

Central African Presbyterian has its congregation concentrated in one village. The Catholic parish, which boasts a cathedral, is one of the oldest in Central Malawi. The first mission school was opened in this area in 1907, and the first baptisms were administered in 1911. All the priests and brothers in the parish were Malawians by the mid-1980s, but they are not from the local villages. Various Catholic groups, which combine praying and religious teaching with assistance to members who fall ill or suffer other hardships, are an important part of village politics. As will be described below, their importance for villagers has been a concomitant of their autonomy from, and even antagonism to, the parish.

In this universe where Christianity is valued and where it is a grave criticism to suggest that a person is not a proper Christian (*wachikhrisitu*), *nyau* appears marginal yet powerful. It is marginal, because it has no recognised place in local politics in most villages.[12] It should be reiterated that this is not because of rigorous ethnic distinctions, but because most villagers consider themselves to be Christians. As noted above, however, *nyau* and Christianity are not necessarily in conflict for those men who have been initiated into *nyau*. Those Christians who perceive conflict usually state that *nyau* is forbidden by the church and they refuse, or are unable, to elaborate. Yet when villagers did talk openly of their disapproval of *nyau* during my fieldwork, it was striking that the secret society was usually associated with the government (*boma*) rather than with some heresy from a theological viewpoint. Many villagers told me that 'there would be no *nyau* in these villages without this government'. For them, *nyau* was an instrument of oppression by Banda's government. In short, despite its marginality in villages, it was powerful because of the government.

The masks of oppression

The everyday forms of coercion and oppression to which all villagers were subjected during Banda's regime included the purchase of Malawi Congress Party membership cards, attendance at political meetings and rallies and, for men, the payment of taxes. Those who did not possess valid membership cards were routinely refused entry to buses and markets. Every 'Malawian', including infants and Mozambiquan refugees, was obliged to have one. Participation in party meetings and rallies was, likewise, an obligation that encompassed everyone in the villages. At rallies, village headmen were often asked by party officials to stand up with their villagers to show their numbers. If too few persons had turned up from a particular village, its headman was publicly humiliated by party officials, who remarked that his village comprised only a handful of people.

The rallies where Kamuzu Banda appeared were, of course, the most important of all. His appearance somewhere in the same district, or even in the same region, usually obliged villagers to attend, and women and schoolchildren had to find time to rehearse, beforehand, songs and dances praising him. Taxation, in turn, was perceived as a continuation of colonial injustice, to the extent that many men maintained that they did what their fathers had done before independence: they moved to live 'in the bush' (*kutchile*) if they were warned early enough of the tax-collector's arrival.[13]

Although village headmen and local party officials were responsible for seeing that the orders of the government were obeyed, the harshest measures of coercion were usually left for strangers and, significantly, for the masked characters of *nyau*. The so-called party membership renewal campaigns were initiated by party 'chairmen' in villages, but because they seldom succeeded in persuading all villagers to renew their memberships, the names of defiant villagers were passed on to officials in other areas. These officials, strangers to the villagers in question, came to visit their houses during the night. They were often accompanied by members of the Malawi Young Pioneers, then the paramilitary wing of the MCP, or by *zilombo*. If the door was not opened, the visitors would break into the house. If its occupants still refused to pay for the renewal of their party memberships, the visitors confiscated property in order to cover the costs of the renewal. The possibility of resistance was extremely limited. The Young Pioneers were notorious for their readiness to use violence; the sight and sound of *zilombo* in the middle of the night have prompted many villagers to make, in horror, the required payments.

The reason why the masked characters of *nyau* inspire fear is twofold. On the one hand, because of their appearance at funerals and their prolonged stays in graveyards, the *nyau* characters are thought to be closely linked to the world of the dead. This aspect of the fear is not explicitly formulated, but it appears to be similar to other dealings with the potentially malevolent spirit world: like witches and the dead, *zilombo* may be capable of inflicting misfortunes. This aspect of the fear is, however, rarely actual, because it is only in exceptional circumstances – such as encountering *zilombo* unexpectedly in the middle of the night – that villagers would perceive *zilombo* as spirits rather than as masked men. The other aspect of the fear is more often actual. This has to do with the fact that in the past non-members of *nyau* were severely beaten, or even killed, if they encountered *zilombo*.[14] Excessive violence, both in initiation procedures and in the relations between *nyau* and outsiders, was forbidden by the government. However, *zilombo* are still thought to be unpredictable and aggressive. It is widely believed that if a non-member encounters *zilombo* and is unable to give money to them, some violence will ensue.

These frightening methods were also employed by party officials to force villagers to attend political rallies. In the morning of the day when a rally was going to take place, *zilombo* 'came out' (*kutuluka*) to go round villages. Carrying long sticks and making animal noises, they were the first sign of the day's rally. In most villagers' views, *zilombo* came out to ensure that no one was able to opt out of the rally. Indeed, there was nothing in the behaviour of *zilombo* to suggest that they had other, more sinister intentions. Those who managed to go to their gardens were followed by *zilombo* who, making fierce gestures and yelling loudly, herded them to the rally 'like goats' (*ngati mbuzi*). Hiding in one's house was of no help either, because *zilombo* could break into the house. They could even interrupt one's bath by banging their sticks on the walls of the bathroom and demanding in falsetto '*tieko, tieko*' ('let's go there, let's go there'). Although their subsequent performance in the rally was, even in the eyes of most Christians, an entertaining relief from the dull rhetoric of party officials and visiting members of Parliament and cabinet ministers, their fierceness and arrogance did not win them any affection from villagers. For the Christian majority, *nyau* was at best a nuisance, at worst the very embodiment of oppression.[15]

It appears that the villagers' view of *nyau* being able to exist 'because of the government' (*chifukwa cha boma*) is perceptive. One village headman in the area went in the early 1980s to ask the district commissioner to grant him powers to prohibit *nyau* in his village. The headman was unsuccessful; the district commissioner explained that Kamuzu Banda wanted people to be free to belong to any denomination they might choose.[16] This perceived association of *nyau* with the government was enhanced by the fact many elders (*akuluakulu*) of the local *nyau* were indeed, at least before the referendum, in public, MCP supporters. Some of the elders had been trained as Malawi Young Pioneers, but, due to their scant schooling, they were unable to find employment. They proudly recounted the story of Kamuzu Banda's visit to a *nyau* headquarters elsewhere in the Central Region. Even they, however, found absurd the idea of Banda's Chewa identity and his initiation into *nyau* (as suggested, e.g., by Short 1974: 8–9). Their respect for Banda did not stem from his being a *nyau* member himself, but from his protection of their *nyau* against the Christian majority.

This *nyau* branch, however, was riddled with internal disputes, rivalries and jealousies. Whenever *zilombo* were supposed 'to come out' for mortuary rites, the event was preceded by disputes and negotiations not only with a village headman and members of the bereaved family, but also among the *nyau* members themselves. The logistics of the rites – such as the timing of the different phases, which masks should appear and how the received tribute of food and money should be divided – were a permanent source of tensions. The tensions over the appearances in MCP rallies became apparent shortly before the referendum. Junior members were increasingly reluctant to force villagers to attend rallies, and some even refused to dance there. At least some members were afraid that they would be attacked by angry supporters of the multiparty cause. Thus, according to this view, a complete inversion was possible; instead of being feared for their fierceness, *zilombo* would themselves be attacked by villagers.[17]

Thus, the politics of *nyau* in southern Dedza at the end of Banda's regime suggests two things. First, the lived-in world of southern Dedza villagers was not constituted by clearly demarcated ethnic distinctions. The 'Chewa' and 'Ngoni' identities were objectified in relation to specific sub-chiefs or chiefs, and to *nyau* and the *ngoma* dance of 'Ngoni'. However, in much of everyday life these identities remained in the background, and participation in *nyau* was open to men from both 'Chewa' and 'Ngoni' villages. Local politics was a more complex affair in which Christianity and the government were more often the explicit parameters of local authority. Most village headmen identified themselves and, as a concomitant, their villages as 'Christians'. The local MCP organisation exercised authority which was, in principle, complementary to the headman's authority, but was often perceived, in practice, as its alternative. As will be seen below, however, the headman's position was by no means free from ambiguity when the multiparty cause was introduced in southern Dedza.

The second general observation to be made about *nyau* is that the government was not simply an external force, but a force that was constituted in an idiom integral to the definition of power relations within southern Dedza villages themselves. For many non-members, *nyau* was a striking instrument of state coercion and oppression. Participation in *nyau* and support for Banda and the MCP were, on the other hand, largely a function of one's fortunes in local village and church politics. Therefore, *nyau* was no more a 'traditional' source of authority than the MCP was a 'modern', or external, source. They both gained significance in relation to the whole field of local politics. In this field, 'the substructure of rural Chewa consciousness', as Kaspin (1993: 54) characterises *nyau*, was objectified by the Christian majority as a tool of oppression.

The coming of *matipati*

In March 1992, the Catholic bishops' outspoken Lenten letter was read in the Catholic churches throughout Malawi. Most southern Dedza villagers, including many local MCP activists, welcomed this remarkable letter. Its subsequent banning as 'seditious' was, however, a bewildering piece of news, because few villagers had thought it undermined Banda's authority. The letter contained, indeed, accounts of 'the growing gap between the rich and the poor', of inequality in medical treatment, of 'a climate of mistrust and fear' and so on, but Banda and the MCP were not named. Nor was the government directly accused. Inadvertently, the banning of the letter polarised the Catholic Church and the government. Villagers suddenly realised that 'Catholics disagree with the government' (*anthu achikatolika akutsutsana ndi boma*). Such a conclusion, despite the long-standing resentment against coercion and oppression, had hardly been articulated before, but even now the realisation did not lead to overt protests or anti-government activities. Comments on oppression, as before, were confided to the trusted few.

The multiparty cause, or *matipati* as it came to be known in southern Dedza, was disseminated by outsiders unobtrusively in the area before the 1993 referendum. No active campaigning for membership recruitment took place in the villages, and the few opposition rallies that were organised in the area drew very small attendances from local villages. Southern Dedza was the constituency of John Tembo, the Minister of State in the Banda regime. It is not clear whether Tembo advised the authorities in the district about the approach to opposition supporters, but it is clear, however, that he was a source of anxiety for both sides. The opposition leaders complained that their meetings were disturbed or even prevented by the authorities in Dedza District. Rumours abounded. Particularly dramatic rumours started from a shooting incident in December 1992. The District Chairman of the MCP shot dead a high-ranking police officer who had been patrolling the chairman's house. The chairman was arrested, and the party denied that the incident was politically motivated. However, for many Malawians, including southern Dedza villagers, it was no coincidence that the police officer had been known for his liberal attitudes towards the opposition campaigning in the district. One rumour even implicated Tembo himself.

In this 'climate of mistrust and fear', *matipati* came to mean in southern Dedza, at first, trouble and short-sighted political aspirations. As was the case apparently in many other areas of Malawi, it was the youth, particularly young men, who were the first to adopt the multiparty cause. Of course, not every youth was impressed by *matipati*; nevertheless, as the most vocal and visible supporters, 'youngsters' (*anyamata*) were perceived by many villagers as epitomes of *matipati*. When opposition rallies took place in Dedza and Ntcheu districts, lorries often came to collect people to attend the rallies. Virtually all who climbed on to the lorries were young men, who shouted 'songs of multiparty' (*nyimbo za matipati*) defiantly at on-lookers as the lorries traversed rural roads. Some of the songs, such as the chanting of '*ndatopa Malawi Kongresi*' ('I am tired [of] the Malawi Congress Party'), eventually became popular tunes. Other songs, especially those containing insults to Banda and praise of opposition figures,[18] contributed, by contrast, to many elders' views of *matipati* as a force prepared to tear the nation apart.

Most southern Dedza villagers expected, during the first four or five months after the announcement of the referendum, that war (*nkhondo*) would be the consequence of *matipati*. Banda and the MCP officials at all levels nourished this fear by claiming that *matipati* was a threat to the nation's unity (*umodzi*). A recurrent trope in the discussions that took place in villages and in gardens was the juxtaposition of current conditions with the anticipated disorder. The discourses about oppression became less pronounced, though not wholly dormant, even in private circles. From time to time, some even envisaged their future as refugees in Mozambique.

In 1986, Dedza District began to receive thousands of refugees from Mozambique. As a result of the peace treaty between the Frelimo government and Renamo rebels in October 1992, the early part of 1993 witnessed a massive return of refugees from Dedza to Mozambique. Southern Dedza villagers, many of whom have relatives and affines in Mozambique, also took a keen interest in politics in Mozambique. For most villagers, however, the perceived fragility of peace made the prospects of exile in Mozambique seem unattractive. The fear, therefore, was that war would erupt simultaneously in the two countries.[19]

The ideas about the registration for voting revealed fears of a backlash, irrespective of which cause would win the referendum. The losing side was widely expected to resort to violence against the suspected supporters of the winners. Although these fears did not, in the end, prevent villagers from registering, in the early months of the referendum process the prevailing mood was to abstain from registration and thereby from voting. Such a mood, superficially, was a mere continuation of the villagers' disillusions about the elections held during Banda's regime. General elections took place regularly then; the last such election was in June 1992. But the 1993 referendum was, however, the first voting exercise in which most of the eligible southern Dedza villagers participated. There is something of a paradox here. During Banda's regime, voting was discouraged by the fact that the vote would make little difference; voting during the referendum was discouraged, by contrast, by the fact that the vote would potentially make a world of difference. At this stage, nevertheless, the difference had not taken on a compelling moral dimension.

The fact that *matipati* initially meant war to many southern Dedza villagers was integral to their perceptions of Malawi as a nation. The invented nature of the president's biography united Malawians by implication in a collective contrivance. 'Peace' (*mtendere*) was ensured, if the diverse interests that constituted the nation remained loyal to the central figure of *Ngwazi*. Southern Dedza villagers were well aware of long-standing dissent within Malawi. Chitumbuka-speakers 'in the north' (*kumpoto*) and the urban population of Blantyre were seen as being particularly weakly committed to the reproduction of the nation.[20] Few southern Dedza villagers questioned the grievances of these dissenting voices. To the extent that they appeared to seek solutions by overthrowing Banda's regime, however, their project was seen as tantamount to dissolving the nation. Southern Dedza villagers' perceptions were not, to reiterate, a sign of silent acquiescence, but an understanding of the necessary entailments of the contrivance to which Banda had bound all Malawians. A danger was envisaged of *matipati* fragmenting the nation by letting loose disparate interests.[21]

Christians or Malawians?

In the end, the multiparty cause did win, even in southern Dedza. In the group of villages where I worked, 58 per cent voted for the multiparty system of government; as mentioned above, the national result was 63 per cent. The results, however, showed great variations within the country. In the Central Region as a whole, the one-party cause received over 60 per cent of the votes, whereas in many areas in the Northern and Southern Regions the multiparty cause received almost unanimous endorsement. Even locally there were great variations in some areas; in Dedza district, for instance, there were reports that, while four-fifths of the voters in one village could have voted for the multiparty cause, in the next village the numbers were virtually reversed in the one-party cause's favour. In the case of these southern Dedza villages, in particular, however, the enthusiasm for *matipati* had become so pronounced on the eve of the referendum that an even greater victory seemed possible. Given the initial suspicion and scepticism, how did this change of heart come about?

It is critical to understand what the referendum came to represent. The value of Christianity both in local politics and in villagers' identity appears as a key to this understanding, and, moreover, the Christian God was invoked explicitly by many villagers in their reflections on the referendum. A crucial preliminary condition was the realisation, after the bishops' Lenten letter had been banned, that 'Catholics disagree with the government'. After the letter, it was widely perceived that the parish priests were supporters of the multiparty cause. This they undoubtedly were, although their sermons hardly touched on the issue until the referendum process was well under way. Their views, in fact, were exposed most clearly when they attended local funerals. Very rarely, at the death of a prominent villager, distinguished by his or her activities in the church, did a priest come to conduct the burial ceremony. After the Lenten letter, such ceremonies became scenes for political contests. In the graveyard, the priest sometimes tried to prevent a local MCP chairman from making a speech; doing this was one of the chairman's duties during Banda's regime. The chairman, in turn, took pains to praise the way in which the church and the government had 'worked together' during the funeral.

The two parish priests, outsiders to the area, were distant figures, however, for most villagers. The priests, the parish clerk and the shepherd, in turn, often complained that villagers' approach to the parish was purely instrumental. The annual 'parish tax' (*mtulo*)[22] was often paid only when a person or a family anticipated a specific event, such as a baptism or a wedding, which required recognition by the church. This suggested, in the parish officials' view, that the parish was selling services to villagers. It would seem, however, that the officials' complaints reflected their more general anxiety over the perceived autonomy of the villages. Although the cathedral was usually packed during the Sunday sermons, premarital pregnancies, adultery, polygyny and belief in witchcraft were, for the parish officials, persistent reminders of the limited success of their teachings. For villagers, the result of these breaches was the 'cutting' (*kudula*) of sacraments which could, at worst, deprive one of a proper Christian funeral. The meaning of the breaches, however, was hardly the same for the parish officials and most villagers. The latter viewed the former's condemnation of witchcraft, for instance, as a criticism of the *practice* of witchcraft, not as a dismissal of its ontological reality.

Christianity is a valued and internal aspect of villagers' own relationships, not a force that derives exclusively from, or is monopolised by, the parish. Local church politics comprises a thriving scene of Catholic groups and offices. Some of these groups cross-cut different villages, others are confined to particular villages, or sections within villages. Every Catholic belongs to the Limana of his or her village or village section, and this group meets usually every week or every fortnight to pray, to listen to a sermon by its chairman or vice-chairman, and to discuss the need for assistance among its members. Limana, which derives its name from a family organisation among the Ngoni (see Philip 1975: 26–7), contributes money or labour when a member falls ill or has a funeral. The group contains some dozen offices, many of which, with the exception of the offices of chairman and vice-chairman, are usually occupied by women. An exclusively female group is Azimayi Achikatolika, which cuts across villages and which also assists its members in need. Women's prominence in the Catholic groups also extends to Regio, the Legion of Mary, an organisation of small groups which the missionaries introduced in the 1940s (see Linden with Linden 1974: 201). With the exception of Regio and some other small groups, the chairperson of each group reports to the parish on the activities of his or her group. The parish has, however, little chance of influencing the functioning of the groups. Villagers themselves choose the officials and establish the agendas.

This universe of Christian belief and practice is not a universe set apart from the rest of sociality, organised by diverse and negotiable relations of kinship, affinity, friendship, party politics and so on. A person's belonging to a Catholic group arises from and, in turn, reproduces a set of valued relationships which does not simply define a distinct 'religious congregation'. During the run-up to the referendum, it was precisely the attempt to compartmentalise Christianity, in conjunction with the perceived assaults on God, that made many southern Dedza villagers give up scepticism and protest.

In particular, it was at two junctures that the Catholic Church was singled out for extensive criticism by prominent MCP leaders. One was the aftermath of the Lenten letter, the other the run-up to the referendum. The speeches made by party officials during Banda's rallies, heard on the radio and spread by subsequent conversations, became increasingly disturbing for most southern Dedza villagers. After the Lenten letter, delegates to the extraordinary meeting of the MCP had already made infamous suggestions which recommended the detention and even killing of the Catholic bishops. Shocking claims followed during the referendum campaign. The bishops and priests alike were accused of hypocrisy in view of their own wealth and well-being. Above all, Banda's vassals – party leaders at district, regional and national levels – insisted that people were in the first place Malawians and only secondarily Christians. Therefore, the word of Kamuzu was to be obeyed, even if it was contradicted by the clergy's views. The cadres themselves appealed increasingly to Christian imagery. Banda was now referred to as *Mpulumutsi*, the Saviour, and his political mission assumed divine qualities. 'God chose Kamuzu' ('*Mulungu anasankha Kamuzu*') was the maxim that outraged southern Dedza villagers the most.

Banda's silence was interpreted as approval of these excesses, and villagers' conclusions usually entertained two possibilities: Banda was seen either as more wicked than had been realised, or as showing definite signs of senility, becoming ever more 'like an infant' (*ngati mwana wakhanda*). In any case, Banda was seen to be implicated in disquieting acts of 'despising God' (*kunyoza Mulungu*). While the party cadres presumably believed that Banda's authority was great enough to warrant excessive claims, many southern Dedza villagers perceived only greed and insolence.

The mainstream Christian churches played a significant role in putting pressure on Banda's government during the referendum process. For example, the threat by the Christian Council of Malawi to recommend a boycott contributed to the government's decision to change the voting procedures it had first announced; the mainstream churches across the spectrum supported the Catholic bishops and came to voice their own criticisms later. An exception, however, was the Nkhoma Synod of the Presbyterian Church. Its open support for the government after the Lenten letter was followed by a substantial donation of money from Banda. Yet although the Presbyterians of southern Dedza belong to the Nkhoma Synod, their views were hardly a simple echo of the Synod's acquiescence. The local Presbyterian and African Church elders were slower than Limana elders and the Catholic priests to comment upon the referendum process in their sermons; towards the end of the process, however, the political arguments among Christians in all three churches in the area had developed novel and daring themes. In the face of the uncertainty of *matipati* and the insolence of the Banda regime, a common justification for the adoption of multiparty politics had become: 'God alone will lead us' (*Mulungu yekha adzatitsogolera*).

This crystallisation of the terms of the ongoing political process emerged, of course, in tandem with a number of other issues. The perceived assaults on God triggered off old grievances against coercion and oppression. Views on compulsory party membership, taxation and the unfair pricing of agricultural products and fertilisers were now debated more openly than ever. A particularly important issue was also the re-starting of labour migration to South Africa. Virtually every man in the area who was born before the 1960s has worked at some point in South Africa, Zimbabwe or Zambia, but Banda's government discontinued labour migration, to the villagers' great dismay, in the early 1970s. The 1974 plane crash in which several Malawian labour migrants were killed, and the labour shortages on Malawian estates have been seen as the reasons for the government's change of policy (e.g. Hirschmann and Vaughan 1983: 87; White 1987: 232). Yet during the referendum campaign, leaders of the MCP explained the ending of labour migration as a protest against the AIDS tests to which Malawian labourers were subjected in South Africa. Many men in southern Dedza were greatly intrigued by the opposi-tion groups, because these were expected to 'open' (*kutsegula*) the South African labour market, if they were elected to power.

Despite this range of grievances and aspirations, Christian idioms and practices were the most pronounced preoccupation on the eve of the referendum, especially among many Catholics. During the Limana elders' meetings at the parish, multiparty activists distributed posters and leaflets, printed in Chichewa, for further circulation in the villages. Special prayers for the referendum were held in the cathedral every Sunday for about a month. Even though the referendum took place on a Monday, however, the last Sunday before it did not witness any special events at the parish. It was rumoured that the priests had been forbidden to arrange any events, because any such action could have been interpreted as a move to mobilise villagers to vote for the multiparty cause.

Instead, the last Sunday before the referendum showed the autonomy and vitality of the Catholic groups in the villages. In many villages, Limana, Regio and other groups conducted all-day and all-night prayers for the referendum. The contents of the prayers and sermons were never un-equivocally inflammatory or millenarian, and they often rehearsed even the long-established prayers for Kamuzu Banda's continued health. Names were not usually named, but those who 'despised God' were warned that they would be proved wrong. Above all, God was repeatedly asked to show mercy, if people chose wrongly in the referendum.

In a marked contrast to the atmosphere during elections under Banda's regime, there was excitement in the air on the day of the referendum and the night before. Many Catholics had attended prayers during the night and arrived to vote before sunrise. Long queues had formed before the polling-stations were opened. Every voter's finger was soiled with ink to prevent multiple voting, and a jubilant idea emerged in villages claiming that the ink represented 'the blood of the black cock' (*magazi a tambala wokuda*). The black cock was the symbol of the MCP and the one-party cause.

Participation in the referendum was thus very high in southern Dedza, but the fear of a backlash had by no means vanished. So, some families adopted a strategy of dividing their votes. Some voted for the one-party cause, others for the multiparty cause. This was thought to undermine the possibility of backlash, because the family had secured support among both causes. Many young people, in particular, felt that they had little leeway and that they were obliged to vote for *matipati* or else face violence from other youngsters. In many cases, however, this did not alienate them from their parents or grandparents, who, to the contrary, encouraged their youth to vote for *matipati*. Women, on the other hand, did not form a group which voted in unison, although Banda had appealed during his campaign for support from 'his' *mbumba*.[23] Participation in the women's league of the MCP had been very rare in the area, and many women cast their votes according to their Christian and kinship affiliations. Because they usually formed the bulk of the local Catholic groups, women had been closely involved in expressing discontent with Banda's regime.

Village headmen, too, did not cast their votes as one uniform group. There were rumours that headmen had been paid by the government to talk positively about the one-party cause, but most headmen were reluctant to engage in party political debates with their subjects. A memorable exception occurred in one village in late March, when the headman and a group of villagers exchanged salient cultural idioms in their debate. Commenting on the emerging multiparty cause in the area, the headman asked whether it was possible for people to leave their old mother in order to start living with a new mother. He received a reply which stated that a new mother had to be found, if the old mother did not cook *nsima*, the staple food. The headman played upon motherhood, perhaps the most valued idiom which expresses moral bonds, in his image of Kamuzu Banda. His opponents, however, made the equally salient observation that moral bonds are built on appropriate performance.

Overall, most headmen's views seemed to be resonant with the general sentiments of their subjects rather than leading the way in the formation of opinions. The relation between the headman and the MCP chairman, also, took various forms in different villages and was calculated to influence headmen's views in different ways. Party chairmen themselves, moreover, by no means voted unanimously in favour of the one-party cause. Many chairmen in villages were also active Catholics, who had been disturbed by the conflict between the government and the church. Their vote for the multiparty cause did not envisage the MCP in the opposition, but was cast as a protest.

Amid all the excitement and triumph after the referendum, it was clear that very few southern Dedza villagers had voted for *matipati* with a particular opposition group or figure in mind. Because very little agitation had taken place and the new 'independent press' was largely a medium for the urban population, the opposition agendas did not produce many rumours. The most appealing of these rumours was the above-mentioned promise to reopen the South African labour market. Some villagers professed a vague allegiance to the UDF rather than to the Aford, which was widely believed to be a party for the northerners. When Chakufwa Chihana had his first rally in the area in September 1993, he was given a cautious reception. Although many more villagers attended this rally than the opposition rallies before the referendum, most were prompted by curiosity rather than gratitude to this veteran dissident. Afterwards, he was condemned in many conversations for talking 'lies' (*mabodza*) and displaying insolence.

There was general irritation about the perceived attempts to manipulate the crowd. On his arrival, Chihana, complete with a Mercedes Benz, was introduced as the 'President'. The persons in the crowd supporting the MCP were asked to stand up to show their numbers. No one stood up. Then the persons supporting the Aford were asked to stand up. A handful of people, mainly from Chihana's entourage, stood up. Many villagers were bewildered and irritated afterwards, because they had been told, on the basis of the standing-up exercise, that everyone supported the Aford. Chihana himself told the crowd that the MCP would finish 'next week', which was interpreted literally and, as a consequence, as a blatant lie. It had been clear to most villagers that the MCP was not going to cease to exist because of their vote for *matipati*.

Indeed, it became apparent after the referendum that the MCP was anything but moribund in the area. The MCP chairman responsible for the whole area had been an unpopular figure and had a reputation of trying to turn funerals into party meetings. A wealthy businessman, he was also frequently absent from the area. After the referendum, he was replaced by a local villager who won instant support with his outspoken concern for the development of the area. At a party rally he addressed the party's visiting district officials with complaints about bus fares, the lack of grinding-mills and so on. By contrast, there were virtually no attempts to establish a local organisation for the opposition parties, and no active campaigning for membership took place. Bakili Muluzi, who was going to replace Banda as the new president in the 1994 elections, was a little-known figure in the area during the fieldwork. It was no surprise, therefore, that the MCP was, after all, successful in southern Dedza in the first multiparty general elections.

In southern Dedza, no backlash or extensive backbiting took place as a result of the referendum. One incident immediately after Banda's accept-ance of the results suggested, however, that the coming of *matipati*, as such, did not resolve all tensions in villages. During the night, after Banda had spoken on the radio, a group of drunken young, mainly unmarried, men rampaged through a village. The only entertaining aspect of their proceedings was their ruthless imitation of Banda's rallies: the impersonator of Banda would utter something incomprehensible, and the impersonator of Tembo would yell '*manja, manja*' ('applause, applause'). The youngsters caused considerable alarm when they declared what would be the consequences of the referendum. Not only, they shouted, would the houses of those who voted for the one-party cause be burned, but also the church would be closed, and *nyau* would take over its building.

Shocked villagers decided that the youngsters had to be brought to the headman's court. They were subsequently made to pay fines, but the headman was at pains to point out that the youngsters had not pronounced their threats by anyone's order. Only two of them had obtained UDF membership cards. However, it is significant that this incident occurred in the only village in the area which has a Presbyterian congregation, and that the youngsters' verbal attacks were directed against this church. Discontent had long been simmering among young Presbyterians over the perceived gerontocracy in the church; some of the church elders were also headman's councillors. The role of the church in articulating the discontent with Banda's regime could thus be forgotten overnight. It is also remarkable that *nyau* appeared now as a force threatening the established order, although none of the young men was a *nyau* initiate at that time. Their jubilant defiance gained momentum from considerable frustration with village and church politics. Therefore, it could merely be a sign of struggles to come.

Conclusion

If the vote of southern Dedza villagers for the multiparty cause was a protest, Christian idioms and belief represent a superficial continuity with the anticolonial protests led by Elliot Kamwana and John Chilembwe in the early twentieth century (see Shepperson and Price 1958). Whereas Kamwana's and, in particular, Chilembwe's protests grew relatively rapidly from *Watch Tower*-inspired millenarianism, however, southern Dedza villagers' protest emerged amid a long-established allegiance to mainstream Christianity.[24] It was only during a period of political transition that the lived-in world appeared to be acutely contradicted by the world of political might. During the decades of Banda's rule, southern Dedza villagers had come to think that they had been made partners in contriving a nation from the fragments of a fantastic biography. The law and order of the contrived nation contrasted with the war and disorder of the nation that no longer gravitated towards the figure of Kamuzu Banda. However, the perceived assaults on God objectified the cleavage between the world of value and the world of contrivance. In a sense, the referendum became a question of allegiances to these two worlds.

There is an urgent need for critical appraisals of Banda's era, and it is particularly important that these are formulated and thoroughly discussed by Malawians themselves. The appraisals will require sensitivity to the variations within the country and to the multiple ways in which Malawians have attempted to order their worlds. In the current refiguring of Malawian politics, the analyses of the past are likely to be weapons for promoting particular interests in the present. This is demonstrated by John Lloyd Lwanda (1993) who, like Banda before him, was practising medicine in Scotland when he made his observations on politics in Malawi. Originally from a Yao area in the Mangochi district of southern Malawi, Lwanda had an active voice in the Malawian diaspora through his own publishing company. In a novel called *The Second Harvest*, for example, Lwanda (1994) describes a 'fictional' African country ruled by 'President-for-Life' Mwari, a former nationalist and one of the architects of the country's independence. The fictional Mwari is determined to stay president till his dying day. In his tribe 'a chief was reluctantly dragged to the throne, but once there it took an earthquake to remove him'. And he does achieve this. It is not surprising that Lwanda became a UDF official and returned to Malawi after the first multiparty elections.

In Lwanda's analysis, Chewa–Ngoni alliance is the key to understanding Banda's grip on power. Banda's era assumes thus an air of tribal conspiracy in which C. Tamanda Kadzamira and her uncle John Tembo, 'proud Ngonis' from Dedza, collaborate with the 'Chewa' president Kamuzu Banda (Lwanda 1993: 46). However, as the idea of a tribal alliance suggests, Lwanda is not concerned about individuals but about ethnic groups. His account of 'tribalism' in Banda's Malawi lists what 'the Tumbuka', 'the Yao', 'the Tonga' and so on have suffered (ibid.: 191–6). As far as 'the Lomwe' are concerned, Lwanda specifies that 'for two decades the rural Lomwe became solid Banda supporters' (ibid.: 192), but subsequently realised that they, too, suffered. Interestingly, Lwanda appears to be unable to specify what 'the Chewa' and 'the Ngoni' gained from 'their' power, other than the promotion of Chichewa as a national language. This, says Lwanda, was 'a sub plot [sic] to increase Chewa educational advantage' (ibid.: 196).

Lwanda's analysis requires discussion not only because of the image it attempts to project on to Banda's regime, but also because of its appropriation of Anglo-American scholarship. Leroy Vail and Landeg White's (1989) article on tribalism in the political history of Malawi is one central source for this intellectual writing in the diaspora. Vail and White, who identified Banda as a 'culture broker for the Chewa' (ibid.: 181), contended that Banda built for himself a 'Chewa' political base (ibid.: 179–80). This required, in addition to his favouritism for Chichewa-speakers from the

Central Region, 'alliance-building' among certain peoples in the Southern Region, particularly Nyanja and Mang'anja. The subtleties of Vail and White's analyses of 'the creation of tribalism' during the colonial era were subverted by this concluding analysis of postcolonial developments. By some sleight of hand, 'ethnic groups' appeared, suddenly, to be real entities, as it were: they engage in 'alliance-building'; they attempt to consolidate a 'political base'. For a Malawian intellectual in the diaspora, this provided a blatantly tribalist vocabulary to analyse the tragedy of Banda's regime.

There is no need, on the basis of these analyses, to question the compassion of both Lwanda and the Anglo-American scholars. Landeg White, for example, was actively involved in putting an end to the cowardly detention of Jack Mapanje, Malawi's foremost poet. Yet it is striking how a scholarly critique of tribalism can, in fact, reproduce tribalism. Vail and White contended that, for instance, Matthew Schoffeleers' studies of the *nyau* cult and Maravi history fostered the Chewa bias of Banda's regime. However, while there is little evidence that 'Schoffeleers became the source of a usable past for the developing ideology of the present' (Vail and White 1989: 182), Lwanda's analysis testifies to White's own usefulness as a source for the developing ideology of 'the second liberation'. My point is not that tribalism does not exist in postcolonial Malawi. For some, such as Lwanda, ethnic identities are painfully fixed and real. But it is, however, quite another thing to portray, without evidence, speakers of certain languages or the populace of a whole region as involved in building alliances along ethnic lines.

The problem, of course, is false concreteness. If taken to be analytic categories, 'Ngoni' and 'Chewa' impute discrete identities to social groups and, as a consequence, make these groups appear as natural units of social life. It is as if we no longer need to understand how such groups came into being in the first place. The evidence presented in this chapter sustains this basic point. It sustains, also, Achille Mbembe's (1992: 5) observation on the multiplicity of identities in the postcolony. The understanding of identity demands that we appreciate the particularities of the social and symbolic universe under scrutiny. In the study of this universe, 'Ngoni' and 'Chewa' are not analytic categories. They are a selection of symbolic constructs from many others which generate meaningful distinctions in the lived-in world. As has been seen, these distinctions are contextual and, among southern Dedza villagers, ethnic distinctions have assumed little significance in political life. Instead, Christianity, *nyau* and activism in the MCP have been more crucial parameters of identity politics. None of these has coincided with only one ethnic category.

Even beyond southern Dedza, it is doubtful whether a tribalist discourse enhances the understanding of Banda's regime. The notion of a 'Chewa political base' ignores the narrow scope of the elite which Banda's patronage created (see Mhone 1992). Moreover, Banda belonged to that category of postcolonial 'master politicians' (Chazan et al. 1988: 159) who engaged in the pragmatic manipulation of their subjects and did not uphold rigid principles. Such observations give no grounds for deploying ethnicity as a privileged analytic category. The conclusion of this chapter must be, therefore, that postcolonialism in Malawi cannot be understood without an appreciation of the variable historical consciousnesses in particular lived-in worlds. The shift from the 'unity', a necessary illusion in many southern Dedza villagers' view, to the avowed 'pluralism' of post-Banda Malawi is bound to require new imaginative responses in the lived-in worlds. In such pluralism, as Lwanda's contribution demonstrates, ethnically delimited categories may become vehicles for the articulation of political discontent (cf. Dubow et al. 1994). Yet there is no obvious reason why the invention of pluralism should be less amenable to imagination than the invention of unity.

Kamuzu Banda once declared: 'My tribe is the whole nation, the tribe of Malawi' (Malawi Government 1966: 620). This, rather than Banda being a culture broker for 'the Chewa', would appear to come close to southern Dedza villagers' view of their first president. A nation created from its founder's imaginary biography can itself only be imaginary. In this sense, southern Dedza villagers have known all along that the nation is an imagined community (cf. Anderson 1983). They have actively interpreted received narratives and images, but nothing ensures, of course, that their interpretations of the current reordering of Malawian political life will sustain the old premises. One thing is certain, however. It takes more than one Kamuzu to muddle fact with fiction.

Notes

1. The Lenten letter is reproduced in Chiona et al. (1992), Lwanda (1993) and Cullen (1994).
2. I conducted my fieldwork between February 1992 and November 1993.
3. I was unable to establish whether or not southern Dedza villagers had found Banda's story unconvincing during the struggle for independence. Elderly villagers' reminiscences of that period would suggest, however, that they were not pre-occupied by doubt. Excitement was the prevailing mood, and Banda's early rallies in Dedza are recalled to have been tumultuous events. Doubt therefore, can be simply an effect of the three decades of autocracy. Certainly the 'alternative' should not be seen as a discourse of the disillusioned youth, because elders, both men and women, often shared their doubt.
4. Some villagers told me that this stranger treated a child of the British royal family and was 'given' Nyasaland as a present. According to a published biography, which was not authorised by Banda, his problems in Ghana stemmed from two sources: from his relationship with a white woman, and from Ghanaian authorities who suspended him from medical practice (see Short 1974: 85). Lwanda (1993: 8) claims that Banda practised abortion in Ghana.

5. These three men are too young to have been involved in the plot from the beginning. Their mention in the account indicates, rather, southern Dedza villagers' knowledge of the history of nationalism in Malawi. Such early nationalists, and Banda's subsequent enemies, like Henry Chipembere, Dunduza Chisiza and Kanyama Chiume, are largely unknown figures among southern Dedza villagers, including most elders. Of the three men mentioned in the account, only John Tembo never fell foul of Banda's regime. Aleke Banda and Gwanda Chakuamba were both detained during Banda's era. The former became the doyen of the UDF, whereas the latter, after a brief involvement in the UDF, returned to the MCP to fill the long-vacant post of secretary-general. John Tembo, in addition to his positions in numerous companies and organisations, was the Minister of State in the President's Office when the events leading up to the 1994 elections took place. He is also the uncle of 'Official Hostess' C. Tamanda Kadzamira.

6. For less Banda-centred accounts of nationalism in Malawi, see, e.g., Shepperson and Price (1958); Rotberg (1966); van Velsen (1966) and Chiume (1975).

7. *Nkhoswe* is the 'guardian' of extended family groups, typically the mother's brother.

8. It is usually a sign of disrespect to call an adult person by his or her first name. However, Banda was commonly referred to as Kamuzu even in his presence.

9. It should be noted that witches also know the art of flying helicopters and aeroplanes. I am aware that in some other areas in Malawi, at least in the Northern Region, Banda is seen as a witch who kills people in order to restore his vitality. I never encountered such an idea in southern Dedza, however. There the image of Banda resembles more that of a white man (*mzungu*) than that of a witch (*mfiti*).

10. The secret society is also commonly known as *gule wamkulu*, literally 'the great dance'.

11. Banda's regime made little modifications to the late colonial structure of 'native authorities'. During independence, the hierarchy has been village headman, group village headman, sub-chief, chief and paramount chief. Banda's claims to the contrary notwithstanding, an ethnic identity has usually been integral to the authority at each level of the hierarchy.

12. The funerals of *nyau* members are a constant source of conflict between *nyau* officials, village headmen and the deceased's family. Although in some villages the headmen accept the full performance of *nyau* ritual in funerals, in most villages the ritual is preceded by much negotiation between the concerned parties. Some headmen reject the ritual altogether. The deceased's family can also be divided over the issue, because it is not always clear whether the deceased would have wanted the funeral to be arranged according to *nyau* or Christian pattern. Some members of the family may also be concerned about their own standing in the church if *nyau* is performed. It should be noted, however, that these problems by no means prevail everywhere in Dedza district. Indeed, only two or three miles from my research area *nyau* appears to be much less contested.

13. One of the concessions that Banda made to the opposition pressures before the referendum was the removal of the so-called poll tax.

14. Because *nyau* is a male secret society, the 'non-members' who face the risk of violence are usually male non-initiates. Women and young children are able to attend *nyau* performances. However, the unpredictable *zilombo* can attack even women.

15. The methods of coercion using *zilombo* were in operation in southern Dedza until the 1993 referendum. Afterwards, *zilombo* still 'came out' before the MCP

rallies, but displayed much less aggression and usually proceeded directly to the site of the rally.

16. 'Freedom of worship' was one of the few civil rights that the Banda regime cherished. Of course, this freedom did not extend to those churches and sects that were 'subversive', such as the Jehovah's Witnesses (see Africa Watch 1990: 63–7).

17. In other areas, however, there were reports that *zilombo* had attacked people who were on their way to opposition meetings.

18. One song demanded 'you should not forget to thank Chakufwa Chihana' (*'musaiale kuthokoza Chakufwa Chihana'*).

19. Some Mozambiquans made sure that they departed from Malawi before the June referendum. Convinced that it was now Malawi's turn to go to war, in their images of home (*kwathu*, 'our place') they depicted Mozambique as a haven of peace.

20. The plight of northerners was a subject of much clandestine discourse in Banda's Malawi. Belief in their superior education, in the lack of development in the Northern Region and in the discouragement of the Chitumbuka language was widely articulated also in southern Dedza. For a historical background, see, e.g., McCracken (1977); and Vail and White (1989).

21. I was often asked about the systems of government in Europe. The apparent success of multiparty politics in Europe produced solemn reflections from many southern Dedza villagers. 'Black people are difficult' (*anthu okuda ndi obvuta*), I was told repeatedly, because 'they hate each other' (*amadana ndi anzawo*).

22. 'Parish tax' needs to be put in inverted commas, because the actual word for tax is *nsonkho*. *Mtulo* has connotations of 'gift', but the more common word for gift is *mphatso*. The fact that *mtulo* was payable annually like *nsonkho* blurred to some extent their semantic boundaries.

23. *Mbumba* is an aggregate of dependants in a matrilineal extended family, overseen by a guardian (*nkhoswe*). For Banda, all Malawian women were his *mbumba* (see also, Hirschmann 1990).

24. I am grateful to Terence Ranger for a comment which helped me to formulate this point.

References

Africa Watch. 1990. *Where Silence Rules. The Suppression of Dissent in Malawi*. London: Human Rights Watch.

Anderson, Benedict. 1983. *Imagined Communities. Reflections on the Origins and Spread of Nationalism*. London: Verso.

Balandier, Georges. 1967. *Anthropologie Politique*. Paris: Presses Universitaires de France.

Banda, H. K. and Young, T. Cullen. 1946. *Our African Way of Life*. New York: Lutterworth.

Barber, Karin. 1986. *Popular Theatre and Public Anxiety*. Unpublished paper.

Barnes, J. A. 1954. *Politics in a Changing Society*. Manchester: Manchester University Press.

Chazan, Naomi, Mortimer, Robert, Ravenhill, John and Rothchild, Donald (eds). 1988. *Politics and Society in Contemporary Africa*. Boulder, CO: Lynne Rienner.

Chiona, J. et al. 1992. 'The Catholic Bishops Speak Out', *Index on Censorship* 21 (5): 15–17.

Chiume, M. W. Kanyama. 1975. *Kwacha. An Autobiography*. Nairobi: East African Publishing House.

Coplan, David B. 1991. 'Fictions That Save: Migrants' Performances and Basotho National Culture', *Cultural Anthropology* 6: 164–92.

Cullen, Trevor. 1994. *Malawi: A Turning Point*. Edinburgh: Pentland Press.

Dubow, Saul, Sharp, John and Wilmsen, Edwin N. (eds). 1994. Special Issue: Ethnicity and Identity in Southern Africa, *Journal of Southern African Studies* 20: 347–474.

Forster, Peter G. 1994. 'Culture, Nationalism, and the Invention of Tradition in Malawi', *Journal of Modern African Studies* 32: 477–97.

Hirschmann, David. 1990. 'The Malawi Case: Enclave Politics, Core Resistance and "Nkhoswe No. 1"', in K. Staudt (ed.), *Women, International Development, and Politics*. Philadelphia: Temple University Press.

Hirschmann, David and Vaughan, Megan. 1983. 'Food Production and Income Generation in a Matrilineal Society: Rural Women in Zomba, Malawi', *Journal of Southern African Studies* 10: 86–99.

Kaspin, Deborah. 1993. 'Chewa Visions and Revisions of Power: Transformations of the Nyau Dance in Central Malawi', in J. Comaroff and J. Comaroff (eds), *Modernity and Its Malcontents. Ritual and Power in Postcolonial Africa*. Chicago: University of Chicago Press.

Kerr, David. 1989. 'Community Theatre and Public Health in Malawi', *Journal of Southern African Studies* 15: 469–85.

Langworthy, Harry W. 1972. *Zambia Before 1890. Aspects of Pre-Colonial History*. London: Longman.

Linden, Ian. 1972. 'The Maseko Ngoni at Domwe: 1870–1900', in B. Pachai (ed.), *The Early History of Malawi*. London: Longman.

Linden, Ian with Linden, Jane. 1974. *Catholics, Peasants and Chewa Resistance in Nyasaland*. London: Heinemann.

Lwanda, John Lloyd. 1993. *Kamuzu Banda of Malawi. A Study in Promise, Power and Paralysis*. Glasgow: Dudu Nsomba Publications.

— 1994. *The Second Harvest*. Glasgow: Dudu Nsomba Publications.

McCracken, John. 1968. 'African Politics in Twentieth-Century Malawi', in T. O. Ranger (ed.), *Aspects of Central African History*. London: Heinemann.

— 1977. *Politics and Christianity in Malawi 1875–1940. The Impact of the Livingstonian Mission in the Northern Province*. Cambridge: Cambridge University Press.

Malawi Government. 1966. *Hansard*. Zomba: Government Printer.

Malawi Information Department. n.d. *The President of Malawi, His Excellency Dr Kamuzu Banda*. Blantyre.

Mbembe, Achille. 1992. 'Provisional Notes on the Postcolony', *Africa* 62 (1): 3–37.

Mhone, Guy Z. 1992. 'The Political Economy of Malawi: An Overview', in G. C. Z. Mhone (ed.), *Malawi at the Crossroads: The Postcolonial Political Economy*. Harare: Sapes.

Philip, K. D. 1975. *Onani Angoni*. Blantyre: Dzuka.

Ranger, Terence. 1983. 'The Invention of Tradition in Colonial Africa', in E. Hobsbawm and T. Ranger (eds), *The Invention of Tradition*. Cambridge: Cambridge University Press.

— 1993. 'The Invention of Tradition Revisited: the Case of Colonial Africa', in

T. Ranger and O. Vaughan (eds), *Legitimacy and the State in Twentieth-Century Africa*. London: Macmillan.

Read, Margaret. 1956. *The Ngoni of Nyasaland*. London: Oxford University Press.

Rennie, J. K. 1966. 'The Ngoni States and European Intrusion', in E. Stokes and R. Brown (eds), *The Zambesian Past*. Manchester: Manchester University Press.

Rotberg, Robert T. 1966. *The Rise of Nationalism in Central Africa: The Making of Malawi and Zambia*. London: Oxford University Press.

Schoffeleers, J. Matthew. 1972. 'The Meaning and Use of the Name Malawi in Oral Traditions and Precolonial Documents', in B. Pachai (ed.), *The Early History of Malawi*. London: Longman.

— 1992. *River of Blood. The Genesis of a Martyr Cult in Southern Malawi, c. A.D. 1600*. Madison: University of Wisconsin Press.

Shepperson, George and Price, Thomas. 1958. *Independent African. John Chilembwe and the Origins, Setting and Significance of the Nyasaland Native Rising of 1915*. Edinburgh: Edinburgh University Press.

Short, Philip. 1974. *Banda*. London: Routledge and Kegan Paul.

Vail, H. Leroy. 1972. 'Suggestions towards a Reinterpreted Tumbuka History', In B. Pachai (ed.), *The Early History of Malawi*. London: Longman.

— 1978. 'Religion, Language and the Tribal Myth: The Tumbuka and Chewa of Malawi', in J. M. Schoffeleers (ed.), *Guardians of the Land. Essays on Central African Territorial Cults*. Gwelo: Mambo Press.

— 1981. 'The Making of the "Dead North": A Study of the Ngoni Rule in Northern Malawi, c. 1855–1907', in J. B. Peires (ed.), *Before and After Shaka. Papers in Nguni History*. Grahamstown: Institute of Social and Economic Research.

Vail, Leroy and White, Landeg. 1989. 'Tribalism in the Political History of Malawi', in L. Vail (ed.), *The Creation of Tribalism in Southern Africa*. London: James Currey.

— 1991. *Power and the Praise Poem. Southern African Voices in History*. London: James Currey.

van Donge, Jan Kees. 1995. 'Kamuzu's Legacy: The Democratization of Malawi', *African Affairs* 94: 227–57.

van Velsen, J. 1966. 'Some Early Pressure Groups in Malawi', In E. Stokes and R. Brown (eds), *The Zambesian Past*. Manchester: Manchester University Press.

White, Landeg. 1987. *Magomero: Portrait of an African Village*. Cambridge: Cambridge University Press.

CHAPTER 5

The potentials of boundaries in South Africa: steps towards a theory of the social edge

Robert Thornton

Anthony Appiah (1991) in a well known article asks whether the post- in 'postcolonial' is the same as the post- in 'postmodern'. Appiah concludes that what is signified by the post- in the first two terms is similar in both cases since both negate a previous authority.[1] Postmodernism negates the authority of the modern as rational[2] while postcolonialism negates the authority of the colonial state as 'modern'. Achille Mbembe (1992) would probably agree with this assessment, citing also the 'tendency to excess and the lack of proportion', the simulacra of power and empty boasts of hegemony, and a sense of subversive play that nevertheless have no material consequences as hallmarks of the 'postcolony'.[3] These relations of power are not consistent with Max Weber's notions of rationality, and thus appear to be dissonant with the fundamental chord of rationalism in modernity. According to Appiah, then, the centrality of rationality and progress in 'the modern' is opposed by both postmodernism and post-colonialism in order to 'clear a space' for a different awareness.

Appiah's and Mbembe's essays have helped to define the ideas of the postmodern and the postcolonial in African studies. In this chapter, I explore ways in which these arguments may be applicable to, or consistent with, contemporary experience in South Africa. Appiah and Mbembe are both familiar with Africa in general, and in particular with Ghana and Cameroon, their countries of origin, but both explicitly exclude South Africa from the scope of their discussion. By contrast, I attempt to understand South Africa as part of Africa. Both Appiah and Mbembe tend to fuse the postcolonial with the postmodern, especially the con-temporary postcolonial experience. Here, I will make a distinction. I shall argue that the current moment in South Africa is indeed postmodern in a number of respects, but it is not postcolonial. In a nutshell, I shall argue that Apartheid was a form of rampant modernism and that post-Apartheid is therefore postmodern. It is also after the 'colonial' of course, but I would reserve the label 'postcolonial' for Apartheid itself.

The postmodern, the modern and the (post) colony Modernism is far from dead in Africa, as elsewhere. Because of their different relations to power, Modernism and postmodernism have quite different meanings and values in the Third World. Despite the fragmentation of modernism in the West, the aporias of reason, the politics of pastiche, the crisis of authenticity and the pervasive presence of simulacra, the Third World appears to be embracing modernism and modernisation as never before. This is occurring just at the moment when Western intellectuals are facing the end of a prophetic positivism and are moving beyond the promises and the premises of the modern with a sense of disillusionment. The newly industrialising countries (NICs) on the Pacific Rim, for instance, appear set to 'inject new vitality into the idea of modernity'. They 'crave modernity' as they move into the twenty-first Century (Lee 1994). For the most part, this appears to be true of African elites as well, who are not only still modernising but seem set to continue their commitment to modernisation well into the future. The postmodern anxieties of the postindustrial West seem irrelevant to them. It may make more sense now to speak of alternative modernisms, or even alternative postmodernisms, each one specific to a particular locale in the global culture-map. With this adjustment, then, Appiah's question still makes some sense. But the very vitality of modernism raises a significant problem for the views put forward by Appiah and Mbembe.

While it is clear that postmodernism and the postcolony have something in common, it may not be the rejection of modernity itself. Instead, we may be witnessing the development of alternative modernisms that selectively choose aspects of Western modernism, especially as these are represented in consumer goods and through the intensification of multi-national capitalism (Lee 1994: 51). The ludic aspects of resistance to colonialism and to the postcolonial state (Mbembe 1992) and the play of images and representations which characterise the neo-traditional contemporary arts and cultures of Africa (Appiah 1991) may have more to do with globalisation and commodification of culture in a way that makes it almost too easy to play. Writing about the seductive power of commodities in the Pacific Rim countries, the sociologist Raymond Lee remarks that the sensualism, playfulness and the ease with which 'hedonism can be translated and transmitted through technology ... have become global culture's principal influence on the transformation of Third World traditionalism. In other words, postmodernism as a postcolonial strategy of ludic inversion fragments and deflates the Western ego, but contrastingly provides a medium for renewed self-assertion among Third World individuals whose historicities are only beginning to come into their own' (Lee 1994: 4).

The force of modernism has always been its opposition to the traditional (Habermas 1985) and its ability to overcome the traditional through more powerful means of representation and production. The global media, transnational distribution of goods and diasporas of peoples, the profligate reproduction of technology of sensualism and ludic excess, however, have made 'the modern' almost irresistibly attractive to most consumers in the Third World. Thus, the force of postmodernism's opposition to modernism is asymmetric to modernism's opposition to traditionalism since both postmodernism and 'the traditional' apparently lack the rhetorical and productive force of modernism. But the consequences of the modern in the period of 'late capitalism' and global culture are not entirely consistent with the agenda of modernism itself, and certainly not with the so-called Enlightenment Project. What is in fact happening is not what modernism led us to expect, and it is not what all the mighty plans of the Modern and modernisation were meant to achieve. It is clear that fundamentalists of all stripes and colours, traditionalists, atavists, right-wingers and racists can take over the powerful representation machinery of late capitalism in pursuit of patently anti-Enlightenment projects. Hybrid, modernised-traditionalism, or 'universal separatism' have proved extremely powerful. This may reflect a new move, not yet named, towards the future, but the postmodern can also be seen as the failure of Modernism to keep its promises, just as the postcolonial can be seen as the failure of colonialism.

Post-Apartheid South Africa, now under an ANC-led Government of National Unity, leads us to extend Appiah's provocative question and to ask whether the post- in post-Apartheid is like the post- in 'postcolonial' or in 'postmodern'. Or, more specifically, is post-Apartheid postcolonial? Is it postmodern? The end of the Apartheid laws and government, and the overwhelming sense of difference felt by most South Africans seem to force some periodisation, and to demand the informal name: 'The New South Africa'. And so, we might then ask whether the label 'post-apartheid' makes sense in ways that are similar to words such as 'postmodern' or 'postcolonial'.

I would assert that South Africa is clearly post-Apartheid. Minimally, it is clearly after Apartheid in the way that the old Soviet Union and Eastern Europe are post-communist. Strangely, both exhibit a nostalgia for the recent past. While there is no nostalgia for either communism or Apartheid, there is a nostalgia for the certainties, however grim, that each offered. What both communism and Apartheid offered were a promise of the future unfolding and a sense of historical majesty that goes with any nationalist narrative, especially when this is paired with a promise (if not the reality) of the rationally administered state. In both cases, it was the failure of prophecy and the fragmentation of the simulacrum of majesty that doomed them. Few, I think, would argue that there is not a 'post-communist condition' – a syndrome of characteristics and factors – in those countries where it once ruled (Lukacs 1994). Similarly, I would argue that the 'post-Apartheid condition' exists too, and that it deserves close attention.

This condition emerges out of the special relationship between modernism, colonialism and Apartheid. Appiah paired the postcolonial and the postmodern, implicitly equating the modern with the colony, and modernism with colonialism. Among other things, modernism provided both a warrant and a means for world domination, and European colonies were one of the consequences of this. In Africa modernity and modernisation cannot be isolated from the colony and colonialism, and all other distinctions pale in comparison. While modernism in Europe drew on the insights of 'primitive art' or on the 'oriental aesthetic', modernism in Africa can be associated only with the practices and ideologies of the European colony in Africa and, after that, with the Euro-American educated elites in the postcolony (Appiah 1991: 347–8). In South Africa, Apartheid stands as a special form of modernism and 'modernisation'.

Appiah thus misses a crucial third term that links modernity and the colony, namely the rational 'progressive' bureaucratic administration.[4] It is 'the administration' that translated the ideas of modernism into the practices of modernity, and which made possible, and justified, their application to the colony as the practices and techniques of power. There is a profound continuity that connects the colony with the postcolony, and this is the resilience of administrative practices themselves. These are culturally revalued in the postcolony but they are not wholly other or wholly different from the colony. The appropriation of the colonial administrative forms is one of the hallmarks of the postcolony. Although the holders of office were replaced, the forms of administration, as form, provide a powerful continuity between the old and the new, the colony and the postcolony. The postcolonial administration often carries out projects that were formulated under colonialism. The modern administration eventually subverts and replaces an indigenous politics, acting as a sort of 'anti-politics machine' (Ferguson 1990). The effect is the same under colonial or postcolonial regimes.

This is particularly true with respect to the continuity of modernism and modernity in the South African 'new dispensation' (the pharmaceutical metaphor is taken for granted in South Africa, consistent with the high status of healers and healing in southern Africa).[5] However well we might understand the effects and traces of modernism and the postmodern in capitalism, globalisation, cultural hybridity and literature, without fully comprehending the role of the bureaucratic administration, we cannot understand South Africa, or Africa.

South Africa is more certainly (more post-?) 'postcolonial' than the rest of sub-Saharan Africa, since the colonies of Natal and the Cape ceased to belong to Britain in 1910, and the rest was only briefly a colony from 1902 to 1910. In comparison with the rest of Africa, the issue of postcolonialism is obscured by the fact that the institutions that might once have been characterised as 'colonial' have long been rendered effectively indigenous.[6] For the bureaucracy, and for the vast majority of educated South African people, there is no 'overseas educated' elite, speaking a foreign language (although they all speak a great many local languages).

What remains, and what ties the 'before' to the 'after' here, is the nostalgia for the administered polity, free from 'divisive politics'. It shares this nostalgia for an absence of politics with the rest of Africa – but, unlike the rest of Africa, the 'disorder of things' (Smart 1993) does not work to enforce a false unity. At least, not yet. Mbembe, for instance, cites Togo, 'until recently the perfect example of postcolonial construction' in which the hyper-valuation of the perfectly administered polity suppresses any form of politics.

The official discourse made use of all necessary means to maintain the fiction of a society devoid of conflict. Postcoloniality could be seen here behind the façade of a policy in which the state considered itself simul-taneously as indistinguishable from society and as the upholder of the law and the keeper of the truth. '[T]he sole party ... claimed to control the whole of public and social life ... proclaiming the unity of the people, among whom no divisions could be allowed to exist ... [D]issidence was denied' (Mbembe 1992: 5).

Examples of this could, of course, be multiplied for all parts of sub-Saharan Africa, including South Africa under Apartheid. But this is precisely the situation which South Africa has now left behind. It is vehemently rejected by virtually all politicians, media personalities and writers, and most ordinary people in all walks of life with whom I have spoken. Even those who were once, apparently, most strongly committed to Apartheid (or to communist centralism, or African Nationalist absolut-ism), today are reluctant to defend these tyrannies. In other respects, however, South Africa now is more African than it has ever seemed before not only because it suddenly sees itself as part of Africa, but also because it now shares the problems of Africa, most notably those that arise from the problematic fusion of Africa and Europe that are summed up under Appiah's rubrics 'postcolonial' and 'postmodern'. It is likely that the embrace of modernity in the Pacific Rim NICs and Third World countries is considerably modified in the specific context of Africa in which languages of European origin dominate the market and are spoken by all elites, and where the institutions of the colonial bureaucracy still define all aspects of politics and statesmanship.

In consequence of this, South Africa is now more postmodern than it is postcolonial, especially in the remarkably postmodern character of the current transition. Remarkable events signal this, such as the 'reconciliation tea party' hosted by Nelson Mandela at his home in Cape Town on 28 July

1995, in which the wives and widows of erstwhile opponents, including Elize Botha, wife of Mandela's most zealous jailer, President P. W. Botha, sat at table with Nonsikelelo Biko, wife of the activist Steve Biko whom agents of the state president killed in 1978.[7] Television talk shows routinely pair previously opposed officers of the South African Defence Force with those from Mkhonto we Sizwe (the now disbanded armed wing of the ANC) who are both part of the same military organisation. In other broadcasts, extreme right-wing Afrikaner nationalists debate with their extreme Black opposites. In one TV talk show in which I recently participated, university professors (such as myself) and teachers were brought together with traditional African healers (*isangomas*, *inyangas*), chiefs, and 'Bushmen' (San), 'Griquas' (Khoikhoi) and others. Indeed, one family of Bushmen, Dawid Kruyper, his wife Sara and child Klein Isak, naked except for their 'traditional' Bushman loincloths, sat in the futuristic, hypermodern air-conditioned Cape Town studios of the South African Broadcasting Corporation and were linked by satellite to Johannesburg![8]

Ironically, the future is what 'the modern' intended to create in Africa. In the late 1950s and 1960s, all new African states, free of colonial domination, promised a modernised future. It was to be governed by a rational administration and would produce wealth and leisure. Above all, it promised a future free of conflict. The modern state, the modern kitchen, the modern chief, modernised agriculture, the bureaucrat with a modern outlook, a modern economy – all this and more. Apartheid promised the same. Thus, Apartheid, both as ideology and as administrative practice, was one of the most virulent varieties of modernism. It was in the name of modernism, not colonialism, that promises were made to South Africans which no government could possibly keep (leaving to one side the question of whether they were worth keeping). Thus, South Africans do not now see these times as something that has come as a consequence of modernisation or modernity. Homelands, 'Betterment', 'Trusteeship', 'Tribal Trust Property', 'De-stocking', 'Population Registration', 'Influx Control' were all fully justified in the eyes of their creators and administrators as modernising agendas. This is what has been rejected with the rejection of Apartheid. The end of Apartheid cannot be seen, then, as a consequence of the modern. Too many atrocities have been perpetrated in the name of The Modern already. The political transition is understood, instead, as the failure of the modern, accompanied by a loss of faith, an occluded vision of modernity as what the future offered. The end of Apartheid is the end of 'modernisation' and therefore may be either a new beginning or a return to the past, to tradition, to primitivism. The end of Apartheid and the collapse of African economies to the north are understood in this way to be of the same moment, and the consequences of the same forces, namely, the end of the rational, modernising order. In South Africa, as in the rest of Africa, this is seen as both liberating and threatening, empowering and impoverishing. Thus, the middle of the 1990s in South Africa may be neither 'postmodern' nor 'postcolonial'. It is rather pre-future, in the condition of the ante-morrow, the *jetztzeit* (Benjamin 1969) of a new-old country that thought it knew all along what would happen, and then didn't know, and thus waits again for the regeneration of a past it has forgotten and the materialisation of a future it does not know. For now, let's just call this a postmodern condition.

The postmodern condition in South Africa

One of the most remarkable things about South Africa is the multiplicity of boundaries that define it, divide it, and thereby give it shape. Apartheid, the political system under which it lived for more than four decades, is synonymous with the meticulous making and marking of difference, especially that difference known as 'race', but also space (Christopher 1994). It was also known for its apparent totalising system of social engineering in which the vision of 'apartness', apartheid, was implemented through massive and violent spatial dislocation of much of its population in terms of a rationalised bureaucratic master-plan of a total differentiation of spheres of life based on race and (what was the same for its architects) culture. The master-plan was accompanied by a master-narrative, taught in all the schools, portrayed in monuments, recited at churches and performed in the sacred rituals of the state. What could be more modern than this? These programmes were instituted as bureaucratic procedures and practices. But bureaucracies tend to see politics as inimical to their own agendas, and, if given the chance, seek to suppress politics altogether. Apartheid was precisely this: an administrative response to political questions, and it sought to suppress politics entirely.[9]

There is, however, an essential contradiction in the concept of a totality based on the dis-integration of the polity, or of a unity based on the logic of division. The motto of the Apartheid state – *eendrag maak mag*, 'Unity is power'[10] – was a lie, but it was also its most fervent hope. Both the essence and failure of apartheid can be seen as the attempt to implement in an administration this oxymoronic conception. The party of Apartheid, the National Party, remained in power longer than any other party in any other post-Second World War democracy.

Despite its remarkable longevity, apartheid (as concept), and Apartheid as a formal system of laws and practices, failed because it constantly undermined the unity it sought through the implementation of difference. In its aftermath, the logic of difference remains, but it now lacks the political, philosophical and aesthetic image of unity of the (total) nation. This could easily be taken as the postmodern condition in which the 'pastiche' is called for, the cobbling together which permits the 'unpresentable to become perceptible' which Lyotard takes as symptomatic

POTENTIALS OF BOUNDARIES IN SOUTH AFRICA   143

of a special 'condition' (Lyotard 1984: 80): 'The postmodern would be
that which, in the modern, puts forward the unpresentable in presentation
itself; that which denies itself the solace of good forms, the consensus of
taste which would make it possible to share collectively the nostalgia for
the unattainable' (ibid.: 81). In Lyotard's attempt to define the postmodern
as the 'paradox of the future (post-) anterior (-modo)' he claims that it is
not our business to supply reality but to invent allusions to the conceivable
which cannot be presented (ibid.: 81).

This is, perhaps, a fair characterisation of the South African predicament. If so, then it should be obvious why Apartheid was the condition
of its own demise, why South Africa should find itself in a characteristically
postmodern predicament (rather than a postcolonial one), and why the
logic of difference and differentiation itself should persist after the demise
of Apartheid itself. It is worth, therefore, distinguishing between apartheid
(lowercase 'a' for the generic concept) and Apartheid (uppercase 'A' for
the named, historical system). The former (apartheid) then refers to the
logic of difference which is, for the most part, still incoherent and ineffable
(like Lyotard's 'unpresentable') but which still pervades all aspects of life
in South Africa. Such a logic of difference is not limited to South Africa,
nor to this historical period. We could, and do, speak of apartheid elsewhere in the world, in the US or in Britain. The latter term (Apartheid)
would refer to the historically delimited, bureaucratic system which implemented the conceptual system. This is the name that it devised for
itself and, if for this reason alone, deserves to be thought of as a proper
name rather than a generic concept. The very fact that 'Apartheid' so
easily slipped into the realm of the generic, and has so readily captured
world attention in the twentieth century, does not suggest a rupture with
modernism but rather indicates precisely its continuity with other modern
or modernising bureaucratic systems.

It is precisely this continuity that makes it so dangerous, since it was
merely an extreme, different in degree, but not qualitatively different.
Apartheid came into being after the electoral victory of the National Party
in 1948, and ceased to exist when the laws were repealed from 1987 to
1993.[11] It originated and came to an end as the result of bureaucratic
decisions. If Mr De Klerk and other members of his cabinet are to be
believed, they reached their decisions acting as administrators. Had they
acted as politicians, of course, they could never have reached the decision
they did in fact reach. Moreover, their decisions were fully consistent with
the history of the administration of the South African government up to
that point. Their decisions to release Mandela, to go for full-franchise
elections and thus to relinquish political power are not comprehensible
within a logic of the political, but only as the consequence of administrative
rationalism. Outside of bureaucracy itself, it could only be seen as irrational.

Thus, it is useful conceptually and historically to restrict usage of the word 'apartheid' in this way – even if it works only on paper and not in speech – since it makes clear that Apartheid is, above all, a form of the modern bureaucratic administration, not a timeless and enduring form of human sociality. It permits us to periodise South African history (past, present and future) in a reasonable way, that is, as history, like any other history, and not as a static ideal type of racism. To do otherwise, it seems to me, risks giving race and racism a foundational status they do not deserve.

Indeed, race is not at all essential to Apartheid itself, as its own institutionalised procedures for race reclassification make plain. The words 'race' and 'colour' themselves are rarely mentioned in the fundamental legal acts that made Apartheid a reality. The legislation needed no higher organising principle beyond the names of the races (or colours) that were already held to exist. Thus, the Population Classification Act (1952), one of the pillars of Apartheid, listed Whites (Blankes), Blacks (Swartes, colloquially 'Kaffirs'), Indians (Indiers) and Coloureds (Kleurlinge), not as fractions of 'race' or types of a general category, but as self-evident, autonomous populations. What is essential is the (re)marking of a difference, on multiple and often arbitrary grounds, in order to exclude those who were understood to be of a different 'nation', but also to enforce an aesthetic vision of purity and rational clarity. Recognition of this as the essential aspect of Apartheid allows us to understand its relation to colonialism and to modernism.

It is nevertheless clear that Apartheid relied on a logic of difference that gave either 'race' or 'nation/nationality' a special place, and produced a set of practices concerned with boundaries between the categories thus conceived. It aimed, above all, to establish the membership of the modern polity in Africa, and to distinguish this with the force of clarity, and of arms if need be, from the 'traditional' polities which both encompassed it and which it, itself, had absorbed.

South Africa today, especially with respect to the edges of difference – or what, more prosaically, we might call 'boundaries' – is a country still (mid-1995) without a permanent constitution, a temporary 'government of national unity', enduring uncertainty about the ownership or access to land and housing, continuing debate about who qualifies as bona fide political actors (that is, whether chiefs and kings do or do not exist 'outside' of politics, and who qualifies as a citizen), uncertainty about virtually all levels of geographic boundary demarcation from provincial to neighbourhood and household, and in which almost all identities – previously legislated and believed to be immutable – are suddenly open to threat and negotiation.

Thus, the South African condition is more postmodern than it is postcolonial. This is especially marked in what Steven Tyler (1987) would call the 'unspeakable' character of contemporary South Africa: there are quite literally no names, no vocabulary, to discuss major aspects and parts of its political being. There is no agreement on what are the boundaries of 'Black', of 'White', of 'Indian' or 'Coloured'. No one knows whether to refer to 'tribes', 'ethnic groups', 'language groups', 'peoples' or 'races'. There is no simple way to 'be Zulu' since the king, the ethnic party (Inkatha Freedom Party), the region (KwaZulu) and the category of 'speakers of Zulu' are all in conflict in some domains, and unresolved in all domains. Not even colour is a reliable signifier any longer. The latest population census reports 6,000 people who list themselves as both 'White' and 'first-language speakers' of Zulu. White TV newsreaders and performers present in Zulu, and the Zulu Chief Minister – and now Minister of Home Affairs – consistently addresses the Zulu masses in English (most of whom do not speak it!).

Nevertheless, these assertions that Apartheid does not depend on race, that boundaries are mutable and open to negotiation, that the categories of South African social life are 'unspeakable' or even 'unthinkable', seem to fly in the face of conventional wisdom. This seems to be especially true with respect to violence. Everyone is familiar, by now, with the endless reports of violence in South Africa which are explained by newspaper journalists as 'ethnic' or 'tribal' violence. Whatever merit the claims I have made so far may have, they seem to contradict what appear to be the facts of the matter. Explanations of violence are characteristically explicit about the tribal or ethnic identity of who 'started it'. Equally characteristically, they are contradictory and confused (Thornton 1990; Minaar 1991). With the implacable logic of the feud, warfare and the evening crime report, perpetrators are in most cases easily identified with their ethnic group, their 'people' or 'race' so that the category may carry the blame and, if possible, revenge be exacted or punishment administered categorically (as the following episode illustrates).

But in South Africa, even here there is confusion. The confusion is not merely circumstantial; it is chronic. In most cases the real causes of violence remain elusive. The certainty with which one ethnic group, one collective or individual actor is named soon dissolves with further investigation. To be sure, there is often deliberate misinformation, deliberate sowing of seeds of doubt and an inevitable harvest of confusion when anyone tries to discover what really happened. But since all participants collude and participate in competing collective imaginations of what really happened, the actual events of violence are not recoverable in the majority of cases. What are recoverable are the stories.

For instance, on Wednesday 26 July 1995, police were sent to quell violence that had flared once again in the hostels of Sebokeng. Sebokeng, a close neighbour of Sharpeville in the Vaal Triangle, was a centre of chronic violence both before and after the 'transition'. Fifteen people died in the fighting before police and army patrols succeeded in controlling it.

The accounts of who caused it are symptomatic of the confusions and complexities of identities.

> Some hostel residents told *The Star* the violence started when a Pedi man killed his Mosotho wife and a Mosotho man after finding out they were lovers.
> Media reports that the two were killed because they refused to contribute money to buy firearms for the hostel were nonsense, a group of women said.
> A Mosotho woman … said the two were killed after they were found having sex by the husband.
> A Basotho faction then concluded that the lovers were killed by Xhosa residents and retaliated. But other residents said the clashes were caused by AmaBhaca and Basotho residents who, together with Inkatha Freedom Party members, were trying to remove Xhosa residents from a section of the hostel to make way for IFP members.
> However, hostel peace committee chairman Vuyisa Lungiswa had a different explanation. AmaBhaca residents and IFP non-residents fought after a *braai* [barbecue]. IFP members were expelled from the hostel in 1992, Lungiswa said, and were now trying to move back. They are feared by present hostel dwellers. Another hostel dweller said the police were collaborating with the AmaBhaca, Basotho and AmaMpondo residents.[12]

In all, fifteen individual or collective actors are named here. Among them are six 'ethnic groups',[13] hostel residents and non-residents, members of a political party, a 'peace committee' member, and the police. All of these were ostensibly directly involved in one murder. All may have played a role in a conflict that, like the Kurosawa film *Rashomon*, or the ten blind men describing an elephant, evidently looks different from each perspective. (It would be enough to drive Agatha Christie mad, although one suspects that Peter Sellers's character, Inspector Clouseau, would be just the man for the job!) The almost unfettered multiplication of actors is patently fictional, but it suggests the drama and play. Here, as Mbembe remarks of Cameroon and of the postcolony more generally, there is 'a distinctive style of political improvisation … distinctive ways in which identities are multiplied, transformed, and put in circulation. But the postcolony is also made up of a series of corporate institutions and a political machinery which, once they are in place, constitute a distinctive regime of violence' (Mbembe 1992: 3).

In the Sebokeng hostel case, multiple shifting and overlapping identities and perspectives (resident or non-resident, lover or spouse, Mpondo or IFP, Xhosa or Bhaca, etc.) make it impossible to assign blame. This episode is typical of countless others that occur daily in KwaZulu/Natal or that have been such an integral part of recent South African history.

In episodes like this one, South Africa is precisely and fully in the process of 'inventing allusions to the conceivable' since there is no agreed-upon reality, as yet, to which a single discourse can be referred. The master-narrative is quite literally gone. The 'state', once all-powerful in

South African eyes, is now suddenly recognised as vulnerable, and non-hegemonic (Gupta 1995; Bayart 1993). Indeed, the concept of 'hegemony' makes little sense since there are no cultural or political grounds on which its power (as hegemonic, as powerful) might be judged. The courts, for instance, act in terms of the 'conceivable' and likely, since laws are of uncertain precedence in the New (old) South Africa in which the constitution has yet to be invented and all government is still 'provisional'. Elections for local government, held on 1 November 1995, were problematic just weeks before they were due to take place since no one knew what a 'local government' would look like, nor even what the centre or boundaries of 'the local' might be.[14]

In a characteristic conceptual sleight of hand, the future constitution is already treated as precedent. Stephen Tyler goes so far as to say that the 'past is the myth modernism invented as the story of its origin'. This is nowhere more true than in South Africa. While Apartheid justified itself as the upholder of the Great Tradition of the West, and promised a future it could not deliver, the current government, lacking a precedent, treats the future as if it were already history. The extended present of South Africa in transition is self-consciously in the process of self-invention and absorbs the past and future into the moment. Mandela is understood to be speaking in a sort of timeless tense, *sub specie aeternitatis*, both at home and abroad, in Parliament or on the rugby field.

The postmodern and the postcolony have fundamental continuities with the modern and colonial. This is especially true in Africa, and in South Africa. Since the colonial in Africa has been defined from the beginning of the twentieth century by its pursuit of modernism, and the by the administrative agendas of modernisation, the end of the colonial is almost inevitably the end of the modern. And yet, the postcolony clings to the modern and to modernisation.

The current master-plan of the South African government is called the Reconstruction and Development Programme (RDP). This evokes the grand plans of European reconstruction after the last war, and the programmes of development (or modernisation) that followed in their wake. It appears to be a programme of modernisation *comme les autres*. What it lacks, however, is certainty. Faith in the inevitability of its realisation has gone, and this more than anything else differentiates it from the grand modernising projects that proliferated from the middle of this century. Nevertheless, this attempt to carry through a modernising project in spite of this aporia must in itself signal a rupture with the past even though the rhetoric is still familiar. This must, in some sense of the word 'post-', be a postmodern project. New grounds for the RDP, or for any other plan of action, must be found to validate its claim to be a fundamental national goal. The modernising project, at least, must be reinvented. The tight bond between the colonial and the modern, between the process of colonial domination and the modernisation, must be subverted. If Apartheid was postcolonial, then postApartheid is postmodern.

Boundaries and an aesthetics of power

The boundaries of South Africa, whether signalled by khaki uniforms or bureaucratic knowledge and practices, are strangely evanescent and yet enduring. They have a presence that makes them stand for themselves. While there is a vast literature on nations, nation-states, the state, ethnicity, and identity, most African countries today are countries, not nations, states or ethnic groups. By 'countries' I mean named areas of land demarcated by international boundaries, but not necessarily possessing comprehensive state apparatuses, full administrative or fiscal coverage of the area so named, or even a coherent self-identity as such. Seen as such, most of Africa consists of countries, not nations or nation-states. Countries seem to exist as a form of nominalism: they are named, therefore they are. They are named because they have boundaries. This is as true for the poorest of them as it is for the most powerful. At some point in the histories of these bits of earth, they acquired boundaries. South Africa, for instance, carries a purely geographic name denoting the southern portion of a continent. Its shape is the result of a history of bureaucratic decisions that might have been otherwise: Lesotho (Basotoland), Botswana (Bechuanaland) and Swaziland might all have been part of it, while Zululand or Transkei (Kaffraria) were not; or some might have been and others not. Other combinations and exclusions were possible. In the end, it is simply as it is: a country within its borders. Actual borders are often determined by factors that have little to do with any real political process: the course of rivers, how far a horse can be ridden, the location of pass, how far a surveyor can see, magnetic variations, illegible or imaginative treaties implemented by guess-work, where one frightened army happened to catch up with another, and so on. These are the events in the histories of countries. It is otherwise for nations. Countries are distinguished from nations, tribes and ethnic groups by the kinds of narratives that define them, and by the rhetoric which evokes them. All postcolonial countries in Africa have recognised and stated in the Organisation of African Unity (OAU) charter that their borders would be maintained even though they are consequences of geographic happenstance and rarely reflect real ethnic, social or linguistic boundaries on the ground. (It is an open question whether this is a good or a bad thing.) A few have changed their names, but none has willingly changed its borders. They cannot be justified functionally, socially or politically. In order that they be taken seriously, governments must refer, again anomalously, to a 'tradition' which everyone knows is recent, not of African origin and often in conflict with the 'nationalist' policies of the governments concerned.

South Africa's borders, similarly, are arbitrary, but to the historical arbitrariness of its external borders are added the many internal borders between provinces (the four old ones and the nine new ones), administrative districts (so-called development regions), the recent nominally-independent homelands (e.g. Venda, Bophuthatswana) and the dependent but self-governing homelands (e.g. KwaZulu), less recently the 'group areas' of Grand Apartheid, the townships, farms, urban areas, suburbs and central business districts, national parks, state lands (some mandated by Queen Victoria!), military preserves, communal tribal lands, Black-owned freehold tenure lands, and many other types of areas and lands. Now there are the phantom boundaries of recently 'absorbed', previously independent or self-governing 'homelands' that cross-cut the new, not yet implemented, boundaries of the nine newly declared provinces whose borders have, again, been decided arbitrarily by committees in Pretoria. All of these boundaries raise questions about who is 'inside' (and inside what) and who is 'outside', who is an enemy and who is a friend, who is a citizen, a 'home-boy', a permanent resident or a refugee, a native, a settler, an African, a South African, and so on. Like the OAU charter that specifies the inviolability of Africa's largely arbitrary boundaries, South Africa today is faced with a problem of boundaries that are both widely recognised as arbitrary and without function, but also considered 'sacred'. Virtually all of them cross-cut others, and divide the country into many different kinds of units without either hierarchical order, such as the Napoleonic rationalisation of the French countryside into *départements* and *préfets*, or a consistent and regular 'tiling' of the terrain with 'counties', as in England. Nor are they consistent with the demarcation of Europe's landmass into 'countries', or the precise jigsaw puzzle of US state boundaries.

There is almost no boundary in South Africa that is not haunted by the ghosts of borders past. A good example is the broad contested region between the Sundays River and the Kei River, still called the Border region in English, with bars, rugby teams and hotels so named. The region was complex from the beginnings of recorded history. White settlement began at the Sundays River in the late 1760s and proceeded with frequent redefinition of the border to the Fish River in 1778 (Bergh and Visagie 1985). Within this Eastern Cape Frontier zone, boundaries shifted continually between Dutch-speaking, German- and English-speaking settlers and transhumant cattle farmers among the Whites, and the Gcaleka, Ngqika, Ndlambe, Gwali, Dange, Ntinde, Gqunukhwebe and others, including the Mfengu, composed largely of factions from the Hlubi, Bhele and Zizi who had been driven into the Xhosa region of the Cape frontier zone in the aftermath of Shaka's consolidation of the Zulu kingdom. Boundaries continued to shift and incorporate more and more of the frontier in the Cape Colony until, in 1856, the remainder of the region was swallowed up by the Colony as a 'humanitarian' measure by the governor Sir George Grey after the collapse of Xhosa independence in the wake of the failed prophesy of Nongqawuse. Nongqawuse, a young girl who saw visions of beautiful cattle and the ancestors of the Xhosa people rising again from the river, ultimately convinced the Xhosa paramount, Sarhili, that his people must burn their crops and kill their cattle in preparation for a great rebirth in which the Whites would be driven from the land.

Great numbers of the Xhosa, as a consequence of this appealing fantasy of power, starved to death, and the remainder, thus weakened, were incorporated easily into the Cape. The frontier shifted by degrees, through failed prophecies, informal agreements and abrogated treaties, but each step left an historical trace of boundaries that can still be perceived today, not so much on the ground as in the beliefs and practices of people who live there. The Cape Frontier is the beginning of the Great Trek and the African National Congress. It is a powerful generator of discourse on boundaries.

The South African boundaries are not mere edges: they are themselves the focus of attention and identity. Today, these aesthetics and metaphysics of boundaries are under pressure in the changing South Africa. Boundaries are being manipulated 'rationally' by governing committees of well-intentioned people, but traditional values, practicalities, practices and habits all attach to the previous and long-standing multiple boundaries and borders. Current political and constitutional debates focus on boundaries – how they are to be created, or destroyed, and how they may attract or repel allegiances – in the New South Africa. Boundaries themselves have a salience that surpasses the merely practical. They are both political problem and political solution. They are entailed by the exercise of power, but undermine power and make possible the escape from it. The politics of boundaries, and the boundaries of the political, and of the political community, all combine in South Africa to create a discourse that goes well beyond the political to the meta-political.

Cross-cutting identities and the integrity of polity

South African identities cross-cut each other in multiple ways and in multiple contexts. There is no fundamental identity that any South African clings to in common with all, or even most other South Africans. South Africans have multiple identities in multiple contexts, depending on factors of expedience, recruitment and mobilisation, and the company one keeps. In many similar multicultural countries or 'hetero-nationalist' states, the same condition applies. In South Africa, however, South Africans have multiple identities in common contexts, and common identities in multiple contexts. A person might be a Zulu, or an Afrikaner, or a Jew in a context of a common political party – perhaps the National Party, the Inkatha

Freedom Party or the ANC. All of the major parties, for instance, are now multiracial (or 'non-racial'), and see this as a powerful source of political strength. A Muslim, or a Coloured, may span many religious, political, social and cultural contexts and thus link them together into a social universe. These identities, then, can be said to be multiple and cross-cutting in that each overlaps a range of contexts, or a common context or institution may contain many identities within it. On the other hand, these differences are also seen as the principal source of conflict in South Africa. The motivation for Apartheid was to prevent – in the mechanical metaphors of the time – 'friction' between the races and nations, since racial difference caused 'friction' between 'race groups', and this caused 'heat', that is, violence. Political commentators and the public today blame political violence on 'tribal', 'cultural' and 'racial' differences.

It is one of the fundamental ironies of South Africa that the endemic conflict that characterised South African history, and that continues today, is the source of both stability and disintegration. This is the compelling insight of Max Gluckman, one of a number of anthropologists such as Monica (Hunter) Wilson and Godfrey Wilson, Isaac Schapera, and Meyer Fortes whose anthropological vision was largely shaped by the South African experience. Indeed, the 'South African experience' has been written directly into the history of anthropology itself. Malinowskian anthropology looked for the order in the whole, the function of each part in making society 'run so smoothly' (Malinowski 1926). In contrast to Malinowski, indeed in direct and conscious critique of the Malinowskian vision, Gluckman argued that conflict was itself a mode of integration. South Africa has puzzled all observers, including both Gluckman and Malinowski, by its apparent surfeit of boundaries across which conflict could erupt. It has always seemed that South Africa was on the brink of political and cultural collapse. For the people of South Africa, the sense that somehow it could never work, yet somehow must work, has been pervasive, a constant sense of suspense. The extremes of this, manifest in apocalyptic visions of bloodbaths, were believed by the political fringe and retailed worldwide by the press. For an anthropologist like Gluckman, it presented a fundamental challenge to the theoretical basis of his discipline, but he argued that it was through conflict itself that societies maintained their coherence, and the rituals of inversions, or courts of law channelled and directed conflict in ways that led to the maintenance of social stability overall. In his essay on the 'social situation in modern Zululand', Gluckman described boundaries as being at the centre of the 'situation', defining interactions between missionaries, Zulu commoners, chiefs and kings, and the various agents of the colonial state. He understood the management of conflict rather than maintenance of order to be at the centre of the political process; ritual played a central role by inverting, masking and mystifying conflict: 'Persons are intricately involved with the same sets of fellows in varied systems of purposive activity. Cross-cutting allegiances and processes of internal development within sets of relation establish ambivalence and conflict within each group. Ritual cloaks the fundamental disharmonies of social structure by affirming major loyalties to be beyond question' (Gluckman 1965: 265).

Thus, Gluckman contended that conflict was itself a form of integration. Certainly, his experience of South Africa must have seemed to confirm this for him, and he generalised it as a principle of political order and stability. But applied grossly to many of the world's conflicts, Gluckman's formulation rings false or naive. In most instances of serious conflict, violence, coercion and other consequences of conflicting aims and claims destroy the polity. Indeed, what seems to have made South Africa unusual is precisely its resilience in the face of long-term endemic conflict. Parties to these conflicts have somehow failed consistently to achieve their ends while southern African society has apparently evolved towards greater and greater political and economic integration while maintaining consistently high levels of violence. Why?

The answer lies in the pervasive 'cross-cutting allegiances' which are both persuasive and permeable, and the ambivalence and ambiguity that they give rise to. Gluckman speaks of the success or failure of conflict itself. The answer to his perplexity, however, lies in the domain of complexities and contradictions of cultural identities more than it does in the success or failure of political processes. South African identities have never polarised sufficiently to permit devastating conflict. They are either too fragmented or too solid to permit the sort of bi-polar conflict that would destroy it. With the exception of the Boer War, in which an external imperial power was directed against the independent Boer states, internal conflict has always stabilised not as a balance of power, but rather as an impotent confusion. This is not a model of conflict as integration, but rather integration through the consistent failure of any single conflict to mobilise two, and only two, sides. It is the very complexity of all possible allegiances, together with the fact that maintaining multiple identities and cross-cutting allegiances has remained possible, that helps to make South Africa uniquely stable and violent at the same time. The factions of Zululand, the gangs of the East Rand, or APLA cadres respond violently to conflicts inherent in the South African social structure, but they never recruit a sufficient following to effect genuine change. This has been true as much for Mkhonto we Sizwe and Apla (the armed wings of the ANC and PAC respectively) as it is for the South African Defence Force, and the mysteriously-sponsored so-called 'third force' of agent provocateurs and violent spoilers.

Countries: failed nationalisms?

On 9 May 1994, Nelson Mandela addressed the people of South Africa on the occasion of the opening of the new Parliament. He did not speak of 'the people' or 'the nation'. As he stood on the balcony of the Cape Town City Hall with the majestic Table Mountain as his backdrop, he pointed to the landscape on which the 'beginning of the fateful convergence' of Black and White had begun. If nations are, as Benedict Anderson (1983) has argued, 'imagined communities', then countries are imagined geometries of landscape. South Africa, the country, is a geometry for conflict and accommodation, but above all it is a landscape. Looking out over the bay to Robben Island on the horizon, he spoke of his own imprisonment and subsequent freedom. With a few gestures to the landscape, he thus summed up over 350 years of history as one might sum up the shape of jelly by pointing to its container.

In the modern theory of nation-states, it is the existence of nations which justifies the existence of states. This was claimed by Hegel, who wished to justify the right of Prussia to conquer the other German-speaking states, and to create a unified master-state. Since the beginning of the nineteenth century, Hegel's theory has become home truth, and is not less strong today. Nevertheless, countries – especially South Africa, and others like it – cannot be justified by the nations they purportedly contain, since they do not contain nations but hetero-glot and hetero-ethnic congeries of peoples. The appeal to nationalism made by the National Party on the basis of an Afrikaner, a Boer or White nation, has failed. The claim to nationalism made by the African National Party is likely to fail as well in so far as, and if, it continues to pursue a 'nationalist' agenda. Countries require other grounds – and Nelson Mandela seems to have grasped this implicitly.

If politics is the art of the possible, then possibilities for legitimacy include the appeal to the earth itself, to the aesthetics of landscape, the native (in the sense 'one born in'), and to autochthony. Failing nations, then, the land is sacred. But land in South Africa is an ambiguous resource, regarded with ambivalence. There is, in fact, very little independent and economically successful agriculture in South Africa, and most of what is there is restricted to a tiny fraction of the country. There is virtually no commercial agriculture in any of the demarcated homelands. The so-called White farms produce the overwhelming bulk of the agricultural product, but most of them are fully mortgaged and could not continue to exist without massive government subsidy. In the face of this, however, it is the land to which appeal is made on all sides. Both White and Black people who call themselves Africans identify with the land, and claim it as their inalienable right. Both appeal to the blood that has been spilt on it, the dead that have been buried in it, the food that can be coaxed from

it and, again and again, the beauty of it. The aesthetic beauty of the
landscape is thus a political resource. The migrant dreams of it while he
is in the mine, and waits to return to his land in the countryside somewhere. In the case of the South African land, aesthetic is power.

City-states and their hinterlands

South Africa is a country stretched as thin as a sheet over three points of
power and wealth. These points, sprawling African conglomerations of
villages, towns, malls, super-highways and dirt tracks, business districts,
industrial parks, townships, hostels, squatter settlements, suburbs, small-
holdings, farms, gardens, parks, public arenas and no-go areas, amount to
city-states, not just cities. They are Johannesburg in the central northern
inland region, Durban on the east coast and Cape Town on the west
coast. There are three or four lesser centres, but for the most part the
three main cities are all that matter, they mark the space around them and
dominate their hinterlands which look to them with desire and anticipation,
loathing and disdain. The violence of the villages far from the vast city
states responds as little to the grand ideas of republic. There is no farm
in the hinterlands that is independent of the capital and administrative
control of the city-state that commands it, and none that can claim to
inspire the idyll of authentic subsistence from the earth and sun, yet there
is none that can claim to be entirely immune to the hope that the earth
will support its children. The city, not by contrast but in sympathy, nurses
its own spasms of violence and hopelessness. The city-state of Johannesburg is, in its turn, like a rural place. Only one train track passes
through it, there are no buses that completely connect it, and people
hurry through it going to other places within and beyond it. Johannesburg
and its hinterlands have names, many names, but no maps. The maps
cannot keep up with the change. These are places where local knowledge
is the best and only guide. Maps show the main roads named for the dead
architects of Apartheid: Malan, Verwoerd, Strydom, and statesmen such
as Jan Smuts and Louis Botha, but the real geography of Johannesburg
lies in the routes to schools, the secluded prayer spots in the rough bush
all over the city, the Portuguese cafés, the sellers of used furniture, fruit
and maize meal. It is like a forest in which only the denizens of the many
eco-zones know its mysterious resources.

Each city-state of South Africa has its own identity and allegiances.
This fact has been implicitly recognised by creating one province, now
named Gauteng (its name in SeSotho means 'place of gold'), out of the
area around Johannesburg. Johannesburg is a young city and one that can
claim autochthonous origin. It sits atop the countless deep galleries of the
mines that brought it into being, like the crown of a giant African termite
mound. Underground, the rock is still dug and pulverised to extract the

gold and other minerals that it contains. The city exists here for no other reason. It is rooted in the hollow chambers created by a century of mining. This in itself is a kind of autochthony.

To think of South Africa as a constellation of city-states avoids the long-ingrained habit of trying to imagine it as a centralised nation on the European model of the 'nation-state' led from Paris, London, Rome or Berlin. The Niccolò Machiavelli of *The Discourses* is more appropriate as an analyst of South Africa than the Karl Marx of *Capital*. The princes and peasants, the palaces and countryside of Machiavelli bear far more resemblance to the intricacies of the real South African country than do the banks and steam-engines of Karl Marx's London, when compared with the city-state and hinterland structure of the South African landscape. Above all, the countryside is emotionally evocative. Autochthony inseparable from the countryside, however, is the politics of chiefs and kings. This dimension of South African politics is probably least understood of all, in part because of the inappropriateness of the models that have been applied. The myths of autochthony seem to be more important here than in most other parts of Africa, where myths of distant origin from Egypt, Ethiopia, Israel, Babylon, ancient West African kingdoms and so on are much more prestigious. Indeed, the autochthons are despised in the rest of Africa.

It is well-known, of course, that the Chief Minister of the Kingdom of the Zulu, and President of the Inkatha Freedom Party, Chief Gatsha Mangosuthu Buthelezi, maintains that he is descended from Shaka, the founder of the Zulu state. His insistence that room be made for permanent recognition of the Zulu monarch, King Goodwill Zwelethini, nearly wrecked the elections. Nelson Mandela, however, is also of chiefly lineage. He renounced the chiefship long ago when he chose the path of the ANC, and it is difficult to say how important this may once have been in securing his original power base among the Xhosa and the educated elites who founded the ANC and who were then its members. It is of little significance now, except that it links him, perhaps ambiguously, to one of the most powerful sources of legitimisation in South Africa.

The chiefs and the so-called traditional authorities in South Africa are ambiguous. Indeed, the 'traditional law' of chiefs and kings has been defined by both the formal state bureaucracy and by the followers of the chiefs as being outside politics. Indeed, the power of traditional authorities and the power of politics seem incommensurable. For many, especially rural South Africans, the authority of the city-states, and the authority of the chiefs are parallel and different. They may function, relative to each other, as points of external reference, as alternative or ultimate courts of appeal. In any case, they offer the individual an escape or alternative recourse: the chief may defend one from the state bureaucracy, while the apparatuses of the bureaucratic state may also act as an escape from 'tradition' and the chief where this is necessary; for instance, in cases of witchcraft accusation, or where Christians may wish to avoid circumcision. The bureaucratic institutions of the city-states and the chiefs are as similar and as dissimilar as the games of draughts (American 'checkers') and chess. Despite the apparent similarity of the games, draughts can not be played with chessmen, nor can chess be played with draughts pieces. In the first case, draughts pieces are not sufficiently differentiated to carry the semantic distinction of chess; on the other hand, the shapes of chessmen make it mechanically impossible to play draughts because they cannot be stacked. The two games are not merely incompatible, but are incommensurable; it is not just a difference of rules, but a difference of fundamental properties. Similarly, chiefs can not be integrated into the politics of Parliament because of the different grounds on which their authority rests. Chiefs still control access to land and control the initiation schools and 'tradition'. Thus any appeal to an African tradition and to autochthony depends upon the existence of chiefs. Any real practice of power in the modern sphere of parliamentary politics, however, must contradict and undermine the power of chiefs. They stand at the inter-section of practical logic of administration, and the meaningfulness and legitimacy of the African identity and origin.

Chief Minister Buthelezi's attempt to negotiate a place for King Good-will Zwelethini in the domain of politics was disruptive and potentially fatal. It was a kind of resistance-politics brinkmanship of holding out to the last possible moment. But more than this, it was a brinkmanship game on the boundary between autochthony and bureaucracy. The king could not be part of parliamentary politics without undermining the nature and basis of his authority, but could not remain entirely outside it without disrupting the legitimacy of the entire system, especially for the large number of Zulu royalists. The compromise that was reached, however, leaves room for many more 'kings' and traditional chiefs to emerge and play an increasingly larger, perhaps parallel role, within the broader field of social power in South Africa.

'Politics' is still not seen as a universal contest in which all possible forms of power are disposed. Rather, 'politics' is a restricted domain of the exercise of particular forms of power for most South Africans. Witches, chiefs, kings, ancestors, God, prophets and doctors all are held to exercise other, different powers. To carry the weight of 'politics', and to bring the legitimacy of the genuine Africanness of its exercise, the chiefs have remained outside politics. Recognising this, Smuts's remark that Africans were not ready for politics rather missed the nature of this dual politics, or rather the differentiation of the polity into the modern and traditional, for the chiefs, as autochthonous authority, are similarly united in their antipathy to 'politics'.

From the view of the Afrikaners, especially those represented by the secessionist AWB and Volksfront, the land is theirs by another logic, the logic of production and utility. It is none the less a claim to the land, not just as resource but as mythical origin and primordial right. In this light, it is easy to understand that surprising alliance between the 'traditional' politics of both the 'White' right-wing and the Zulu chief minister. Both necessarily resorted to the identity-giving power of the land, and the landscape, and appealed in their different ways to a pure Africanness.

Politics and meta-politics

The key to South African politics, then, is that it is not just politics at all. All politics, they say, is local politics. This is true where politics concerns itself with the legitimate exercise of power and with control over the distribution of scarce resources, or over the behaviour of the members of the polity. This is what we usually mean by normal politics. As such, all normal politics is, from the outside, essentially boring. By contrast, South African politics is not boring. This is because it is not merely local. In fact, it is a politics about politics, a meta-politics. South African politics has constantly attempted to explicate and examine the grounds of its very being. This is a politics which has not been able to take for granted the nature or number of its primary actors. It is a politics that seeks not merely to distribute power, or to acquire or maintain power, but to define the nature of power itself. Many different political visions contend with one another in the political arena; even the limits and nature of the arena itself are questioned and tested. A universal politics in which all persons are the primary units has only just been achieved, this late in the twentieth century.

The transition to 'transition' from apocalypse

When Captain James Cook came to South Africa on his way to his fatal impact with the Hawaiians, he noted the constant tension that seemed to exist between the 'races', the English and Boers, the White and the Hottentots. He gave the colony just twenty years before, he thought, it would end in bloody violence. At the end of the 1980s it seemed that Captain Cook had been off by a precise factor of ten; that is, it had taken 200 years to dissolve into a bloodbath, not the twenty that he had then predicted. Now, it seems he must have been just plain wrong.

For most of its existence, the sense of the end of history, the coming of bloody and final conflict, has characterised South Africa's view of its own history. It is still the central element of the political vision of the many in the White right-wing, and of some Black ultra-nationalists of the PAC and its allies. It is a vision of a 'rolling apocalypse' in which the predicted end is only just put off by another war, another proclamation, another bomb, by segregation, by Apartheid, by the end of Apartheid, by 'one settler, one bullet', and now by elections. Everyone now feels that South Africa is in 'transition'. But South Africa is not simply in 'transition' to a final state, or to some other 'end of history'. To be successful, it must remain in a sort of permanent transition. Like Trotsky's idea of a 'permanent revolution', South Africa seems likely to remain in permanent transition, just as it once seemed to exist perpetually just ahead of apocalypse. It is important to maintain this sense of transition since there can be no end to history in South Africa that is not also apocalyptic. That much is correct about the baleful visions of the racists of all colours and persuasions. But history does not end. This is a postmodern condition, and the ability and willingness to recognise it is a sign of a new kind of political maturity.

Notes

A version of this paper was first presented at the Second Inter-University Colloquium of the Standing Committee on University Studies of Africa (UK) and the Netherlands African Studies Association for the panel entitled 'Post-colonial South Africa in the Making', convened 13–16 May 1994, at the International Centre for Contemporary Cultural Research in Manchester, UK. In its current revised form, it was presented to the History Workshop entitled 'Democracy: Popular Precedents, Popular Practice, Popular Culture' at the University of the Witwatersrand, 13–15 July 1994.

1. Most other writers in this area would agree that this is a principal feature of postmodernism, for instance: Habermas (1985: 4), Bertens (1995); Tyler (1987: 3); Lee (1994: 12). On the other hand, Smart (1993) emphasises 'shift' and 'qualitative transformation' from the modern, rather than 'opposition'. All agree on some sort of punctuated continuity with the modern, however.

2. Appiah refers explicitly to Max Weber's understanding of rationality here, especially that in 'The Protestant Ethic and the Spirit of Capitalism', translated by Talcott Parsons (London, 1930), p. 13 (Appiah 1991: note 6).

3. Mbembe's formulation, which has been developed in response to post-colonialism in Cameroon, bears a strong resemblance to Max Gluckman's ideas about rituals of rebellion (Mbembe's 'subversive play') and the 'frailty of authority' (Mbembe's 'simulacra of power'). Gluckman developed these concepts to account for his experience and research in South Africa and Zambia from the 1920s to the 1940s (Gluckman 1955; 1963; 1965). It seems to me that these similarities are founded on similar cultural and political developments in these different times and places. Early in this century in southern Africa, and especially in South Africa, the withdrawal of British imperial power left a bourgeoisie and elite struggling for ways to assert their power and to control a country which looked, for all practical purposes, to be so diverse as to be largely ungovernable. Strictly speaking, South Africa was already 'postcolonial' after 1910. The simulacrum, subversive play and the 'carnivalesque' were well developed in South Africa by the 1930s when Gluckman conducted his research. This is the topic of another paper, in progress.

4. To be fair, of course, Appiah's remarks which provide the introit for this

discussion are directed principally at art and literature, not at social or political organisation. Mbembe's 'Provisional Notes on the Postcolony' is about social and political aspects and is consistent with Appiah's understandings (Mbembe 1992; see also Bayart 1993).

5. Though the necessity and passion for healing the body-politic after war that exists in Zimbabwe, for instance, does not exist in South Africa (Ranger 1992: 74).

6. Provided, of course, we do not commit the facile and tempting but racialist confusion of 'colonial' with 'White', especially 'White in Africa'. I use 'colonial' here in the rather stricter sense of external government control of most aspects of administration, politics and economy. It was as much a part of the Apartheid ideology to pretend that all White South Africans were 'European' and somehow of another external order – that is, 'colonial' – as it was to pretend that Black South Africans were not part of the same complex polity. These views constitute two sides of the same Apartheid ideology, and both are also false.

7. *The Star* 26, 28 and 31 July 1995.

8. The idea for this was certainly not mine! These programmes are organised quickly and without serious thought by producers in the studios. They represent a kind of unfiltered but televised conversation, much as one might have 'in the field'. Dawid Kruyper, who sat virtually nude in Cape Town, is a farm worker in the Western Cape who has 'discovered' his Bushman identity, and has sought to reclaim it by adopting the dress he has seen in pictures and films of Bushmen in Botswana, Namibia and Angola. His only language is Afrikaans. The programme, 'Two Way', was shown in South Africa on NNTV on Sunday 30 July 1995.

9. See, for instance, Foucault on this: 'Once knowledge can be analysed in terms of region, domain, implantation, displacement, transposition, one is able to capture the process by which knowledge functions as a form of power ... There is an administration of knowledge, a politics of knowledge ... which, if one tries to transcribe them, lead one to consider forms of domination designated by such notions as field, region, territory' (Foucault 1980: 69).

10. This motto is the Afrikaans version of the motto of the old Suidafrikaansche Republiek, known as the Transvaal, the Boer republic founded in 1854 and eventually conquered by the British in 1902. Under the old republic, the Dutch spelling was used: *eendracht maakt macht.*

11. I shall use this distinction throughout the remainder of this discussion. The significance of this distinction, however, was strongly brought home to me during discussion of the original version of this paper at the SCUSA colloquium conference. In his report on it for *Anthropology Today*, J. Hutnyk notes my 'contentious ... distinction between a historically past "capital A" apartheid [sic] and the continued legacy of "small a" apartheid [that] drew the suggestion that the problem was one of a rhetorical democracy in a context of unchanged economic, social and psychological exploitation and inequality' (Hutnyk 1994: 25). Anyone currently living in South Africa, however, as opposed to those who examine it from without, would accept that the end of Apartheid is empirically real (legal, economic, structural) and that change has been pervasive.

12. *The Star*, 26 July 1995.

13. Even the number of 'ethnic groups' is problematic here. Some of these groups, like the AmaBhaca, are often considered to be part of the larger Xhosa category, while the Pedi are classified as 'Sotho'. 'IFP' is virtually identical to 'Zulu' here, but this category or 'tribe' is itself problematic.

14. Akhil Gupta, for instance, argues (1995) that instead of treating the 'local'

as an unproblematic and coherent spatial unit, we must pay attention to the 'multiply-mediated' contexts through which the state comes to be 'constructed'. Although he writes from the context of northern India, the question is nowhere more apposite than today's South Africa. Gupta and Ferguson (1992), Appadurai (1991), and Thornton (1988) make similar points.

References

Anderson, Benedict. 1983. *Imagined Communities: Reflections on the Origins and Spread of Nationalism.* London: Verso.

Appadurai, Arjun. 1991. 'Global Ethnoscapes: Notes and Queries for a Trans-national Anthropology', in Richard G. Fox (ed.), *Recapturing Anthropology: Working in the Present,* Santa Fe, NM: School of American Research.

Appiah, Kwame Anthony. 1991. 'Is the Post- in Postmodernism the Post- in Postcolonial', *Critical Inquiry* 17 (Winter): 336–57.

Bayart, Jean-François. 1993. *The State in Africa: The Politics of the Belly.* London: Longman. (First published as 'L'état en Afrique: La politique du ventre', Paris: Fayard, 1989.)

Benjamin, Walter. 1969. 'Theses on the Philosophy of History', in his *Illuminations.* Translated by H. Zohn. New York: Schocken.

Bergh, J. S. and Visagie, J. C. 1985. *The Eastern Cape Frontier Zone, 1660–1980: A Cartographic Guide for Historical Research.* Durban: Butterworths.

Bertens, Hans. 1995. *The Idea of the Postmodern: A History.* London: Routledge.

Christopher, A. J. 1994. *The Atlas of Apartheid.* Johannesburg: Witwatersrand University Press.

Ferguson, James. 1990. *The Anti-Politics Machine: 'Development', Depoliticization, and Bureaucratic Power in Lesotho.* Cambridge: Cambridge University Press.

Foucault, Michel. 1980. *Power/Knowledge. Selected Interviews and Other Writings, 1972–1977.* Edited by Colin Gordon. New York: Harvester Press.

Gluckman, Max. 1955. *Custom and Conflict in Africa.* Oxford: Blackwell.

— 1963. *Order and Rebellion in Tribal Africa.* London: Cohen and West.

— 1965. *Politics, Law and Ritual in Tribal Society.* Chicago: Aldine.

Gupta, Akhil. 1995. 'Blurred Boundaries: the Discourse of Corruption, the Culture of Politics, and the Imagined State', *American Ethnologist* 22 (2): 375–402.

Gupta, Akhil and Ferguson, James. 1992. 'Beyond "Culture": Space, Identity and the Politics of Difference', *Cultural Anthropology* 7 (1): 6–23.

Habermas, Jurgen. 1985. 'Modernity – an Incomplete Project', in Hal Foster (ed.), *Post-Modern Culture.* London: Pluto. (First published in English as 'Modernity versus postmodernity', *New German Critique* 22 [Winter, 1981].)

Hutynk, John. 1994. 'African Research Futures: Postcolonialism and Identity', *Anthropology Today* 10 (4): 24–5.

Lee, Raymond L. M. 1994. 'Trend Report: Modernisation, Postmodernism and the Third World', *Current Sociology* 42 (2): 1–66.

Lukacs, John. 1994. *The End of the Twentieth Century and the End of the Modern Age.* Tichmore Fields.

Lyotard, Jean François 1984. *The Postmodern Condition: A Report on Knowledge.* Translated by Geoff Bennington and Brian Massumi in *Theory and History of Literature* 10. Minneapolis: University of Minnesota Press.

Malinowski, Bronislaw. 1926. *Crime and Custom in Savage Society*. London: Routledge and Kegan Paul.

Mbembe, Achille. 1992. 'Provisional Notes on the Postcolony', *Africa* 62 (1): 3–37.

Minaar, Anthony de V. 1991. *Conflict and Violence in Natal/KwaZulu: Historical Perspectives*. Pretoria: Human Sciences Research Council.

Ranger, Terence. 1992. 'Afterword: War, Violence and Healing in Zimbabwe', *Journal of Southern African Studies* 18 (3): 698–707.

— 1993. 'The Communal Areas of Zimbabwe', in Thomas J. Bassett and Donald E. Crummey (eds), *Land in African Agrarian Systems*. Madison: University of Wisconsin Press.

Smart, Barry. 1993. *Postmodernity*. Key Ideas series. London: Routledge.

Thornton, Robert. 1988. 'Culture', in Emile Boonzaier and John Sharp (eds), *South African Keywords: Uses and Abuses of Political Concepts*. Cape Town: David Philip.

— 1990. 'The Shooting at Uitenhage, South Africa, 1985', *American Ethnologist* 17 (2): 217–36.

Tyler, Stephen. 1987. *The Unspeakable: Discourse, Dialogue and Rhetoric in the Postmodern World*. Madison: University of Wisconsin Press.

PART TWO

Identity degradation, moral knowledge and deconstruction

CHAPTER 6

'Producing' respect: the 'proper woman' in postcolonial Kampala

Jessica A. Ogden

The urban experience for Ugandan women was framed by an early and persistent stigmatisation. Their participation in town life, indeed their very presence in town, was denigrated. Against that background arose a struggle for respectability through economic and symbolic means, through hard work and marriage. The forms this struggle has taken differed from the colonial to the postcolonial periods, and in the different socio-economic strata that comprise the city. My concern here is primarily with ordinary women living in a densely settled, lower-income neighbourhood of post-colonial Kampala; women who have little formal education, few specialised skills, and generally no access to waged employment. Many came to town following the failure of rural marriages. They came to forge new futures for themselves, and they came to take their places, often permanently, as immigrants, not mere sojourners.[1] This chapter explores the continuities and discontinuities in the social constructions of womanhood in the shift from the colonial to the postcolonial eras; how the women themselves have renegotiated the devaluation of their persons in those constructions. Specifically, it is shown that, as participants in postcolonial Kampala, women actively generate the means and meanings by which they can obtain respect and respectability, and be identified as Proper Women.

From the earliest days of colonialism, women's entry into Africa's emerging towns and cities was accompanied by a particular kind of moral discourse: a combination of the strict patriarchal/patrilineal social organ-isation of the rural areas, and the Victorian, middle-class, Christian morality introduced by the colonial project (see Jeater 1993). Women's participation was evaluated in distinctly sexual terms, their considerable economic and political contributions, ably recounted by White (1990) among others, neither recognised nor appreciated. In fact, the focus on the sexuality of African urban women, and their presumed immorality, had a direct impact on the kinds of economic options open to them. In southern Africa for example, such was the anxiety about the power and perversity of urban women's sexuality that they were not considered employable for domestic service by the European settlers (Schmidt 1992: 8; Jeater 1993: 245).

The lack of opportunities for urban women to find work for wages forced them to find means of generating income within the informal economy. The most logical and lucrative niche to exploit was providing sexual services to the African male wage labourers living in town without their wives. White (1990) shows that businesswomen in colonial Nairobi were shrewd, and that their economic activities were central to the functioning of the emergent African urban economy, indeed of the colonial system itself. Thus, despite the fact that they were reviled as immoral and unworthy of respect, the participation of women in the cities was a crucial element in the administration of colonial government.

The repercussions of the moral economy on ordinary women coming to town during the colonial years in search of a better life are not, perhaps, easily assessed. How has this colonial history and its discourse influenced the postcolonial construction of identity for women in Kampala? How have ordinary urban women engaged with and/or renegotiated this semantic field on the way to engendering respect and the moral right of residence in the city? And finally, how is the presence of AIDS influencing these processes? This chapter addresses these three fundamental questions of postcolonial urban life and identity.

The national, the local and the postcolonial

Uganda's postcolonial existence has been riven with civil war and economic plunder. Since independence in 1962, power has changed hands seven times, each time through violent takeover or outright civil war. It was not until 1986, when Yoweri Museveni's National Resistance Army (NRA) finally won its protracted 'bush war', fought since 1980 against Obote's second dominion and then against the Okellos's dictatorship, that relative peace and stability began to make way for economic recovery.

The National Resistance Movement (NRM) government is not without problems or critics. There continue to be bloody insurgencies in the north where a group of former Okello supporters defy efforts at reconciliation. Museveni has been criticised for resisting multipartyism, although he has agreed, in principle, to bow to the will of the people in this matter. The NRM has, however, made it a priority to introduce democracy at every level of decision-making in the country through the development of Resistance Committees,[2] by sanctioning freedom of speech, and by allowing a relatively free press. In 1987–88 the NRM government invited the IMF/ World Bank, albeit with some reluctance, to begin to restructure the economy (Hansen and Twaddle 1991; see Lateef 1991; Ochieng 1991; Mugyenyi 1991, for a discussion of structural readjustment in Uganda).

Thus, after more than two decades of social and economic destruction and outrage, a new government came to power in Uganda, and brought with it renewed hope for peace and a return to economic prosperity. It is not insignificant, however, that in that same period the AIDS pandemic tightened its grip. Despite, or maybe because of this history, the NRM government took the distinctively courageous step of making the presence of AIDS in Uganda known to the outside world. The foreign scientific community was welcomed into Uganda in order to combat the epidemic (see Museveni 1992: 269–78). By 1994, however, HIV seroprevalence among women attending antenatal clinics in Kampala was close to 35 per cent. Thus today urban women, whose sexuality has historically been considered dangerous, have another reason to be feared and reviled. As a result, these women have to cope with yet another threat to their personhood.

In my effort to understand the impacts of HIV/AIDS on the lives of Kampala women, I found that it was important to understand the past and present meanings associated with womanhood and feminine identities, in part by asking about the norms and ideals that circumscribe women's behaviour. Through many conversations, some in group discussions, the notion of the Proper Woman, *omukyala omutufu*, emerged. Although the perceived importance of being a Proper Woman varied, sometimes according to a woman's own circumstances, I found a significant degree of consistency in the definitions offered by individual women of what being *omukyala omutufu* involved in a specific neighbourhood (Ogden 1995).

The neighbourhood of my study, Kifumbira I, is at once representative and also distinct within the slums of Kampala. Kifumbira I is part of Kamwokya II ward, Central Division, located about six kilometres from the city centre. Socio-economically heterogeneous, Kamwokya II is densely populated and includes some of Kampala's poorest, as well as some of its better-off residents. The ward has a thriving localised economy, although its 'industry' is largely unenumerated, and exists almost entirely within Kampala's growing and vibrant informal economy (see Wallman and Baker, forthcoming).

Kifumbira I, which is one of the ten RC1 zones that comprise Kamwokya II, is itself densely populated, ethnically heterogeneous and socio-economically diverse. It is an hour-glass-shaped wedge that extends from one border of Kamwokya into the heart of the commercial area of the ward. Although there are a few relatively affluent families living at the zone's perimeter, the majority of the population live clustered in the densely settled, unplanned 'slum' in the centre of the zone, and it is here that I carried out most of my fieldwork.

Because Kamwokya, like similar suburbs of Kampala, grew up during the long period of insecurity, the area was almost totally unplanned. There are no municipal facilities to speak of – no planned sewerage system (all waste flows in open sewers that cross-cut the area like so many rivers), and only a rudimentary sanitation service. The Catholic Church, which has a strong presence in Kamwokya, recently installed a standing water pipe in each zone.

Housing has also developed haphazardly. In Kifumbira I most of the dwellings have been constructed so that each room houses an independent household. Whole families (and sometimes extended families) may live in a single room which serves as both living and sleeping space for all household members. The dwellings are often poorly constructed – generally mud-bricks with old iron-sheeting roofs – and the interior walls rarely reach the ceiling. Thus, as well as there being little privacy within a household, there is little privacy between households. This situation lends itself to tension and suspicion between neighbours.

The rhythm of everyday life and neighbourhood knowledge   The economic activities of those living in this part of Kifumbira I are diverse. Generally speaking, the residents are not employed within the formal sector. The men are largely casual labourers and hawkers working in the city centre. They are engaged at every level of the informal economy, and their considerable skill at manipulating whatever resources may be at their disposal enables them to make ends meet. Women here also generate family income in a great variety of ways, but most look for ways to do so from home. The women I worked with in Kifumbira I sold charcoal and tomatoes and other daily necessities from outside their houses; they sold locally-brewed alcohol by the glass from home; they made mats and other handicrafts; they cooked and sold fried snacks such as *sambusas* and *chapati*. Others, unable to earn from home, tried to find evening work such as selling cooked food at the local candlelight market or selling sweet bananas and milk in the evening along the road. The consensus among the women was that it was important that they bring in some money, but it was equally important that they be able to attend to chores in the home and to look after the small children. Domestic help was an option for only a very few women in Kifumbira I.

Work is not organised co-operatively. Neighbours may help each other, however, in a number of ways. Young children wander freely among neighbouring households, and are seen as the collective responsibility of an area. If a mother has to go on some nearby errand, she may – if she is on good terms with her neighbours – just go knowing that the children will be looked after. Similarly, a woman vending from her house who is on good terms with her neighbours can trust that if she is away when a customer comes, her neighbour will sell on her behalf and give her the money later.

Against that background emerges a pattern of daily life for the women of Kifumbira I. During the day most men are away, either working, looking for work, schooling or socialising and trying to think up new and better ways to support their families. Some women go early to Kalerwe market to get cheap 'morning' prices, greeting and chatting with friends along the way. The bulk of the day for the women, though, is spent outside in the areas around their homes. It is here that they peel piles of potatoes and plantains and cook on small charcoal fires; pound ground-nuts; wash clothes and dishes; sell their wares; bathe, feed, enjoy and discipline their children; sew, knit, weave and crochet for profit or relaxation; and socialise with their neighbours. There are few times during the day when a woman will be inside her hot and stuffy house: when cleaning the house itself; when she and/or her children are eating; when she is resting or bathing; and if a special guest comes for a visit that requires either decorum or privacy.

Thus life for the women of Kifumbira I is both 'domestic' and intensively public. Networks are close-knit, and mobility is generally restricted to areas within the zone. Personal finances are strained, and families are often *in extremis*. The scrutiny under which these women live out their days is intense: what an individual does, when, with whom and in what manner is general neighbourhood knowledge. It is not surprising, therefore, that there are strong ideas about what constitutes a good or a bad neighbour, a good or a bad woman, and that most people work hard to make their behaviour and the ideals appear to match. What I call the Proper Woman covers a whole constellation of these norms and values. The concept is a normative one derived from the Luganda phrase, *omukyala omutufu*. This concept has a particular significance in everyday postcolonial practice within the changing moral economy of the neighbourhood.

This evidence advances arguments originally raised by analysts of colonial urban Africa, notably the members of the Rhodes–Livingstone Institute, later the Manchester School at the University of Manchester (see Hannerz 1980; Werbner 1990), and members of the East African Institute for Social Research in the 1950s and early 1960s (Parkin 1990); and on the link to Kamwokya II research, Wallman (ed.) (1996) and Ogden (1995). Colonial research highlighted the importance in African urban contexts of the neighbourhood as a locus of sociality, particularly for women, but through them for the community generally (e.g. Southall 1961b: 224). Many of the networks formed were close-knit and dense (Mitchell 1966; 1969; Boswell 1969; Southall 1961a; 1961b). Normative control was high, and was effected at least in part through gossip and the formation of 'gossip sets' (Gluckman 1963; Epstein 1969a; 1969b; Paine 1967). It was in these women-centred neighbourhood groupings that important norms and values were generated and negotiated. In postcolonial Kampala, it is in the neighbourhood that the notion of the Proper Woman – as a normative framework for the demeanour and respectability of resident women – derives its greatest power and significance (cf. Bohman 1984 for similar in urban Colombia).

Men, women and an emergent moral economy in the city: colonial discourse

Like other cities in colonial Africa, Kampala drew migrant labour from the rural hinterland, and these men lived and worked side by side with local Baganda. Most of the non-Baganda men came as temporary wage labourers and so did not expect to stay in Kampala. Low wages and stringent housing codes discouraged workers from bringing their wives and families to join them.

Women also came to Kampala. Like the men, they came to town in search of their fortune, to make a new start. The terms of their entry into the city were different from the men's, however, and they did not come to join a waged workforce. They came instead mainly to fill economic and social niches opened by the lack of wives, and many regarded themselves as immigrants rather than short-term migrants (see Southall 1961a; Southall and Gutkind 1957). The reasons women made this migration were probably as various as the women themselves, but certain patterns are foregrounded in the colonial literature. A common theme is of escape and the 'runaway' woman (cf. Schmidt 1992). Many migrated to Kampala when a failed rural marriage made life in the village difficult or impossible. City life represented an alternative to staying in an unhappy marriage, marrying into a polygamous situation or remaining unmarried and largely unappreciated in the natal home (Southall and Gutkind 1957; Obbo 1980; Swantz 1985; Halpenny 1975).

Women, having migrated to Kampala by themselves, were clearly not in a position to rely on male support or on the support of their family (Rakodi 1991), and so were compelled to make the city work for them economically. The city, with its growing population of mostly unaccompanied male migrant labourers in need of wifely services, complied. Migrant women found – and indeed generated – occupational niches that they could fill using skills carried with them from the rural areas, such as brewing various types of local alcohol and selling cooked food. Despite the range of economic niches filled by these single migrant women, however, the dominant stereotypes assumed that most of them supported themselves through some manner of commercial sex work (Southall and Gutkind 1957; Obbo 1980).

The stereotype representing town women as prostitutes was eventually written into policy. In the 1950s, single women in Kampala were criminalised through the Vagrancy Acts and the Prevention of Prostitution Acts (Obbo 1975). This law defined as a prostitute 'any woman who habitually gives her body indiscriminately for profit or gain, or who persistently indulges in promiscuous intercourse with men though she derives no gain or profit thereby' (Obbo 1975: 290).

Almost any woman could be guilty of prostitution by this definition, and the City Council and Kibuga officials (African appointees) periodically arrested single women who were found in low-income areas of the city (Obbo 1980; and see also, on a similar control in colonial Harare, Schmidt 1992: 120; and in Gwelo, Jeater 1993). Ultimately, however, the laws were difficult to enforce, and failed to deter the continuing flow of women into the growing conurbation. In fact, as early as 1953–57, Southall and Gutkind found that in one suburb women made up nearly 40 per cent of the population. By the early 1960s, the sex ratio in Kampala had more or less evened out (Obbo 1980). The trend has now gone a stage further. A recent analysis of the 1991 census shows that in some age groups women now significantly outnumber men (Pons and Wallman, forthcoming).

The abundant colonial accounts of Kampala are, to a considerable extent, directed by a colonial agenda on 'adjustment' and 'adaptation'. The pressing question, constantly raised, was: How were Africans adjusting to urban life? A dominant concern was the instability of urban marriages (Southall and Gutkind 1957; Halpenny 1972; Mandeville 1975; Parkin 1976; and Obbo 1980; 1987). Explanations offered by colonial-era anthropologists for the instability and lack of conventionality of urban unions included sex-ratio differentials; ethnic mixing; high numbers of single women uninterested in marriage; relatively high numbers of 'barren', divorced and economically independent women (none of whom was considered an ideal marriage partner); the relative weakness of corporate kin groups; and the fact that many women and men migrating to towns wanted to escape tradition and custom (e.g. Southall and Gutkind 1957; Parkin 1976; Mandeville 1975; Obbo 1980; White 1990).

Because of the complexity and variety of conjugal relationships observed by the colonial ethnographers, most made some attempt at classification, ranging from Parkin's distinction between permanent and temporary unions (1976)[3] to Mandeville's contrast between 'marriage' and 'free marriage' (1975). Southall and Gutkind (1957) broadly describe three types of 'temporary' sexual unions ('prostitution', 'lover relationships' and 'free marriage') and two recognised forms of marriage (customary and Christian). Unions starting out as temporary often became 'permanent' at a later time, just as some customary marriages became Christian. In some cases men and women would move in together as a means of 'testing the relationship out' before making a longer-term commitment. A further pattern was widely observed, though not adequately explained: the everyday practice of men and women, looking for the stability, respectability and prestige which a permanent conjugal union alone provides.

Compared with the wealth of rural conventions and customs, changing though these were, the rules regulating sexual relations between men and women in town were relatively undefined, more negotiable, more informal, less explicitly formulated or collectively crystallised. Although by no means all urban conjugal arrangements were informal, sexual relationships

between women and men were significantly influenced by the ambiguity
and complexity of the city, and were subject to experimentation and
innovation. The conditions of the city (and of the quickly changing rural
hinterlands, cf. White 1990 and Schmidt 1992), lent a particular kind of
fluidity to conjugality that perplexed colonial observers, and, no doubt,
some members of the local population also. The very lack of formality
and specificity in conjugal arrangements must have contributed to the
stereotyping of urban women as 'prostitutes'.

A simple dichotomy, much in need of deconstruction, has been used
to discuss the contested placement of women within the moral economy
of the town. In this dichotomy women are classified as either 'independent'
or 'dependent', a distinction which is misleading because it does not
adequately account for the great variation in living styles adopted by urban
women. Although it is an over-simplification, this distinction has nevertheless become too prominent a part of the sociology of Kampala to be
ignored or even dismissed lightly. The dichotomy also importantly reflects
one significant difference between Baganda and non-Baganda women in
Kampala: the difference in their rights to hold land, a difference important
for the emergence of a small class of typically older, childless Baganda
women known as *banakyeyombekedde*. Under a special agreement dating
from the establishment of Uganda as a protectorate, Baganda women
secured the legal capacity to inherit, purchase and own freehold land in
their own right. This gave Baganda women a choice not shared by other
women in the region: they could either do what their families would
expect of them and get married, or they could remain single and become
economically independent land-owners (Obbo 1980: 44). In the Uganda
context, this economic independence was often accompanied by sexual
freedom (Halpenny 1975; Obbo 1980), and few *banakyeyombekedde* ever
married (or remarried) formally (Mandeville 1975).

Despite the range of income-generating activities women engaged in,
the importance of sex work for the economic independence of Kampala
women looms large in colonial studies. Three categories of sex worker are
described in that literature: 'true prostitute', *malaaya* and 'good-time girl'.
'True prostitutes' were women for whom sex was a business. They charged
a pre-set fee to men who could be total strangers. According to Halpenny
(1975), 'true prostitutes' were those women whose 'total income [was]
dependent on sexual relations with innumerable men in rapid succession ...
charging a flat fee per occasion' (ibid.: 283). These women might have saved
their money, bought some property and eventually retired as *banakyeyombekedde*. By contrast, *bamalaaya* were women who did not consider themselves to be 'prostitutes', but who typically had a number of sexual partners
who would give them food, money or other gifts for their subsistence. In
the literature they were regarded as commercial sex workers despite the fact
that they apparently never demanded money in exchange for their services.[4]

Thirdly, the literature describes a 'mixed' form of prostitution, 'a convenient complement to beer selling, mat making, plantain and charcoal selling or sewing', practised by women entrepreneurs, who generally refused to set a fee for sex and other services, 'simply waiting to receive presents and indicating clearly whether they [were] adequate enough' (Southall and Gutkind 1957: 86). For the man, the arrangement was an opportunity for a trial union, without having to make a long-term commitment to a wife. For the woman, the man with whom she lived was her 'husband' for the duration of her residence. 'Good-time girls' were young women who spent time in local bars exchanging sex for beer and companionship (Southall and Gutkind 1957). It may be that these young women were labelled *bamalaaya* by some, or even prostitutes by others.

The flexibility of these categories is significant. They could be combined with other forms of generating income, or practised during some periods and not during others, or given up altogether. This ambiguity was recognised by the ethnographers. Southall and Gutkind, for example, acknowledge that in one parish (Mulago), all single, unemployed women were labelled prostitutes, despite the fact that there were only four self-proclaimed prostitutes living there at the time. 'Town women, it is felt, are bad women, and they are to be used for pleasure but not to be married. All women who work for wages tend to be put in this category. The good woman, according to this set of ideas, is the one who stays at home in her husband's room, refuses to speak to strangers and remains unprofitably idle' (Southall and Gutkind 1957: 77).

These negative stereotypes of urban women persist in postcolonial discourse. Obbo, for example, was told that 'urban migration is bad for women because it corrupts their virtue, leads to marital instability, and erodes traditional norms' (Obbo 1980: 27–8). The reason urban women were held in contempt, Obbo argues, is that not only had they broken away from and altered the system of male control over their lives; they had transgressed against a more fundamental virtue: that aspect of gender ideology that places the onus of the community's moral virtue on women (ibid.).

More recent analysts may have had some success in shaking off this postcolonial heritage. The reality for many single women in Kampala today, as in other postcolonial Third World cities, is that multiple partner strategies have become an economic necessity. As Schoepf et al. (1988) point out, the deepening economic crisis of African countries has meant that women may rely more on multiple partner relationships than they did in the past (see also Schneider 1989; Larson 1989). This presents new kinds of terminological difficulties, a point that has become increasingly apparent in the work of AIDS researchers. The effort to describe the complexity and variety of non-monogamous sexual relationships in less stigmatising and non-moralistic ways has led to the generation of new terms, such as 'commercial sex worker', 'multiple partner strategies', and 'lateral linkages' (see, e.g., Overall 1992).

The colonial legacy is still very much apparent in daily conversation in Kamwokya. The old stereotypes of urban women as sexually dangerous, and the dominant stereotypes of urban women as immoral and not worthy of respect, continue and have an important effect on normative and ideal constructions of femininity and womanhood. Although laws instituted during Amin's regime banning women from wearing mini-skirts, wigs and trousers have long since been revoked, there continues to be active public debate about the appropriate deportment of urban women. During my fieldwork, this postcolonial moral discourse was most vividly evoked in local press accounts of mini-skirted or otherwise 'scantily clad' women being physically or verbally harassed in the streets of the city.

The women I spoke to in Kifumbira had this to say on the subject:

— A woman should not put on expensive (i.e. modern) clothes, because the way one dresses can make her be respected. When a housewife puts on mini-dresses, people will not respect her.
— At times you can meet a woman and you see that the way she dresses does not fit her age. Even you, the person who has met her, feel ashamed ... She even finds it difficult to walk in such a dress because she cannot make strides.
— I think the type of dresses that shame us are those ones which have a slit.
— Doesn't such a woman have a daughter? Why doesn't she take the skirt to a tailor to have [the slit] blocked? Now, if you have a daughter and you put on a slit, she will also. How will the public differentiate between you, the mother, and your daughter?
— The way one dresses shows what she is. A woman should put on a dress or skirt which is not tight, and should not put on short dresses which stop at the knee, making her look like a stick!

This discourse on the deportment and morality of urban women is also reflected in current usages of commercial sex worker terminology and categorisation. Although one no longer hears about the 'true prostitute' or the 'good-time girl' as such, there are clearly distinctions between the professional who makes her living by frequenting the large downtown hotels exchanging sex for money, and the otherwise ordinary woman who may be compelled, for any variety of reasons, to have multiple sexual partners, either serially or concurrently, from whom she receives gifts, food and/or money in exchange for sex, household chores and companionship. Depending on her relationship with her neighbours and general deportment, *any* single woman living alone may be referred to as *malaaya* by other women.

Thus the semantic context in which Kampala women must define themselves today is the product of a particular colonial history, and of postcolonial social and economic developments. The (negative) social identity imputed to the colonial era women immigrants has had a lasting impact on local stereotypes. In postcolonial Kampala these stereotypes provide the semantic basis for the particular set of norms and ideals that residents have come to know as *omukyala omutufu*, the Proper Woman.

Relationships between women and men: love, sex and marriage *Omukyala omutufu*, the Luganda phrase for the 'Proper Woman', is literally *mukyala*, meaning wife, or married woman, and *mutufu*, the proper/right/correct one. In brief, 'the proper housewife'.

Other terms within the same semantic field are used in Kifumbira I to differentiate between types of sexual relationships roughly glossed as 'friend' (*mukwano*), 'lover'/'sweetheart' (*muganzi*) and 'husband' (*muame*). In that order is an understood spectrum from the most casual, tentative, exploratory and least committed, to the opposite extreme of a committed, long-term and ostensibly monogamous relationship. *Mukwano* is ambiguous when used for a sexual relationship; it is simply the Luganda word for 'friend', and it is usually young people who have these relationships. In most cases a woman will date her *mukwano*, and he will give her gifts and enjoy 'good times' with her (maybe in exchange for sex), but he will not be seen as a potential 'husband'. *Muganzi*, on the other hand, implies a greater commitment to the relationship, although that commitment is not always the same on both sides. A woman does not usually live with her *muganzi*, but she may aspire to do so and (so) may have his children.

When a relationship becomes more established, and both partners are willing to make a longer-term commitment, they usually start to live together. A man who has made such a commitment to a woman and demonstrates a willingness to 'look after' her (financially and emotionally) is *muame*. Ideally, the man should be formally introduced to the woman's family and a series of gifts and feasts should be made on both sides to seal the union. Most young couples do not have the financial means this requires, however, and many people live together as husband and wife for years before a formal introduction is made. One key informant explained that although her husband has not been 'introduced', he is known to her family, is recognised as the father of their children, and often accompanies her to the village for weddings and funerals. Thus this couple, like many others, are recognised as husband and wife by the community in which they live as well as by their extended family, despite the lack of ritual and legal formalities.[5]

The key to urban 'marriage' today is, therefore, a demonstrated commitment to a long-term, permanent relationship.[6] On the wife's part this implies sexual fidelity. Although a 'husband' may tacitly be expected to have casual sexual liaisons outside marriage, it is important to note that the ideal of male sexual fidelity has gained currency in recent years due to AIDS.[7] 'Marriage' gives a woman respectability because a married woman is necessarily constrained in her behaviour. Of a single woman living alone, it is often said that 'what she likes is what she does' (*kyayagara kyeyekolera*). Her behaviour is thought to be unpredictable and probably immoral, and is assumed to include trying to steal other women's husbands.

Postcolonial analysis of sexual relationships in urban Uganda must accept as valid the integrity of this dynamic semantic field. Bledsoe remarks upon the futility of trying to pigeonhole phenomena that are inherently ambiguous and fluid, and argues cogently that 'we need to abandon the search for categorical precision and confront squarely the fact of ambiguous conjugal unions' (Bledsoe 1990: 121). Bledsoe argues further that conjugal relationships are in fact becoming *more* fluid in the postcolonial era as women increasingly depend on childbearing as a means for pressing economic claims on their partners; a process through which 'marriage becomes almost incidental to a woman's reproductive career' (ibid.: 119). Marriage is not, however, incidental to the construction of a woman's identity. On the contrary, it is central to it, and the 'fluidity' or ambiguity of this status enables a woman to maximise her chances for obtaining respect and respectability, and for becoming a Proper Woman in the eyes of her community.

'Producing': the moral identity of mothering and childbearing   Childbearing, or 'producing', a central feature of a secure marriage, is an important element in constructions of womanhood. Yet 'producing' is not appropriate in all situations, and a pregnancy may threaten, rather than confirm, self and future. The situations of inappropriate motherhood are becoming, with the incidence of AIDS, increasingly frequent; and so too are contradictions of female identity becoming more acute. The gravity of motherhood is most apparent in three central arenas of a woman's existential life. These are: the construction of the self as 'woman' on the basis of motherhood; the personal security derived through childbearing; and the prestige, social esteem and respect which motherhood confers upon a woman whose children are born within 'marriage'.

There is a vast Luganda terminology for matters relating to childbearing and associated dysfunctions, and this plethora of linguistic detail in itself indicates the social importance of procreation. The term denoting a barren woman – that is, a woman who has never conceived – is *omukazi omugumba* or, simply, *mugumba*. Of a woman who 'produces slowly', or has only a few children spaced many years apart, it may be said that *ekizaala gumba*, she produces like a barren person. If a woman has *ever* conceived – even if only once, and even if the child subsequently died (before or after birth) – she is *kufisa*. *Kufisa* (sub-fertility or secondary infertility) derives either from syphilis or from a failure to conduct the proper rituals at a girl's first menstruation. Although the woman referred to as *kufisa* or *ekizaala gumba* has no or few living children, she has at least experienced pregnancy, and so 'knows how it feels to be a woman', and so will not be referred to as *mugumba*.

Much is said about 'bad' childbearing. A woman who has many closely spaced pregnancies may be told *oyosera ng'embwa*, or 'you produce like a dog'. Nevertheless, it is said that *nzaala mbi ekira obugumba*, or 'bad pro-creation is better than barrenness'. One woman said that it is even better, from the point of view of womanhood, to give birth to sick or malformed children than to 'produce nothing at all'. A woman in such a situation may be pitied, but it is nevertheless considered preferable to being *mugumba*, for at least she 'knows what it is like to produce'. She has received 'the gift of motherhood that a barren woman can never have'. To be a woman one has to have 'produced'.[8]

Thus the primary importance of childbearing is its place as a culturally construed essence of womanhood, as a central feature in the construction of female selves. As one woman put it: 'even the title is enough. The title *Mama* makes a woman so happy. Even a man feels so happy to be called *Taata* [Father]. That happiness comes from all the good things a child does for its parents.'

The second aspect for discussion is the security for the future that children should ensure. For women this security is two-fold. On the one hand, they hope and expect that their children will take care of them in their old age. As one informant put it: 'a woman who does not produce children will not have the benefit of assistance in her old age when she can no longer support herself'.

Childbearing also provides security of a different order by stabilising a marriage and, more significantly, by ensuring some measure of in-heritance should the child's father die. In relation to the first point, many women fear that if they do not produce children for their lover, they do not have much of a chance of becoming his wife. As one woman remarked: 'You produce also to sustain the existence of the clan. When a woman does not produce, the husband's clan cannot grow. You may be dropped for that one who can contribute.'

Similarly, if a woman bears only children of one sex, she may fear that her husband will send her away and get another woman to try for children of the opposite sex. Mama Catherine, for example, had spoken during her pregnancy about using some form of family planning so that she could stop producing after this, her third, child was born. Even her husband said the same, explaining that he felt three children were enough in these difficult times. When the third daughter was born, however, both agreed that they would have to keep trying for a boy.

The legitimacy conferred upon a union by the birth of children extends to the treatment of a woman by a deceased husband's family. I was given this illustration:

> A mother is much respected [by her in-laws]. For example, if a man is married to two women one of them might be barren. He can love the barren one so much, even more than the mother. Time may come when the husband dies. At that time the barren one can be chased away [by his relatives] because she has no child. She might not even get any of his property, yet the co-wife and her children do. So you see the mother would be highly respected more than the barren one, yet their husband loved the barren one more.

The birth of children, thus, validates urban marriages in the absence of a formal ceremony. This validation has taken on new significance in the era of AIDS, and may be one compelling reason to continue child-bearing even when one or both partners are infected with HIV.

The third personal arena for which the significance of childbearing is manifest is in the respect and prestige conferred upon mothers who are also wives. Mothering gives one entrance into the community of adult women which is closed in many ways to barren women and to single mothers. A married mother expressed this widely shared opinion: 'When a woman does not produce she gets no respect. Even when mothers come together, such a woman is not accepted among them, because they will say that she will have nothing to contribute in their discussions. They will always ask her to leave.'

A single mother supported that opinion from her own experience:

> Single mothers do not get much respect, especially when they are not employed. Your parents feel that you have not honoured them. The community fears and despises you. You can only get support from others in your own situation. As a single mother you are not accorded full status as an adult woman, and men just approach you as if you are a prostitute. You also get chided by other women. Although you are a parent, it is as though you do not know how to do things properly in the home. For example, if some neighbours are cooking communally for someone's funeral, they will make a point of not asking you to join. You are made to feel that because you don't have a husband you cannot cook nicely. They say that when you don't have a man, you can just do what you like. They also fear that you will take their husbands.

Respect, discipline and the contested terrain of empisa   Underlying such statements is a powerful yet contradictory, highly contentious and ever uncertain process. It is a process that stamps a neighbourhood with the distinctive imprint of a postcolonial moral community, stigmatising the 'barren' woman, marginalising the single mother and, at the expense of other women, privileging the married mother. I refer to the process of giving and receiving respect, and self-respect no less than respect for others. In everyday discourse neighbours have the presentation of respect in mind when they speak of *empisa*. Its meaning, not matched by a single English word, depends on its many contexts of use. 'Discipline' is the working translation that Kifumbira I women always volunteered in our conversations directly on the topic of the Proper Woman. In everyday discourse, *empisa* has the sense, at its simplest, of 'conduct'. More inclusively, by association with ideas of character, personhood, self-respect (*okwewa ekitiibwa*) and respect for others (*okusamu ekitiibwa abalala*), *empisa* is a complex moral concept: being reserved, respectful, sensible.

Empisa comes with socialisation; in a sense, it is socialisation. Parents teach it to their children and if one is from a 'good' family one will have *empisa* as an adult. Hence someone's lack of *empisa* in the eyes of others reflects badly on the person's parents and, fundamentally, on his or her mother, who is more readily blamed than the father when children misbehave, act disrespectfully, or look dirty and unkempt. Women complain, however, that in the slum areas of town their own example may not be enough. From the time they can walk, their children are playing with, and being influenced by, all the other children in the area. It is impossible to isolate one's child, and many mothers fear that their children's up-bringing is out of their hands. A significant part of that difficulty is attributed to living conditions which are so cramped. Women are able to laugh at their predicament, as they did in the following part of a group discussion:

— Most of problems here in town originate from many people staying in one house. There might be a house with six rooms and therefore six renters. Something surprising/shaming can happen! Maybe one of the six will decide to bring a schoolgirl home during the day and they lock themselves in the house. You cannot see what is happening, but you can hear them uttering obscene words, words which you yourself cannot let past your mouth ... Our children learn bad manners, because even if you try to teach them *empisa* the neighbours will spoil them. And what makes things worse is the fact that our rooms are small. The whole family is squeezed in the room when the parents are playing sex in the bed. The kids can hear everything. This spoils kids! The situation is not good.

— It is hard because of these small rooms we sleep in! A man may come home when he is drunk and he starts pulling your arm ...

— But for you [the woman], you try to keep the respect by telling the man that children are there listening, and ask 'aren't you ashamed?' When you have *empisa* you have to wait until the kids are asleep.

— You might think the kids are asleep when they are actually awake. A kid can be naughty in a way that he/she sleeps at first and wakes up when you are in the act. When the kid hears you he/she becomes eager to know what is taking place!

Empisa must be everyday practice at home, and it is largely the woman's responsibility to see that it is. Beyond the home must come the *empisa* of the neighbourhood. Maintaining good relations with one's neighbours through *empisa* is felt to be one of the keys to urban survival.

Empisa is most obviously displayed in the neighbourhood by the rituals surrounding greeting. The importance of greeting as social and moral behaviour has long been recognised by social anthropologists and Kifumbira I presents no exception (e.g. Malinowski 1944; La Fontaine, 1972; Goody 1972; Reisman 1977; Baxter 1990). By exchanging appropriate greetings, women acknowledge their mutual participation in a moral community. By withholding greetings, a woman shows her rejection, not only of other individuals, but of the wider moral community as a whole. Women would often complain that to get the short distance from home to the shop and back could take up to an hour, because they would have to stop and greet everyone along the way. Behind this 'complaint', of course, is a statement of belonging and of proper womanhood.

Those who do not greet properly are considered suspicious, difficult and troublesome, and are cut off from inter-neighbourhood exchanges and networks. This was illustrated graphically by one such woman whose child was severely malnourished. When asked why no one in the neighbourhood was giving her any help, her immediate neighbour, Mama Catherine, explained that no one wants to help a person who spends her time making quarrels and disturbing the peace: 'She is always accusing us of stealing her things. She is the one who steals, but we just leave her alone.'

The tensions created in the neighbourhood by someone who lacks *empisa* can result in accusations of witchcraft. Again, and interestingly, the 'bad neighbour' is said to be the one who raises the accusation. Making the accusation merely confirms that a person lacks *empisa*. Only the envious and isolated would deliberately bring a quarrel with neighbours through witchcraft accusations. Mama Beth spelled this out:

> If you stay around here long enough you will notice two things: there are some women who co-operate with their neighbours. These are *muliranwa gwenkolagana naye*, 'good neighbours'. There are also those people who just stay in their houses and do not even greet those who live around. They stay separate and keep to their own things. Such people don't co-operate. They make quarrels and get suspicious and jealous of everyone. They can even accuse their neighbours of witchcraft. For example a woman who never greets may see you stop a moment outside her door. If her child should happen to fall sick the next day she can even accuse you of harming her child.

The orthodox expectation is that women who have *empisa* have well-mannered children, co-operate with their neighbours, greet properly and welcome visitors into their homes. They avoid quarrels when possible, and make an effort to stay 'cool' when conflict is unavoidable. In short, they are active and engaged members of a distinct moral community. 'A woman fails utterly to be a Proper Woman,' I was told, 'when she does not have *empisa* and quarrels all the time with others. It is the way one behaves that makes one a Proper Woman.'

Thus, greeting and trying to maintain harmony with one's neighbours are indications of *empisa*, and show that one is a good neighbour. They do not in and of themselves, however, indicate proper womanness. 'A Proper Woman is a good neighbour,' one woman said, 'but a good neighbour is not always a Proper Woman.'[9] To be both a Proper Woman and a good neighbour one needs to be 'married'. Single women who are not, by definition, *omukyala omutufu*, are in principle assumed not to have *empisa*. This issue was discussed during an argument between an older and a younger woman:

> Younger woman: ' ... supposing I never married but a man comes to my house and I produce children with him. Can't I look after my children like any other mother although they don't have a proper father there to look after them?'
>
> Older woman: 'A rebel woman is not counted as a Proper Woman. *She is doing her own things*. She is not counted at all.'

Marriage, while not guaranteeing a woman *empisa*, is in some ways a prerequisite. A woman living alone has no one there to control her behaviour; she 'does her own things'. There is nothing or no one to restrain her sexuality.[10] People will wonder why she is alone, and will assume it is because no man wants her, and no man wants a woman without *empisa*. The argument is circular, and many women get trapped in its spiral. Today even young widows – of whom there are increasing numbers – are suspect. These women are all the more reviled because their partners are assumed to have died of AIDS, and therefore their identity is not only suspect but spoiled. One such woman was an informant who worked hard to establish herself as a Proper Woman after her husband's death, and was finally able to establish a reputation as a celibate Catholic woman working solely to give her children food and a roof over their heads. It was, however, a fragile status, and she had to labour to maintain it.

Not all of the women felt equally strongly about the importance of the Proper Woman in the neighbourhood. Mama Jacob, an 'independent' woman with a rather chequered past, insisted that in the slum everyone was equal, and that one could have *empisa* without being a Proper Woman. To Mama Jacob, *omukyala omutufu* is a high prestige status that comes only with money and a stable, properly-conducted marriage. She felt that despite their poverty, the women of Kifumbira's 'slum' are decent and morally upright people. *Empisa*, she claimed, is important because one has to live well with one's neighbours. *Omukyala omutufu*, on the other hand, belongs to the world outside the slum.

In everyday discourse there are simple alternatives for bringing together the Proper Woman, marriage and *empisa*. A woman can redefine 'marriage' or the 'Proper Woman' to include her own situation, or she can reject the relevance of the ideal altogether. Mama Jacob's opinion was based both on observation and lived experience: the women in her neighbourhood are, like her, unmarried but none the less good and decent women. In the day-to-day life of the neighbourhood, having *empisa* is enough. But for those who aspire to it, and this includes most women in Kifumbira (including Mama Jacob), 'marriage' gives a woman an extra measure of legitimacy, respectability and status, even within the slum.

Underlying the attitude of many women to marriage is the assumption that men do not have *empisa*. Informants say that a man might take a 'wife' and then get bored and want to get another one. To justify himself, he might antagonise his wife into quarrelling with him, and accuse her of 'going out' for sex and not keeping house properly, of not being *omukyala omutufu*. In the meantime, he himself might have already started with a new girlfriend. A woman's best defence in this situation is to arm herself with *empisa*. As Mama Beth told me, 'At all times a wife must be cool. Even when her husband abuses and mistreats her. She should show him through her example the proper way to behave, otherwise they cannot go forward in their marriage.' If a wife is successful, her husband will ask himself, 'Why do I abuse my wife?' and in time he will stop, enabling the couple to negotiate the obstacles and to build a better marriage. If the husband does not change his ways, however, then the wife is justified in leaving him, her proper womanhood intact. If, on the other hand, the wife allows herself to be drawn into the quarrel, or if she does not look after the home and children well, then it is felt that she is not serious about the marriage and is 'just doing her own things'. Mama Beth said that such people will always be alone, because no one would want them for a spouse.

Women enforce and reinforce this use of *empisa* among themselves. Margaret and Jane, both RC1 women's secretaries, told me that when a woman comes to seek advice about how to handle a difficult husband, she is advised to be patient and to try to keep the marriage together. Margaret gives this advice: 'Please, you stay there and don't quarrel. Give him what he needs and be quick in your work at home. He will be shamed. He will come back.'

In practice, women do follow such advice. It is realistic and successful enough, given the backing of neighbourhood opinion, to be taken by women as a serious conjugal strategy. An example is useful:

Mama Catherine was taken critically ill with a searing headache. Early in her illness rumours were rife that her husband, Taata, had taken an 'outside' girlfriend who was 'charming' Mama Catherine, making her ill. Rumour had it that the

same woman had used a love charm on Taata to lure him away from his ailing
wife. Mama Catherine ignored this gossip. She knew her husband was having
an affair, but refused to be party to gossip about witchcraft. She simply continued
to behave in the normal way, and did not accuse her husband or complain
about his affair. One day, however, Taata found that the tea prepared by the
outside woman tasted peculiar, and became afraid that he truly was being
charmed. He left her immediately, never returned, and to this day has not taken
another outside lover. Mama Catherine was praised by the other women for
her behaviour. She showed that she had *empisa*, and got her husband back in the
end.

Women learn, and teach each other, that respect can be won by seizing
the moral high ground. Used in conjugal politics, women's *empisa* generates
more than mere personal identity. *Empisa* becomes a force, some women
would say *the* force, for a stable and successful marriage. From a doctrinaire
outsider's point of view, *empisa* could, admittedly, be viewed as a means of
suppressing women's needs. Rather than giving voice to their mistreatment
and seeking proactively to change their situation (as some Euro-American
feminists might wish them to do), women in this context are admonished
to show inner strength, character and dignity through *empisa*. A woman's
capacity to elicit change – to be powerful and empowered – arises from
her relative success in being a Proper Woman, and it is through this that
she acquires the respect of her spouse and of the neighbourhood as a
moral community.

The power of *empisa*, and of being a Proper Woman, largely derives
from the history of women's involvement in urban life and their management of the stereotypes stigmatising urban women, making them appear
morally suspect. AIDS has introduced a new dimension to this context.
The relationship between the presence of AIDS and the meanings associated with the Proper Woman is not straightforward. On the one hand, the
rhetoric of the anti-AIDS campaigns seems to underscore and give added
legitimacy to the notion and practice of *empisa*. On the other hand,
however, it raises new imperatives for sexual and marital relationships.
Moreover, familiar suspicions and fears have taken on new resonance.
The question is: what is it about *empisa* and childbearing in the postcolonial
time of AIDS that 'produces' spoiled identities?

'Producing' spoiled identities? Childbearing and womanhood in the time of AIDS

Women living in Kifumbira I, and places like it, today face unprecedented
challenges to their capacity to construct positive identities for themselves.
Few are more vital than the challenges posed by AIDS. Urban Ugandan
women are no strangers to challenge, of course. From the earliest days of
their participation in the project of urban life, women in Kampala have

faced harsh choices and taken tough decisions. As Southall puts it, the 'unavoidable conflict' confronting urban women in the late colonial period was that

> the dutiful wife of a stable marriage wins the respect of her husband and general high esteem, yet her jural status may be even lower than it is in the rural community ... On the other hand, the free-lance woman may forfeit respectability and general esteem, yet can undoubtedly win an economic and jural status as an independent business woman and property owner which is not open to her respectable sister. (Southall 1961a: 22)

Economic crisis and over-crowding, however, have restricted women's 'free-lance' options in important ways. Although women continue to be skilful in generating income within the informal economy, they are finding it increasingly difficult to earn a living and support their children by themselves (cf. Obbo 1991). This must be one reason why many women in this area want to be married. But also, and importantly, women want husbands and the legitimacy, respectability and security that 'marriage' should provide. The respectability that women acquire through marriage is one important means by which they enter into the moral community of the postcolonial neighbourhood. Bearing and rearing children is a vital factor: having children confirms womanhood and self. But motherhood is not unconditionally appropriate, and impropriety is increasingly associated with mothering as a result of AIDS. In situations where mothering would once have been an identity asset, it has now become a potential liability. Even bearing children within a recognised marriage can be seen as scandalous, if that marriage has been, or is regarded to have been, touched by AIDS. Young widows, facing uncertain futures, seek security in new relationships, and bear children to seal those relationships, often with predictably tragic results.

A new orthodoxy is emerging. Important segments of the community have come to regard such behaviour as irresponsible and foolish. Older women, themselves beyond childbearing, and some of the more educated or sub-elite women, shake their heads and click their tongues in dismay at the lack of *empisa* women have in the face of AIDS. They wonder what could motivate a woman to continue to 'produce', well knowing she is effectively producing children destined to die or, worse, be orphaned.

The women of Kifumbira I do not lack education about AIDS. They know that the HIV virus is transmitted through sexual intercourse with an infected person. Many also know that the virus can be transmitted to a foetus by an infected mother. Therefore, most women are intuitively aware of the degree of risk that accompanies unprotected intercourse. As Mama Jacob once sagely remarked: 'No one can confidently say the spread of AIDS has reduced ... Maybe you are safe if the man has had no previous partners. Otherwise, as long as you are a couple [are sexually active], one partner will definitely bring the disease. You can't claim that a person can protect him/herself. The two protect each other by abstaining from sex outside their relationship.'

Thanks largely to the government's rapid and candid response at the outset of the epidemic, Uganda has had an active and well resourced AIDS education and intervention campaign to which Mama Jacob's well-informed remarks are testimony. Over the years, Ugandans have learned that to avoid infection and/or transmission they should 'Love Carefully' and 'Stick to one partner' by 'Zero Grazing'. An organisation known as TASO (The AIDS Support Organisation) provides counselling, education and training for people with AIDS and those who care for them. The AIDS Information Centre provides free testing, and has a 'post-test club' which provides a supportive and constructive environment for anyone needing extra help after a test, whether the result is positive or negative. The Catholic Church has set up a comprehensive AIDS programme, including home care, food relief, free clinic and school for 'AIDS orphans', and an organisation based in Kamwokya called Youth Alive that delivers a strong and consistent message to young people about avoiding AIDS by 'behaviour change' or sexual abstinence. These are just a few of the organisations that abound in Uganda, most with bases in Kampala, whose sole aim and purpose is to bring about the end of the epidemic. The messages of the anti-AIDS campaign would seem powerfully to reinforce the notion of the Proper Woman, and in particular *empisa*. As we have shown, *empisa* is a means of eliciting sexual fidelity from one's partner, and for building the firm foundation of a stable and lasting marriage. If one is successful in achieving the proper balance between sexuality and restraint it could be the difference between life and death.

There are few other viable interventions. Condoms are regarded with a great deal of suspicion, and can be used only for sex outside 'marriage'. It is notable in this regard that in Kifumbira I none of six women who gave detailed reproductive life histories had *ever* used any form of modern contraception. All of the women reported that they would reject the use of condoms with their main partner. Besides the primary draw-back, that condom use precludes the chance of conception, condoms have become synonymous with sexual misconduct and the breakdown of marital fidelity. Suggesting that one's main partner use condoms is tantamount to admission or suspicion of 'outside' sex, both of which seriously jeopardise whatever semblance of conjugal harmony and trust there may be in the union.[11]

Celibacy, the only other recommended prophylaxis, is simply not considered to be an option by married women of any age or by the majority of unmarried women in their childbearing years.

I asked a group of women in Kifumbira I if they would use a prophylactic vaginal cream, that would not be immediately apparent to their partners, and that would 'kill' the HIV. The women unanimously agreed that it would be preferable to the condom, and were enthusiastic about the idea. In Mama Catherine's words: 'one can't afford to refuse that "medicine" because one can't abstain from sex – for example a young woman can't. And even if a woman wants to protect herself, her husband can refuse. We could use that "medicine" more than a condom.' I then asked them how they would feel about this cream if it was also contraceptive, and would kill sperm. Predictably the response was qualified:

> Mama Catherine: 'It would be good "medicine" and we would appreciate it because of AIDS, but when it comes to destroying sperms, then that is bad.'

> Mama Johnny: 'That medicine should be for people who have stopped producing but it wouldn't be good for young girls who are still producing because they won't do without producing children.'

AIDS threatens to subvert very radically the constructed status of wife and mother. Nevertheless, the women of Kifumbira I continue to privilege the values associated with childbearing, motherhood and marriage when making sexual and reproductive decisions. In the face of AIDS women turn to 'discipline' as *empisa* to provide one possible, if flawed, solution, because it is through *empisa* that urban women are able to demonstrate their moral rectitude and self-respect, and to effect the proper balance between sexuality and restraint. The postcolonial discourse and practice of *empisa* gives women agency in effecting positive change. The extent to which the women themselves currently recognise this remains to be determined. Should they come to do so, however, it may have a positive effect on their capacity to manage their lives effectively despite this epidemic.

Conclusion: postcolonial women, respect and morality in the neighbourhood

> To be defined as respectable ... is to be considered as a regular or normal human being; that is as a member of that category of persons perceived as morally acceptable, as other than evil, and so on. (Ball 1970: 328)

Ball suggests that the post-Victorian era has been characterised by the emergence of a 'cult of respectability' (1970: 329). This interest in Respect emanates from the (Christian) contention that morality is an individual affair between one person and his or her conscience (Seidler 1986: 2). As expressed through colonial discourse, policy-making and, naturally enough, evangelism, this 'autonomy of morality' notion had an important impact on the moral categories of the colonised African populations (Jeater 1993). This chapter has argued that these processes are implicated in the negative stereotypes of urban women which persist well into postcolonial times. It is argued further that postcolonial women have responded to this moral devaluation by generating and manipulating the meanings which enable them to construct positive identities through childbearing and marriage. Women have used the city to their own advantage and, in the process, the neighbourhood – as the focus and locus of women's lives – has become the moral community to which they are answerable.

In present-day postcolonial Kampala the making of respect and respectability, couched in terms of the Proper Woman and *empisa,* continues to depend upon the special localism of women. The construction of feminine identities occurs within this semantic field. Women in Kifumbira engender respect (produce positive identities) by demonstrating *empisa,* and by 'producing' children within locally sanctioned marriages. A new dimension of the postcolonial context – AIDS – may have far-reaching effects upon these processes, not all of which are necessarily negative (cf. Ogden 1995a; and 1995b).

It is unfortunate, and surprising in light of this and related research (e.g. Jeater 1993; Schmidt 1992; White 1990; Overall 1992), that little debate about respect-making has arisen in feminist scholarly literature. This may partly be attributed to the fact that studies of 'Respect', like its cognate 'Morality', have fallen largely beyond the sociological purview (with some exceptions, such as Ball 1970). It may also be a consequence of the presupposed subordination of women that has crippled so much feminist scholarship. One positive outcome of the débâcle of AIDS may be renewed scholarly interest in, and concern for, processes of the moral economy, and the proactivity of women within those processes. In this endeavour, we may be increasingly compelled (as many already have been, e.g. Jeater 1993; and White 1990; also, if differently, Parkin 1990) to address our colonial legacy critically – as it appears in scholarship and, indeed, in social processes themselves. If we manage to turn the colonial era on its head and ask not what these processes did to women, but how women have participated actively in their generation (as per Schmidt 1992: 1), we may be able to come some way towards a more balanced understanding of the postcolonial, and at the same time address the potential utility of our work.

Notes

The research for this study was conducted under the aegis of a project funded by the Overseas Development Administration, entitled *The Informal Economy of Health in African Cities: Structural, Cultural, and Clinical Dimensions of the Management of STD and Paediatric Crisis by Women Resident in Kampala.* That study was a multidimensioned, multidisciplinary, collaborative effort conducted under the direction of Professor Sandra Wallman, University of Hull, UK and Dr Jessica Jitta, Child Health and Development Centre, with the assistance of associates in each institution. The project being reported here articulated with that study on a number of levels.

While acknowledging the assistance of colleagues on that project, I note that the views expressed here are entirely my own and are not necessarily those of the sponsoring agency nor of my colleagues.

1. Throughout this chapter, by 'the women of Kifumbira I' I refer to a very specific population. In Kampala there is no singular category 'woman'. The following comments about marriage, childbearing and *empisa* may not apply in the same way to the many elite and sub-elite women living in the capital, although they are present in the general normative scheme of their lives. They will also apply differently to women of varying ages and statuses, and these issues will be touched upon in my analysis.

2. The pyramidal Resistance Committee (RC) system is rooted at the village level (RC1) in a committee of nine directly elected representatives. At the next level, the RC2 or parish level, representatives are elected by the RC1 members; the RC3, or district level, delegates are in turn elected by the RC2, and so on up to the level of the National Resistance Council itself. The committees are made up of a chairperson; vice-chairperson; secretary; finance secretary; secretary for mass mobilisation and education; secretary for information; secretary for women; secretary for youth; and secretary for defence. The RC1 and RC2 members play a key role in the daily lives of residents. They arbitrate disputes between neighbours, family members and spouses; they can liaise between local residents and officialdom on a number of levels; they provide an organisational infrastructure through which projects for local improvements can be channelled; and they can provide individual assistance. The RC system seems to be extremely popular at the village and parish level, and is an element in the general sense of optimism that pervades the country.

3. 'Permanent' marriages were those contracted according to 'tribal custom', religious ceremony (Christian or Muslim) or by a District Registrar. Sometimes relationships were made 'permanent' solely by the payment of bridewealth or by the birth of children. The length of time the couple had been together and the degree of harmony between them were also taken into account in ascribing 'permanent' status to a union. A 'temporary' marriage, on the other hand, was one secured in town. No bridewealth was paid, and the woman often entered the union childless. If she got pregnant, however, there was a chance that the union be considered 'permanent'.

4. White provides a detailed analysis of the various prostitution forms as they existed in Nairobi during the colonial period. She notes that in the *malaya* form, 'taken from the proper, dictionary Swahili word for prostitute – the woman stayed inside her room and waited for the men to come to her ... and in Nairobi as elsewhere, *malaya* prostitutes provided the most extensive set of domestic services for sale, including food, bathwater, conversation, and, when a man spent the night, breakfast' (White 1990: 15).

5. Although this means that the relationship is recognised as legitimate while both parties are alive, the legitimacy does not always persist after death, and these issues have become increasingly complicated by the escalating numbers of AIDS deaths. The lack of formal legality of so many marriages has meant that many widows are left destitute by their husbands' families. They may lose everything, including home and children. Thus at a time when a widow may be facing her own imminent illness and death, she is left with no means of support. Laws are beginning to change in order to protect these women and ensure their rights to their husbands' property, but the process is slow and is leaving many behind.

6. Some of the older women maintained that these partnerships are not proper marriages, but are *kakwundo kakubye eddirisa,* or 'bat knocks on the window marriage'. As Mama Beth, the Auntie of Kifumbira explained: 'The type of marriage we have these days is *kakwundo kakubye eddirisa.* These days boys convince girls: "First you come and cook for me, then we shall look into the matter later." This *kakwundo kakubye eddirisa*! The girl passes behind the house and enters quietly. The so-called bridegroom will get one of his friends and say, "My friend, come and we will have a bottle of beer." This is not marriage. You are only a proper couple if you introduce yourselves to the parents ... even then you still have a debt for a church wedding!'

7. One male informant, an RC1 in Kifumbira, was especially concerned that I realise the extent to which men are remaining monogamous these days. He said that most of the men in Kifumbira I have families in the village, and are in town only to earn money to support them properly. These men, argued the RC1, have no money to give to 'prostitutes'. They go home as often as possible to be with their wives. He said: 'Don't let these women deceive you that it is only the men who spread AIDS. Even we are changing.'

8. A Luganda proverb describes the fact that 'barren' women lack some essence of womanhood: *amabeere kiruvu n'omugumba agamera* translates roughly as 'breasts are like a moustache – even a barren one develops them'. According to Kisekka (1973), and my informants who confirmed her interpretation, this saying highlights the fact that a moustache is a symbol of manhood, but growing one does not in itself make one a man. Likewise, breasts are an outward sign of femininity, but having breasts alone does not make one a woman.

9. This echoes a similar distinction made by prostitutes in colonial Nairobi: 'The values *malaya* women articulated had to do with being good neighbours and responsible tenants and loyal friends (although not always loyal spouses) ... they did not describe their prostitution as separate from their other urban relationships' (White 1990: 77). The *malaya* prostitutes described by White were not interested in 'joining the ranks of respectable society' (ibid.: 224), but they were shrewd enough businesswomen to realise that their prospects of accumulating wealth were directly dependent upon securing the trust of their communities, and particularly of their (women) friends and neighbours. Thus, the *malaya* prostitutes were 'good neighbours', but they were almost certainly not 'Proper Women'.

10. Obtaining and maintaining a balance between sexuality and restraint is a key indication that a woman has *empisa.* Marriage is important because it enforces restraint and legitimates sexuality (see Ogden 1995b).

11. In addition to these broad points, it is worth mentioning that the AIDS situation has given rise to a significant condom mythology. The general moral behind the condom myths is that both the condom and the man who wears it are likely to be hiding something. Many people believe that men puncture condoms, thereby protecting themselves but permitting semen to flow. People also say that condoms burst during sex, especially the condoms available cheaply around town because these have been sent from Europe past their expiry date. People fear condoms will come off and 'get lost' inside the woman. Others say that having sex with a condom is like eating a sweet in its wrapper, or taking a shower with clothes on. Finally, there are rumours that developed countries send condoms impregnated with HIV in an effort to destroy African people.

References

Ball, D. W. 1970. 'The Problematics of Respectability', in Douglas (ed.), *Deviance and Respectability*.

Baxter, P. T. W. 1990. 'Oromo Blessings and Greetings', in A. Jacobson-Widding (ed.), *The Creative Communion: African Folk Models of Fertility and the Regeneration of Life*. Uppsala: Uppsala Studies in Cultural Anthropology.

Bledsoe, C. 1990. 'Transformations in African Marriage and Fertility', *Annals of the American Academy of Political and Social Sciences* 510: 115–25.

Bohman, K. 1984. *Women of the Bario: Class and Gender in a Colombian City*. Stockholm: Studies in Social Anthropology.

Boswell, D. M. 1969. 'Personal Crisis and the Mobilisation of the Social Network', in Mitchell (ed.), *Social Networks in Urban Situations*.

Douglas, J. D. (ed.) 1970. *Deviance and Respectability: the Social Construction of Moral Meanings*. New York: Basic Books.

Epstein, A. L. 1969a. 'The Network and Urban Social Organisation', in Mitchell (ed.), *Social Networks in Urban Situations*.

— 1969b. 'Gossip, Norms and the Social Network', in Mitchell (ed.), *Social Networks in Urban Situations*.

Fardon, R. (ed.). 1990. *Localising Strategies: Regional Traditions of Ethnographic Writing*. Edinburgh and Washington, DC: Scottish Academic Press and Smithsonian Institution Press.

Gluckman, M. 1963. 'Gossip and Scandal', *Current Anthropology* 4: 307–16.

Goody, E. N. 1972. '"Greeting", "begging" and the presentation of respect', in La Fontaine (ed.), *The Interpretation of Ritual*.

Hakansson, T. 1994. 'The Detachability of Women: Gender and Kinship in the Processes of Socio-Economic Change Among the Gusii of Kenya', *American Ethnologist* 21 (3): 516–38.

Halpenny, P. 1975. 'Three Styles of Ethnic Migration in Kisenyi, Kampala', in Parkin, (ed.), *Town and Country in Central and Eastern Africa*.

Hannerz, U. 1980. *Exploring the City: Inquiries Towards an Urban Anthropology*. New York: Columbia University Press.

Hansen, H. B. and Twaddle, M. 1991. 'Introduction', in Hansen and Twaddle (eds), *Changing Uganda*. London: James Currey.

Jeater, D. 1993. *Marriage, Perversion and Power: The Construction of Moral Discourse in Southern Rhodesia, 1894–1930*. Oxford: Clarendon Press.

Kisekka, M. 1973. *Heterosexual Relationships in Uganda*. PhD thesis, Ann Arbor: University of Michigan.

La Fontaine, J. S. (ed.). 1972. *The Interpretation of Ritual: Essays in Honour of A. I. Richards*. London: Tavistock.

Larson, A. 1989. 'The Social Context of Human Immunodeficiency Virus Transmission in Africa: Historical and Cultural Bases of East and Central African Sexual Relations', *Review of Infectious Diseases* 11: 716–31.

Lateef, K. S. 1991. 'Structural Adjustment in Uganda: The Initial Experience', in Hansen and Twaddle (eds), *Changing Uganda*. London: James Currey.

Malinowski, B. 1944. *A Scientific Theory of Culture and Other Essays*. London: Routledge and Kegan Paul.

Mandeville, E. 1975. 'The Formality of Marriage: a Kampala Case Study', *Journal of Anthropological Research* 31: 183–95.

Mayer, P. 1971. *Townsmen or Tribesmen? Conservatism and the Process of Urbanisation in a South African City*. London: Oxford University Press.

Miller, N. and Rockwell, R. C. (eds). 1988. *AIDS in Africa: The Social and Policy Impact*. Lewiston: Edwin Mellin.

Mitchell, J. C. 1966. 'Theoretical Orientations in African Urban Studies', in M. Banton (ed.), *The Social Anthropology of Complex Societies*. Association of Social Anthropologists Monographs. London: Tavistock.

— 1969. 'The Concept and Use of Social Networks', in Mitchell (ed.), *Social Networks in Urban Situations*.

— (ed). 1969. *Social Networks in Urban Situations*. Manchester: Manchester University Press.

Mugyenyi, J. B. 1991. 'IMF Conditionality and Structural Adjustment Under the National Resistance Movement', In Hansen and Twaddle (eds), *Changing Uganda*. London: James Currey.

Museveni, Y. 1992. 'AIDS is a Socio-Economic Disease', Address delivered to the 1st AIDS Congress in East and Central Africa, Kampala, 20 November, in Y. Museveni, *What is Africa's Problem?* Kampala: NRM Publications.

Obbo, C. 1975. 'Women's Careers in Low Income Areas as Indicators of Country and Town Dynamics', in Parkin (ed.), *Town and Country in Central and East Africa*.

— 1980. *African Women: Their Struggle for Economic Independence*. London: Zed Books.

— 1987. 'The Old and the New in East African Elite Marriages', Parkin and Nyamwaya (eds), *Transformations in African Marriages*.

— 1991. 'Women, Children and a Living Wage', in Hansen and Twaddle (eds), *Changing Uganda*. London: James Currey.

Ochieng, E. O. 1991. 'Economic Adjustment Programmes in Uganda, 1985–8', in Hansen and Twaddle (eds), *Changing Uganda*. London: James Currey.

Ogden, J. A. 1995a. *Reproductive Identity and the Proper Woman: the Response of Urban Women to AIDS in Uganda*. PhD thesis, University of Hull.

— 1995b. 'AIDS, Family Planning and the Proper Woman in Kampala: Fears and Expectations.' Paper presented at the XIth International Conference on STD and AIDS in Africa. Kampala, Uganda, December 1995.

Overall, C. 1992. 'What's Wrong with Prostitution? Evaluating Sex Work', *Signs: Journal of Women in Culture and Society* 17: 705–24.

Paine, R. 1967. 'What is Gossip About? An Alternative Hypothesis', *Man* 2: 278–85.

Parkin, D. 1969. *Neighbours and Nationals in an African City Ward*. London: Routledge and Kegan Paul.

— 1976. 'Types of Urban African Marriage in Kampala', *Africa* 36: 269–85.

— 1990. 'Eastern Africa: the View from the Office', in Fardon (ed.), *Localising Strategies*.

— (ed.). 1975. *Town and Country in Eastern and Central Africa*. Oxford University Press.

Parkin, D. and Nyamwaya, D. (eds). 1987. *Transformations in African Marriages*. Manchester: Manchester University Press.

Rakodi, C. 1991. 'Women's Work or Household Strategies?', *Environment and Urbanisation* 3 (2): 39–45.

Reisman, P. 1977. *Freedom in Fulani Social Life: An Introspective Ethnography*. London: Routledge and Kegan Paul.

Schmidt, E. 1992. *Peasants, Traders and Wives: Shona Women in the History of Zimbabwe*. London: James Currey.

Schneider, B. 1989. 'Women and AIDS: an International Perspective', *Futures* 21 (1): 72–90.

Schoepf, B. G., Schoepf, C., Engundu, W., WaNkara, R. and Ntsomo, P. 1988. 'AIDS and Society in Central Africa: a View from Zaire', in Miller and Rockwell (eds), *AIDS in Africa*.

Seidler, V. 1986. *Kant, Respect and Injustice: the Limits of Liberal Moral Theory*. London: Routledge and Kegan Paul.

Southall, A. W. 1961a. 'Introductory Summary', in A. W. Southall (ed.), *Social Change in Modern Africa*. London: Oxford University Press.

— 1961b. 'Kinship, Friendship and the Network of Relations in Kisenyi, Kampala', in A. W. Southall (ed.), *Social Change in Modern Africa*. London: Oxford University Press.

Southall, A. W. and Gutkind, P. C. W. 1957. *Townsmen in the Making: Kampala and Its Suburbs*. Kampala: East African Institute of Social Research.

Summers, C. 1991. 'Intimate Colonialism: the Imperial Production of Reproduction in Uganda 1907–1925', *Signs: Journal of Women in Culture and Society* 16 (4): 787–807.

Swantz, M. L. 1985. *Women in Development: A Creative Role Denied?* London: C. Hurst.

Wallman, S. 1996. 'Ethnicity, Work and Localism: Narratives of Difference in London and Kampala', *Ethnic and Racial Studies* 19 (1).

— et al. 1996. *Kampala Women Getting By: Wellbeing in the Time of AIDS*. London: James Currey.

Wallman, S. and Baker, M. 1996. 'Which Resources Pay for Treatment? A Model for Estimating the Informal Economy of Health', *Social Science and Medicine* 42 (5): 671–9.

Wallman, S. and Pons. V., 1994. 'Where have all the young men gone?' Paper presented at the meeting of the British Association for Population Studies, August.

Werbner, R. P. 1990. 'South-Central Africa: The Manchester School', in Fardon (ed.), *Localising Strategies*.

White, L. 1990. *The Comforts of Home: Prostitution in Colonial Nairobi*. Chicago: University of Chicago Press.

CHAPTER 7

Witchcraft, violence and identity: different trajectories in postcolonial Cameroon

Cyprian Fisiy and Peter Geschiere

One of the most striking aspects of postcolonial Africa is the emergence, or rather the re-emergence, in public discourse of 'witchcraft', 'sorcery', '*sorcellerie*', or whatever term people use. After colonial conquest and the imposition of novel forms of state organisation, colonial authorities were, in general, intent on banning the whole issue of 'witchcraft' from the public domain.[1] Independence brought no immediate changes in this respect. In Cameroon, for instance, the new national government initially tended to ignore 'witchcraft' – a traditional relict, according to the new elite, which could only divert attention from the urgent task of modernising the country (Rowlands and Warnier 1988). Even in the early 1970s, Geschiere's interest in the role these conceptions of the occult played in the new inequalities was seen by new elites as the rather unhealthy interest of a foreign anthropologist.

However, all this changed in the wake of the continuing Africanisation of the state. As Bayart (1989) shows, with a wealth of detail, the modern state can no longer be considered as a *Fremdkörper* in Africa. True, the postcolonial state still bears the marks of its colonial origins; but, especially since the end of the colonial period, it has been invaded by African conceptions and forms of organisation. The consequence is that local discourses on the occult with their implications for power and violence, inequality and success, have overrun the new public domains created by the state. Nowadays, in Cameroon, as in most African countries, the discourse on witchcraft and sorcery is omnipresent, especially in the more modern sectors of society: in sports and in politics, in the health service and in the educational institutions, in urban settings as much as in the village. Witchcraft has become one of the favourite topics of the popular press, and it tends to dominate speculations on new form of entre-preneurship and accumulation (Fisiy and Geschiere 1991; and Geschiere 1995; see also, van Binsbergen 1981; Rowlands and Warnier 1988; Austen 1993; Bastian 1993). *La sorcellerie* is now in the full spotlight of public debate, and the official authorities no longer seem to be intent on dimming this light; the contrary is the case.

This vociferous emphasis on occult forces directly affects issues of identity and inequality, of violence and new forms of accumulation. Local discourses on witchcraft and sorcery have always centred on power and inequality, on the tension between individual ambition and communitarian control, and on the spectre of the 'sovereign subject' who tries to emancipate him/herself from this control in ways which might be secret, but certainly not always reprehensible (Jewsiewicki 1994; cf. also Guyer 1993, Geschiere 1982; and Laburthe-Tolra 1977). Not surprisingly, these conceptions are invoked, more and more openly, to interpret new inequalities, new forms of power and their drastic consequences for local relations. The debate is not so much whether recourse to the occult as such is permitted, but rather which uses of these forces are acceptable and which are not.[2]

The modernity of witchcraft

Of crucial importance is the impressive capacity of local discourses on witchcraft and sorcery for incorporating the images and objects of the modern world. In Cameroon in the 1970s, for instance, magical objects bought from mail-order firms in Europe played a central role in the rumours of witchcraft. The witches were also supposed to follow bureaucratic procedures: for instance, by using a *cahier* with lists of their potential victims, just as the *sous-préfet* uses his feared census lists of tax-payers and tax-defaulters. Witchdoctors make ostentatious use of books on 'Eastern Magic' and Christian symbols. Witchcraft rumours can also attain truly global dimensions: in Douala, for instance, witches are supposed to work with the Mafia in Italy. And nearly everywhere in Africa, there is a close conceptual connection between the new objects of wealth and witchcraft (Fisiy and Geschiere 1991; and Geschiere 1995; see also, Ciekawy 1989; Auslander 1993; Bastian 1993). Far from being a 'traditional' relict which will 'automatically disappear with electric light' – as several Dutch priests in Cameroon assured Geschiere in the 1970s – witchcraft discourses seem to offer an idiom of choice for trying to understand and control the modern changes. Admittedly, the view, so tenacious among Euro-American observers, of witchcraft as a 'traditional' obstacle to change, is not totally unfounded. In many situations, these discourses do seem to have a traditionalising tenor, opposing development and change. Yet, in other contexts, the same discourses seem to intertwine very easily with new developments – such as the penetration of money, the emergence of wage labour and the spread of new consumer goods, as well as with new forms of individualism and violence, or whatever form 'modernity' takes in Africa. There seem to be surprising convergences between discourses on the occult – with their emphasis on individual accumulation and debt[3] – and a capitalist world-view.[4]

This linking of local conceptions of the occult to the modern is, we emphasise, still the subject of great uncertainty. Highly different interpretations of the articulation of sorcery/witchcraft with the new forms of wealth are possible. A crucial factor is the role of the state. Nearly everywhere, state officials, while fearful of this treacherous domain, feel compelled to intervene in it, precisely because of the modern dynamics of discourses on the occult. The precise nature of the state interventions can vary strikingly, however. Another important factor is the varying role of the witchdoctors, the most visible representatives of the world of the witches, who seem more and more intent on claiming their place in the public sphere but, again, do so in highly different ways.

Three case studies from Cameroon: witchcraft, kinship and new forms of accumulation

The aim of this chapter is to compare briefly, against the background sketched above, three case studies from different parts of present-day Cameroon. The three cases illustrate different regional trajectories in the articulation of sorcery/witchcraft, personal identity and modernity. A central factor is the varying role of the state. In the East Province, since the end of the 1970s, the state courts have begun, quite abruptly, to condemn witches, often without any concrete proof of physical aggression, mainly on the basis of the expertise of the *nganga* (witchdoctor). This is all the more remarkable since it is completely in contradiction to the preceding judicial practice.[5] In the Centre and South Provinces, the courts seem to be more circumspect, although here, as well, there is strong popular pressure on the state to intervene. In the Western Provinces – the third area to be discussed below – there are, as yet, hardly any examples of parallel interventions by the state; here, people seem to feel that the threat of witchcraft has to be dealt with in other ways.

In a broader sense, these three cases exemplify different patterns in the relation between witchcraft, identity and violence, and different interpretations of the tension between the new forms of individualism and the community. The striking variations in the role of the state offer a concrete point of departure for exploring the different scenarios illustrated by these cases.

However, before introducing our case studies, a few more general remarks may help unravel the conceptual knot of witchcraft, violence and new forms of inequality in postcolonial Africa. First, the strong ambivalence of witchcraft discourses *vis-à-vis* issues of equality and inequality, of personal ambition and communitarian control. Elsewhere, we have discussed the ambiguity between 'levelling' and 'accumulative' tendencies in these discourses (Fisiy and Geschiere 1991). At least in our Cameroonian cases, *evu*, *djamb*, *liemba* or whatever term is used, can be the weapon of both the weak and the powerful. Generally, these notions are closely linked to jealousy: this is what we call the levelling side of witchcraft: the spectre of poorer people, notably kin, who use occult forms of aggression, or threaten to do so, in order to force their richer fellow men to share their wealth.

The same occult forces, however, are supposed to be used by the rich and the powerful themselves in order to further their ambitions and to enhance their accumulation of wealth and power; in our terms, the accumulative side of these beliefs. It is this ambivalence which makes the implications of local ideas on witchcraft and sorcery for the new forms of accumulation so highly complex. The new inequalities often take on new dimensions and therefore increase the fear of the jealousy and the occult aggression of the poor. But these same occult powers are thought to be the secret cause of the success of the new rich and even place them outside the reach of their fellow men.[6]

The same ambiguity marks the relation of these discourses to violence. Basic to the very notion of witchcraft is the idea that violence is omnipresent. Eric de Rosny – a French priest in Douala who after a long period of training was initiated as a *nganga* (healer) – describes as the culmination of his initiation a sudden and piercing realisation of all the violence around him (de Rosny 1981; see, for a parallel example from Europe, Favret-Saada 1977). It was only due to the secrets his 'professor' had taught him that he could control his panic. The threat is all the greater since witchcraft/sorcery, at least in this region, mostly refers to aggression and hidden violence from close by; the most dangerous forms of sorcery are nearly always supposed to come from within the intimacy of the 'house'.

However, the same discourses on occult powers are used for the control of violence. In southern Cameroon, the *nganga* is supposed to be able to heal and check the violence of the witches, only because (s)he is a 'witch who has beaten all records'. The *nganga* thus becomes a good example of how the very belief in witchcraft can serve to channel and contain internal aggression. This reminds one of the 'eufunctional' view of witchcraft beliefs, already mentioned, which was so strongly emphasised by classical anthropology. Marwick, for instance, saw witchcraft as a 'social strain-gauge' which helped to reproduce the social order (Marwick 1965: see also, Gluckman 1955 and, for an ironical comment on this rather surprising image of witchcraft as 'tamed' and 'domesticated', Douglas 1970).

Developments in postcolonial Africa make it ever more difficult to retain such a positive image of witchcraft beliefs. One is rather struck by how easily such beliefs can generate violence in daily life and in forms which certainly do not remain hidden.[7] In eastern and southern Cameroon, the *nganga* are now experimenting with new ways of violence in order to discipline the 'suspects'. Rumours about new forms of witchcraft are no longer contained by the verbal violence of accusations but lead to a general panic which seems to require more Draconic measures. In this context, the state adds its own kind of violence.

A final remark concerns the close connection of witchcraft with kinship and moral identity, which further complicates its implications for the new forms of wealth. In the Cameroonian societies discussed here, witchcraft can be seen as the dark side of kinship. Witches are supposed to have a special hold over their kin. Basic to these beliefs is the shocking realisation that there is jealousy and aggression within the family; that is, among the very people with whom one has to live and collaborate (see de Rosny 1981; 1992; Geschiere 1994; cf., for parallel examples, Meyer 1992; and Bastian 1993).[8] Paradoxically, the same discourses are used to try to incorporate the new opportunities for enrichment created by broader politico-economic developments. These also reinforce the emphasis on personal ambition and a quest for individual autonomy, which in these societies are in themselves certainly not wrong.[9] Yet, the same discourses can be used also to slander such ambitious persons, to attack their moral identities and make them suspect as witches. Nowadays, such suspicion is directed especially at modern entrepreneurs who try to break away from the old order and its restrictions. But when problems arise, the *nganga* will use the same witchcraft beliefs to try and replace these people within their family. Even in urban contexts, witchcraft is always linked to the family. A *nganga* will therefore emphasise that his (or her) occult healing powers can only work if the family agrees to collaborate (de Rosny 1981; 1992; Geschiere 1995).

Unravelling the complexities of this conceptual knot clarifies why people, at least in some parts of Cameroon, tend to invoke the help of outside agencies, notably the state. These complexities show also how treacherous the field is in which the state is intervening. A crucial factor in this context is the relation between state officials and local experts for dealing with the threat of witchcraft. The latter are usually the *nganga*, but in some areas also the chiefs and their associations. We shall see that there are important regional variations in this respect.

The confusing intertwining of witchcraft and kinship also raises questions concerning variations in the kinship organisation itself and its varying capacity for accommodating the new inequalities. To what extent do such variations affect the relation between witchcraft discourses, identity and violence?

New witch-trials in the east: judges in alliance with witchdoctors
The first witch-trials in Cameroon took place in the East Province, which fits a widespread stereotype that, here, witchcraft is particularly rampant. In general, the east is seen to be one of the most backward parts of the country, part of the forest area to which access has remained difficult.

But this stereotype also reflects the great problems, during colonial and even postcolonial times, of incorporating the strongly segmentary societies of the east into the state and the market economy. The Maka, for instance – among whom Geschiere did fieldwork over a longer period of time – lived until the colonial conquest (1905–10) in family villages which were small, exogamic and completely autonomous. Within the village, family elders exercised strict control over women, young men and other dependants of their group. But between villages no form of central authority existed, and the state of hostility was constant.[10] At most, villages claiming common descent and intermarrying regularly could meet to resolve their conflicts. But such reconciliations were always precarious; the basic hostility might flare up again.

To these societies, the state, as it was imposed by the colonial conquest, with its claims of automatic obedience, was a complete novelty. Consequently, the colonial authorities had great problems, not only in 'pacifying' these areas (it took the Germans five years to subdue the relatively small Maka group) but also in mobilising people's labour for the market economy. The French, who during the First World War conquered this part of Cameroon, instituted a highly coercive system of labour control, since they believed that only government coercion could make these 'backward' people produce surpluses for the *'mise en valeur'* of the area. The precarious articulation of the old, 'tribal' order with the authoritarian forms of control imposed by the state, still marks present-day relations in the villages (Geschiere 1982).

People in Yaoundé (the capital of Cameroon) tend to refer to the *'mentalité primitive'* of the Maka and other groups in the east as the main reason why the state had to intervene in this province, especially against the proliferation of witchcraft. The following case exhibits a pattern which in many respects is characteristic of the witch-trials by the state courts in the east.[11]

On 17 May 1983, the Tribunal of Abong-Mbang sentenced a fifty-seven-year-old bachelor named Mentanga from the village of A. to five years in jail, a fine of 30,000 CFA francs (equivalent to £70 at the time) and to pay compensation of 5,000 CFA francs (£12) to the wronged party. The latter was a *'guérisseur traditionnel'* (traditional witchdoctor) called Baba from the same village. The accused had been handed over to the gendarmes by the village chief and Baba himself.[12]

Baba (forty years old), himself a native of the village, left shortly after independence, to work in various professions in Yaoundé and other cities. Before the court he explained how he had returned to the village in 1980:

Since that time, I practised traditional medicine. Indeed, around 1981–82, I decided that I had to purify the village. I posed an ultimatum to all killers to hand over their evil objects [*maléfiques*] to me. Eighteen persons did so and I took care to treat them. However, Mentanga stubbornly refused to declare himself. Therefore, during the month of May 1982, I armoured [*j'ai blindé*] the whole village by my own means; the results were soon to follow. The next month, Mentanga came to hand over his *fétiches*, followed by an angry crowd. Overcome by shame, Mentanga tried to kill himself by swallowing the panther's whiskers from one of his *fétiches*. However, I quickly dealt him a blow so that the package with whiskers fell on the ground. I picked them up and handed them to the village chief. The latter decided to hand the culprit over to the tribunal.

Mentanga told the court a different story. He did not know whether or not he was a '*sorcier*', '*parce que je ne suis pas Dieu*' ('since I am not God'). The package with the panther's whiskers had been given to him by a friend when they came home, half-drunk, from the plantations. The friend had not told him what the contents were and he had not opened it. When he woke up next day, he could not find the package. He called Baba and asked him to look for it and the witchdoctor had indeed found it in his bedroom. '*Je ne connais rien de la pratique de la sorcellerie*' ('I don't know anything about practising witchcraft'). But the judge paid little attention to the defendant's denial (just as in most other cases in our sample). He concluded that Mentanga had indeed tried to impede Baba's work in all sorts of ways. Moreover, he had panther's whiskers in his possession and everybody knew that they are used '*pour lancer le sort*' (literally, to 'throw fate', that is to kill people magically, from a distance). And Mentanga could not really explain how he came into possession of this package. The judge concluded that '*les dénégations vaines du prévenu doublées de ses déclarations contradictoires tendent uniquement à perdre le Tribunal*' ('the futile denials of the suspect and his contradictory statements are only meant to confuse the court'). And the defendant was convicted.

Baba, the witchdoctor, had asked for compensation of 500,000 CFA francs (£1,200). The judge was indeed prepared to grant him a certain compensation, with the argument that a witchdoctor is 'provoked' and 'morally damaged' by a witch 'who hinders him while doing his work'. But the judge deemed Baba's claim excessive and reduced the compensation to 5,000 CFA francs (£12). On 6 December 1983, the Appeal Court of Bertoua confirmed this sentence on all points.

The course of events in this case contained elements of surprise, not only for outsiders but for the villagers as well. Yet one can detect in it many current elements from the local discourse on occult forces. The panther's whiskers, which Baba took from Mentanga and which caused so much consternation, are often mentioned as a favourite weapon of the witches. Common also is the fact that the accusations originated from within the circle of close kin: for some time there had been persistent rumours about poor Mentanga's witchcraft. These rumours apparently originated from his own family.

A basic element in the witchcraft discourse of the Maka – and in other parts of the forest area of south Cameroon – is the notion that witches have a special substance which the Maka call a *djamb* in their belly which permits them to leave their bodies. Potentially, everybody has a *djamb* but only special people take the trouble to develop it. These are the true *mindjindjamb* (witches). At night, when the owl calls, they leave their bodies and fly away along invisible threads (the *tand-i-djamb*) to the *sjumbu*, a kind of witches' sabbath where they meet their accomplices. The climax of these nightly encounters are huge cannibalistic banquets. Each witch has to offer one of his (or her) relatives. The witches eat the heart of their victim, who immediately falls ill. He will surely die, unless he finds a *nganga* strong enough to force the witches to lift their spell. The *djamb* belief of the Maka has many more aspects. Most important is that the forces of the *djamb* lend themselves for all sorts of uses, including more positive ones. *Djamb* is indispensable for the exercise of authority (the *djamb idjuga*) or, in former days, to have success in war (the *djamb-le-domb* – 'witchcraft of war'). And it is only because he (or she) possesses such a highly developed *djamb* that the *nganga* can heal.[13] But the dark core of this imagery, the cannibalistic feasts where witches betray and eat their own kin, is a true obsession for the Maka.

These obsessional fears were at the base of the evil rumours about Mentanga. In many respects, the accusations against him corresponded to the classic pattern of Maka witchcraft. However, other cases before the Bertoua court also illustrated the innovative character of the witchcraft discourse. In one case a whole group of young men were convicted for bewitching their former schoolteacher whom they blamed for their bad results at school. In another case, the accused was supposed to have constructed a secret airstrip behind his house where 'aeroplanes magiques' (magical aeroplanes) landed at night; his access to modern goods was seen as a deadly menace to the village. In this case, the link with new forms of wealth was clearly imagined. In general, access to new consumer goods is still fairly restricted in the relatively poor Maka area (compared, for instance, to the more developed western parts of the country).

Yet in the same region, where the inequalities within the villages are still limited, new forms of success seem to be self-evident targets for witchcraft rumours. Ambitious farmers, who profited more than their co-villagers from new opportunities in cocoa and coffee cultivation, were often associated with the world of the *djamb*; their modern houses with tinned roofs have long been the object of strong witchcraft fears (Fisiy and Geschiere 1991). In a neighbouring village, only a few kilometres from Baba's, one of the few retired Maka civil servants was recently accused of *kong* (a novel form of witchcraft, closely related to the new forms of wealth, to which we will return below). This accusation, made in public by a young, aspiring female *nganga*, caused great unrest in view of the accused's prestige, but has not yet been followed up or concretely resolved. It is highly improbable that it will lead to a court case, like the one above. It is no doubt characteristic that all of the thirty-eight accused persons in the witch-trial files we could study clearly had a very modest background. Apparently, the *nganga* are reluctant to take rumours about more wealthy or powerful figures to the courts.[14]

The most conspicuous innovations in the case above concern the role of Baba, the *guérisseur traditionnel*, who is a good example of the more modern type of *nganga*, increasingly prominent throughout the region during recent decades. In striking contrast with the *nganga* of earlier days, the new ones make themselves much more conspicuous. Whereas Baba's predecessors used to live in fairly modest houses, often somewhat at the margin of the village, Baba's house – his 'hospital' as he called it – was in the middle of the village at the main junction. It was indicated by no fewer than three big signs, saying: 'Baba Denis, *professeur-guérisseur*' [professional healer], *Astrologue* [astrologist] and *Rose-Croix* [Rosicrucian].' The latter sign shows that Baba associated himself with the new Cameroonian elite which contains a strong element of Rosicrucians (President Biya himself is supposed to adhere to this movement).

When he was interviewed by Geschiere, Baba emphasised his modern identity. He spoke at length of his important contacts in the capital (without going into more detail), showed his collection of books on magic and his *cahiers* with notes on all the cases he treated, and referred to his occult knowledge as his science. Most strikingly, he maintained a somewhat frightening martial air. Rumour had it that he served in the army but was discharged for pilfering and even spent some time in jail. But this only strengthened his fearsome reputation among the villagers: people generally believe that it is in jail that one meets the truly dangerous *marabouts* who can teach you all sorts of secrets.

Despite this modern identity, Baba played on local ideas in order to build up his reputation among the villagers. Like the *nganga* of earlier days, he spoke of his confrontations with the witches as 'combats', in which he had to 'surprise', 'vanquish' and 'disarm' them. For the Maka, as said before, a *nganga* can only do such things because he himself is something of a super-witch. There is a strong belief throughout this area that a *nganga* can be initiated by his own 'professor' only if he is prepared to sacrifice one of his own relatives (just as the witches are supposed to do). The *nganga* can only heal because he (or she) has killed (see also Mallart [1981] on the Evuzok of south Cameroon and Copet-Rougier [1986] on the Kako, to the north-west of the Maka). Like his predecessors, Baba had the moral identity of a highly ambivalent and dangerous figure in the eyes of the people.

202 IDENTITY DEGRADATION, MORAL KNOWLEDGE

The most significant innovation was Baba's novel use of these powers. In former days, *nganga* intent on neutralising the dangerous powers of witches were supposed to compel the witches to give up their forces so that both they and their victims could be healed. In general, witchcraft affairs in the villages had a fairly open ending. Persistent accusations could lead to a public palaver in which the elders would admonish both the accused and the accusers to put the matter before a *nganga*; but even those cases seldom came to a conclusive verdict. People felt rather that such affairs should be arranged in private, for instance by enlisting the help of a *nganga* who had to settle the score in his (or her) own hidden ways.

Modern *nganga* like Baba seem to be much more intent on bringing matters into the open, most drastically by handing over the suspects to the gendarmes. In the 1970s, the *nganga* still tended to be afraid of making themselves too visible to the state. Of course, some of them also had their clients among the highest ranks of the new state elite, but these were private, more or less hidden contacts. Most *nganga* tended to be rather afraid of the gendarmes since they were not at all sure to what extent the state condoned their practice. Apparently, Baba had no such fears. By delivering the witches to the gendarmes, he related his role as *guérisseur traditionnel* to the new public sphere around the state – apparently with considerable success. To the judges, he became an indispensable ally as an expert witness: apparently, it is only the *nganga* who can furnish definite proof in difficult witchcraft affairs.[15] To the villagers, this had made him into a new kind of broker in their relations with the fearsome authority of the state.

What do these cases say about the intricate articulations of witchcraft, violence and identity? To what extent do the new relations between witchdoctors and judicial authorities give new dimensions to this conceptual complex? We might give a more 'traditional' reading of the first case, and similar stories from the witch-trial files. On this interpretation, they would reflect the old struggle of the local community to maintain control over ambitious individuals in its midst: people like Mentanga who used old secrets in order to prevail over his fellow-villagers, or more innovatory witches like the owner of the 'magic' aeroplanes who used his occult powers to get access to the miracles of modern technology. In this vein, these stories exemplify the levelling impact of the witchcraft discourse, helping to restore communitarian values against personal ambition.

If we focus on what actually happens in daily life, we find reflected the other side of the same discourse, which can also serve to affirm the strong emphasis on personal ambition in these societies.[16] In fact, it is Baba, the traditional witchdoctor, who uses the local conceptions of the occult to further his own ambitions and to give the role of the *nganga* a new kind of prestige. He is the one who emerges from the story as a 'sovereign subject', who tries to emancipate himself from the communitarian restrictions on the *nganga* role. His collaboration with the gendarmes and the courts gives this role a new scope and he clearly tries to establish himself as a new kind of broker between the village and the authoritarian state. To the villagers, a 'modern' *nganga* such as Baba, precisely because he is linked to the coercive apparatus of the state, seems to be better qualified for dealing with the proliferation of witchcraft.

The case has similarly ambivalent implications if we focus on the relation between *djamb* and violence. At first sight, the violence seems to come from the witches: Mentanga with his panther's whiskers or the nightly thunder of the 'magic' aeroplanes of his fellow-witch. But, again, in the everyday world, Baba is the one who unleashes a formidable amount of violence, which is, moreover, of a new type. The forceful way in which he publicly exposes his 'suspects' is already remarkable and rather different from the more subtle ways in which *nganga* proceeded in earlier days. Even more striking is the fact that he does not proceed by trying to neutralise Mentanga's powers in order to 'cure' him, as *nganga* used to do. Instead, he delivers him to the gendarmes. Since colonial times, the latter have become for the villagers the very incarnation of violence. People believe that every suspect who is brought to their office receives first of all a 'warning', in the form of a thorough thrashing. In the case above – as in most of the witchcraft files we were able to consult – the judge added his own kind of violence by condemning the accused to a long period in jail. Because of the collaboration of the *nganga* with the gendarmes and the judges, witchcraft rumours now can suddenly unleash violence of a new kind in the village.[17]

The south: witchcraft and the dilemma of the state   Elsewhere in Cameroon, the judicial authorities seem to be more reluctant to intervene so directly in witchcraft affairs. But especially in the South and the Centre Provinces, where local forms of organisation have similar segmentary tendencies as in the east, there seems to be strong popular pressure on the state to intervene. This was clearly illustrated by the following case with which we were confronted during a brief period of research in Kribi, a small town on the coast of south Cameroon.

In 1991, the villagers of N., a small locality thirty kilometres to the northeast of Kribi, dragged an old man to the gendarmes in town. They insisted that he had already killed several people by means of witchcraft and that the village had to be rid of him. The state attorney looked into the matter but, after a few days, he ordered the gendarmes to release the man since there was no concrete evidence (*preuves tangibles*; 'tangible proof') against him. The consequences were dramatic. A few months later, the villagers set the house of the old 'witch' on fire and he died in the flames. This was brought to the attention of the gendarmes who immediately came to the village and arrested seventeen persons, all young men.

In February 1992, when we arrived in Kribi, the young men were still in prison. We had the chance to discuss this case with Mr Ela, the new state attorney (the successor to the one who had released the old man). Mr Ela, who originates from the same province, complained that the case put him in an impossible dilemma. He insisted that he was a 'positivist': in principle, the court should consider cases of witchcraft only if there was concrete proof of physical aggression (the *preuves tangibles* mentioned before); in this sense his predecessor had acted rightly. This meant also that, now, he could not simply release the young men; that would be condoning murder. On the other hand, if the court convicted the young men for having killed the old man, people would say that the state protected the witches and this was also not acceptable. Therefore, his predecessor had acted wrongly after all: he should at least have kept the old man in prison for some time until the excitement in the village had died down.

According to Mr Ela, the new state attorney, the whole affair was typical of the pressure exercised by the population on the judicial authorities. He maintained that in most of these cases, the initiative did not come from the courts but rather from below. He and most of his colleagues were rather inclined to stick to the 'positive spirit' of the law.[18] The great problem was, however, that on this point the law did not 'correspond to our culture'. The state could not neglect the urgent demands of the population to intervene against witchcraft. When we interviewed him in 1992, the state attorney was clearly doubtful about how to resolve this dilemma.

In this case again, the link between witchcraft and violence is highly ambivalent. Moreover, it is complicated by the role of the state, albeit in strikingly different ways from our first case. To the villagers, it was clearly the old man who had released violence in the village by his dark powers. In the upshot, the roles were reversed: the young men committed violence by killing the old man.

Several factors can explain why witchcraft rumours had such a dramatic effect in this case. First of all, according to some, the old man had been accused of *kong*, a new form of witchcraft. Briefly, at this point, *kong* stands for the individualism of the new rich who are supposed to enslave their own people mystically to further their personal pursuit of riches. Even though the old man in question seemed quite poor, he was apparently suspected of killing his own kin to accumulate in secret the new and much coveted objects of wealth. The new rumours about this link between hidden violence and new forms of accumulation had recently created a real panic in this area.

This can be related to the general politico-economic profile of this area, which in some respects is highly different from the east. Historically, the Kribi area was one of the first parts of the country to be deeply penetrated by the colonial market economy. In German times, it suddenly became the centre of the highly spectacular but equally short-lived boom in rubber. It was also one of the first areas of missionary activity (the American Presbyterians were already active here prior to the German conquest). However, after the collapse of the trade in wild rubber from 1913 onwards, the area stagnated despite several large-scale plantation schemes and logging concessions. This series of abrupt changes deeply affected local patterns of organisation. The 'customary chiefs', whom the colonial authorities tried to impose upon the local, highly segmentary forms of organisation, never succeeded in really establishing themselves. Instead, especially after independence, the region became the scene of a true proliferation, quite exceptional for Cameroon, of all sorts of in-dependent churches and other religious movements.

This makes it all the more surprising that, in the case described above, there is no intermediate role for an equivalent to the *nganga* who figured so prominently in the cases in the east. Indeed, during the 1970s, a new anti-witchcraft movement, called Bissima, which was supposed to be especially effective against *kong*, spread through the Kribi area. In recent years, however, it was felt that most witchdoctors, even the Bissima ones, had already been corrupted by the very forces they were supposed to combat. This might be one of the reasons why the villagers decided not to invoke the help of a local specialist, but rather took the old witch directly to the gendarmes.

The case shows clearly that, in the absence of any 'traditional' expert who can act as intermediary, popular pressure on the state to intervene against witchcraft can put the state officials in a very difficult position.[19] Indeed one can sympathise with the second state attorney's complaints about his impossible predicament. The case shows also that, without such an intermediary figure, the link between witchcraft and violence can become particularly direct.[20]

The west: zombies and the hidden violence of the new rich Especially in the Western Provinces of Cameroon, a different pattern has evolved in the relation between witchcraft, new forms of individualism and violence. Here, for some decades now, rumours have abounded about a new form of witchcraft related to *kong* (mentioned above) which is equated with the new forms of wealth and which evokes specific patterns of violence and counter-violence.

Different terms are used for this new form of witchcraft: it is called *ekong* in Douala, *nyongo* in the south-west, *ekom* among the Bakossi and *famla* in the Grassfields of the west and the north-west. A general name is *kupe*, after Mt Kupe (100 kilometres to the north of Douala) which plays a central but mysterious role in these beliefs. The basic story, however, is nearly the same. These witches are no longer supposed to eat their victims as in older forms of witchcraft, but to transform them to zombies and put them to work. Often these witches are said to transport their victims 'in lorries' to Mt Kupe where they have to work on 'invisible plantations'. Throughout Cameroon, Mt Kupe has thus become associated with mysterious, and suspicious, wealth.

Elsewhere, we have tried to place these beliefs in a broader historical and regional context (see Fisiy and Geschiere 1991; and also Geschiere 1995; see also the very vivid descriptions of de Rosny [1981 and 1992] of his own experiences with *ekong* and healing in Douala; also Ardener [1970] on the Bakweri; Balz [1984] and Ejedepang-Kogé [1971] on the Bakossi).[21] Most people see Douala as the place from which these new forms of witchcraft have originated. This has a special significance since Douala is the main port of the area and the historical point of entry for the European trade. Indeed, these new forms of witchcraft are often explicitly connected to the growing impact of the Europeans and their commercial activities, particularly since the nineteenth century. The belief seems to have spread only later into the hinterland, together with the new consumer goods. It emerged towards the end of the colonial period in the Grass-fields, where it coincided with the rise of new entrepreneurs from these areas. More recently, it reached the south, the centre and the east where it is called *kong*.

Characteristically, again, these beliefs also reinterpret old elements in a new context. Even this 'modern' form of witchcraft, often associated with the new cities, is still closely connected with the familiar framework of kinship: a witch is still supposed to deliver a close relative in order to become a member of the feared *ekong* associations and healing is possible only if the *nganga* succeeds in reuniting the family. But these old elements are now expressed in a new idiom, which has strong commercial – one could even say, capitalist – overtones. *Ekong* witches are said to 'sell' their relatives; the witches go at night to the 'market of sorcery' – as already mentioned, a particularly powerful image in these areas of the country – and it is from there that they bring back their riches; they transport their victims 'in lorries' to the mystic 'plantations' on Mt Kupe.[22]

In this form as well, the link between witchcraft and new forms of wealth is highly ambivalent. The rumours about *ekong*, *famla* or *kupe* all seem to express a deep distrust of the new rich, who are supposed to owe their success only to a new form of hidden violence, breaking through the old communitarian restrictions. At the same time, these stories betray a true fascination with the new consumption goods which are seen as the manifestations *par excellence* of these hidden forces. Moreover, the concrete effects of these rumours and accusations often seem to be quite limited.

Warnier (1993) observes that *famla* rumours are circulating about nearly all successful entrepreneurs from the Grassfields, without really affecting their position.

This Grassfields area – including the francophone Bamileke and the anglophone Bamenda – is of particular interest here. It is from this area that, especially after independence, a true commercial bourgeoisie emerged; it is now supposed to dominate the Cameroonian economy. As could be expected, rumours about *famla* or *kupe* are therefore particularly strong throughout this region. But it seems also that these societies have their own mechanisms for both legitimating the suspect forms of new wealth and containing, at least to a certain degree, the threat of the new forms of witchcraft. This affects both the role of the state and the implications of these witchcraft discourses for the exercise of violence in this area. It is quite striking that here, despite the general unrest about *famla* and *kupe*, there are as yet no parallels to the witchcraft trials in the east. Neither are there clear signs of popular pressure on the state to intervene against these new forms of witchcraft. People seem rather to put their trust in local mechanisms for dealing with the violence evoked by these new witchcraft rumours.

A very interesting manuscript, unfortunately not yet published, by Patrick Mbunwe-Samba from the north-west, *Witchcraft, Magic and Divination*, is a rich source of stories about *kupe* and *famla* (Mbunwe-Samba 1989). A characteristic example is the following story about Mr P., who worked as a headmaster in several towns of the north-west. The story concerns his frightening experiences when he returned to his home area but it also concerns his final triumph. The following is a direct quote from Mbunwe-Samba's text:

> After many transfers in his long career, Mr P. settled to teaching among his own people in the village of N. in Noni area in Bui Division. In this village, stories started circulating that he was planning to give schoolchildren in for *kupe*, that in actual fact he had buried a pot in the school in which children's fingernails were cut and stored and that the eventual outcome would be that one day, when lightning struck, it would destroy a large number of school-children all at once; some said fifty would die! As these stories developed the village population began to get more and more anxious and disturbed. It is not certain what was the last straw but we are told that the Parent–Teachers' Association (PTA) of the school organised a secret meeting at which they resolved that Mr P. was practising witchcraft and that the Senior Divisional Officer (SDO) should be asked to transfer him. The PTA sent to Mr P. a copy of the letter they had written to the Senior Divisional Officer. He replied demanding that they prove their baseless allegations.
>
> Instead of waiting to get a reply from the SDO to their petition, the group came to the school and drove Mr P. away from the class and then began to plan to kill him by attacking his entire household. The headmaster of the school was forewarned of the plans being made to take Mr P.'s life and he

sneaked into Mr P.'s house, in time to warn Mr P. and his children. They narrowly evaded capture, escaping by the back door. The story of this dramatic escape is told in many versions in Nkor today, some even saying that Mr P. transformed and disappeared!

If this plan had succeeded it would have shown how a few people can scheme and manipulate a group to create problems which could have far-reaching consequences.

We are told that Mr P. did not take the threat lying down. In the following days, the forces of law and order descended on Nkor and eight people were arrested and detained at Kumbo, the divisional capital. We were informed that the case was actually taken to the magistrate's court. The case was tried and the suspects were discharged and acquitted on technical grounds, because it was argued that women were among the men but were not together arrested.

It is revealing to note that Mr P. stood as a candidate in the parliament elections of April 1988; the results from the Noni area show that there was a lot of support for him in spite of the feelings of some Noni people about the case. This was indeed a very encouraging sign. In our last interview with some Noni people in July 1989 it was remarked that the population of N. has now realised that there was actually no truth in the accusations against Mr P. The villagers have now come to realise that there was a clique behind the entire drama and are now friendly with Mr P., with whom they not only drink, but also exchange visits.

The fact that Mr P. succeeded in standing for parliamentary elections as a candidate for this area allows the story to be seen in its correct perspective and reveals the intrigues of some interested parties, who thought that they could challenge his candidature in this way. (Mbunwe-Samba 1989: 56–8)

This story has several surprising aspects. One is that it was the Parent–Teachers' Association which took the initiative to unmask Mr P.'s supposed dabbling with new forms of witchcraft. Normally, this would be dealt with by the chief and his disciplinary society (the *kwifon*), which are still very powerful throughout this region. According to some there were private grievances behind all this. Mr P. had been an enterprising politician during the heyday of multiparty politics in the years around independence, astutely switching from party to party. Rumour had it that some people were using the PTA to settle old scores. This was also one of the reasons why only part of the community joined in the actions against Mr P.

This might also help to explain another surprising aspect of the story, namely its happy ending. Despite all the backbiting, Mr P. succeeded in being nominated by his home community as a candidate in one of the most prestigious elections in the area. This is a pattern which recurs in similar stories from the north-west and the west: accusations of *kupe* or *famla* against ambitious individuals create problems for them but ultimately do not seem to harm their careers.[23] Elsewhere we argued that this may relate to the particularly important role of chiefs in this area (Fisiy and Geschiere 1991; 1993), which is one of the ways in which the west and the north-west differ greatly from the segmentary societies from the eastern and southern forest areas, discussed above. Both in the west and the north-west there is a strong tradition of chieftaincy which goes back centuries before colonial rule. In many respects, the chiefs in these areas seem to have consolidated their powers despite all the changes in colonial and postcolonial times. Even to the modern elites from this area, who now live in cities elsewhere in the country, chieftaincy is still a crucial issue. In various ways, the chiefs have succeeded in co-opting these new elites into the associations of their court.

It is therefore quite striking that the chief does not figure in Mbunwe-Samba's story. But in most of his other stories, chiefs do play a central role. In some cases, they appear to support local accusations of *kupe* against ambitious individuals. But in others, they protect the accused and seem rather intent on associating with them and their new wealth. As Fisiy has emphasised elsewhere, all this depends notably on whether the new wealth is 'dedicated' to the chief (Fisiy 1992; see also Fisiy and Geschiere 1991). In precolonial times, accumulation of wealth through trade abroad was very important in these societies. The chief was supposed to act as a kind of pivot in the enrichment of his subjects: it depended on his powers whether or not they had success in their dealings with parties from outside the realm (Warnier 1985). Wealth, accumulated outside the chief's control, was seen as asocial and indeed as associated with witchcraft. But wealth which was legitimated by the chief's blessing was viewed as the fruit of rightful personal ambition.

Most chiefs in this area are intent on participating in the new forms of wealth as well. They create novel, 'pseudo-traditional', titles at their courts which are bought by the new elites who have succeeded in making careers in the new centres of power outside the chiefdom (but who are often not qualified by descent to assume the existing titles). Thus the chiefs succeed both in profiting directly from the new wealth of their subjects abroad and also in incorporating them in the traditional associations around the court (Goheen 1993; forthcoming). Another effect is that the new wealth of these subjects, which in too many cases is highly suspect, is legitimised – one might say 'whitewashed'. In these areas, the chiefs seem to be acting as catalysts for legitimising the new forms of wealth, a capacity which is blatantly missing in the segmentary societies of the forest discussed above.

From all this an original pattern emerges in the relations between witchcraft, individualising tendencies and violence. The *famla* and *kupe* imagery express strong suspicions *vis-à-vis* the new forms of wealth which are attributed to dangerous individual ambitions and new forms of hidden violence. It can evoke violent reactions, as in Mbunwe-Samba's story about the conflict between Mr P. and the PTA. But the chiefs have been able to make their control over wealth and violence evolve, so as to keep up with modern changes. By incorporating the new forms of wealth within the traditional associations of their court, they are supposed to keep the hidden violence of *famla* and *kupe* in check. Therefore, they are also in a position to control the counter-violence *kupe* and *famla* rumours evoke.

This is certainly important as a background to the success of new entrepreneurs from these societies: here, the new forms of individual success are, at least to a certain extent, still incorporated in the communitarian institutions of the chief's court (see also Warnier 1993). This is, again, in sharp contrast to the general distrust of the new forms of wealth in the forest societies, which still seem to constitute an unresolved problem there. It can explain also why the state is far less involved in witchcraft affairs in the west and the north-west, despite the general unrest about *kupe* and *famla*.[24] The chiefs still seem to be able, at least to a certain degree, to control the violence and the counter-violence called forth by the rumours about these new forms of witchcraft.

One can wonder, however, whether these Grassfields chiefs will retain the moral power to do so in the future. Their close alliance with the new elites and the selling of new titles seem to involve them also in a quite ruthless pursuit of the new forms of wealth.[25] Goheen, writing about the neighbouring chiefdom of Nso, quotes a powerful image from her informants which clearly summarises the doubts of the population: will these businessmen and civil servants who buy the novel titles from the chief really turn out to be his 'new leopards' with whom he will ride at night, transformed into a lion, in order to protect the realm? Or will they prove to be 'witches of the night' who will corrupt his power from the inside? (Goheen, forthcoming).

Conclusion

The preceding comments may have indicated some of the reasons why witchcraft discourses have come to play such a prominent role in debates over identity and violence in postcolonial Cameroon. The curious bifocality of these discourses – centred on conceptions of kinship and domestic intimacy but at the same time addressing personal ambition and individual pursuits of wealth/power – makes them obvious idioms for trying to interpret the increasingly worrying inequalities within African societies in postcolonial times. Whatever the differences between these local discourses, they always raise the questions of which means are acceptable and which are unacceptable in the pursuit of personal ambitions, and how to relate such ambitions to the maxim of solidarity among kin. In postcolonial Africa, these have indeed become urgent questions.

In many African societies – certainly in the Cameroonian cases discussed above – the tension between kinship and communitarian control on the one hand and the quest for individual autonomy on the other seems to have been an old leitmotiv (albeit differently expressed in the segmentary forest societies of south and east Cameroon, and the more hierarchical chiefdoms of the west and the north-west). But with the new opportunities for enrichment for the few and the rapid impoverishment of the many in postcolonial days, this tension has become ever more pronounced. It is no coincidence that this also coincides with an upsurge of rumours about witchcraft and sorcery which now seem to overrun the new public spheres built up around the state as well. It is not just a whim that modern consumer goods, which symbolise the new forms of success, play such a prominent role in these rumours, alongside the old preoccupation with kinship. The continuing strength of these discourses is precisely that they still seem capable of relating the two. This is one of the reasons why discourses on *ekong, famla* or *kupe* – which relate witchcraft to both kinship and new forms of entrepreneurship in a most spectacular way – could spread so rapidly throughout western and southern Cameroon since the end of the colonial period.

The preceding comments may have shown also that it is risky to generalise, despite the spread of such notions across old cultural boundaries. The various cases indicate that references to similar witchcraft conceptions can have highly different implications, and that the tension between kinship and the new opportunities for enrichment can be 'acted out' in highly different ways. A concrete starting point for trying to understand such differences is the highly variable role of the Cameroonian state in the various regions discussed above. There is a most direct link here to the varying ways in which witchcraft rumours can trigger violence. It is indeed quite striking that, within one country, state officials can follow such different strategies: in the east, the state courts and the gendarmes seem quite eager to respond to popular pressure to intervene against the proliferation of witchcraft; in the south, there are similar pressures, but the judicial authorities react much more cautiously; in the west, the state hardly plays a role in such affairs and local societies seem much more inclined to arrange such matters themselves.

In this chapter, which offers no more than a first and rapid comparison, such differences were mainly related to the role of the chiefs who, in the west, still serve as a crystallisation point for legitimising the new, suspect forms of wealth. In the segmentary societies of the south and the eastern forests, such crystallisation points are clearly lacking. Consequently, the new forms of accumulation seem to remain an unsolved problem there.

However, it might be worthwhile to try and deepen this comparison. No doubt other, more hidden factors may be at stake as well. It is to be expected that the close link between witchcraft and kinship, so strongly emphasised above, does play a role here as well. An obvious question, already raised in the Introduction, is whether differences in the ways in which kinship is organised affect the relation between witchcraft, new forms of personal ambition and the role of the state. Indeed, both Warnier (1993) and Rowlands (1993) stress that there are fundamental differences between kinship discourses, and their implications for new forms of accumulation, in the Grassfields and in the forest regions. In the Grassfields societies, kinship itself would offer certain forms of protection against the 'strategies of disaccumulation' which are so dominant in the kinship organisation of the forest societies. Such differences can help us to understand why the panic about novel forms of witchcraft, which are related to the new forms of wealth, is much greater in the forest region, and why, in this region, there is consequently such a strong popular pressure on the state to intervene. It can also explain why, in the Grassfields, people still seem more inclined to put their trust in local mechanisms for dealing with such threats.

Related to this are important differences in the texture of the witchcraft/sorcery discourses themselves. In the forests, especially among groups like the Maka or the Beti, discourses on *djamb* and *evu* are extremely fluid; any distinction between good and evil, or between acceptable or unacceptable uses of the occult forces is relative and undermined by the extremely diffuse tenor of these discourses. In contrast, the discourses on the occult in the Grassfields societies seem to be more compartmentalised; the chief and the institutions of his court legitimise and confirm prevalent distinctions between proper and improper aspects of the occult. Such differences are again directly related to varying possibilities for legitimising and incorporating the new forms of wealth with their suspect backgrounds. The diffuseness of discourses on *evu* or *djamb* in the forest societies explains not only why they are so omnipresent and all-pervasive there but also why they can generate a true panic and a feeling that only an appeal to outside agencies, such as the state, can help.[26] Historically, there is a tragic paradox here. During the first decades of colonial rule, it was precisely these segmentary societies, not used to any kind of central authority, which strongly resisted the imposition of the state and the new forms of domination and violence it brought. Now, these same societies seem to feel themselves so unable to solve their internal conflicts that they appeal to the state to intervene in the most private of spheres, that of witchcraft and kinship.

The preceding explorations into the intricacies and the inherent logics of discourses on the occult, and their relations to the new inequalities, suggest two directions for further comparative research which may be of special interest, in regard to future developments in postcolonial Africa.

The first direction concerns the precarious relations between the state, on the on hand, and, on the other, 'traditional healers', witchdoctors or other experts from the local societies for dealing with witchcraft. The possibilities or impossibilities for collaboration between the two will affect directly the relation between witchcraft rumours and violence. Clearly, 'traditional healers' are now, nearly everywhere in postcolonial Africa, intent on modernising themselves and attaining some kind of position in the public sphere. An important issue is how the official authorities react to such efforts.

The case above from the Kribi area shows that state officials can be put in an impossible dilemma where there is strong popular pressure on them to intervene against witchcraft when there are no local experts available who can act as intermediaries. In this case, the predicament led to violence of a most undiluted kind: the summary execution of the old man, supposed to be a witch, by the villagers. In the cases from the east, on the contrary, the judicial authorities showed themselves to be quite eager to collaborate with local *nganga* (witchdoctors). But this collaboration also had quite shocking consequences: the 'witches' were subject to the violence of the gendarmes and the state prison while the *nganga* tended to become violent, disciplining figures instead of healers.

The more or less official collaboration between the state elite and *nganga* in the east is, as yet, quite exceptional in Cameroon. How precarious this relationship still is can be seen from the ambiguous position of the national Association of Traditional Healers. This association has had a semi-formal status for more than ten years now. Many *nganga* sport their membership card as some sort of proof of official recognition. But the government has refused formally to recognise the association, which is all the more surprising since, in private, many members of the state elite highly value the services of such *nganga*. The official reason for withholding recognition is that it is so difficult to make a distinction between 'bonafide' and 'malafide' *nganga* within the association. But according to others, the problem is rather that the association has been captured by people from the north-west, the area of the strongest opposition to President Biya's government.

On this point, more detailed comparisons might be enlightening, for instance with countries such as Zimbabwe or Ghana where similar associations have been recognised for some time. There are crucial issues at stake here. The question to what degree and under what conditions 'traditional healers' will succeed in claiming a position in the new public sphere around the state touches upon a nodal point in the intertwinement of witchcraft beliefs, identity and violence. An advantage is, moreover, that this point can be studied in fairly concrete terms, which is fairly rare in this field.

A second direction for comparative research concerns the question of the limits to the connection between witchcraft and kinship. In the Cameroonian societies studied above – and in many other situations in Africa – this link is still very close. Discourses on witchcraft still succeed in encompassing both the world of kinship and the fascination with the new forms of riches. One can wonder, however, if this will remain possible in view of the growing inequalities in postcolonial Africa, which seem more and more to overstretch the elasticity of the kinship patterns.

Of particular interest in this respect is Bastian's recent study of the role of witchcraft in the relations between Igbo urbanites and villagers. After all, the Igbo have a reputation both for the capacity of their home communities to retain the loyalty of urban migrants and for their talents to profit from new economic opportunities. Bastian (1993: 134) still emphasises, for the Igbo as well, the close link between witchcraft and family, but she adds that 'an impersonal quality is creeping into Nigerian witchcraft'. Does this mean that here it is no longer self-evident that witchcraft refers back to the basic networks of family and kin? In our Cameroonian examples this is not (not yet?) the case.[27] But it is clear – for instance in rumours on the *famla* of rich Bamileke entrepreneurs who are supposed to compete among each other with such occult means – that the link with kinship is becoming ever more tenuous.

One can wonder what will happen if witchcraft beliefs are indeed cut loose from their kinship moorings. It might mean that the hold these beliefs have over people's minds will slacken. Elsewhere, we have tried to show that it is precisely this close link with the intimacies of kinship that makes witchcraft appear such an inescapable reality to many Africans (Fisiy and Geschiere 1991). In the near future, however, this loosening of the connection between witchcraft and kinship may foster the idea that witchcraft is completely out of control. There is a very real danger that this might call forth further feelings of panic and even more arbitrary forms of violence.

This seems to make all the more urgent the question of how more peaceful forms of collaboration can be realised between the official authorities and the local mechanisms for containing fears about witchcraft; more peaceful, that is, than the frightening witch-hunts unleashed by the collaboration of state courts and local *nganga* in East Cameroon.

Notes

An earlier version of this text was presented at a conference entitled *Violence et la production du sujet souverain* at the Maison des Sciences de l'Homme (Paris, May 1994), organised by Bogumil Jewsiewicki. We thank Georg Deutsch, Bogumil Jewsiewicki, Achille Mbembe, Achim von Oppen, Wim van Binsbergen and especially Richard Werbner for their comments on earlier versions of this text. Geschiere worked on the text while he was research fellow at the Forschungsschwerpunt Moderner Orient (Centre for Modern Oriental Studies) in Berlin. He thanks the Centre for providing a highly stimulating environment.

1. There were debates in several colonies on how to deal with the numerous anti-witchcraft movements. Official support for such movements – even for the less violent ones – would mean a recognition of the reality of witchcraft as such.

Experts, such as the 'witchdoctors', were in general looked upon highly unfavourably by the new authorities. The consequence was that the local populations firmly believed that the state protected the witches. (Fields 1985; see also National Archives Bureau [in SW Cameroon], file Aa 1934,16 for a drawn-out discussion on these issues in Nigeria and the Cameroons, during the 1930s and 1940s; and National Archives Yaoundé, files 1 AC 416/D, 1935, and APA/900/CF, 1950, for similar discussions in French Cameroon.)

2. Especially from this last paragraph it may have become clear that there are serious terminological problems in this field. Recently, several authors have emphasised that terms such as 'witchcraft' or 'sorcery' should be avoided because of their Eurocentric associations (see, for instance, Schmoll 1993; cf. Crick 1979). Indeed, the introduction of these terms in Africa by anthropologists (along with missionaries and other Northerners) is a good example of one of the central topics at the SCUSA conference on postcolonial identities – namely, the role of 'Euro-American scholarship in constructing postcolonialism and identity' (introductory text for this conference by Werbner and Ranger 1994). A particular problem is that these terms have a strong pejorative tenor whereas the African terms they are supposed to translate often have a broader array of associations: the latter refer to occult forces which are often employed to harm, but which can be used constructively as well. Moreover, these African discourses are often so fluid that it is highly dubious to try and make sharp distinctions between more destructive and more constructive uses of these forces. Thus, the general use of terms such as witchcraft or sorcery risks reducing a rich world-view, in which man's environment is animated by all sorts of spiritual forces, to an ugly core. A more neutral translation – for instance, 'occult forces' – would therefore be preferable. However, this problem is complicated by the fact that these European terms have now been widely appropriated by Africans. They are now generally used by newspapers as much as by Radio Trottoir. Public debates are waged in these terms (in Cameroon in the 1980s, for instance, the Ministry of Scientific Research tried to launch a large-scale research project on *Sorcellerie et Développement*). Therefore, we decided to retain these terms, despite their obvious disadvantages. After all, it seems urgent that scientists try to relate as much as possible to ongoing debates in the societies they study (cf. Fisiy and Geschiere 1991). Finally, we do not follow the classical distinction proposed by Evans-Pritchard between witchcraft and sorcery since it does not apply very well to the Cameroonian societies studied here, and certainly not to the modern dynamics of these discourses.

3. Compare the notion, very common in the western parts of Cameroon, of the 'market of sorcery', which apparently goes back to precolonial times: a secret place where some succeed in appropriating wealth and others lose whatever they had (Geschiere 1995; and Ejedepang-Kogé 1971).

4. This 'modernity' of witchcraft/sorcery in Africa was long neglected by anthropologists, although witchcraft/sorcery, as such, was one of their favourite topics. The classic anthropological studies of witchcraft, however, analysed it nearly exclusively within the local context (Douglas 1970), concentrated on witchcraft accusations, and related these to tensions within the local communities. Moreover, the strong interest was in 'eu-functional' aspects of such accusations, in how they helped to restore the social order. Such a view is, indeed, difficult to reconcile with the impact – ever more manifest since the 1960s – of witchcraft conceptions on modern politics, sports or new forms of entrepreneurship. In retrospect, apparently, anthropologists were slow in picking up the modern dynamics of witchcraft discourses. As recently as 1991, we found it difficult to compare with other studies

in this field (Fisiy and Geschiere 1991; see also Geschiere 1982; but also van Binsbergen 1981; and Rowlands and Warnier 1988). However, important since then is a sudden wave of studies on different patterns in the intertwinement of local witchcraft conceptions and broader politico-economic developments (Ciekawy 1989; Niehaus 1993; van Kessel 1993; and especially the contributions in Comaroff and Comaroff 1993). This new attention to witchcraft comes especially from anthropologists interested in the impact of the state or, even broader, in the meeting of the local and the global. As Richard Werbner suggests, it might be interesting to analyse in more detail to what extent this broader background leads to different views on witchcraft as compared to older anthropological studies (see personal communication and Geschiere 1995).

5. We stress that, in colonial times and during the first decades after independence, state courts rather tended to persecute witchdoctors (for defamation and breach of the peace), which made people complain that the state was protecting the witches. As one of Geschiere's informants in the east explained to him in the early 1970s: 'You Whites do not believe in witchcraft. Therefore, the state of the *colons* refused to intervene against the witches. But now, all this is going to change. Nowadays, it is Africans who are in command and they know witchcraft is all too real here. Soon the law will be changed, so that judges will be able to deal with the witches.' Apparently, not even a change in the law has been necessary for this. The state courts in the east are now condemning witches on the basis of an existing, but extremely vague, article on *sorcellerie* in the Cameroonian *Code penal* (which is copied from the French *Code*). See Fisiy 1990a; and Fisiy and Geschiere 1990.

6. This ambivalence – which is so marked in the forest societies of southern and eastern Cameroon, but certainly not only there – becomes even more complex if one relates it to distinctions between good and evil (or acceptable and unacceptable uses of the occult). In several contributions on the modern dynamics of witchcraft discourses in Comaroff and Comaroff (1993), a strong emphasis is placed on witchcraft as something evil (see especially the fascinating chapters by Bastian and Auslander). However, between the lines it becomes clear that the same forces can also be put to a more respectable use (to protect the home and the accumulation of wealth). No doubt, societies will differ in the degree to which they clearly distinguish between more respectable and more destructive uses of the occult (it would be very interesting to know more of the variations in this respect). However, it seems to be in the very nature of witchcraft discourses that they always tend to relativise and undermine such distinctions (Fisiy and Geschiere 1990; 1991; Geschiere 1994). It is precisely this diffusing impact which makes these discourses so 'good to think with' for interpreting the new inequalities and modes of accumulation.

7. In his in-depth study of the history of a community in Zimbabwe and on the basis of the shocking stories of his informants about their experiences during the liberation war, Werbner (1991: 150) makes an important contrast between 'sorcery-as-usual' in peacetime crises and 'sorcery-as-arbitrary' in wartime. The cases below seem to show that economic tensions – notably the growing uncertainty about the new forms of wealth, even if they remain largely imagined – can serve also to make the relation between witchcraft rumours and violence quite arbitrary.

8. An interesting question for further comparative research is to what extent this equation of kinship and witchcraft is general to Africa. It seems that there is, in any case, in many areas of the continent, a close conceptual link between witchcraft and intimacy.

9. See Guyer (1993) on the strong emphasis on 'multiple self-realisation' for a

man, as characteristic for these societies. According to Laburthe-Tolra (1977), the exercise of violence, especially homicide, was crucial in this drive for self-realisation.

10. The Maka characterise the former relations between the villages as *domb* – a term which they now translate as 'war'. This translation can have incorrect associations: war was not continuous; rather there was a constant threat of aggression, manslaughter and raids. For the general ethnographic background, see Geschiere (1982).

11. Fisiy succeeded in consulting altogether twenty-two files of witch-trials in the archives of the Court of Appeal of Bertoua (the capital of the East Province), covering a period between August 1982 and December 1984. Most files also contained copies of an earlier trial of the same case before one of the *'Tribunaux de Première Instance'* in this province. Moreover, Geschiere collected detailed information on six other cases in various Maka villages. See Fisiy (1990a and b), and Fisiy and Geschiere (1990).

12. Sources for this case: *Jugement du Tribunal* d'Abong-Mbang, 1196/COR; *Cour d'Appel* Bertoua, dos. 83.400.971/PG/BE, 6–12–1983; and Geschiere's investigations in the village. The names of the accused are pseudonyms. However, we have retained the real name of the *guérisseur* Baba Denis since he has become a public figure through his regular appearances as an expert witness before the state courts.

13. See above on the moral ambivalence of discourses about the occult. It seems that in the forest societies of southern and eastern Cameroon, of old highly segmentary in nature, these discourses are extremely fluid, making any distinction between more positive and more negative uses of the occult forces extremely precarious. In this respect there seems to be a certain contrast to the more hierarchical societies of the western parts of the country (see below and Geschiere 1994).

14. Many of the cases which came to court rather indicated the inverse pattern: apparently they were triggered by the fears of more prominent figures in the village (party officials, municipal counsellors, richer farmers) who suspected that they were bewitched by poor neighbours and asked the *nganga* for help. In a few cases about which we could collect more detailed information, it appeared that there were also witchcraft rumours concerning these prominent villagers. It is no doubt typical that these were not taken up by established *nganga* such as Baba.

15. Baba, and a colleague of his, a certain Aliguéna, who enjoyed a similar prestige in this area, played a decisive role in eight of the twenty-two court cases, the files of which we could consult. In none of these eight cases was any of the accused acquitted. On the difficult question of how to constitute 'proof' in witchcraft trials see Fisiy (1990a and b).

16. See Guyer (1993), quoted above, on the drive towards 'multiple personal self-realization' in the societies of the equatorial forest. In the Maka area, this emphasis on personal ambition is restrained by strong levelling mechanisms (the close link between witchcraft and jealousy; the segmentary implications of the kinship discourse). In an earlier publication, Geschiere (1982) described the tension between personal ambition and levelling mechanisms as characteristic for this society, in the past as well as nowadays.

17. The new possibilities of getting some sort of official recognition – for instance as a useful expert witness for the judicial authorities in their interventions against witchcraft – give the *nganga* role a more violent tenor. Modern *nganga*, such as Baba, are often much more aggressive in their accusations than their predecessors. They themselves take the initiative to point out witches (clearly, they try in this way to recruit new clients, who are told that they urgently need the services of the

nganga to protect themselves against these witches). And they do not deem it necessary to shroud their accusations in vague allusions, as *nganga* used to do in the 1970s. By handing over the accused to the gendarmes, instead of curing them, these modern *nganga* become highly punitive figures. One wonders if this affects their capacity to heal (see Geschiere 1995).

18. In this respect he differed from his colleagues in the east, who do feel that the law allows them to convict witches without '*preuves tangibles*'. Apparently different interpretations of the law are possible on this point. According to our information, the *Cour Suprême* in Yaoundé (the capital) did uphold the verdict of the Bertoua court in the few cases where the convicted 'witches' appealed against their conviction. The state attorney in Kribi maintained that neither he nor his colleagues had received clear guidelines from above in the matter.

19. In the Kribi area the relation between state officials and the witchdoctors – in this region particularly numerous – was fraught with suspicion (much more so than, for instance, in the east). The state attorney we interviewed cited several cases where he had intervened against witchdoctors and their fraudulent practices. He emphasised also that he had never called up a witchdoctor as witness. This makes the whole issue of how to constitute proof against supposed 'witches' practically unsolvable (see further, Fisiy 1990a and b; and Geschiere 1995).

20. In 1995, Geschiere had the opportunity to discuss the preceding case from the Kribi area once more with Mr Ela, the state attorney. This time, this official was more certain how he should deal with such affairs. Apparently, in the meantime, he had developed his own strategy. He emphasised that popular pressure on the courts to intervene in witchcraft affairs was even stronger than before. However, he knew now how to deal with them and he did not need a *nganga* for this. His current strategy was to have the accused arrested – if only for his (or her) own protection – and then to organise a large court session at which the whole village had to be present. If it became clear that there was no evidence against the accused, he (or she) could safely return to the village. In this way he had solved also the case in the village of N. (of the seventeen young men who had murdered an old 'witch'). He had summoned the whole village to a court session. There, he had demonstrated that there was no evidence at all against the old man. Consequently the villagers had accepted his verdict that the young men should be punished for their deed. All of them had been sentenced to eight years or more in prison and there had been no protest from the village.

21. There are, of course, close parallels to these beliefs elsewhere in West Africa (see, for instance, Austen 1993, who places such African interpretations of capitalism in a truly global context).

22. The word 'plantations' has particularly strong connotations in this area. At the end of the nineteenth century, the Germans created here one of the few large-scale plantation complexes in West Africa. The recruitment of plantation-labour – at first through direct coercion or by the intermediary of the chiefs, later through more commercial forms of wage labour (a true labour market had already developed by the thirties) – affected the whole western part of Cameroon.

23. A parallel story recorded by Fisiy refers to another village in the same area (Fisiy and Geschiere 1991). For the more general ethnographic background, see Aletum and Fisiy (1987); Fisiy (1993); and Goheen (forthcoming).

24. Indeed, from the case above of Mr P., a reverse pattern emerges (when compared to the cases from the south and the east). In this case, it was Mr P., the accused, who appealed to the court (and not his accusers). Apparently, the court was determined not to become involved in this case. It more or less protected Mr

P. against the witchcraft accusations, but it refused to deliver a clear verdict with an excuse that seemed quite thin (the fact that women had been among Mr P.'s attackers but had not been arrested). The contrast with the readiness of the courts in the east to intervene in a most unequivocal manner against the witches is quite striking.

25. For quite shocking examples of this (chiefs literally selling the land of their subjects to Fulani pastoralists in order to profit from the new regulations under the Land Reform Act), see Fisiy (1992); see also Goheen (forthcoming).

26. This emphasis on different tenors of witchcraft discourses, in relation to variations in the kinship organisation, can indicate also that the contrasts discussed here do not simply coincide with an opposition between segmentary societies and more hierarchical chiefdoms. In the South-west Province of Cameroon, for instance, local societies were of old also strongly segmentary in character; but here all sorts of distinctions in the discourse on the occult seem to have been supported by a whole network of more or less secret societies (see, for instance, Balz 1984 and more in general, Geschiere 1995). In this area there has, as yet, hardly been any pressure on the state to intervene against witchcraft. In a broader comparative perspective, one can mention, for instance, the Igbo of East Nigeria: again, highly segmentary societies but with more compartmentalised discourses on the occult, lacking the all-pervading diffuseness of the *evu* of *djamb* concepts (cf. Bastian 1993).

27. A young witchdoctor and two of his helpers with whom we talked in Kribi were the only ones among our informants who insisted that in their area, '*la sorcellerie*' was no longer tied to kinship. Unfortunately, we did not have the opportunity to check what they meant by this in more concrete terms. The few cases from this area about which we have more detailed information still followed the familiar pattern of ultimately relating witchcraft accusations to the intimacy between kin. See also Meyer's recent and very interesting thesis on the intertwinement of kinship, witchcraft and beliefs in the devil in southern Ghana (Meyer 1995).

References

Aletum, A. and Fisiy, C. F. 1987. *Socio-political Integration and Institutions of the Nso Fondom*. Yaoundé: MESIRES.

Ardener, E. 1970. 'Witchcraft, Economics and the Continuity of Belief', in Douglas (ed.), *Witchcraft Confessions and Accusations*.

Auslander, M. 1993. '"Open the Wombs!": The Symbolic Politics of Modern Ngoni Witchfinding', in Comaroff and Comaroff (eds), *Modernity and Its Malcontents*.

Austen, R. A. 1993. 'The Moral Economy of Witchcraft: an Essay in Comparative History', in Comaroff and Comaroff (eds), *Modernity and Its Malcontents*.

Balz, H. 1984. *Where the Faith Has to Live. Studies in Bakossi Society and Religion*. Basle: Basler Mission.

Bastian, M. 1993. '"Bloodhounds Who Have No Friends": Witchcraft and Locality in the Nigerian Popular Press', in Comaroff and Comaroff (eds), *Modernity and Its Malcontents*.

Ciekawy, D. 1989. 'Witchcraft and Development in Kenyan Politics: Complementary or Conflicting Ideologies', paper presented to the American Anthropological Association.

Comaroff, J. and Comaroff, J. (eds). 1993. *Modernity and Its Malcontents, Ritual and Power in Postcolonial Africa*. Chicago: University of Chicago Press.

Copet-Rougier, E. 1986. 'Catégories d'ordres et réponses aux désordres chez les Mkako de Cameroun', *Droit et Cultures* 11: 79–88.

Crick, M. 1979. 'Anthropologists' Witchcraft: Symbolically Defined or Analytically Undone?', *Journal of the Anthropological Society of Oxford* 10: 139–46.

de Rosny, E. 1981. *Les Yeux de ma Chèvre, Sur les Pas des Maîtres de la Nuit en Pays Douala.* Paris: Plon.

— 1992. *L'Afrique des Guérisons.* Paris: Karthala.

Douglas, M. (ed.) 1970. *Witchcraft Confessions and Accusations.* London: Tavistock.

Ejedepang-Kogé, S. N. 1971. *The Tradition of a People.* Ejedepang-Koge: Bakossi Yaoundé.

Favret-Saada, J. 1977. *Les Mots, la Mort, les Sors – La Sorcellerie dans le Bocage.* Paris: Gallimard.

Fields, K. 1985. *Revival and Rebellion in Central Africa.* Princeton, NJ: Princeton University Press.

Fisiy, C. F. 1990a. *Palm Tree Justice in the Bertoua Court of Appeal: The Witchcraft Cases.* Leiden: African Studies Centre.

— 1990b. 'Le Monopole Juridictionnel de l'Etat et le Règlement des Affaires de Sorcellerie au Cameroun', *Politique Africaine*, 40: 60–72.

— 1992. *Power and Privilege in the Administration of Law: Land Law Reforms and Social Differentiation in Cameroon.* Leiden: African Studies Centre.

Fisiy, C. F. and Geschiere, P. 1990. 'Judges and Witches, or How is the State to Deal with Witchcraft? – Examples from Southeastern Cameroon', *Cahiers d'Études africaines* 118: 135–56.

— 1991. 'Sorcery, Witchcraft and Accumulation – Regional Variations in South and West Cameroon', *Critique of Anthropology* 11 (3): 251–78.

Geschiere, P. 1982. *Village Communities and the State: Changing Relations among the Maka of Southeastern Cameroon.* London: Kegan Paul International.

— 1994. 'Domesticating Personal Violence: Witchcraft, Courts and Confessions in Cameroon', *Africa* 64 (3): 323–41.

— 1995 *Sorcellerie et Politique en Afrique. La Viande des Autres.* Paris: Karthala.

Geschiere, P. and Konings, P. (eds). 1993. *Les Itinéraires d'accumulation au Cameroun/ Pathways to Accumulation in Cameroon.* Paris: Karthala.

Gluckman, M. 1955. *Custom and Conflict in Africa.* Oxford: Blackwell.

Goheen, M. 1993. 'Gender and Accumulation in Nso', in Geschiere and Konings (eds), *Les Itinéraires/Pathways.*

— (forthcoming). *Men Own the Fields, Women Own the Crops: Gender and Power in the Cameroon Highlands.* Madison: University of Wisconsin Press.

Guyer, J. 1993. 'Wealth in People and Self-realization in Equatorial Africa', *Man* 28 (2): 243–56.

Jewsiewicki, B. 1994. *La Violence et la Production du Sujet Souverain, Réflexions sur les Sociétés Post-Coloniales et Post-Soviétiques Avec une Place Spéciale pour l'Afrique.* Call for papers for a seminar on violence, Paris, MSH (May).

Laburthe-Tolra, P. 1977. *Minlaaba, Histoire et Société Traditionnelle Chez les Beti du Sud Cameroun.* Paris: Champion.

Mallart Guimera, L. 1981. *Ni dos ni Ventre,* Paris: Société d'ethnographie.

Marwick, M. 1965. *Sorcery in Its Social Setting: A Study of the Northern Rhodesian Cewa.* Manchester: Manchester University Press.

Mbembe, A. 1992. 'Provisional Notes on the Postcolony', *Africa* 62 (1): 3–37.

Mbunwe-Samba, P. 1989. *Witchcraft, Magic and Divination – A Personal Testimony.* Typescript. Bamenda.

Meyer, B. 1992. '"If You are a Devil, You are a Witch and If You are a Witch, You are a Devil" – the Integration of "Pagan" Ideas into the Conceptual Universe of Ewe Christians in Southeastern Ghana', *Journal of Religion in Africa* 22 (2): 98–131.

— 1995. *Translating the Devil, an African Appropriation of Pietist Protestantism. The Case of the Ewe in Southeastern Ghana, 1847–1992.* PhD thesis, University of Amsterdam.

Niehaus, I.A. 1993. 'Witch-hunting and Political Legitimacy: Continuity and Change in Green Valley, Lebowa, 1930–91', *Africa* 63 (4): 498–529.

Rowlands, M. 1993. 'Economic Dynamism and Cultural Stereotyping in the Bamenda Grassfields', in Geschiere and Konings (eds), *Les Itinéraires/Pathways.*

Rowlands, M. and Warnier, J.-P. 1988. 'Sorcery, Power and the Modern State in Cameroon', *Man* 23: 118–32.

Schmoll, P. G. 1993. 'Black Stomachs, Beautiful Stones: Soul-eating among the Hausa in Niger', in Comaroff and Comaroff (eds), *Modernity and Its Malcontents.*

van Binsbergen, W. 1981. *Religious Change in Zambia: Exploratory Studies.* London: Kegan Paul International.

van Kessel, I. 1993. '"From Confusion to Lusaka": The Youth Revolt in Sek-hukhuneland', *Journal of Southern African Studies* 19 (4): 593–614.

Warnier, J.-P. 1985. *Echanges, développement et hiérarchies dans le Bamenda précolonial Cameroun.* Stuttgart: Steiner.

— 1993. *L'Esprit d'entreprise au Cameroun.* Paris: Karthala.

Werbner, R. 1991. *Tears of the Dead: the Social Biography of an African Family.* Edinburgh and Washington, DC: Edinburgh University Press and Smithsonian Institution Press.

Werbner, R. and Ranger, T. 1994. 'African Research Futures: Postcolonialism and Identity in Africa'. Statement of Purpose for the Second Inter-University Colloquium, Manchester and Oxford: SCUSA.

CHAPTER 8

Identity, alterity and ambiguity in a Nigerien community: competing definitions of 'true' Islam

Adeline Masquelier

Changing visions of otherness in Arewa

Is the Qur'an one or many? The issue is a burning one for villagers of Arewa, speaking Hausa and living in the town of Dogondoutchi, on the southern fringe of Niger. A multiplicity of arguments 'based' on the Qur'an overwhelms appeals against or in favour of particular religious practices or principles. A growing number of Muslims feel confused and bewildered. For some followers of the Prophet, to answer 'yes', acknowledging the many Qur'ans, is attractive. Recognising that more than one Qur'an exists opens the way to justifying the emergence of several Muslim traditions, while facilitating their peaceful co-existence within one community. With this comes also the prospect of legitimising access to differing truths (each Qur'an defining its own particular brand of truth) and lessening the current competition for the power to define Muslim realities.

The problem of the one book for all Muslims has not always been so hotly debated. Until quite recently, villagers of Arewa, who knew one kind of Islam exclusively, hardly ever questioned the dictates of a faith that had come to define the status quo for most Nigeriens, educated or illiterate, rural or urban, wealthy or impoverished. Communities were split, nevertheless, by religious debate, but the arguments were primarily about the nature of spirit and human relationships. Some Muslims would argue that, if spirits intervened in people's lives, they should either be exorcised or simply ignored. Against that, followers of the spirit possession cult known as *bori* would claim that spirits are a necessary – and indeed inevitable – presence in people's lives and that driving them away merely compounds difficulties. Such was the ongoing argument in 1988–89, during my first fieldwork in Dogondoutchi, when I often heard the chief of *bori* complain against learned preachers, the *Malamai*, for insulting the cults' devotees during their preaching. I witnessed, occasionally, bitter confrontations between the followers of the Prophet and the *bori* spirits' mediums and heard a wealth of rumours about the dishonest practices of several local *marabouts* (Masquelier 1992b; 1993a; 1994).

The situation was, however, not that of a clean break, or a divide into neat oppositions. Although in the past, Muslims and *bori* adepts have fought, scorned or offended each other, their visions of the world were not, and are not, irreconcilable. Muslims and non-Muslims have identities which are and have been fluid, multilayered, and often overlapping or intersecting.[1] Muslims as town-dwelling villagers find the *bori* cult to be a useful foil against which they make more of themselves and their own identity, as it were, looking good in contrast to the provincial cult adepts. At the same time, when it looks as though Islam was, and remains, bent on repressing what is locally referred to as 'traditional' culture, there is evidence that the *bori* cult has evolved in conjunction with Islam.

Today, despite the intensity of former confrontations, the moral debates that have long pitted *bori* values against Muslim conventions no longer appear to be relevant. The Prophet's followers' fight to devalue cult members and their efforts to eradicate the 'sinful', polytheistic practices of *bori* have been eclipsed by a *jihad* waged by Muslims against Muslims. The current discussions and disputes now centre on the nature of Islamic knowledge, the way one practises Islam, and the constitution of Islamic authority. This much emerges from the sweeping wave of reforms that have been instituted in the last four years by a minority of Muslim fundamentalists[2] eager to purify Islam and to free itself from the hegemony of Muslim elders. The *'yan izala*,[3] as these fundamentalists are called locally, have successfully managed to carve out a niche for themselves in their attempts to impress upon Nigerien communities an alternative moral order based upon what they claim to be a literal reading of the Qur'an.

In this chapter I want to focus on the current debate that opposes mainstream Muslims (commonly referred to as *'yan tariqa*) and *'yan izala* for the control of truth. In the process of assessing differing truths or defending the superiority of one over another, Muslims of either persuasion explore and question the whole notion of knowledge (and its multiple sources, forms, and levels) in ways they never have before. Much of what was taken for granted as Islamic doctrine must now stand the light of scrutiny. What used to be natural is now disputable. Much of what remained embodied must now become objectified so as to justify its legitimacy. What was known as common sense has to be articulated as knowledge. Practices that were justified by an appeal to tradition must currently find justification in Qur'anic sources.

Knowledge, while remaining the stuff of everyday social life, is also progressively more sacralised. It is no longer enough to distinguish knowledge simply from common sense. Knowledge must more than ever become 'linked to doing and its embodied signs; objectified knowledge [must be] displayed and legitimated in practice' (Lambek 1993: 25). As adversaries struggle to articulate bits and pieces of Islamic knowledge so as to demonstrate the superiority of their perspective, they construct themselves in contrast to their opponents because, since they both claim an Islamic status, that is all they can do to define their own Muslim distinctiveness. Thus, out of these particular arguments emerge novel images of identity and alterity that redefine the boundaries of humanity and morality. Here I discuss one set of images through its expression as rumours that circulated while I was in Niger in 1994. As will be shown, these rumours focusing on the *'yan izala*'s otherness primarily serve to highlight an essential *difference* between two kinds of Islam and to explain why one is necessarily better than the other.

Much of the early literature on the construction of the Other has focused on ethnic stereotypes, analysing them as little more than 'catalogues of nasty things which a majority has said about a minority' (McDonald 1993: 222). It is only more recently, with such works as Said's (1978) and Fabian's (1983), that anthropologists have been encouraged to scrutinise nations', cultures', communities' and their own propensities to posit cultural facts as things observed rather than heard, invented or transmitted. In an effort to examine critically how we/they construct and perceive difference, social researchers have focused on contextualising and historicising the processes through which persistent tropes are created to define otherness and locate margins. What emerges out of recent studies is that 'otherness is always the context of deploying one's own concerns' (Al-Azmeh 1993: 129). As we shall see, the Mawri construction of *'yan izala* as others offers a prime example of how the 'dominant preoccupations of the self-defining center determin[e] where and how the relevant difference [is] seen, sought or understood' (McDonald 1993: 226).

The spread of Islam in Arewa

Prior to the French conquest of the territories which now make up the Republic of Niger, Arewa had remained almost totally impermeable to the influence of Islam at a time when most of the neighbouring Hausa states were under the domination of the Muslim empire of Sokoto. In this area of subsistence agriculture and barter exchange, war was the basic source of wealth and power for the ruling aristocracy, as well as the only avenue to fame and fortune for commoners. Religious power was in the hands of indigenous priest elders (*'yan kasa*), while defence and political management were entrusted to the descendants of the Bornuan warriors who had conquered the area in the seventeenth century. Though the propagation of Islam in Arewa and elsewhere in Niger owes much to French colonial policies (Fuglestad 1983) that stimulated religious conversion — especially after Muslims came to be perceived as useful servants of the administration instead of potential trouble-makers — it is only after independence in 1960 that adherence to the religion of the Prophet intensified dramatically. Islam soon became the common denominator between the various ethnic groups that made up the population of the young republic of Niger and it was clearly a major catalyst in the construction of national unity and identity (Bernus 1969: 208).

With the emergence of an indigenous elite who at independence turned to Islam to reaffirm its own identity *vis-à-vis* the French, Islam has become increasingly associated with status, power and *arziki* (a complex word-bundle which signifies wealth, prosperity and well-being). In Arewa and elsewhere, trade is virtually monopolised by Muslims, who have largely succeeded in silencing spirit devotees and in making them relinquish the last ties they ritually held over the marketplace (Masquelier 1993b). The major administrative positions of Dogondoutchi are also monopolised by followers of the Prophet whose prosperity eloquently demonstrates to would-be converts that the social veneer offered by Islam is an indispensable element of success when building a career in commerce or politics.

For a silent majority, especially women, who obediently conform to Islamic custom, the spirits remain powerful mediators capable of reaching a distant God faster and more effectively than prayers in Arabic. At the same time, these villagers know that it is only by professing allegiance to the Prophet that they will see doors open up before them. The wealth and accomplishments of respected *Alhazai* (individuals who have gone on the pilgrimage to Mecca) also constitute a powerful incentive to turn to prayer for those who are constantly told that such prosperity is an undeniable sign of God's will.

Today in Arewa, many have turned their backs on the spirits to espouse the values of the Qur'an. The spots where Muslim scholars used to prostrate themselves during the five daily prayers are no longer burned by *bori* devotees eager to purify the land from what they saw as corrupt and polluting practices. On these very sites, a small mosque or a simple neighbourhood site of worship often stands, testifying to the vast expansion of a faith which, according to some sources, counted not one adherent in the entire town of Dogondoutchi as late as 1946.

Yet, wherever Islam has taken roots in Arewa, it has drawn on a variety of traditions and resources to adapt itself to the local cultural landscape. Though it has often been described as a cohesive, homogenous and invariant force, Islam, in Niger as elsewhere, is 'composed of many realities, some structural, some organisational and institutional, but which are overall highly fragmentary' (Al-Azmeh 1993: 4). Despite earlier regimes' efforts to promote Islam as *the* religion of the Nigerien people through the construction of mosques, the establishment of a Muslim university in Say, and patronage of the Hajji to Mecca, a sense of ethnic identity generally prevails over a sense of being Muslim. For many villagers, turning to Islam is essentially a way of fitting in and conforming to what have become 'normative' practices in communities where followers of the Prophet often outnumber *bori* mediums ten to one. The extent to which an individual follows (or seems to follow) the precepts of the Qur'an varies greatly. Thus, while some Mawri appear to be devout Muslims, others are less so, even if they claim an Islamic status and don an Islamic robe (*riga*).

It is precisely in these multiple, though sometimes tenuous, distinctions that we can appreciate one of the characteristics of the postcolony, namely the 'distinctive ways in which identities are multiplied, transformed and put into circulation' (Mbembe 1992: 3). In his work on Islamic discourse among Pakistani immigrants in Britain, Al-Azmeh (1993: 1) notes that 'there are as many Islams as there are situations that sustain it', hence the plural use of Islam in the title of his book (see also, el-Zein 1977). But how do we describe the ways in which Islamic universalistic principles have taken shape in various social and historical contexts without categorising Islam as 'a plastic congeries of beliefs and practices'? (Eickelman 1987: 18). There lies one of the main challenges for the study of Islam.

This chapter does not attempt to offer a response to the problem of how to emphasise the multiplicity of Islamic expressions without reducing Islam to an essentialist core; rather it aims to analyse the current Islamic situation in a Nigerien community where the 'regime of unreality' (Mbembe 1992: 7) that constitutes the postcolony has been reinforced by the spread of fundamentalism and of its 'invented traditions' (Hobsbawm 1983). Many Mawri (Arewa villagers) thus call themselves Muslim simply because they ostentatiously attend the Friday prayer at the mosque and fast during Ramadan even though they may sustain different, and even opposed, views of what it means to follow the Qur'an. For some, identifying oneself as a follower of the Prophet does not preclude sacrificing to a deity in times of crisis or attending a *bori* ceremony every once in a while. Nor does it mean that one should refrain from dancing or stop wearing amulets that allegedly protect one from misfortunes and health problems. The relative absence of *ulema* (learned men, initiated into sacred knowledge) in Mawri communities and the reworking of indigenous elements into Muslim epistemologies have greatly contributed to the richness and diversity of Islam as a localised practice.

Truth, tradition and innovation in competing Muslim discourses

It is precisely the syncretised habits of their Islamicised brothers, and the creative synthesis of Muslim values with indigenous principles, that the *'yan izala* are intent upon eradicating. Constantly using the Qur'an as the ultimate reference enables these conservative Muslims to justify their roles as reformers of the faith, something which in turn gives a moral legitimacy to their claim that they are the custodians of truth and piety. The founder of the *izala* movement is Malam Ismaila Idris, a Fulani born in 1937 in Katagum, Nigeria, who started his religious career by working for *Jama'at*

Nasir Islam, a powerful educational organisation headquartered in Kaduna (Isichei 1987: 203). In 1974, after his views led to trouble within the organisation, he left to become an Imam in the army. There, too, his religious opinions eventually contributed to his discharge. In 1978, he founded the *'yan izala*, with its headquarters in Jos. Malam Idris's teachings centred round his hostility to the Tariqa brotherhoods (the main ones being the Qadiriyya and Tijanniya) which are of paramount importance in Nigerian as well as Nigerien Islam (Isichei 1987).

Though it is not hard to imagine how Idris's views became disseminated into southern Niger by itinerant preachers and enthusiastic followers of the master, it is more problematic to trace the early history of the Islamic movement in Arewa. I was told by the older members of *izala* that ten years ago the local leaders had no followers in Dogondoutchi. They were forced to keep their meetings secret for fear of being thrown into jail on charges of conspiracy.[4] Today, *izala* scholars enjoy a growing popularity, most notably among the younger Muslim segment of the population that is particularly receptive to the *izala* ban on conspicuous consumption. In contrast to the Nigerian situation where most of the followers of Malam Ismaila Idris are poor, the local organisation counts a few prosperous merchants in its ranks.

Nevertheless, *izala* appears to be a populist movement aimed at rallying the disenchanted and making war on a society that has long privileged extravagant spending and conspicuous generosity. The rapid splintering of the extended family and the nuclearisation of farming in postcolonial times has meant that many young men have progressively ceased to count on the support of their elders for putting together a brideprice or paying their taxes. Instead of relying on the pooled resources of the extended farming unit, individuals have become increasingly responsible for their own subsistence (Sutter 1979; de Latour Dejean 1982). Being on one's own does not mean that one is relieved from social and economic burdens. On the contrary, household heads face heavy social and financial pressures from friends, relatives and dependants, all the more so if they are salaried workers or if they engage in seasonal migrant labour. Often, the demands for money put on those who enjoy the luxury of a regular income are beyond what their generally meagre resources can bear. The incessant demands for money or gifts and the pressing need for cash (rendered even more acute by the devaluation of the local currency in 1994) have made it difficult for villagers to feed the very social networks which serve as bulwarks against the depredation of an increasingly urban-centred and bureaucratic economy. In times of falling living standards, rising crime and disintegrating family ties, the *izala* message about thriftiness and the conservation of scarce resources has been favourably received by young men eager to unburden themselves from many costly financial obligations without appearing selfish or disrespectful of tradition.

The Qur'anic injunction to stop spending resources simply to create or maintain social ties thus serves to define more sharply the notions of individuality, free enterprise and private property that have already come to characterise postcolonial Nigerien society. In addition to promoting frugality, the *'yan izala* have successfully learned to use communal prayers and sermons as tools of propaganda and mobilisation, and loudly advertise their views as well as upcoming events through the use of microphones and loudspeakers strategically positioned throughout the town. They have also inserted themselves firmly in the local 'cassette culture' (Manuel 1993) by disseminating their ideas and principles through cassette tapes of their sermons. In so doing, they have accelerated the local commoditisation of a religion that increasingly facilitates access to learning through the production and marketing of a wide array of religious goods from newspaper cartoons and Islamic databases to Qur'anic bumper stickers (Starrett 1995).

The contrast between the more liberal trend of Islam and the fundamentalists is striking. The more liberal trend of Islam played, and continues to play, a crucial role in minimising sectarian competition while promoting national unity. Yet, as liberals, Muslim clerics and healers, in particular, have virulently rejected all of the *'yan izala*. The *'yan izala* themselves have exacerbated local animosities and driven a deep wedge where there existed only minor fissures between local factions. They have particularly angered liberal elites who see the *'yan izala* as a pack of trouble-makers manipulated by greedy and power-hungry charlatans exploiting people's credulity as well as their resources. Some members of the educated elite also believe that the movement is financed by foreign powers who wish to destabilise the country and eventually impose an Islamic Republic they will control from afar. Whether or not the *izala* organisation receives financing from Saudi Arabia and Kuwait, as is alleged by some, it is clear that its views arouse passionate resentment among devout *'yan tariqa* who followed the precepts of the Qur'an long before the *'yan izala* started advertising novel religious values.

By preaching in favour of conservative reforms aimed at cleansing Islam from corrupting practices and immoral traditions which others before them tried to eradicate, the *'yan izala* are redirecting the course of the ongoing, and at times latent, debate on spirituality, morality and truth that has long shaped *'yan bori* and Muslims' relations in addition to concretising their mutual enmities. According to *'yan izala*, what is at stake now is not to whom one prays – i.e. the spirits or Allah – but *how* one prays. What matters is not the authority that Muslims hold over non-Muslims but the legitimacy that *izala* practices must gain to overshadow a Muslim tradition tainted by decades of sinful innovations. What needs to be done, first, is not to convert spirit followers to the religion of the Prophet but to convince those who call themselves Muslims that they should abandon all practices that are innovative (*bidea*) and therefore *haram* (forbidden). In their eyes, the ills of the present are mainly due to a failure to conform to the sacred scriptures, and the only way to deal with the consequences of this failure is to return to the true form of Islam.

As can be expected, such a course of action has angered not the *'yan bori* – for whom all Muslims are simply people who have strayed from the path of the spirits – but the more liberal Muslims who do not see why customs that have been transmitted for generations should suddenly be abandoned because some say that they are now sinful. *Malamai* (Muslim clerics/healers) have virulently rejected all of the *'yan izala*'s claims and principles as nonsensical innovations that have no place in a religious tradition they like to think of as ancient, despite its recent history in Arewa. Eager to appear as reformers rather than as revolutionaries, and anxious to offer proofs of their good faith, the *'yan izala* retort that the *malamai*'s aggressive response to their preaching only serves to strengthen their already firm determination to eradicate syncretism and restore Islam to its purer form. One should expect, the *'yan izala* cleverly point out, that as providers of amulets and other Qur'anic medicines from which they derive a substantial income, the *malamai* would object to these reforms: it is they, after all, who stand to lose the most, economically and socially, if villagers come to see that *laya* (amulets) and *rubutu* (washed-off ink from Qur'anic tablets drunk as medicine) are *haram* (forbidden), and stop acquiring them.

What interests me about the nature of this dispute between fundamentalists and mainstream Muslims is the process through which each party is able to redefine itself by constructing its opponent as the Other, an Other that lacks authenticity, legality and worthiness. By constructing *izala* practices as lacking a fundamental legitimacy, mainstream Muslims reassert their own authority over a moral order whose superiority was only reaffirmed, up until recently, when pitted against *bori* values and conventions. Conversely, *izala* members validate the authenticity of their practices not by contrasting them with those of *bori*, but by measuring them against the rites and principles of mainstream Islam. Hence, the *bori*, which in the past endured the repeated attacks of Muslim elites eager to distance themselves from 'animists', has – at least partially – lost its relevance as a signifier of backwardness and immorality. In fact, those Muslims who not long ago most vehemently stigmatised the possession cult to reassert the moral superiority of their own faith must now suffer the spiteful critiques of zealous conservatives in need of an accessible target.

For them, in turn, it is the *'yan izala* rather than the *'yan bori* who have become fundamentally other, others whose difference makes them a prime object of Muslim contempt. Hence, for one of my neighbours, an old woman whose son had left the family compound soon after admitting to being a *dan izala*,[5] the new enmity that characterises the relations between 'yan izala and liberal Muslims was far greater than the animosity 'yan bori and Muslims had long felt towards each other. 'The 'yan izala hate us and we hate them,' she had said to me one day. 'A Muslim can let a dan izala die, even if it is his brother. He will do nothing for him, he will not help with the burial[6] – unless he is forced to.'

Although those who have clearly benefited from the mutual antagonism that shapes the liberal Muslim/'yan izala dialogue seem eager to emphasise the inherent incompatibility between the two, many would rather minimise the perceived differences in an effort to contain the rising tension. As a respected Alhaji put it,

> For years and years, there have been Christians, 'yan bori and Muslims. They have lived in peace, they have not insulted each other. And now, these ['yan izala] arrive and they start insulting everyone ... They have misinterpreted the Qur'an ... [They don't realise that] there is only one Qur'an. The difference between Tijanniya and Izala is that I, I know that nowhere in the Qur'an does it say it is OK to insult others.

Besides pointing to the fact that 'yan izala behave offensively and make wrongful use of the Qur'an, Alhaji constructed an idyllic pre-izala period where all people, be they spirit mediums, Muslims or Christians, had the right to approach God by treading the path that suited them. Although Alhaji too, like the 'yan izala, appeals to the past to legitimise his conception of the present, his version of the utopian golden age differs starkly, of course, from that of the fundamentalists: where his creation of the past is characterised by the peaceful co-existence of the various faiths and guarantees everyone equal access to religious truth, that of the fundamentalists bluntly asserts the pre-eminence of Islam (in a mythical, un-syncretised form) as the only path to salvation.

It is true that most Muslims have been more tolerant of indigenous religion in this area than they have been in northern Nigeria. I have heard local Muslim scholars observe, for instance, that 'yan bori follow one path (hanya) while masu salla (those who pray) follow another. Yet, one can hardly say that these various paths to God have co-existed peacefully side by side. Bori, I have shown elsewhere (Masquelier 1993b, 1994), has routinely constituted a statement of protest and defiance in the face of Islamic hegemony for those who felt estranged from the central loci of power and wealth. Today, bori followers still seek periodically to contest the ascendancy of Muslims over the terms of trade and politics, and serious clashes ensue from such ritualised, though no less political, displays of anger and force. In a similar manner, and despite some villagers' reluctance to be implicated in the debate over the legitimacy (or lack thereof) of izala views, confrontations within communities, between neigh-bours and among kin inevitably occur. One only needs to attend the bi-weekly sermon organized by the izala association, or listen to the conversations liberal Muslims have about *izala* worship, to see that, rather than giving voice to shared values, every gesture, speech or rite enables people to contest each other's rights, question each other's truths and to widen oppositions.

Conversions, conventions and innovations

The *'yan izala* describe themselves as reformers devoted to eradicating the indigenous elements that have become incorporated into local Islamic values and practices. The motto of their brotherhood speaks of the need to reject *bidea* (innovations) and to bring *sunna* (the saying and practices of the Prophet). Nowhere in the Qur'an, *'yan izala* claim, is it said that people can wear amulets or drink the washed-off ink that has been used to write a Qur'anic verse. To do so, they say, amounts to creating another god through the object of one's fetishisation and, by implication, to insulting Allah by doubting his powers to heal and to comfort those who put their trust in Him. A member of *izala* told me that the Prophet went as far as tearing off the amulets worn by some of his followers, and later warned them that such *gris-gris* (charms) would only bring them problems.

Dancing and playing the drums are also prohibited by the *'yan izala* because, according to a Dogondoutchi preacher,

> it is Satan who pushed people to beat the drums and to dance. Satan will tempt someone by saying: 'You can do this, just try it.' He uses flattery and so the person is very tempted to do the wrong thing. During a celebration, it is Satan that makes you give *kari* [gifts of money] to the dancers, and that's bad because it forces people to spend more money than they have; after that they have nothing.

The practice of thriftiness which *'yan izala* are encouraging by arguing that the Prophet never said you should spend more than you can afford – because your primary responsibility is to care for your close kin, not to entertain your neighbours – is not welcomed by Mawri villagers for whom generosity and gift-giving go hand in hand with sociality and friendliness.

Being able to part with large sums of money, whether to pay for a dowry, to entertain one's guests during an infant's naming ceremony, or simply to provide monetary favours, is what earns a man prestige, respect-ability and popularity (see Gregoire 1992: 147; Nicolas 1986). The fact that he is generous with his wives, that he can provide for needy relatives and that, on occasion, he spends lavishly to entertain neighbours and acquaintances makes him more desirable as a friend or a patron, thus further increasing his reputation as a successful and prosperous individual. By being generously provided for by her husband or father, a woman is assured not only material comforts but also the status that comes simply from being a rich man's wife or child. Because some of the habits preached by *izala* leaders appear so antithetical to culturally acceptable norms of sociality, most Mawri generally ignore and even question the *'yan izala*'s injunction against ostentatious displays of generosity and what is seen as the needless spending of, at times scarce, resources. Many villagers I know would rather become heavily indebted to fulfil monetary obligations than be exposed as selfish, antisocial or, worse, stingy.

As noted earlier, those who espouse the tenets of *izala* philosophy are by and large young men who welcome the ban on needless expenditures and gift-giving that have become such a burden for many household heads, especially since the recent devaluation of the CFA franc.[7] Because they are enjoined not to show devotion to those who expect (or order) them to commit sinful actions – that is, actions that the local Muslim tradition tolerates but which are expressly forbidden by the *izala* doctrine – many *'yan izala* who have openly criticised their elders have been forsaken by their parents or have cut all ties with their families. 'The Prophet told us to respect our parents,' a local tailor, and a *dan izala* since 1989, once volunteered, 'but if your father asks you to do something that is not what God wants of you, then you need not feel respect for him because those who want you to go against God's will deserve no respect.' For many fathers and older men, the *'yan izala*'s avoidance of expected sociality, their lack of filial piety, and their shift to a type of individual accumulation reminiscent of the Protestant ethic reflect yet other aspects of the rupture between a precolonial past (remembered in terms of sharing, commensality and nurturing kinship ties) and the contemporary postcolony (experienced in terms of greed, deceit and competition). Just as in other African societies where the capitalist spirit has started hindering the authority of the gerontocracy (Parkin 1972), older folk decry the *izala* attitude of 'each man for himself' which, as far as they see it, threatens the redistributive ethos.

Though most mainstream Muslims would probably agree that the alleged selfishness of fundamentalists is part of the growing trend towards self-orientation that characterises postcolonial identities, they do not perceive it as a consequence of the exigencies of modern life (in contrast to, say, migrant labour). In their eyes, the *izala* ethos is largely motivated by greed and a desire for power. This is, of course, what makes *izala* reforms unacceptable to the great majority of liberal Muslims who object that fundamentalists, by and large, are dishonest and cynical opportunists taking advantage of people's fears and doubts.

Aside from incurring the wrath of their kin for formulating reactionary opinions of local Islamic customs or pointing to their elders' lack of education and piety,[8] members of *izala* have made foes among neighbours and former friends because of their insistence that the 'traditional' prayer schedule local Muslims have adopted is incorrect. They have created their own schedule of prayers (three of the five prayers take place half an hour after the *'yan tarika*'s prayers) which, they insist, reflects more accurately the teachings of Muhammad. When to pray, how to pray and what to say during prayers have become perhaps the most hotly contested aspects of Islamic practice, and certainly those around which most of the dispute between *izala* and Muslims has intensified.

According to *'yan izulu*, when asked by a man what constituted the most important activity in Islam, the Prophet allegedly answered, 'Praying on time.' *'Yan izala* also stress that it is praying on time, more than anything else, which will ensure that one goes to heaven. Since it is God's will that those who know teach those who do not know, *izala* preachers are eagerly enjoining all those who attend their sermons to learn how to pray 'the right way'. In 1994, a Dogondoutchi preacher warned during one of his bi-weekly sermons that 'Those who "spoil the prayer" [i.e. pray incorrectly] will not receive rewards [*lada*], and they will not go to heaven. If you don't learn how to pray the right way and you do as you please, God does not accept your prayer.' There again, as in the traditional rhetoric used against *'yan bori* to convince them of the advantages of a Muslim way of life – if you don't pray, no malam will attend your child's naming ceremony or bury you when you die (see Masquelier 1994) – an *izala* preacher professes ominous warnings intended to steer would-be converts into the proper path so as to ensure their ultimate redemption, a redemption that is based as much on external signs of piousness as on schedule, symbols and style.

Imaging and imagining alterity: the animalised other

Mawri villagers, regardless of their religious persuasion, often insist on the animality of multiple spirits (*iskoki*) who roam the earth in search of human company or the opportunity to commit evil deeds. Spirits, my friends told me, can take on a human appearance[9] at will when they do not simply remain invisible (Masquelier 1992a). They commonly exhibit hooves when, intent upon tricking or harming someone, they disguise themselves as human beings. In other words, despite their extraordinary plasticity, something in their human-like appearance usually gives away their in-humanity. Thus villagers who meet a pretty, and usually innocent-looking, maiden on the road, and notice the camel-, horse-, or donkey-hooves sticking from under her wrapped skirt, know better than to anger her. Of course, while some chillingly recall how they noticed the hooves just in time to escape the spirit's trap, others, less fortunate, do not allegedly live long enough even to regret their lack of observation.

Among the creatures displaying animalistic features that set them apart from fully human beings is a category of sorcerers (*mayu*) who possess the ability to fly like birds. These sorcerers are not explicitly likened to birds; they have no wings. Yet, their ability to propel themselves in the air

– thanks to the jet of fire that comes out of their anuses – emphasises their distinctiveness at the same time that it makes them ominously powerful.

Difference is also what mainstream Muslims attempt to stress when describing or criticising *izala* members.[10] Hence, women comment endlessly on the *hijabi*, the ample veil that cloaks *izala* women down to their ankles and hides their bodies from the public eye.[11] Villagers criticise *izala* men for wearing long, pointed beards: *'yan izala* are jokingly referred to as *masu geme* ('those who wear a beard'), a particularly ironic statement given that beards are usually associated with Christian missionaries and, by extension, infidels. They are also the object of scornful comments because they wrap their turbans only once around their heads, letting the rest of the fabric hang freely behind their backs, as do other Muslims in the Middle East.[12] But in a fundamental way, it is not just that the *'yan izala look* different. They *are* essentially different. Though one may have a fundamentalist as brother or son, such a relationship is never alluded to[13] for to do so would only render more difficult the task of constructing '*izala*-ness' as an alien category. Since the representation of *'yan izala* as bizarre and foreign is an important step towards justifying the discursive war waged against them, Muslim fundamentalists have become the prototypical *Other* in the eyes of many villagers eager to hold on to their own tradition.

Not surprisingly, such construction of otherness as problematic identity involves an emphasis on the animality of the *'yan izala*. Liberal Muslims widely suspect that after they die, *'yan izala* turn into donkeys. According to the rumours that circulated in Muslim circles in 1994, anyone attempting to exhume the body of a deceased *dan izala* would invariably find the carcass of a donkey in place of human remains. In 1992, a well-known religious figure of Dogondoutchi had allegedly insulted the *izala* congregation during the Friday prayer at the *Grande Mosquee*, warning them that if any of them dared touch his Qur'an, he would die. The man had added that if anyone ever dug up the corpse of a *dan izala* the day after the burial, he would find a donkey in the dead man's tomb. 'This is because they turn into animals as soon as they die,' he was said to have concluded. Implied in such a statement was the certainty that, despite their determined efforts to claim unique access to truth, and therefore to eternity, the *'yan izala* would never go to paradise. After all, they are nothing but beasts.

Of donkeys and dogs: animal metaphors and Islamic others

While many of the individuals with whom I talked with knew of no specific case that would substantiate the widely suspected notion that their religious adversaries turned into pack-animals after death, I nevertheless heard a particular story that allegedly happened in the small village of Tsakari, north of Dogondoutchi. It is a story which might appear sensational, but it is far from exotic to those for whom these tales of animalised Muslims have come to signify a particular experience of change, alienation and conflict. That is why in the discussion that follows I foreground the rumoured meanings Mawri villagers give donkeys and thus animality in the context of current arguments over religious identity. Rumours of inhumanity, and in particular fundamentalist inhumanity, constitute a form of social consciousness that is revealing of the ways rural Nigeriens objectify and assess their own situation in a swiftly changing and increasingly unstable postcolonial world.

These tales of the *'yan izala*'s plasticity were sometimes met with healthy scepticism on the part of villagers who had no real interest in perceiving fundamentalists as animals or animal-like. 'These are only stories mean people spread to make the *'yan izala* look bad,' my friend Iyale had thus snapped at a young man. 'We know the stories *they* tell about *us* are not true. So why should I believe *your* stories?' Clearly, not everyone in Dogondoutchi gives credence to these tales of shape-shifting. Nevertheless, it is relevant to ask, why donkeys and not dogs or hyenas?

The following is an account of one of the most popular versions of the rumour that was circulating in 1994. A young man who had just finished his Qur'anic studies in Nigeria was returning home to his family. His proud father decided to have a feast (*walima*) to celebrate his son's return. He slaughtered several goats and rams, had his wives prepare a lot of dishes and invited his son to eat. 'I do not eat the meat of a pagan,' the son was said to have uttered in response to his father's request. Having secretly embraced the *izala* faith while in Nigeria, he was now obliged to reveal that according to his 'new' religion, his father was an infidel, and therefore no longer someone with whom he could eat a meal. Feeling deeply insulted, the father became so angry that he beat his son to death. Soon after, he was brought to the judge to be tried later for the killing of his son. When asked why he had committed such a crime, the father simply answered: 'I did not kill my son, I killed a donkey.' Puzzled by such a statement, the judge sent people to the guilty party's compound to shed light on what had happened. Those who went saw no trace of the son's corpse, but found instead the cadaver of a donkey that appeared to have been severely beaten.[14]

Was the father ever found guilty of the death of his son? The story did not say. What is suggested, though, is that, in addition to being fundamentally different from other humans, *'yan izala* are, by definition, ambiguous beings. Yet, they do not visibly exhibit this essential ambiguity until after their deaths, when they can shed the human shell that was concealing what was perhaps their true nature. Whether or not they actually assume their former identity after they die, they are masters of deception, and this, too, makes them different. 'They are not like us,' Hajiya Bibata, a loquacious neighbour, said once about the *'yan izala*. 'You cannot marry one of them, and they cannot marry you.' By way of an explanation, she had added that she would not marry her daughter to a *dan izala* any more than she would give her in marriage to a Fulani, a butcher, or a blacksmith.

This statement is illuminating because it captures succinctly what '*izala*-ness' is for so many Dogondoutchi villagers caught up in a 'struggle for the hegemonic control of interpretation of how the world should be seen' (Fischer and Abedi 1990: 97). Not unlike Fulani who, though they may have lived in the area for generations, remain newcomers enveloped in an aura of mystery and foreignness that prevents Mawri villagers from knowing and trusting them, *'yan izala* are seen as outsiders who have come to cause trouble and wreak havoc within what used to be tightly-knit families. Villagers often note that *izala* preachers come from Nigeria or Benin, or simply from another part of Niger, to emphasise their alien status and the fact that they are intruders. Like the Fulani, their differing set of moral standards and cultural values renders their assimilation into Mawri society difficult, if not impossible. The well-known proverb, 'a Fulani never reveals his insides', which points to the Fulani's characteristic reluctance to trust non-Fulani, could well apply to stereotypes of *'yan izala*, other villagers' view of fundamentalists being that they are essentially untrustworthy and deceitful. Note that the encroachment of foreigners in Mawri communities is not unprecedented. Despite the fact that the progress of Islam was slow in this area of Niger, the colonial period witnessed the coming and going of itinerant Nigerian Muslim preachers eager to spread the words of the Qur'an. More recently, there has been a regular influx of *malamai* from Nigeria. Local villagers are used to foreigners settling in their midst to provide the community with enlightenment, advice and Qur'anic medicines.

Returning to Hajiya's comparison of *'yan izala* to blacksmiths, it is relevant to note that, as specialised professionals and because of their control over the transformative capacities of fire, smiths constitute a sort of *nyamakala* group; that is, a cluster of clans that 'own the right to arcane spiritual and technological practices and are therefore able to offer special services to the rest of society' (McNaughton 1988: 3). Butchers, too, constitute a group apart because of the fact that they slaughter animals and shed blood, thereby attracting spirits who feed on it. Customarily, they should not marry women other than daughters of butchers because they have little status and are held in low esteem by their fellow-villagers.

Should a non-*nyamakala* woman marry a butcher, it is said that she will find that, when she stays in her husband's house, the calabash she keeps under her bed will fill itself with blood during the night. This, people assert, shows what happens to those who do not marry one of their kind. Butchers, in fact, like fundamentalists, are different enough to be endowed with animality by Mawri villagers wishing to objectify them tangibly as other. In contrast to the animal characteristics of *'yan izala* that become prominent only at death, those born in a butcher lineage exhibit their animality only before birth. I have repeatedly heard people say that during the nine months of her pregnancy, it is not a human foetus that the wife of a butcher is carrying, but the foetus of a dog. Only when it is about to be born does the 'puppy' turn into a child with human features.

Are donkeys to horses what *'yan izala* are to *'yan tariqa*?

Much of the research on the significance of animals in human discourse has followed Lévi-Strauss's (1962) insight that natural species are chosen to embody emotionally charged ideas or particular moral configurations because they are good to think with rather than good to eat. Making sense of totemic representations entails, in many cases, understanding the connection between dietary prohibitions concerning animals and the animal classificatory scheme (Douglas 1966; Leach 1964; Tambiah 1969; Sahlins 1975). In the context of African myths, the role of dogs and hyenas as a 'moral waiting to be identified' (Gottlieb 1992: 117) has been well explored (Beidelman 1961; 1975; 1986; Calame-Griaule and Ligers 1961; Gottlieb 1986). Though, in the case at hand, donkeys are more situated in the material world of everyday life than in the immaterial universe of myth, they, like the hyenas of Dogon mythology, present people with a counter-image of their own humanity. Donkeys offer an expression of otherness that Mawri villagers redeploy to reassert their own moral and social identity. Yet, in contrast to the dogs of Beng culture or the tricksters of Kaguru thought, they are not constructed through the projection of negative human traits on non-human characters. Rather, it is they who lend their animality to human individuals who are otherwise so different from other Mawri that they can only be constructed as beastly alter egos.

What place do donkeys occupy in the Mawri bestiary system of classification? To answer this question, it is useful to define first what donkeys are for Mawri villagers. In addition to being thought unintelligent and lazy, donkeys cannot remain faithful to their owners and only follow the hand that feeds them. I was told several times that to win a donkey's attachment, one only has to offer him food. Given the Mawri ready scorn for those who let the rumblings of their stomach deafen their reason, the donkey, in his greedy opportunism, is a quintessential figure of contempt.

A well-known Mawri story illustrates the stupidity of donkeys by depicting them as animals who will stubbornly remain in the middle of the road even when a vehicle approaches at great speed. Dogs bark at cars from the side of the road, and camels flee at the sight of an automobile, but donkeys linger, passively waiting to be hit by the oncoming vehicle. Used to pull carts or as pack animals to transport heavy and bulky goods over short distances, donkeys are often beaten mercilessly by their owners. They are resilient and strong, they need little care and they cost far less than a camel. Yet they are not valued in the way cattle or camels are, despite their usefulness in rural communities where only a privileged minority can afford to buy automobiles or trucks.[15]

I once told a group of friends with whom I was discussing the various moral qualities attributed to certain members of the animal world that the two beasts of American politics were the elephant and the donkey. My unreflective statement gave rise to what I interpreted to be rather sarcastic outbursts of laughter on the part of my audience who simply could not fathom why anyone would pick the ass as an emblem of their political party, much less why anyone would trust a candidate who chose to run as 'donkey' in a political campaign. My futile attempts to contextualise the metaphoric use of asses, elephants and bulls (of the stock market) only met with further disapproving clicks of the tongue and I could tell from my friends' annoyed glances that, in their memories, Clinton the democrat would be for ever associated with 'asinine' politics.

To understand the lowliness of the donkey as a symbolic category, it helps to contrast it with the horse, in Mawri opinion a far nobler animal than its equine cousin. Horses carry people but donkeys are generally used to transport bulky loads (bricks, fodder, bags of millet, etc.). Horses are intimately associated throughout Hausaland with the public image of traditional rulers and of heroic warriors but donkeys are the beasts of the common man. In precolonial times, when horses were locally in short supply, the wars chieftaincies waged against each other were fought to acquire booty[16] in the form of horses, cattle, millet or cowries from one's defeated opponents (de Latour 1982: 243). Prisoners acquired in battle could be used as slaves but they often served as a medium of exchange for horses that could not be acquired easily by other means.

To this day, horses are associated with prestige, nobility and material success and their role as a status symbol has been only partially eclipsed in rural communities by cars and trucks. In each Mawri chieftaincy, an individual would traditionally be nominated as *sarkin doki* (chief of horses) to oversee the stables of the ruler. Today, such a title is mainly honorific since *chefs de canton* (county customary chiefs) and many village *sarakuna* (pl. of *sarki*; chief) have replaced their stallions with Land-Rovers or Peugeots. In Dogondoutchi, horse races were always a popular event that drew huge crowds of onlookers to the race tracks on the outskirts of the town. Without implying here that horse races are to the Mawri what cockfights are to the Balinese (and that, just as 'much of Bali surfaces in a cock ring' [Geertz 1973: 417], much of Arewa surfaces in a horse track), it is clear that horses evoke the masculine qualities of military men and chiefly figures, and that they are valued as such. The male villagers I knew and talked to were certainly fond of horses[17] and many young boys prided themselves on knowing how to ride their fathers' or their uncles' horses. Of late, increasingly tight budgetary resources and the prohibitive costs of maintaining stables have forced town officials to stop holding horse races, but older men still talk of the days when they would all ride richly bedecked horses as part of the chief's escort in local parades.

Relevant as well to this discussion is the use of equine imagery to shape the dramatic processes of spirit possession in the gendered idiom of mounting and penetration.[18] During possession, as well as in everyday life, the devotee is referred as the horse (*doki*) of the spirit. A member of the *bori* may thus be addressed as *dokin* Gurmunya, that is, the 'horse of Gurmunya', Gurmunya being a lame spirit of Zarma origin who possesses only women. Possession is hence metaphorically equated with the sexual act wherein the medium is mounted (*hau*) by the spirit, just as the rider mounts his horse.

Going back to the identification of fundamentalists with donkeys, it is not as alter egos to humans but *in contrast* to the noble horse that donkeys are given their full significance by Mawri intent upon vilifying their Muslim brethren. In other words, it is because donkeys are not horses that they are useful when one is figuring out a way to objectify how *'yan izala* are different from other Muslims. These relationships underlying the alleged connections between Muslims and animals can thus be rendered in the following proportion:

dan izala : *dan tariqa* : : donkey : horse.

For those who ultimately share, believe, and circulate the tales of 'animalisation', it is significant that these tales strike at the core of the problem that is currently tearing apart Mawri families and communities. By stressing the similarity between fundamentalists and donkeys, villagers deny the *'yan izala* not only humanity but also – and perhaps more importantly – reason and knowledge, the very qualities which, ironically, members of *izala* have singled out to legitimise their identity and defend their reforms in the face of hostility, competition and ignorance.

Conclusion

In this chapter, I have described the tense relationships between fundamentalist and mainstream Muslims as I encountered them in Dogondoutchi during the summer of 1994. The last few years have seen sweeping changes in the way some Muslims, who define themselves as *'yan izala*, interpret the Qur'an and practise their religion. Using sermons and prayer sessions as tools of propaganda and mobilisation, and constantly referring to the Qur'an to justify their roles as reformers of the faith, these fundamentalists are gaining a growing number of adherents. I have focused here on the mutual antagonism that colours the relation between the two Muslim factions and on the stories through which liberals construct fundamentalists as the prototypical Other.

Traditionally, very few Muslims completed Islamic studies or even knew how to read Arabic in this part of West Africa. Through their focus on education and preaching, the members of *izala* emphasise a return to the Qur'an and *hadith* in an effort to purify Islam from all the syncretistic practices that have moulded it in its present form. As critics of a local tradition they reject as sinful, *'yan izala*, just as others reformers elsewhere, 'are acting within spaces of doubt and ambiguity to create alternative ways of knowing Islam and being a Muslim' (Horvatich 1994: 823). It is their clever use of ambiguity and doubt that gives their movement such powerful momentum. At the same time, the very fact that they define their religious activism as an *alternative* to the orthodoxy is what enables their opponents to displace them as animalised alter egos who do not deserve even to come into contact with the sacred Qur'an.

Like Kafka's Gregor Samsa who, one day, finds himself metamorphosed into a monstrous beetle, *'yan izala* end up eventually having to assume their animality. But, unlike Gregor, whose transformation from human to bug occurs during life, Mawri fundamentalists find themselves shape-shifting at death, that is, when they stop being in control of either their identities as social actors, or their corporeality as living organisms. More important perhaps is the fact that in contrast to Gregor, who fights to reassert his fundamental human core despite his physical existence as a mere insect, *'yan izala*, the rumours imply, are overcome by their asinine qualities when the spirit has left the body, which is when no human essence remains to contradict their beastly appearance. Death, then, becomes the moment of truth during which the deceit of those who allegedly preached the truth becomes unveiled. It is followed by perhaps the most insulting moment for those who during their lifetimes strove for recognition and respect: instead of being remembered as members of their patrilineage that left their imprint on the world, *'yan izala* will dissolve into oblivion as surely as their donkey skin will fall prey to the worms. Already disowned by their parents during their lifetimes, they now cease entirely to exist as humans even in social memory, since they do not even leave human remains that could attest to their prior existence.

Notes

1. Those who are neither *'yan bori* nor Azna (the latter are descended from the first occupants of Arewa and theoretically are still in charge of propitiating the local deities who originally helped the settlers to establish themselves in the area) are generally referred to as Muslims, regardless of whether or not they devoutly perform the basic Muslim duties and live according to Muslim tenets. Hence, a

villager may call himself *musulmi* (Muslim) because he ostentatiously accomplishes the five daily prayers and fasts during Ramadan even though he may not understand a single word of Arabic. And in local bars where beer flows quite freely, many of the patrons identify themselves as Muslims, more perhaps as a way of fitting in than because they have adopted a religious code of conduct. This does not mean that there is no conformity to Islamic tenets, but rather that there are differing ways of living one's life as a Muslim and differing degrees of piety and religious motivation.

2. Though it is often associated with bigotry and fanaticism, the term 'fundamentalist' is at least less inadequate than the currently available alternatives (such as Islamists, for instance). I use the word purposefully, aware that, as Munson (1993: 152) remarks, it reflects our own hostility towards the movement which we purport to describe. Though it is not the term that Mawri villagers, by and large, use to refer to the members of this conservative Islamic movement, it connotes adequately the negative sentiments mainstream Muslims feel towards *'yan izala*.

3. The term *izala* is used to describe both the Islamic organisation – sometimes also referred to as *kungiya addinin Islam* (association of the religion of Islam) – and the membership of the association.

4. A few years ago, three of the Dogondoutchi leaders were in effect imprisoned for a few days on the urging of *malamai* who denounced them as criminals with evil intentions towards the local population. They were freed later when it was found that the charges were unsubstantiated.

5. Literally 'son of *izala*'; sing. of *'yan izala*.

6. As I have shown elsewhere (Masquelier 1994), the struggle for power between *'yan bori* and Muslims has often centred on the control over burial practices. Moreover, one of the most effective ways that *malamai* pressure villagers to adopt a Muslim identity and to follow Muslim rules is to threaten to refuse to bury them ritually and to dump them simply in a hole. Failing to attend the burial of one's brother or even to pay condolences to the spouse or children of the deceased is a sign of utmost disrespect that provides a good indication of how strained the relations between the two siblings must have been.

7. I do not know to what extent the recent devaluation of the local currency has contributed to the popularisation of *izala* views on expenditure and thriftiness and, at this point, can only suspect a possible connection.

8. A song that was written to criticise and poke fun at the *'yan izala* describes *'yan izala*'s relations to other Muslims in the following manner:

The son does not greet his father
Unless his father greets him
Even when they are kin, they split [presumably because of irreconcilable
    differences]
Their insults to the neighbours spoil [their relations]
With your merchandise you cheat people.

9. Spirits can also take on the appearance of a harmless animal, such as a donkey or a goat, to trick humans or help them. When they take the form of human beings, they may make themselves look like somebody with whom a person is familiar, such as one's grandmother or one's friend, in order to communicate with this person without unduly frightening her or arising her suspicion.

10. The Mawri are not alone in focusing on animality to index differences between themselves and others. McDonald (1993: 226) notes how classical writers made sense of their barbarians and savages through a metaphoric of *feritas* that, in

contrast, helped to emphasise their own *humanitas*. One need only look at travellers' and colonials' accounts of foreign populations to gather further evidence of the common use of animalistic features to describe Wild Men whose strangeness served to highlight the fundamental humanity of their observers.

11. Mack (1992: 93n) notes that 'in Muslim West Africa, a women's veil is her home, the compound walls protecting her from public view'. Until *'yan izala* made their wives and daughters wear veils, this general observation clearly applied to Arewa where Mawri women did not traditionally veil. Women can cover their heads and shoulders with a wrapper when walking in a public space if they wish. Yet, all they need to wear to obey the conventions of propriety and modesty is a small headscarf which, symbolically more than practically, covers their hair.

12. The song that every child knows and which is aimed at ridiculing the *'yan izala* describes them in the following manner:

> If you see a child with an abundant beard
> With a lower jaw as long as the mane of a horse
> With a turban wrapped only once around his head
> Don't look any further, it is them [the *'yan izala*].

13. Whenever I learned that someone I knew, and had conversations with, was kin to an *izala* member, it was always because a third party shared this information with me. I cannot remember a single instance where my interlocutors admitted to me that someone in their family had become a *dan izala*.

14. There are many inconsistencies in this story which should cast doubts on the veracity of the reports for any perceptive individuals. For instance, it is not clear why the son's corpse should still be in the compound (as donkey or as man) at the time of the judge's inquest since Muslims bury their dead right after death has been established and the corpse washed and prepared.

15. That much is obvious from the selective use of animalistic imagery to convey the specific moral qualities associated with each political party during the first democratically held elections in 1993. The democratic ideals of the UDFP (Union Démocratique des Forces Progressistes) were represented by the elephant, a symbol of potency and freedom; the party is also referred to in Hausa as *Sawaba*, liberty. The noble camel embodied the resilient strength of the RDA (Rassemblement Démocratique Africain). The stork, an emblem of faithfulness (these birds always come back to the same nest after their migratory travels, I was told), lent its name (*Chamoua*) and its aerial grace to the small UPDP (Union des Patriotes Démocrates et Progressistes). Thus, while the elephant or the stork are effective vehicles for embodying moral qualities that would be valued by an electorate about to choose their next president, the donkey evokes only negative traits for Nigerians of the contemporary postcolony.

16. Regardless of the motives invoked when attacking a neighbouring village, war meant above all pillage and the capture of slaves. Mawri never fought to establish territorial domination over land but rather to extort as much wealth as possible in the form of cattle, millet or prisoners.

17. Mawri villagers, like their Hausa neighbours, clearly value horses in the way that Fulani herders value their cattle and Tuareg pastoralists think of their camels.

18. In its interconnection with the idiom of marriage – for instance, the *bori* initiate is called a 'bride' (*amarya*) regardless of gender – the equestrian theme is prevalent in several other possession cults (see Matory 1993; Boddy 1989; Deren 1991).

References

Al-Azmeh, Aziz. 1993. *Islams and Modernities*. London: Verso.

Beidelman, T. O. 1961. 'Hyena and Rabbit: a Kaguru Representation of Matrilineal Relations', *Africa* 31 (1): 61–74.

—— 1975. 'Ambiguous Animals: Two Theriomorphic Metaphors in Kaguru Folklore', *Africa* 45 (2): 183–200.

—— 1986. *Moral Imagination in Kaguru Modes of Thought*. Bloomington: Indiana University Press.

Bernus, Suzanne. 1969. *Particularisme Ethnique en Milieu Urbain: L'Exemple de Niamey*. Paris: Institut d'Ethnologie.

Boddy, Janice. 1989. *Wombs and Alien Spirits: Women, Men and the Zar Cult in Northern Sudan*. Madison: University Press of Wisconsin.

Calame-Griaule, G. and Ligers, V. 1961. 'L'Homme-Hyène dans la Tradition Soudanaise', *L'Homme* 1 (2): 89–118.

de Latour Dejean, E. 1982. 'La Paix Destructrice', in J. Bazin and E. Terray (eds), *Guerres de Lignages et Guerres d'Etats en Afrique*. Paris: Editions des Archives Contemporaines.

Deren, Maya. 1953. *Divine Horsemen: the Living Gods of Haiti*. New York: McPherson.

Douglas, Mary. 1966. *Purity and Danger. An Analysis of the Concepts of Pollution and Taboo*. London: Routledge and Kegan Paul.

Eickelman, Dale. F. 1987. 'Changing Interpretations of Islamic Movements', in William R. Roff (ed.), *Islam and the Political Economy of Meaning: Comparative Studies of Muslim Discourse*. London: Croom Helm.

el-Zein, Abdul Hamid M. 1977. 'Beyond Ideology and Theology: The Search for the Anthropology of Islam', *Annual Review of Anthropology* 6: 227–54.

Fabian, Johannes. 1983. *Time and the Other: How Anthropology Makes Its Object*. New York: Columbia University Press.

Fischer, Michael M. J. and Abedi, Mehdi. 1990. *Debating Muslims: Cultural Dialogues in Postmodernity and Tradition*. Madison: University of Wisconsin Press.

Fuglestad, Finn. 1983. *A History of Niger: 1850–1960*. New York: Cambridge University Press.

Geertz, Clifford. 1973. *The Interpretation of Cultures*. New York: Basic Books.

Gottlieb, Alma. 1986. 'Dog: Ally or Traitor? Mythology, Cosmology, and Society among the Beng of Ivory Coast', *American Ethnologist* 13 (3): 477–88.

—— 1992. *Under the Kapok Tree: Identity and Difference in Beng Thought*. Bloomington and Indianapolis: Indiana University Press.

Gregoire, Emmanuel. 1992. *The Alhazai of Maradi: Traditional Hausa Merchants in a Changing Sahelian City*. Translated by Benjamin H. Hardy. Boulder, CO: Lynne Rienner.

Hobsbawm, Eric. 1983. 'Introduction: Inventing Traditions', in E. Hobsbawm and T. Ranger (eds), *The Invention of Tradition*. Cambridge: Cambridge University Press.

Horvatich, Patricia. 1994. 'Ways of Knowing Islam', *American Ethnologist* 21 (4): 811–26.

Isichei, Elizabeth. 1987. 'The Maitatsine Risings in Nigeria 1980–85: a Revolt of the Disinherited', *Journal of Religion in Africa* 17 (3): 194–208.

Lambek, Michael. 1993. *Knowledge and Practice in Mayotte: Local Discourses of Islam, Sorcery and Spirit Possession*. Toronto: University of Toronto Press.

Leach, Edmund. 1964. 'Anthropological Aspects of Language: Animal Categories and Verbal Abuse', in E. J. Lennenberg (ed.), *New Directions in the Study of Language*. Cambridge: Cambridge University Press.

Lévi-Strauss, Claude. 1962. *Totemism*. Harmondsworth, Sussex: Penguin Books.

McDonald, Maryon. 1993. 'The Construction of Difference: An Anthropological Approach to Stereotypes', in Sharon MacDonald (ed.), *Inside European Identities*. Providence, RI: Berg.

McNaughton, Patrick R. 1988. *The Mande Blacksmiths: Knowledge, Power and Art in West Africa*. Bloomington: Indiana University Press.

Mack, Beverley B. 1992. 'Harem Domesticity in Kano, Nigeria', in Karen Tranberg Hansen (ed.), *African Encounters with Domesticity*. New Brunswick, NJ: Rutgers University Press.

Manuel, Peter. 1993. *Cassette Culture: Popular Music and Technology in North India*. Chicago: University of Chicago Press.

Masquelier, Adeline. 1992a. 'Encounter with a Road Siren: Machines, Bodies and Commodities in the Imagination of a Mawri Healer', *Visual Anthropology Review* 8 (1): 56–69.

— 1992b. '"The Doguwa is Like the White Man": Images of "Others" in *Bori* and Muslim Discourse', paper presented to the American Ethnological Society Meeting. Memphis.

— 1993a. *Ritual Economies, Historical Mediations: the Poetics and Power of Bori among the Mawri of Niger*. PhD thesis. University of Chicago.

— 1993b. 'Narratives of Power, Images of Wealth: the Ritual Economy of *Bori* in the Market', in Comaroff and Comaroff (eds), *Modernity and Its Malcontents: Ritual and Power in Postcolonial Africa*. Chicago: University of Chicago Press.

— 1994. 'Lightning, Death and the Avenging Spirits: *Bori* Values in a Muslim World', *Journal of Religion in Africa* 24 (1): 2–51.

Matory, J. Lorand. 1993. 'Government by Seduction: History and the Tropes of "Mounting" in Oyo-Yoruba Religion', in Comaroff and Comaroff (eds), *Modernity and Its Malcontents: Ritual and Power in Postcolonial Africa*. Chicago: University of Chicago Press.

Mbembe, Achille. 1992. 'Provisional Notes on the Postcolony', *Africa* 62 (1): 3–37.

Munson, Henry Jr. 1993. *Religion and Power in Morocco*. New Haven, CT: Yale University Press.

Nicolas, Guy. 1986. *Don Rituel et Echange Marchand dans une Société Sahelienne*. Paris: Institut d'Ethnologie.

Parkin, David J. 1972. *Palms, Wine, and Witnesses: Public Spirit and Private Gain in an African Farming Community*. San Francisco: Chandler.

Sahlins, Marshall. 1975. *Culture and Practical Reason*. Chicago: University of Chicago Press.

Said, Edward. 1978. *Orientalism: Western Representation of the Orient*. New York: Pantheon.

Starrett, Gregory. 1995. 'The Political Economy of Religious Commodities in Cairo', *American Anthropologist* 97 (1): 51–68.

Sutter, John. 1979. 'Social Analysis of the Nigerian Rural Producer', Vol.2, Part D of the *Niger Agricultural Sector Assessment*. Niamey: USAID.

Tambiah, Stanley J. 1969. 'Animals are Good to Think and Good to Prohibit', *Ethnology* 8 (4): 423–59.

CHAPTER 9

Contested authorities and the politics of perception: deconstructing the study of religion in Africa

Rijk van Dijk and Peter Pels

Recent critiques of anthropological texts have led to a wide acknow-ledgement of the power relations expressed and produced by their rhetoric. The fieldwork encounters on which many of these texts are based are unevenly and unequally translated into them, and the texts themselves remain largely beyond the control or influence of the anthropologist's interlocutors. At the same time, the authority of these texts relies heavily upon the ability to represent the voice of the 'other' people encountered during research. Ethnography, therefore, has always depended on poly-phony, but has also, paradoxically, denied this polyphony by subsuming it under a dominant authorial voice. This chapter suggests that this paradox is not just a textual phenomenon, but emerges from more general, and to a large extent irresolvable, contradictions between intellectual authorities that confront each other in the practice of research.

Inspired by literary criticism, a number of scholars have argued that this paradox may be resolved by experimenting with 'dialogical' or 'poly-phonic' texts in a search for compositions that are more true to the fieldwork situation (Clifford 1986a; Marcus and Fischer 1986; Tedlock 1987).[1] Their efforts have produced many interesting insights into the construction and deconstruction of ethnographic authority, but the ques-tion remains as to whether the authority of the ethnographer is not too entrenched to allow for a successful use of these strategies. Others have argued that experiments with 'dialogue' can never completely dislodge the power of authors to edit out voices at will (Pool 1991b). The dilemma of critical approaches to anthropological texts is that, while literary criticism can identify relations of power that constitute texts, textual experiments cannot change these relationships (Fabian 1991: 193–4). Ethnographic dialogue is always contextualised by a dialectics of power relationships that conditions and inhibits it (Comaroff and Comaroff 1992: 11; Schrijvers 1991). As Arjun Appadurai recently put it, theories of the intertextual have to be complemented with theories of the inter*con*textual (Appadurai 1995).

One step towards formulating questions about the interaction of contexts is, we feel, a 'democratising' of the capacity to deconstruct authoritative statements in the study of religion. Classical anthropology of religion was, to a large extent, premised on denying the authority of the religious authorities under study, if not during fieldwork, then at least in ethnography (Evans-Pritchard 1962) – a form of 'deconstruction' in its own right (cf. van Binsbergen 1991: 337). By outlining the (often deemed faulty) processes of reasoning, or the social conditions that lay behind religious expressions, anthropologists have usually argued that these expressions have to be judged on their political and social, rather than their literal, content and claims to knowledge. 'Deconstructionism', in contrast, took the anthropological subject for its object, and analysed the ways in which its claims towards ethnographic authority were themselves part of strategies of cultural imperialism. This endeavour drew regularly upon religious metaphors to attain its critical ends (ethnography as 'allegory' or 'occult document': Clifford 1986b; Tyler 1986).

Both these positions, however, remain based on textual strategies that define a subjective locus relatively isolated from the 'contact zone' (cf. Pratt 1992) in which knowledge about the others' religion was produced. Our intention is to bring out a number of contexts in which the religious or magical 'object' itself becomes a 'subject': that, in other words, a deconstruction of the anthropological subject by its object is a perfectly common occurrence, especially during fieldwork (but also, and increasingly, in wider contexts). We maintain that it is necessary to democratise deconstruction in this way, if not to unsettle anthropological claims to authority, then at least to restore agency to those whom these claims commonly reduce to 'objectivity' (or a 'voice'). We think such a step is necessary for the reorientation of research into religion in a postcolonial world.

To anticipate the direction into which our conclusions will go: we feel it is not only necessary to engage critically with the ability to construct an 'other' textually – as implied in the concept of *ethno*graphy – but also to rethink the extent to which the practice of fieldwork is based on an interaction between contexts standing in a relationship of inequality. As the following case studies will show, the distinctions between textual authority and oral communication, between objective observation and (inter)subjective production of knowledge, and between 'science' and 'religion', are not just suppositions of anthropological theory, but also political *tactics* actively deployed and resisted, by both ethnographer and the people he or she confronts.[2] In other words, they are not merely elements of the texts anthropologists produce, but also of the (political) contexts in which they and their interlocutors need to move.

By bringing the active challenge to ethnographic authority by people written about to the fore, we hope to raise some doubts about the matter-of-factness with which ethnographers maintain their identity as scholarly writers who do their research in some 'field' far away from 'home'. By this, we do not merely want to draw attention to the intellectual distancing that goes on when an ethnographer deploys the knowledge gained 'out there' in the home context; we also want to suggest that, in a world where an Indian writer residing in Britain can expect an armed Iranian on his doorstep any minute, 'fieldwork' is coming closer to 'homework' than we usually think.[3]

We suggest that the study of religion in Africa is particularly suitable for a discussion of such developments. As many anthropologists have observed, the anthropological study of religion tends to reflect, more than any other anthropological topic, the preconceptions of the Western observer. This is probably the reason why so little has been written (except autobiographically) about fieldwork on religion, because in it, the 'veil of objectivity' (Jules-Rosette 1978) is so easily torn away (see van Binsbergen 1991: 340; Douglas 1982; Olivier de Sardan 1992: 9; Stoller 1989b: 39). Since the first descriptions of 'fetishism' on the West African coast in the sixteenth century (see Pietz 1985; 1987; 1988), Europeans have been fascinated by the magic which they attributed to African thought and which seemed so different from their conceptions of 'rational' value, to the extent that some twentieth-century debates about rationality exclusively focused on African magic and religion (Evans-Pritchard 1976; Hollis and Lukes 1982; Wilson 1970). Given this tension within the Western tradition between scientism and occultism (about which more below), the study of religion in Africa can be expected to provide particularly poignant examples of the kind of cultural politics we want to discuss in this chapter.

We propose to do so by presenting two cases in which the tactical behaviour of both the anthropologists and their interlocutors challenges the hegemony of their attitudes towards each other's production of (scientific, religious and magical) knowledge. We first discuss an element of anthropological fieldwork which, although it has always exerted a powerful influence on the anthropological imagination, has in practice been rare: the *initiation* of the researcher into secrets held by local religious leaders. Here, ethnographers (act as if they) accept the hegemony of the 'other' cultural practice while being initiated. The result is that the assumed hegemony of the anthropologists' world-view and their assumptions about 'objective reality' undergo a severe trial from which they emerge changed.

This role of initiation has what one might call a 'subdominant' history in anthropological thought. Even within academic anthropology itself, the assumed objectivity of anthropological knowledge was slightly subverted by the corridor-talk conception of fieldwork as a form of initiation, a subjective transformation supposed to make one into a real anthropologist.[4]

Being initiated as a member of a local cult was, since the inception of intensive fieldwork, part of the methodological arsenal of anthropology (cf. Spencer and Gillen 1899). In the postcolonial era, and especially since the resurgence of 'occult' inspiration marked by Carlos Castaneda's *The Teachings of Don Juan* (1968), the possibility that initiation by non-Western religious authorities would subvert or deconstruct the hegemony of Western assumptions about knowledge (and, consequently, about power) has become debated more and more (see van Binsbergen 1991; Stoller and Olkes 1987; Turner et al. 1992).[5]

Of course, anthropological researchers have always, to some extent, put their everyday conception of the world at risk during fieldwork (as the endless considerations of 'culture shock' show). But situations in which researchers subject themselves more or less willingly to a formal initiation, from which it is hard to withdraw at will and at short notice, seem to be rare. In our second case, we give an example of a confrontation between ethnographer and interlocutors that is far more prevalent, yet even less studied by anthropologists. It shows how van Dijk was obliged to go through a penitential exercise after having produced a text in a popular magazine which insufficiently recognised the inspirational authority of religious leaders in the field. In this case, the existence of the text was, for the Born-Again religious leaders which it discussed, evidence of the lack of allowance that the ethnographer gave to their religious authority in the co-production of knowledge. Thus, the Born-Again preachers challenged van Dijk's unconscious assumptions about his authority to write, and as a consequence initiated an ideological struggle about the proper sources of knowledge. The conflict between authority based on observation (van Dijk's) and authority based on inspiration (the preachers') articulated a difference that, left unchallenged, would threaten the integrity of the niche in Malawian society that the preachers had created for themselves. As it was, both parties had to engage in a *bricolage* of tactical steps to restore their former positions, in which both the project of the ethnographer and that of the preachers could be safeguarded from the threat posed by their differing approaches to authoritative knowledge.

The politics of perception

A discussion of such topics can hardly avoid asking what is more in heaven and earth than that which is 'dreamt of in our philosophy'. The authority of different possible perceptions of the world is, in these situations of an anthropologist's initiation into and confrontation with 'other' religious realities, contested in ways which are, for both sides, uncomfortable. Anthropologists commonly react to these situations in two ways: either they declare specific scientific assumptions about how reality is to be perceived to be the most valid; or they declare the 'other' assumptions about authoritative knowledge to be part of a 'discourse' or a 'definition of the situation' that needs to be understood in its own right, to assess how this specific context is constituted. The first reaction posits the sovereignty of a scientific subject, the second the right of that subject to define its object, and both, therefore, maintain or resurrect a hierarchy of perception, a hierarchy that the deconstructions of ethnographic authority during fieldwork, to which we referred above, have challenged in the first place. To the extent that distinctions between the 'natural' and the 'supernatural', between 'scientific' and 'religious', or between 'real' and 'occult', constitute the authority of the ethnographer, we have to acknowledge that they are *themselves* part of a politics of perception that informs the power relationships between anthropologists and interlocutors, and the contexts in which they live.

By insisting on an account of this politics of perception, we want to draw attention to the fact that judgements of admissible evidence about the constitution of the world – and, by default, of the otherworldly – rely on hierarchies of perceptual faculties that can no longer be regarded as self-evident. As recent studies in the 'anthropology of the senses' show, neither the number nor the ranking of the senses in Western epistemologies is 'natural': they vary both historically and culturally (Classen 1993; Howes 1991). More important, perhaps, is the observation that this is not merely a question of different cultural or historical classifications of the senses, but of the material relationship between the human organism and its environment. Studies in the physiology of perception stress the difficulty of disentangling different senses from each other within the work of perception (Classen 1993: 5). Even more, it has become clear that new technologies of perception – writing, linear perspective, printing, photography, film – have created new sensory possibilities and new sensory regimes.[6] By stressing the *politics* of perception, we want to emphasize that these bodily, technological and cultural repertoires of perception make up a *contested* terrain, and that the extent to which one privileges a 'natural' over a 'supernatural', or a 'scientific' over a 'religious' conception of the world is the outcome of a struggle over how to perceive, rather than the reflection of a given 'objectivity'.[7]

The existence of such struggles is demonstrated by the fact that anthropologists' involvement with occult knowledge[8] generally provoked a rethinking of the limits and possibilities of human perception. When North Asian and American shamanism captured the imaginations of travellers and philosophers in the eighteenth century, scholars such as Diderot, Herder and Goethe speculated on the relationships between the hypersensitivity of the shaman and that of the poetical and musical genius (Flaherty 1992). In the nineteenth century, Alfred Russel Wallace's conversion to spiritualism changed his theories about human evolution and led him to postulate a 'higher sense than vision' to account for the way in which spiritualistic mediums could contact the other world (Wallace 1896), and involved him in a discussion with Edward Tylor that may have led Tylor to 'see' for himself what evidence could be mustered for the existence of spiritualistic phenomena (Pels 1994; Stocking 1971). As we shall see below, present-day anthropologists who were initiated into occult secrets display a similar desire to redefine hierarchies of perception (see, in particular, Stoller 1989b).

The critique of Western hierarchies of perception and their influence on the constitution of the objects of anthropology has focused pre-dominantly on the critique of 'visualism', or the way in which the hegemony of the eye in Western epistemologies has determined what can, and cannot, be admitted as 'fact' (Fabian 1983; Tyler 1984). Often, such critiques themselves have to fall back on Western classifications of the senses, positing the oral/aural (Fabian 1983), the olfactory (Stoller 1989b) or the tactile (Pels 1993: 1–20) against the hegemony of vision. We ourselves, in our interpretation of the two cases that are the subject of this chapter, have not been able to escape such ethnocentrism, particularly where we rely on metaphors of tactility or the sense of touch. This should not obscure the fact that sensory regimes and their tactical con-frontations are more complex than that: if vision can be realised through different physiological, technological and cultural media,[9] it is also possible to distinguish different perceptual possibilities within the realm of the oral/aural (between, for instance, interrogation and dialogue) or within that of tactility (for instance, the difference between the exchange of blows and of caresses). Moreover, because a sensory regime is itself based on a combination and hierarchy of senses, the analysis of the interaction between them remains a crucial part of any study of the politics of perception.

In the cases studied, the politics of perception of the ethnographer are usually informed by a fairly stable combination of 'visualist' politics – one-sided 'observation' combined with representation in writing (for a critique, see Fabian 1983: ch. 4) – and a form of the control of the oral/aural through interrogation (for a critique, see Rosaldo 1989). Deconstruc-tions of this sensory regime by religious authorities during fieldwork employ other forms of perception, that often invert the Western hegemony of vision and interrogation by forcing the researcher to 'listen' passively or 'feel' instead of to 'supervise', 'question' and 'observe'. For Western scientists the most elusive challenge to their sensory regime is that which puts forward definitions of reality based on an 'inner' vision or 'inspiration'. As indicated above, we do not pretend to provide answers to metaphysical questions about the validity of such perceptions. However, we feel that a study of the politics of perception in the practice of studying religion in Africa can restore initiative and agency to those who are usually simply objects of study. In a postcolonial world, where it is becoming increasingly obvious that religion is going to continue playing a major role in modern politics (cf. Geschiere n.d.; van der Veer 1994), such a democratising of deconstruction promises to be a further step in the disengagement of scientific politics from Western 'scientistic' prejudice.

Sorcerer's apprentice: objectivity, occultism and liminal politics

The mainstream attitude of anthropologists towards occult knowledge is perhaps best represented by the work of Edward Evans-Pritchard who, convinced that Zande witchcraft was based on faulty premises, deconstructed its belief system by analysing its 'closed' reasoning and the social mechanisms that supported it. His account of research into 'witchdoctor' practices shows how the identity of the classical anthropologist relied on a specific politics and hierarchy of the perception. Evans-Pritchard, afraid that participation – his becoming a witchdoctor himself – would change the phenomena to be 'observed', reduce his ability to observe critically while participating, and lower his esteem among Azande (as Zande nobles would not become witchdoctors), decided to send his assistant as a proxy (Evans-Pritchard 1976: 67–8). By having two witchdoctors – who both knew their pupil would tell everything he learned to the anthropologist – compete for the tuition of his assistant, he created a rivalry which guaranteed that few secrets would be withheld (ibid.: 69). Moreover, by forcing one of the witchdoctors to effect a cure on someone in his house, he managed to detect fraud in the 'extraction' of witch-substance from a patient, and led the healer to confess it in private (ibid.: 102–4). Not only does Evans-Pritchard display his extraordinary talent for power-play during fieldwork in this passage, he also shows that this power was directed, in the first place, at the *visible* manifestations of witchdoctors' powers (the extraction of evil substance) and, in the second place, at breaking the conditions of secrecy under which oral communications were ordinarily transferred, thereby imposing his own control. His research was a politics of controlled supervision, or 'observation'. The objective anthropologist, a powerful *voyeur*, produced a denial of equality in fieldwork practice even before this was turned, in his textual production, into a 'denial of co-evalness' (cf. Fabian 1983).

The publication of Carlos Castaneda's *The Teachings of Don Juan* (1968) produced an, in his own case short-lived, occult revival in anthropology. The dismissal of Castaneda from the anthropological canon, after the suspicions that his Don Juan was a hoax became too prominent to ignore, tends to cover up the momentary significance of his work. Not only was Castaneda's an outstanding 'ethnographic experiment' with dialogue more than ten years before this became fashionable, its fraudulence discloses an important argument about ethnographic authority: that the authenticity of a fieldwork account is something which is very difficult to check, and that anthropologists are trusted and judged on the basis of the *words about* their experiences, and not their experiences themselves.

Recently, a number of interesting contributions to the literature on this topic have been published, dealing mostly with Africa (van Binsbergen 1991; Favret-Saada 1980; Fidaali 1987; Gibbal 1994; Olivier de Sardan 1988; 1989; 1992; Stoller 1989a; 1989b; Stoller and Olkes 1987; Turner et al. 1992). Paul Stoller has given an account of how, over a long period of fieldwork in the Songhay region of Niger, he became apprenticed to a number of different local sorcerers and healers (Stoller and Olkes 1987). Stoller presents himself as an anthropologist relying on a self-image of 'objectivity' that is increasingly subverted by his experiences as a sorcerer's apprentice. Early in the book, he describes his dilemma by referring to Evans-Pritchard and Castaneda, the alternatives being to refuse to become involved, or to become involved but not believed by one's colleagues. However, the 'real reason' why he hesitated is his fear of the physical and psychological danger that might be involved, and how becoming an apprentice would change him as a person. He anticipated the lure of occult knowledge and the possibility of becoming 'a more powerful person' (Stoller and Olkes 1987: 25–7), but, pondering the 'Evans-Pritchard question' at a later stage, Stoller writes: 'Although no red-blooded modern anthropologist would send a proxy, the question still stood: When does the anthropologist say: "Enough, I cannot become more subjectively involved"?' (ibid.: 38).

'Objectivity', for Stoller, seems to mean that the researcher *is not being changed* by his research experiences, and impossible though this is, it is precisely the kind of immunity against the experience of another reality that Stoller identifies with Evans-Pritchard's power-play.[10] When Stoller's first teacher, the *sorko* Djibo, tells him just to listen and memorise, Stoller wants to tell him that, as an anthropologist, he is supposed to ask questions and direct informants (Stoller and Olkes 1987: 31) just as Evans-Pritchard manipulated his. Yet Stoller does not conceptualise his activity as political: his role-switching from anthropologist to sorcerer's apprentice is described only in terms of 'ethical' contradictions (ibid.: 111, 180; see below, note 14 in particular, for the topic of covering 'ethnic' with 'ethic', or cultural politics with the cloak of professionalism).

The 'veil of objectivity' (cf. Jules-Rosette 1978) of Stoller is eventually ripped off by his perception of a physical change: at one point he finds himself partly paralysed at night, and panics at the thought that a nearby sorceress is testing him. By reciting a charm of defence against bewitchment, the paralysis disappears. 'Before my paralysis, I *knew* there were scientific explanations of Songhay sorcery. After Wanzerbe [the place where the paralysis occurred] my unwavering faith in science vanished' (Stoller and Olkes 1987: 153) and with it, his 'unwavering faith' in anthropological objectivity.

Here, it should be noted that such extraordinary physical perceptions are also the basis of the change of mind that other anthropological apprentices to occult teachers undergo: Jean-Marie Gibbal describes his sensation of a strange, invisible presence during and after attending a possession ceremony, and how he was 'overtaken by waves, vibrations, and shaking that had me participating physically in a rite whose meaning partially escaped me' (Gibbal 1994: 81). Gibbal also refers to Fidaali's (1987) conclusion that the practices of the healer to whom Fidaali was apprenticed relied on 'an archaic, coalescent perception of the world that is anterior to language. This perception is made possible by mobilizing all the senses and working at a level of attention sensitive to the body's internal messages' (Gibbal 1994: 158).

Lastly, Wim van Binsbergen, although he hardly devotes attention to the perceptual process in his account, relates how an illness – difficult to explain, and not cured, by Western medicine – drove him to join a healing lodge that did, indeed, cure him. Again, a perception of inner, physical change preceded a transformation of reality.

This challenge to Western sensory regimes led Stoller and Gibbal to question the hierarchy and politics of perception. Stoller devoted a whole book to it (1989b) which Gibbal cites approvingly. This rethinking of human sensitivity also led them to question the ways in which it is represented in writing and to discuss the possibilities of 'evoking' something that is hard to make present by ink on paper only (Gibbal 1994: 150; Stoller 1989b: 153).[11] One of the textual strategies they both employ is to incorporate the 'observer' and his doubts into their accounts of fieldwork, and such personal narrative is also the option that others with similar problems of representation chose (although they are less optimistic about the results: van Binsbergen 1991; Jules-Rosette 1976).

Jean-Pierre Olivier de Sardan has criticised both Stoller and Gibbal for incorporating, through their first-person narrative, an ethnocentric 'occult exoticism' into Songhay magic and religion. He argues that in their attempt to explain Songhay magic and religion to a Western audience, they take 'fashionable' European occultism as their model rather than Christian or everyday magical routines (Olivier de Sardin 1992: 14).[12] And indeed, contrary to Stoller's idea that European – and, by implication, anthropological – metaphysics is characterised by an 'escape from the senses' (Stoller 1989b: 153), we have indicated that (hyper-)sensitivity, poetic expression and occultism have been debated conjointly in Europe since at least the Enlightenment, despite the temporary hegemony of specific perceptual regimes. This lends considerable weight to Olivier de Sardan's contention that this rhetoric of the experiencing 'I' tends to downplay the banality and matter-of-factness of Songhay magic and religion in favour of a rarefied idea of the occult.

Indeed, Stoller's textual solution to the questions of representation raised by his experiences is, as we have already indicated, not a solution to his dilemma. Stoller is not aware of the fact that the incorporation of the researcher and of individual 'voices' into an ethnographic text was a (subdominant) strategy of ethnographers even before the advent of professional anthropology.[13] Thus, his claim to present a more profound 'respect' for indigenous knowledge (again, a rhetoric as old as cultural relativism itself) through texts that give an 'authentic' voice to it (Stoller 1989b: 27, 153) is, like other so-called 'postmodernist' initiatives, not much more than a new professionalism in anthropology, now perhaps more influenced by aesthetic than by natural science models (cf. Pels and Nencel 1991).[14] His text hides, therefore, a profound *complicity* of ethnographic and magical authority that has been, we submit, present in anthropology since its inception: both the shaman and his apprentice are experts in cultural knowledge who set themselves apart from a lay public. Indeed, Stoller claims authority on the basis of a knowledge of 'the Songhay world' that, to use his own words, 'few Songhay know directly' (Stoller and Olkes 1987: 227–8).

It would be too simple to leave the discussion at this level of ethnographic, that is, textual, strategies. At that level, Olivier de Sardan's accusation against Stoller can be turned back upon himself by the argument that his endorsement of the 'banal', everyday, reality of Songhay magic and religion shows a European, mainly Marxist, preoccupation with the 'masses' as they are classified from a conceptual framework just as authoritarian.[15] Noting a (largely textual) complicity between ethnographic and magical authority should not obscure the profound contradictions and tactical *bricolage* of the 'contact zone' in which this authority is built up.

Wim van Binsbergen's account of becoming a *sangoma* can remind us of this. He acknowledges that, gratifying though the combination of the authority of an anthropologist with that of a *sangoma* may seem to be, it does not resolve the contradiction between their respective contexts, even if this means relinquishing ethnographic authority at home:[16] 'I refuse to deconstruct my knowledge of sangomahood if, in the process, that means that I am professionally compelled to kill its powerful images on the operation table of intellectual vivisection. At the same time, it would be a waste not to ultimately subject this knowledge to the kind of systematic academic commentary I and especially many of my colleagues have shown ourselves capable of' (van Binsbergen 1991: 337).

Another transformation of these contradictions is the way in which van Binsbergen's newly acquired authority, though it may set him off from a 'lay audience' in Botswana, could also be (and was) perceived as an act of 'humility' by them: his initiation, in particular, could be seen as a subversion of the rejection of *sangoma* practices that they have learned to expect from White and Christian culture (ibid.: 337–9). Initiation, is, as many scholars now agree, based on putting one's body at the disposal of the initiators (cf. Comaroff 1985; Jackson 1983), and therefore a form of communication (of, among other things, humility) that can better be described in terms of the sense of touch rather than that of vision (Pels 1993: 1–18).

Perhaps the most telling example of the way in which the contradictions between sensory regimes, despite the willingness of the ethnographer to relinquish his own, remain the condition of such liminal situations, is Stoller's account of the search for a sick man's 'double' by *sorko* Djibo in order to cure him. When Djibo has released the 'double' from a pile of husks, he turns to Stoller:

> 'Did you hear it?'
> 'Hear what?' I asked dumbfounded.
> 'Did you feel it?'
> 'Feel what?' I wondered.
> 'Did you see it?'
> 'What are you talking about?' I demanded.
> Sorko Djibo shook his head in disbelief. He was disappointed that I had not sensed in one way or another the man's double as he, Djibo, had liberated it. He said to me: 'You look but you do not see. You touch, but you do not feel. You listen, but you do not hear. Without sight or touch,' he continued, 'one can learn a great deal. But you must learn how to *hear* or you will learn little about our ways.' (Stoller 1989b: 115, emphasis in original).

Stoller takes this remarkable dialogue as an argument for the recognition of the cultural importance of sound, probably because of Djibo's emphasis on hearing. But he does not note that Djibo launches an out-and-out attack on Stoller's *complete* routine of perception. Stoller's 'non-seeing' and 'non-touching' will not prevent him from learning, Djibo says. But 'non-hearing', in particular, will prevent Stoller from learning about Songhay ways. Not only does Djibo say that Stoller cannot perceive as a Songhay *sorko* should, he also inverts the hierarchy of perception common to the West, by putting the aural sense first. We already noted that Stoller was not supposed to pose questions, nor was he allowed to write down the magical formulas he had to learn before he had committed them to memory completely. This shows to what extent Djibo's politics of perception redefined the relationship between anthropologist and informant even before Stoller's perception of reality itself had changed, and how powerless Stoller's textual strategy of incorporating his personal sense-perception in his account is in bridging the gap with Djibo's paradigm.

Stoller also does not show how his perception of his own, North American, world has changed under the influence of his apprenticeship in Songhay.[17] Perhaps this is another way in which these political contradictions, this time in the guise of 'home' versus 'field', are maintained. Murray Last pointed out to van Binsbergen that the true test of his sangomahood would be to continue practising as one, and, up to now, van Binsbergen maintains a group of clients in Francistown – which implies that many of the contradictions he notes in his account are also maintained.[18] The continuing existence of an irresolvable contest of authorities, however, does not imply that these contradictions, themselves, remain stationary. Van Binsbergen's performance of a sacrifice to his wife's ancestors in Belgium (van Binsbergen 1991: 319) is only one way in which, for a sorcerer's apprentice, 'fieldwork' can become 'homework', and the immunising of the anthropologist against his 'field' that Evans-Pritchard demonstrates becomes harder and harder to maintain.

So, if contradictions between sensory regimes turn out to condition a practice in which anthropologists more or less willingly undergo the influence of the other's mode of perceiving because of the continuity between ethnographic and magical authority, they can be expected to appear more forcefully in situations where such a partial community of interest does not prevail, and that, in the study of religion in Africa, is probably more often than not the case. We turn now to an examination of one of these more prevalent situations.

The deconstructed ethnographer, or perception, penance and intellectual survival

The following case from van Dijk's fieldwork in Blantyre, Malawi, shows a conflict between researcher's and researched's strategies of perception and representation. The ethnographer's textual representations were confronted with the oral performances of young to very young preachers (some only nine years of age) that showed divine inspiration. These performances provided a channel for dissent from the oppression of the Banda regime, and the gerontocratic structure of Malawian society in general, by stressing inspiration as the real source of power and authority. Inspiration combined with oral performance, both forms of authority that could neither be institutionalised nor laid down in tangible texts, were key strategies used to steer free of any sort of political involvement with this establishment. Van Dijk's entry into, and attempts to record, the field of activities of the young preachers brought him into direct conflict with these strategies. The young preachers distrusted van Dijk's perception through observation, of distanced seeing and hearing, and stressed a tactile experience – of being '*touched*' by the Holy Spirit – that should be communicated orally and in public to show what such experiences really mean.

Since the early 1970s, Malawi's urban centres have seen the rise of a number of Christian fundamentalist groups and organisations led by young itinerant preachers, varying in age between nine and thirty (see van Dijk 1992; 1993; forthcoming). These preachers aim at a purification of social life and their work can be interpreted as a modern transformation of earlier puritan movements in Malawi. Puritanism, present in Malawi since the early 1930s in the form of various anti-witchcraft movements, provided the means and the basis for the younger generation to challenge the authority of elders both in political and religious terms (the so-called *Mchape* movements, see Richards 1935; Ranger 1972; Fields 1985). In modern urban conditions the younger generation again presented a puritan ideology to assert themselves against the gerontocratic mode of political and religious control, still paramount in Malawian society in the 1970s, 1980s and early part of the 1990s. By a Christian fundamentalist ideology of high morality, sin and redemption, and obedience to leadership, the preachers were able to deprive the coercive Malawian regime of the opportunity to define this movement as subversive and as a threat to the nation's 'peace, calm, law and order'. The young preachers obtained room for manoeuvre, a safe niche in the heavily supervised and controlled life of Malawian society, which they used to set up organisations, large revival meetings, 'crusades' and even meetings of a more secretive nature that were and still are held at night in the townships or on top of certain hills.

Within this niche the preacher-leaders, rather than relying on notions of formal membership, have promoted an ideology of 'Born-Again' identity to mark off their group from the outside world. While a system of supervision in the full sense of the word (with records, fees and exclusive membership of one denomination as against another) is absent, the young preachers know for certain who belongs to the core-group that 'prays' with them and who usually does not, and they keep in contact with one another on a regular basis. In this way it doesn't really matter whether a person is 'praying' with this preacher or that as long as the person remains within the Born-Again circle.

In the city of Blantyre, where van Dijk concentrated his research, this circle consisted of a broad network of a variety of Born-Again preachers and their adherents. They conducted a range of weekly if not daily revival, prayer and healing meetings, that maintained its contours by the identity of being 'Born-Again'. A Born-Again is allowed and even stimulated to maintain his or her membership of other Christian denominations as long as he or she is prepared to display commitment to the rather strict Born-Again ideology. This ideology includes a range of restrictions on personal conduct and morality, but above all propounds the view that a continuous channel or, perhaps better, a lifeline, to the power of the *Mzimu Woyera*, the 'White' or Holy Spirit, should be maintained. Ecstatic frenzies, speaking in tongues, visions, the ability to heal by prayer and laying-on of hands are direct and tangible signs of the flux and momentum of this empowering channel. Any transgression of the many do's and don'ts directly affects the power flowing through this channel and may therefore jeopardise the spiritual wall that the Born-Agains have erected to ward off evil spiritual forces from outside their circle.

The spiritual circle is thus embodied by the Born-Agains themselves and the network of organisations and activities which they have been able to set up. Unlike other puritan movements, the circle does not exist in the materialised form of a closed community or compound. The Born-Agains do not need such physical boundaries, and the spiritual ones which define their circle serve a clear purpose in an urban setting, with its mobility and continuously changing sets of social relationships. Every 'true' Born-Again is the carrier of this spiritual circle of defence, irrespective of the social networks in which an individual may be engaged. A real breach of the circle occurs when the channel of inspirational power from the heavenly forces is either not maintained, or denied and exchanged for a different, sometimes contesting line of power. Therefore, the Born-Agains, leaders and followers alike, repudiate involvement in the Malawian political system as well as involvement in the authority structure of other important social or religious organisations. Likewise, the power and authority that can be derived from what they call, in derogatory terms, 'book-knowledge' is abhorred, and the authority of mainstream church leaders, pastors, priests and bishops is questioned on the grounds that it is not based on the power of inspiration. It was such a challenge to inspirational authority that occasioned a breach of confidence between the ethnographer and some of the young preacher-leaders in Blantyre.

After almost a year of intensive contact with a number of young preachers and their followers in Blantyre, van Dijk published a short article in one of Malawi's most widely read monthlies, *Moni* (April 1989). The article was written from the point of view of a distanced observer who has had some experiences that might be sufficiently interesting to the general public to be published. The article opened by introducing the author and his academic interest in the subject matter and set out to describe the activities of the young preachers in Blantyre. One of the paragraphs that displays the author's stance as an observer ran as follows: 'With the "infilling" of the Holy Spirit, as many youngsters have been explaining, one suddenly feels as having stepped into the world of light. Every meeting, therefore, is filled with ecstatic prayers, shouting and speaking in tongues to create the exact state of mind wherein the baptism by the Holy Spirit can take place.'

Here the use of inverted commas for 'infilling' indicated how the possession by the Holy Spirit was perceived by some of the interlocutors, while the word 'ecstatic' underscored the distancing attitude of the author towards these forms of experience. The magazine came out and was sold on the streets of Blantyre on a Saturday morning, and on the afternoon of the very same day a message reached van Dijk that his presence was requested at a special meeting with a group of preachers, first thing Monday morning. The topic of discussion would be his text.

That particular Monday morning, in one of the townships of Blantyre, van Dijk met with a group of apparently hostile preachers who positioned themselves in a semi-circle facing the other end of the small room where van Dijk had to sit. On a small table in the middle of the room the magazine was turned open on the page that showed van Dijk's article. One by one, the preachers expressed their utmost concern with the contents of the article. Van Dijk was confronted with questions about the way in which he depicted the Born-Agains: 'Why do you use the word "ecstatic" when God blesses us with his Holy Spirit descending upon us all?'; 'Why do you say we, preachers, speak against the authority of the elders, while in fact we are preaching against sin?'

Above all, one specific criticism appeared again and again: 'You have stayed with us, you have eaten with us, you have participated in our meetings and now you have written about us. Have you been intending to be rude? Are you a spy of the Pope?' After some discussion and clarification it was decided that at the revival meeting of the coming Saturday van Dijk would publicly denounce the Pope and the allegation of being a spy for the Holy See. Furthermore, the preachers strongly demanded that he would also, and above all, acknowledge the power of inspiration by the Holy Spirit in his work, and that this inspiration was a necessary part of his scientific interest.

The next Saturday, during a large revival meeting held in one of Blantyre's conference centres, van Dijk was called to the pulpit to declare the sincerity of his intention not to offend the Born-Agains of Blantyre and to acknowledge the points on which the preachers had insisted on the preceding Monday. As his penitential exercise was met with appreciative cheers, applause and laughter, it seemed to restore some mutual trust and confidence. It did not lead, however, to a further appreciation of his scientific interest. Some weeks later, it became clear that his authority to put things down in writing was still suspect. When he tried to conduct a small survey of the socio-economic position of some of the followers, this procedure of obtaining information in written form was simply refused to him: the completed forms were confiscated by some young preachers. Despite having explained and discussed the purpose and method of this form of data-collection at length, he was asked why he needed the forms and whether he was going 'to write or to understand'. Clearly, the process of obtaining knowledge by means of methods that were directly associated with 'book-knowledge' conflicted with the preachers' basic notions of how the 'truth' about the Born-Again movement could be ascertained.

At first sight, it seems that the sheer fact of writing and publishing about the inner characteristics of the movement and its ideology caused confusion and resentment. In retrospect, however, the challenge to van Dijk's authority to write can be related to a politics of perception seated at a deeper level. The questions with which the preachers confronted him, when accusing him of rudeness and spying, were basically a deconstruction of the authority he assumed in his text, that was subsequently related to other texts and to the interrelations of the contexts in which they could be put to use. The preachers were familiar with the use of the written word, many having completed at least junior certificate secondary schooling while some of them had obtained higher education. Their authority depended on text: the divine inspiration of the Gospel. In other words, it was not the text as such, as much as the indications it provided about a politics of perception that properly belonged to a realm outside their spiritual circle – the realm of gerontocratic power, often associated with witchcraft – that caused anxiety among the preachers.

The preachers were disconcerted by certain signs in van Dijk's text that raised doubts about the basis of his assumption of authority. His putting a word like 'infilling' between inverted commas could be perceived by the preachers as indicating intellectual distance from their discourse and activities, something that the description of their behaviour as 'ecstatic' would only reinforce. His description of the preachers' protest against the power of elders made theirs a *particular* interest that denied the universality of the purification from sin they aimed to achieve. Moreover, there were also suspicious intertextual relationships: originally, *Moni* was a magazine with Roman Catholic orientation and, in the same issue, the opening article discussed the Pope's coming visit to Malawi (in June 1989), where he would be received by President Banda. In relation to wider, global and local, contexts, this was not a recommendation for van Dijk's text: the Roman Catholic hierarchy was seen by the preachers as being closely allied with the main bulwarks of political power, and many preachers feared any sort of interference with their activities by the repressive political machinery. In the eyes of the preachers, the Roman Catholic Church was the prime example of how far removed from inspirational knowledge and power religious authority can become. It was the lack of divine inspiration that supposedly made the Roman Catholic Church so prone to collaboration with the political elite as it seemed (at that time).[19]

In the light of these intertextual and intercontextual relationships, the fact that van Dijk's article, in the view of the preachers, did not explicitly acknowledge a form of revelation and inspiration was unsettling. The politics of perception that the article seemed to suggest to them was closer to 'book-knowledge' than to the inspiration by which van Dijk was supposed to be touched in every nerve of his body. The other aspects of his scholarly behaviour, such as interviewing, observing and participating in their meetings, did not challenge the preachers' model of inspiration directly; indeed, a desire to obtain some form of inspiration seemed the most likely explanation of van Dijk's eagerness to communicate, observe and participate. In the end, this inspiration would even assure him academic success as well. But because the authority of the article was supported by a notion of distanced academic observation, it was unclear whether it would support or threaten the integrity of the Born-Agains' spiritual defence. There was no indication in his article that van Dijk was prepared to support it against the evil outside world. Was van Dijk, by writing this article, a 'spy of the Pope' and, by implication, a potential government informer? And if not, what had made him write this article at this exact moment in time? Was God's hand in it? Was it that, by revelation and inspiration, he had heard a call to write something that would explain to Malawian Catholics something of the true power of God, which could not be vested in ecclesiastical hierarchies, but was manifested in the divine inspiration of those who are 'saved' by becoming Born-Again? The anxiety that these questions produced could only be set at rest by a public, oral performance acknowledging the inspiration of the Holy Spirit.

Thus, the Born-Again preachers seemed to react to a perceptual regime implicit in the article that declared them to be an object of observation (seeing and hearing) without granting them the subject position that they felt they deserved on the basis of their experience of being 'touched' by the Holy Spirit, and of their perception of truth by inspiration. And whatever one might want to say about the grounds of the truth at which the preachers arrived, their interpretation of the perceptual strategy of ethnography, as represented by van Dijk's article, was accurate in the sense that it correctly identified a politics of perception whereby controlled observation and interview became dominant at the expense of the preachers' 'inner tactility'. Text-book-knowledge was the sign of an 'informative' regime of perception corresponding to 'a political situation of more or less direct control', a regime at odds with the 'performative' strategy (Fabian 1990: 19) – divine inspiration as testified by public, oral representation – that served the preachers to subvert, and dissent from, a system of political oppression.[20] The preachers' uncertainty about the role this kind of distanced perception of their activities could play within the broader context of Roman Catholicism and Malawian politics occasioned them to ask for a public penance that would safeguard their spiritual survival in the circle of defence they had carved out in Malawian society. For the ethnographer, the display of public humility was a necessary – but, in the 'field', only temporary – act of intellectual survival as well.

Discussion

The two cases presented above are too isolated to allow for conclusions. Their in-depth analysis, however, does point to a number of issues in which these contests of authority affect the future of research into religion and religious movements in Africa. These can be summarised under three headings: the politics of perception, the question of representation, and the blurring of the boundaries between 'home' and 'field'.

The politics of perception, or tactility and fieldwork tactics   Few ethnographers will fail to recognise the situation whereby informants with whom
an interview was arranged let them feel their superfluity and irrelevance
by keeping them waiting or not showing up at all. Elsewhere, Pels has
argued that such events, which require physical co-presence of ethnographer and informant, or the feeling of the absence of it, can best be
described by a metaphor of 'tactility' or the sense of touch (Pels 1993: 1–
18). Such 'tactile' perception, a type of 'feeling' not identical with emotion,
makes one, when it is recognised as such, attentive to those events in a
fieldwork process that rely on co-presence, the movement and positioning
of bodies, and immediate perceptions that defy description in exact terms;
anyone but the most disembodied researcher dealing with the anthropology
of sexuality will be familiar with these problems.

Wim van Binsbergen has also drawn attention to the similarity of the
problems which researchers into trance-healing and sexuality face (personal
communication). In the study of religion in Africa, such problems of (the
representation of) tactile perception are readily apparent once we consider
the possibility that a researcher participates directly in ritual.[21] Pels found
little difficulty in dancing to Luguru ritual rhythms – something with which
some researchers from an older generation might have more problems –
but rarely mustered sufficient spiritual energy to endure the hardships of
sitting and kneeling on wooden benches during one of the interminable
Catholic services he attended. Van Dijk felt uncomfortable when he had
to occupy the pulpit to deliver his penance, while van Binsbergen has also
drawn attention to the hardships of dancing during the ceremonies he
attended both before and after his initiation (personal communication).

It is hard to say right now what a more sustained attention to tactile
perception will attain in the study of religion in Africa, especially since
scientific rhetoric seems to have little room for its description, which
leans towards narrations of subjective experience rather than objective
generalisations. Two directions of enquiry, however, suggest themselves.
First, that a politics of tactile perception seems an obvious tactic for the
people observed to get their own back from a researcher who tends to
rely exclusively on sight and (controlled) sound for obtaining his information. The physical hardships of initiation are an example of this, as
van Binsbergen pointed out; the condition being, of course, that the
researcher puts his body at the disposal of his informants. Second, tactile
perception seems closer to the kind of 'inner' perception (of paralysis or
disease and its cure, of trance-like vibration) that seems to occasion many
of the conversion experiences that anthropologists, as sorcerer's apprentices, undergo. A phenomenology of perception that does not privilege
distanced vision and controlled sound seems necessary to future research
into religion in Africa, although it remains unclear to us to what extent
this will include moving towards psychotherapy or conversion.

Text and context: the question of representation As we have tried to show by presenting the two cases, alternative forms of textual representation do not seem to solve the problems of the politics of representation: the contradictions between paradigms of perception and the contests of authority associated with them are not affected by literary experiments. That does not mean, however, that the issue of representation itself becomes obsolete; on the contrary, by identifying its politics, we have urged a recognition of the fact that the politics of perception and its representation are themselves part of the contexts in which religion is studied in Africa today. It is just as much part of the object of study as it poses a problem for the subjects that study it.

The practical relevance of this issue of representation becomes, perhaps, most clear when one considers the current question of the professional-isation of 'traditional' medicine in Africa (cf. Last and Chavunduka 1986). Clearly, if an African government aspires to register and professionalise 'traditional' healers, a whole array of questions about what is represented by 'traditional', and how this representation affects the practitioners in question, arises: does it not change their work completely by, for instance, shifting the emphasis from religion to medicine?; what kind of politics of representation is involved?; are healers represented by a Ministry of Health official or by one of their own members in a separate body?; is the leadership of this separate body representative of 'traditional' healers as a group? It is also clear that, in such cases, given the simultaneous existence of institutions based on a scientific model of medicine, the whole set of contradictions between perceptual paradigms will be operative. If, as van Binsbergen has argued in his paper, his healing practice is based on a practical knowledge that is hard to convey in scientific writing, how can one call for the registration and professionalisation of 'traditional' healers, as this requires precisely the kind of textual representation that van Binsbergen says is so difficult to achieve? The point to be made here, of course, is that clinical practice has, for a long time, been faced with similar problems, and that a more thorough comparison of African healing with clinical reasoning – in particular, that of the Western medical practitioner, whose reasoning may be as fuzzy and practical as that of his African counterparts (see Ginzburg 1983) – is necessary.

In addition to the area of healing and therapy, another field in which the practical relevance of representation, and its relation to perceptual regimes, comes to the fore is the institutionalisation of religion in Africa and its role in (de-)legitimising changing forms of political power. On the one hand, since the advent of the democratic political changes on the African continent many of the established mission churches have involved themselves in practical politics by offering religious legitimations for imagined 'Africanised' or 'traditional' forms of democratic power. Such contemporary concepts of 'indigenisation' often bypass the indigenisation of Christianity practised by Africans since the first missionary encounter (through, for instance, 'witchcraft' and 'devilry': Meyer 1992) and, as a consequence, downplay the political significance of their (missiological and ethnographic) regimes of perception and ignore their potential conflict with locally held perceptions of political power and its legitimacy.[22] As Bayart (1989) has shown for Cameroon and other West African societies, political power is often perceived in olfactory and tactile terms, of a *politique du ventre* of *manger* and *bouffer*. Schatzberg (1993), too, alludes to tactile perceptions of the legitimacy of political leadership, as physically-felt forces of leadership that benefit or hurt the local population (see also Geschiere, n.d.). In other words, the representations of 'tradition' and 'Africanity' by the established mission churches, while influencing the discourses on democratisation in Africa, have seldom been related to the perceptual regimes that mediate both politics and religion.

On the other hand, the increasing institutionalisation of African churches puts them in a position in which their leaders not only read and adopt, but also criticise the analyses made of their (political) development by European academics. When Matthew Schoffeleers recently interpreted the South African Zionist churches as politically conservative and acquiescent, his views were heavily challenged by Zionist leaders (Schoffeleers 1991; Ngada 1992). In a manner recalling the Born-Agains' challenge to van Dijk's *Moni* article, Zionist leaders argued on several occasions that 'book-knowledge' and observation give only partial accounts of protest (see also Hallencreutz and Palmberg 1991). The central theme of, among others, Bishop Ngada's intervention in the debate about Schoffeleers' interpretation of the Zionist churches was also what spiritual experiences really might do to a person living in harsh circumstances of political coercion, and why these can hardly be represented in text. In all these cases, the conventions of representation and the politics of perception of academic anthropology play a role and call up protest. They remind us that the solution of the problems of representation adopted by Stoller, and, with more misgivings, by van Binsbergen and Jules-Rosette – of self-representation by a narrative of personal experience – need not be the only one available.

The interpenetration of 'field' and 'home'   The issue of the professionalisation of 'traditional' medicine also shows to what extent these issues can no longer be 'localised' in a 'field' away from 'home'. As Dutch psychiatry increasingly has to face the necessity of confronting or incorporating, for instance, Surinamese *winti* practitioners or Ghanese *imams*, similar problems arise within the Dutch nation-state. The postcolonial world is a world of migrants, and we do not need to stretch our imaginations very far to recognise that anthropologists were, with colonial administrators and missionaries, some of the first professional migrants to herald the coming of a world in which global inequalities are increasingly a feature of everyone's everyday life. Yet, few researchers have taken academic anthropology or its so-called 'amateur', missionary and administrative counterparts as an element of a globalisation movement that transformed religious practice in Africa. Just as the issue of experimental representation often serves as a cloak to hide irresolvable political contradictions in anthropological practice, just so did the historiography of anthropology use a professional self-image to deny or ignore its rootedness in colonial practice (cf. Pels and Salemink 1994). The two cases presented above seem to suggest that anthropologists have used a number of tactics in the field, and textual strategies out of it, that keep 'home' and 'field' apart. It is becoming clear, however, that they do this against a background of an increasing interpenetration of cultural realms that eventually questions any form of cultural hegemony, whether based on distanced, ethnographic observation, or on a privileging of the olfactory or tactile, or on another perceptual regime.

In the field of the study of religion in Africa, this interpenetration of cultural realms should lead to a recognition that the identities of both subject and object, of scholarly and religious authority, have a long history of mutual (de)construction. In the field of the study of missions in Africa, for instance, it is remarkable that the concepts of 'culture' and 'history' have worked for so long to reify 'European' and 'African cultures', keeping the 'contact zone' in which so much of religion in Africa has been (de)constructed out of the analysis (as is shown, for instance, by the fact that only recently, the concept of 'syncretism' has been subjected to critical scrutiny; see Stewart and Shaw 1994). In the field of Christian missions, at least, this gap is now quickly being filled (for an overview, see Pels 1993: 1–18). As van Dijk's work with Born-Again preachers in Blantyre shows, present-day religious developments are also very much shaped by the assessment that religious leaders make of globalised forms of religious and political organisation and their intercontextual relationships. Lastly, now that a growing number of scholars acknowledges that, when confronted with magical healing, the researcher cannot fall back simply on a number of scientific conventions of authority, it seems necessary to consider the legitimacy, and acknowledge the political necessity, of this deconstruction of authority and identity by those whom anthropologists study.

Notes

We would like to thank Wim van Binsbergen for discussing the topic of this paper with us while it was being written, and Dick Werbner for his productive editorial comments.

1. These scholars are often designated 'postmodernists', but the use of the term in this way – usually meant as derogatory – is highly problematic (Pool 1991a).

2. For the distinction between 'strategies' (implying a decontextualised subjective position from which strategies are drawn up) and 'tactics' (implying a *bricolage* of political calculation without a single locus), see de Certeau (1984: xix, 36–7).

3. We owe the fruitful juxtaposition of 'fieldwork' and 'homework' to discussions with Smadar Lavie during a conference in Amsterdam in June 1993.

4. Compare also C. G. Seligmann's statement that 'Field research in Anthropology is what the blood of the martyrs is to the Church' (cited in Lewis 1976: 76).

5. A closely related argument can be set up for those anthropologists who underwent a religious conversion (cf. Jules-Rosette 1976); however, we do not have the opportunity to go into the relationship between initiation and conversion, interesting though this may be (but see Pels 1994).

6. This has been argued by scholars as diverse as Walter Benjamin, Marshall McLuhan and Walter Ong. Martin Jay (1993: chs 2 and 3) gives an overview of the changes that occurred within European 'scopic', that is, visual, regimes through technological innovation.

7. It should be noted that this position does not deny that some sensory regimes can be more practically effective – more powerful – than others; we hesitate, however, in equating the practical success of these more powerful regimes (in the domination of nature as well as of humans) with a higher 'truth'.

8. We do not use 'occult' with the derogatory meaning it has acquired, but take it to refer to knowledge that has been rejected by the dominant intellectual establishment (cf. Webb 1974).

9 Which led Martin Jay to distinguish between alternating 'models of speculation, observation and revelation' within the history of Western 'scopic' epistemologies (Jay 1993: 236).

10. Despite Stoller's assessment, however, we should point out that Evans-Pritchard's politics of perception was more complex: by identifying himself with Zande nobility, he could not become a witchdoctor and therefore had to send a proxy.

11. Van Binsbergen also uses the term 'evocation' (1991: 333), but as his account differs in a number of respects from those of Stoller and Gibbal, it will be dealt with elsewhere. 'Evocation' is also important for Stephen Tyler (1986).

12. It is unfortunate that Olivier de Sardan does not elaborate on the latter in his paper. However, Malinowski pointed out sixty years ago that it is possible to look for magic in Western prayer, advertisement and legal procedure (Malinowski 1935), and, one might add, in medicine (e.g. psychiatry and the placebo effect).

13. Which is the reason why we argue in the introduction that the paradox of polyphony (of simultaneously relying on and suppressing it) has *always* been integral to ethnography. See, for the relationship between the experiencing 'I' sensitive to polyphony, and the observing 'eye' that tries to reduce it, Pratt (1985). Olivier de Sardan also notes (*contra* Stoller) that the experiencing 'I' is just another form of realism, not an escape from it (1989: 130; 1992: 10).

14. Professional 'ethics' seem, moreover, to be a specifically 'ethnic' preoccupation of the US American academy, given that the AAA code of ethics was both the first, and is the most frequently redrafted, ethical code in anthropology (see Fluehr-Lobban 1991).

15. Van Binsbergen, personal communication; see also his comments on anthropology's 'Faustian rationality' (van Binsbergen 1991: 336). Stoller suggests Olivier de Sardan's 'intellectual arrogance' without accusing him directly (Stoller 1989a: 116).

16. Van Binsbergen writes: 'The practical knowledge I claim to have acquired

(enough to convincingly play the role of a *twaza* novice and to come out as a fully-fledged *sangoma*), is at the same time more profound and complete, more personal and idiosyncratic, and (as all practical knowledge) more superficial and patchy, than that which my learned colleagues have produced on this topic over the decades' (van Binsbergen 1991: 333). One longs for a lengthy elaboration of the contradictions sketched in this paragraph.

17. He writes: 'If I have discovered anything from my experience of Songhay sorcery, it is that sorcery is a metaphor for the chaos that constitutes social relations – Songhay and otherwise. We all suffer *zamba*, a good friend's betrayal [Stoller has just been robbed by his most trusted assistant]. Things crumble and are reconstituted in all societies; we are *all* in sorcery's shadow.' This discovery that 'things fall apart' is hardly novel and is shared by writers as different as Yeats and Achebe. It is similar to the arbitrary closure of the hermeneutic circle that Michael Taussig offers when ending a discussion of Peruvian phantasies of Western cannibalism by saying that we are all cannibals (Taussig 1987: 241), an observation that goes back, in anthropology at least, to Lévi-Strauss (1977: 441).

18. Van Binsbergen, personal communication.

19. This position of the Roman Catholic Church *vis-à-vis* the political regime changed dramatically when the Catholic bishops' Lenten letter of 1992 initiated unprecedented, concerted and mass protest against the Banda regime. The church took the lead in changing the coercive political climate and was more or less able to force the ruling party and Banda to negotiate the more democratic system that was eventually installed in 1994.

20. In the same way, the suspicion of the preachers about the kind of supervision suggested by the questionnaire which van Dijk handed out some time afterwards can be interpreted.

21. For an exploration of such participation, see Turner et al. (1992), although we feel uncomfortable with its emphasis on vision (e.g. 'seeing' spirit manifestations) and the consequent lack of questioning of the 'evidence of the senses' (ibid.: 4).

22. We might add that the politics of representation of missiology and missionary ethnography – especially the relation between cultural relativism and political conservatism – is a little researched field in any case.

References

Appadurai, Arjun. 1995. 'The Production of Locality', in R. Fardon (ed.), *Counterworks: Managing the Diversity of Knowledge*. New York and London: Routledge.

Bayart, J.-F. 1989. *L'état en Afrique. La politique du ventre*. Paris: Fayart.

Castaneda, Carlos. 1968. *The Teachings of Don Juan*. New York: Ballantine edn, 1969.

Classen, Constance. 1993. *Worlds of Sense. Exploring the Senses in History and Across Cultures*. London and New York: Routledge.

Clifford, James. 1986a. 'Introduction: Partial Truths', in J. Clifford and G. Marcus (eds), *Writing Culture*. Berkeley: University of California Press.

— 1986b. 'On Ethnographic Allegory', in J. Clifford and G. Marcus (eds), *Writing Culture*. Berkeley: University of California Press.

Comaroff, Jean. 1985. *Body of Power, Spirit of Resistance*. Chicago and London: University of Chicago Press.

Comaroff, Jean and Comaroff, John. 1992. *Ethnography and the Historical Imagination*. Boulder, CO: Westview Press.

de Certeau, Michel. 1984. *The Practice of Everyday Life*. Berkeley: University of California Press.

Douglas, Mary. 1982. 'The Effect of Modernisation on Religious Change', *Daedalus* 111: 1–19.

Evans-Pritchard, Edward. 1962. 'Religion and the Anthropologists', in his *Essays in Social Anthropology*. London: Faber and Faber.

— 1976. *Witchcraft, Oracles and Magic among the Azande*. Abridged with an introduction by E. Gillies. Oxford: Clarendon Press, 1st edn, 1937.

Fabian, Johannes. 1983. *Time and the Other: How Anthropology Makes Its Object*. New York: Columbia University Press.

— 1990. *Power and Performance. Ethnographic Explorations through Proverbial Wisdom and Theater in Shaba, Zaire*. Madison: University of Wisconsin Press.

— 1991. 'Dilemmas of Critical Anthropology', in L. Nencel and P. Pels (eds), *Constructing Knowledge. Authority and Critique in Social Science*. London: Sage.

Favret-Saada, Jeanne. 1980. *Deadly Words: Witchcraft in the Bocage*. Cambridge: Cambridge University Press.

Fidaali, K. 1987. *Le pouvoir du Bangré. Enquête initiatique à Ouagadougou*. Paris: Presses de la Renaissance.

Fields, Karen. 1985. *Revival and Rebellion in Central Africa*. Princeton, NJ: Princeton University Press.

Flaherty, Gloria. 1992. *Shamanism and the Eighteenth Century*. Princeton, NJ: Princeton University Press.

Fluer-Lobban, C. 1991. *Ethics and the Profession of Anthropology*. Philadelphia: University of Pennsylvania Press.

Geschiere, Peter. n.d. *Le viande des autres. Sorcellerie et pouvoir au Cameroun*. Unpublished manuscript.

Gibbal, Jean-Marie. 1994. *Genii of the River Niger*. Chicago: University of Chicago Press; 1st edn (in French) 1988.

Ginzburg, Carlo. 1983. 'Morelli, Freud and Sherlock Holmes: Clues and Scientific Method', in U. Eco and T. A. Sebeok (eds), *The Sign of Three*. Bloomington and Indianapolis: Indiana University Press.

Hallencreutz, C. F. and Palmberg, M. (eds). 1991. *Religion and Politics in Southern Africa*. Uppsala/Stockholm: Almqvist and Wiksell.

Hollis, Martin and Lukes, Steven (eds). 1982. *Rationality and Relativism*. Oxford: Blackwell.

Howes, David. 1991. *The Varieties of Sensory Experience. A Sourcebook in the Anthropology of the Senses*. Toronto: University of Toronto Press.

Jackson, Michael. 1983. 'Knowledge through the Body', *Man* 18: 327–45.

Jay, Martin. 1993. *Downcast Eyes. The Denigration of Vision in Twentieth-century French Thought*. Berkeley, CA: University of California Press.

Jules-Rosette, Benetta. 1976. 'The Conversion Experience', *Journal of Religion in Africa* 7: 132–64.

— 1978. 'The Veil of Objectivity: Prophecy, Divination and Social Inquiry', *American Anthropologist* 80: 549–70.

Last, Murray and Chavunduka, Gordon. 1986. (eds). *The Professionalisation of African Medicine*. Manchester: Manchester University Press.

Lévi-Strauss, Claude. 1977. *Tristes Tropiques*. New York: Pocket Books; 1st edn, 1955.

Lewis, Ioan M. 1976. *Social Anthropology in Perspective. The Relevance of Social Anthropology*. Harmondsworth: Penguin.

Malinowski, Bronislaw. 1935. *Coral Gardens and Their Magic*, Vol. 2: *The Language of Magic and Gardening*. Bloomington: Indiana University Press.

Marcus, George and Fischer, Michael. 1986. *Anthropology as Cultural Critique*. Chicago: Chicago University Press.

Meyer, Birgit. 1992. '"If You are a Devil, Your are a Witch and if You are a Witch, You are a Devil," The Integration of "Pagan" Ideas in the Conceptual Universe of African Christians in Southeastern Ghana', *Journal of Religion in Africa* 22 (?): 98–131.

Ngada, Archbishop N. H. 1992. 'Politics and Healing in the African Zionist Churches', *Challenge*, February 1–3.

Olivier de Sardan, Jean-Pierre. 1988. 'Jeu de la croyance et "je" ethnologique: exotisme religieux et ethno-égo-centrisme', *Cahiers d'études africaines* 28: 527–40.

— 1989. 'Le réel des autres', *Cahiers d'études africaines* 29: 127–35.

— 1992. 'Occultism and the Ethnographic "I". The Exoticising of Magic from Durkheim to "Postmodern" Anthropology', *Critique of Anthropology* 12: 5–25.

Pels, Peter. 1993. *Critical Matters. Interactions between Missionaries and Waluguru in Colonial Tanganyika, 1930–1961*. PhD thesis. University of Amsterdam.

— 1994. 'Spiritual Facts: The Conversion of Alfred Russel Wallace', paper presented to Seminar, *Conversion*. Amsterdam: Centre for Religion and Society, June.

— and Nencel, Lorraine. 1991. 'Introduction: Critique and the Deconstruction of Anthropological Authority', in L. Nencel and P. Pels (eds), *Constructing Knowledge. Authority and Critique in Social Science*. London: Sage.

— and Salemink, Oscar. 1994. 'Introduction: Five Theses on Ethnography as Colonial Practice', *History and Anthropology* 8 (4).

Pietz, William. 1985. 'The Problem of the Fetish I', *Res.* 9: 5–17.

— 1987. 'The Problem of the Fetish II: The Origin of the Fetish', *Res.* 13: 23–45.

— 1988. 'The Problem of the Fetish IIIa: Bosman's Guinea and the Enlightenment Theory of Fetishism', *Res* 16: 105–23.

Pool, Robert. 1991a. 'Postmodern Ethnography?', *Critique of Anthropology* 11: 309–31.

— 1991b. '"Oh, Research, Very Good!": On Fieldwork and Representation', in L. Nencel and P. Pels (eds), *Constructing Knowledge. Authority and Critique in Social Science*. London: Sage.

Pratt, Marie Louise. 1985. 'Scratches on the Face of the Country, or: What Mr. Barrow Saw in the Land of the Bushmen', *Critical Inquiry* 12: 119–43.

— 1992. *Imperial Eyes. Travel Writing and Transculturation*. London and New York: Routledge.

Ranger, Terence O. 1972. 'Mchape and the Study of Witchcraft Eradication', paper presented to the Conference on the History of Central African Religious Systems. Lusaka.

Richards, Audrey. 1935. 'A Modern Movement of Witch-Finding', *Africa* 8 (4): 448–61.

Rosaldo, R. 1989. *Culture and Truth*. Boston: Beacon Press.

Schatzberg, M. G. 1993. 'Power, Legitimacy and Democratisation in Africa', *Africa* 63: 445–61.

Schoffeleers, Matthew. 1991. 'Ritual Healing and Political Acquiescence: the Case of the Zionist Churches in South Africa', *Africa* 60 (1): 1–24.

Schrijvers, Joke. 1991. 'Dialectics of a Dialogical Ideal: Studying Down, Studying

Sideways, and Studying Up', in L. Nencel and P. Pels (eds), *Constructing Knowledge. Authority and Critique in Social Science*. London: Sage.

Spencer, W. Baldwin and Gillen, Francis. 1899. *The Native Tribes of Central Australia.* (New York, 1968.)

Stewart, C. and Shaw, R. 1994. (eds). *Syncretism/Antisyncretism.* New York and London: Routledge.

Stocking, George W. 1971. 'Animism in Theory and in Practice: E. B. Tylor's Unpublished "Notes on Spiritualism"', *Man* 6: 88–104.

Stoller, Paul. 1989a. 'Speaking in the Name of the Real', *Cahiers d'études africaines* 29: 113–25.

— 1989b. *The Taste of Ethnographic Things. The Senses in Anthropology.* Philadelphia: University of Pennsylvania Press.

Stoller, Paul and Olkes, Cheryl. 1987. *In Sorcery's Shadow. A Memoir of Apprenticeship among the Songhay of Niger.* Chicago: University of Chicago Press.

Taussig, Michael. 1987. *Shamanism, Colonialism and the Wild Man.* Chicago: University of Chicago Press.

Tedlock, Dennis. 1987. 'Questions Concerning Dialogical Anthropology', *Journal of Anthropological Research* 43 (4): 325–47.

Turner, Edith with Blodgett, W., Kahona, S. and Benwa, F. 1992. *Experiencing Ritual. A New Interpretation of African Healing.* Philadelphia: University of Pennsylvania Press.

Tyler, Stephen A. 1984. 'The Vision Quest in the West, or What the Mind's Eye Sees', *Journal of Anthropological Research* 40: 23–39.

— 1986. 'Post-Modern Ethnography: From Document of the Occult to Occult Document', in J. Clifford and G. Marcus (eds), *Writing Culture*. Berkeley: University of California Press.

van Binsbergen, Wim. 1991. 'Becoming a Sangoma: Religious Anthropological Field-Work in Francistown, Botswana', *Journal of Religion in Africa* 29: 309–44.

van der Veer, Peter. 1994. *Religious Nationalism.* Philadelphia: University of Pennsylvania Press.

van Dijk, Rijk. 1992. 'Young Puritan Preachers in Post-Independence Malawi', *Africa* 62 (2): 159–81.

— 1993. 'Young Born-Again Preachers in Malawi: the Significance of an Extraneous Identity', in P. Gifford (ed.), *New Dimensions in African Christianity*. Ibadan: Sefer Books.

— forthcoming. 'Fundamentalism and Its Moral Geography in Malawi: the Representation of the Diasporic and the Diabolical', *Critique of Anthropology*.

Wallace, Alfred Russel. 1896. *Miracles and Modern Spiritualism.* London: George Redway; 1st edn, 1874.

Webb, James. 1974. *The Occult Underground.* La Salle: Open Court.

Wilson, Bryan (ed.). 1970. *Rationality.* Oxford: Blackwell.

Colonial and postcolonial identities

Terence Ranger

'Postcoloniality' has meant three main things. It has meant, first, the coming of Third World identities and spokesmen into the First World. As a leading 'postcolonial' theorist, Gyan Prakash, has written: 'The third world, far from being confined to its assigned space, has penetrated the inner sanctum of the first world ... arousing, inciting and affiliating with the subordinated others in the first world. It has reached across boundaries and barriers to connect with minority voices in the first world: socialists, radicals, feminists, minorities, etc.' (Prakash 1990: 403).

Hybridity – the cultural condition of Third World intellectuals in the West – is asserted to be the condition of all contemporary society. Old European national identities are undermined by the ludic play of ethnicity. White male chauvinist dominance is undermined by the deconstruction of gender and even sex.

'Postcoloniality' has also meant privileging particular methods and problematics so as to subvert the self-confident rationality of imperial science. In contemporary Africa and Asia expatriate scholars have to accept partnership or apprenticeship as a condition of doing research at all. But in any case these methods and problematics have proved attractive to many Europeans setting out to study Africa and Asia, who themselves want to forswear any imperial arrogance. The International Development Studies Centre at Roskilde University, for instance, has produced as the latest of its Occasional Papers, a volume on *Issues of Methodology and Epistemology in Postcolonial Studies*. Its editor, Signe Arnfred, is frank about her intention:

> Most of the researchers assembled at the seminar, as well as the majority of speakers, are in fact engaged in what would normally be called development studies. The point of introducing the term 'postcolonial studies' in this context is twofold: 1) to create a distance to 'mainstream' development studies, where epistemological reflections are not much developed, and 2) to stress the importance of researchers' awareness of history and of relations of power. (Arnfred 1985: 1)

Arnfred asserts that the concepts of 'existing social science – economics,

272 POSTCOLONIAL IDENTITIES IN AFRICA

sociology, social anthropology, etc. – are vastly inadequate' for grasping contemporary African and Asian realities. Their assumptions need to be deconstructed: an 'approach [which] has been especially fruitful in the hands of social groups previously not seen as producers of science, like first world women, and third world women and men'. The old colonial relations of dominance and authority need to be replaced by social science as dialogue, as participation, in which 'the researcher herself becomes an object for research' and 'the roles researcher/researched may be partially reversed'. New concepts must be developed to deal with worlds that do not exist sociologically merely because they have not been named, but which are there 'right in front of our noses'. Many such unnamed worlds are being explored – and named – by feminist researchers; others are being recovered by those working on consciousness and identity (Arnfred 1995: 1–11).

The third sense of 'postcolonial' is descriptive. It means the contemporary state of ex-imperial societies in Africa and Asia and also the attempts being made to describe them in ways which have meaning. The chapters in this book are admirable examples of 'postcolonial' studies in this sense. The Africa of this book is certainly recognisable, whereas Africa in all too many monographs and in the media is not.

Nevertheless, it seems to me that when one combines the three senses of 'postcoloniality' – assuming that to make sense of contemporary Africa involves adopting the problematics and methods of 'postcolonial theory' – a paradox arises. It is similar but not identical to the paradox described by Thomas Blom Hansen in his comments on 'postcolonialism' and the West. Hansen asks whether there really is any global political project linking Third World intellectuals with First World socialists, radicals, feminists and minorities:

> Is this really so ? Or are we merely experiencing a rebirth of good old Third Worldism dressed up as hybridity in the rather Western and universalist idiom of poststructuralism? I question the real intellectual advance of a political–intellectual construction like postcoloniality, being made in the name of historisation, which ultimately ends up with a highly generalising and sweeping statement about the state of the global intellectual–political struggle as structured along clear frontlines: The stubborn, Cartesian modernising elites of the West versus an emancipatory rainbow coalition of hybridised Third World people along with all kinds of metropolitan minorities. (Hansen 1995: 125)

Hansen thinks this essentialises the West to the point of caricature; that it ignores the Western romantic critique of Cartesianism; and that it projects 'a common hybridised future' which 'certainly militates against the quest for difference on which it is built'. It privileges categories of Western thought even while denouncing them, and dangerously allocates Africa and Asia to the realms of the romantic irrational.

The paradox with which I am concerned in this Postscript also springs from the making of an essentialised contrast; this time between colonial Africa and postcolonial Africa. There is no doubt, of course, that postcolonial theorists dislike colonialism and despise its social sciences. The colonial period was a time of distortion through power: power was used to force Africans into distorting identities; power relations distorted colonial social science, rendering it incapable of doing more than reflecting colonial constructions. But at the same time many postcolonialist accounts of contemporary Africa – some even in this book – oddly privilege colonialism.

In the context of the argument of 'post-coloniality' even scholars like Patrick Chabal and Filip De Boeck, whose work as a whole certainly does not attribute order and rationality to colonialism, can easily be misread. Thus when Patrick Chabal writes of contemporary 'great instability' and says that 'incompetence, greed and the lust for power have unleashed untold violence on ordinary men and women', there *seems* to be an unintended implied contrast with a period of relative stability and competence. Similarly Filip De Boeck writes of a contemporary 'breaking up ... of the "taken-for-granted" quality of a world that goes without saying for those who experience, live in and belong to it', which 'jeopardizes cohesive cultural systems and destroys embodied cultural identities'. When he adds that 'many people in Central Africa have no choice but to continue living in a world that is falling apart in front of their own eyes', there *seems* to be an unintended implied contrast with a previous period in which the world was *not* falling apart and *could* be taken for granted. Offered 'a collapsing African reality that grows more complex, chaotic and violent every day', Africans themselves might be forgiven for expressing a preference (as they often disconcertingly do) for the apparent authoritarian stabilities and disciplines of colonialism. Yet when Chinua Achebe wrote *Things Fall Apart*, it was the coming of colonialism rather than of postcolonialism that he was describing.

I believe myself – as I am sure Chabal and De Boeck also believe – that these dichotomies are misleading. I believe that colonialism was much less coherent, simple and lucid than such dualism suggests; I also believe that the modernising project, whether for good or ill, still has much life in it in postcolonial Africa. It seems to me that if one were to attack colonial societies with postcolonial problematics and methods one would come up with a very different picture of colonial realities – a picture that has very many similarities to and connections with postcolonial Africa.

The contributors to this book themselves suggest the need to break down the barriers between postcolonial Africa and its past. Chabal stresses the need to 'reconnect the present with the precolonial and colonial past'; De Boeck thinks that 'recent africanist academic discourse has perhaps too narrowly focused on the postcolonial situation' and that one ought to reach 'beyond the fractures inflicted by the postcolonial world' and to draw on 'precolonial sources'. Jessica Ogden insists on the connections between colonial and postcolonial images of urban women in Uganda. Nevertheless, the emphasis of this book, and very properly so, is on Africa in the present. It seems to me, therefore, worthwhile to consider the relation between colonial and postcolonial societies in a little more detail.

The first point, I think, is that so far from colonial identities being exclusively ascribed and monolithic, colonialism was an original and necessary source of hybridity, if we define that as a mix of First World and Third World cultures. (If we were to define hybridity as a mix of various African cultures then it had existed in Africa for hundreds of years.) Ulf Hannerz, author of several works on global hybridisation (Hannerz 1987; 1991; 1992) says that his 'own interest in creole culture was stimulated especially in connection with field work in Nigeria, and certainly creolization, in culture as in language, is particularly typical of what were colonial, and are by now more likely postcolonial situations' (Hannerz 1995: 36). As Jonathan Friedman writes, 'Creolization was once something that happened to the colonial others of the world, [but] now, in this age of fragmenting hierarchies, there is no longer an exemplary centre from which to view the other': creolisation has come home to the metropole (Friedman 1995: 22).

Hannerz remarks that the colonial power 'invented' Nigeria. My second point concerns the other great colonial 'invention': ethnicity. Inventing ethnicity *did* involve ascribing monolithic identities, and also involved tremendous upheaval and affront to the 'taken-for-granted' world. Many historians have described how under colonialism bounded ethnicities replaced previously much more fluid, multicultural and multilinguistic networks of interaction and identity.[1] But we have perhaps stressed too much the intellectual processes which underlay the production of ethnic units – the dialectic between colonial inventors and African imaginers – and not enough the great disruption involved in drastically narrowing down the African religious, social and economic world while at the same time enlarging the administrative and political.

I quote here one recent account of these disruptions because it deals with the Congo and thus provides a stimulating colonial background to De Boeck's postcolonial Zaire chapter. Kajsa Eckholm-Friedman and Anne Sundberg write:

> In pre-colonial times there were no 'ethnic groups'. They were formed during the colonial system ... In pre-colonial times there were independent political units in the Congo area, first larger kingdoms and then lesser chiefdoms. These units were dynamic constructions, some of which expanded at the expense of weaker units ... The expanding units incorporated individuals from other groups through the mechanism of slavery ... and the motor process was external trade.

As an immediate result, colonization led to a breakdown of the indigenous social order. The former political units disappeared, hierarchies broke down and people were forced to participate in the projects of the intruders. (Ekholm-Friedman and Sundberg 1995: 204)

After much turmoil, 'a reorganization occurred where older men, especially the various types of chiefs, re-established their dominance over other social categories by means of political relationships to the white sector and new types of economic translations. A new kind of indigenous society was formed and one of its characteristic features is the co-existence of different "ethnic groups".' (ibid.)

To this day, therefore, the southern Congo is divided into bounded ethnic groups, whose dominance is certainly not a result of postcolonialism rather than colonialism; nor is the influence of the Congo's 'uncaptured kings', whose power derives from the colonial ethnic reorganisation rather than from precolonial slave-based states.

Ekholm-Friedman has written of 'creation' as well as of 'catastrophe' in the Congo, the 'creation' being precisely the emergence of ethnicities (Ekholm 1991). Jan Vansina's magisterial survey of the whole equatorial region comes to very different conclusions. So far as he is concerned, colonial ethnicity, customary law and other invented 'traditions' represented the death of the true equatorial tradition of society and governance. The violence of early colonialism was disruptive enough; the 'new kind of indigenous society' formed during middle colonialism was yet more alienating, and decisively cut off postcolonial equatorial Africa from precolonial culture. Vansina writes:

As told by most history books ... it seems as if colonies sprang up complete in all details like mushrooms after a rainstorm. This view obscures the most important process that actually occurred: the conquest of equatorial Africa. It obscures its most important fact: that the conquest took 40 years to complete, that is, 40 years to destroy the equatorial tradition. It passes over the violence of an apocalyptic conquest. A combination of war, destruction by fire, disease and hunger finally succeeded in breaking overt African resistance by 1920, at the cost of an estimated half of the total population of the area. (Vansina 1990: 239)

Physical violence was accompanied by cultural violence. Colonial agents and missionaries destroyed 'most outward manifestations of the old tradition'; at the same time they 'first built their own cognitive view of rural African society and then imposed it on daily life before or during the 1920s. The only concession to the equatorial way of life was to preserve some cultural flotsam and jetsam, and to erect a structure called customary law, which was utterly foreign to the spirit of the former tradition. Customary law was the headstone on its grave' (ibid).

Thus, several decades before De Boeck's finding that things were falling apart in Zaire, 'the familiar old ways of life were reeling' and there was 'a tragic chasm between the physical and the cognitive realities'. 'New explanations and major adjustments' of the equatorial tradition were required, but they were not achieved. A Christian youth revolution ridiculed all tradition without being able to replace it: 'witchcraft now ran un-checked'. It all sounds very much like the postcolonial societies described in this book. Vansina concludes:

> The equatorial tradition finally died in the 1920s ... The conquest prevented the tradition from inventing new structures to cope with a new situation. Instead the colonial government invented them ... The whole structure made sense only in the cognitive world of the Europeans, not in the equatorial tradition ... The cognitive part of the old tradition, its very core, went into irreversible crisis. The peoples of the rainforests turned into cultural schizophrenics ... When independence loomed, insecurity exploded. The rural population sensed that there was no turning back to an unsullied age of ancient tradition. (Vansina 1990: 415)

This violent insecurity led to great outbursts of witch-finding: 'Variants of neo-African tradition were gestating in cities and the countryside.' And the transition to independence – to postcolonialism – took place 'without the guidance of a basic new common tradition'. Today, 'the people of equatorial Africa are still bereft of a common mind and purpose' (Vansina 1990: 48).

I have elsewhere questioned the deep pessimism of Vansina's view of the last seventy years in equatorial Africa.[2] Nevertheless, it is a much more convincing account of colonialism in equatorial Africa than either that given 'in most history books' or that implied by the colonial/post-colonial dichotomy. Other re-readings of colonial society also bring it closer to the postcolonial. Take, for instance, Richard Werbner's striking evocation of the wink as the postcolonial gesture *par excellence*. Yet the combined attitudes which produce the wink certainly existed in colonial Africa as well as in postcolonial. European imperial power, in its military and police manifestations, had to be taken very seriously. But at the same time European behaviour, ideas, dress, pomposity, mangling of African languages and ignorance of African societies, all made them ridiculous. The culturally creolised peoples of the East African coast, acute observers as they were of the minutest shifts of power in the Indian Ocean, responded to the rivalries of French and German and English and Scots with the mimicry of the *Beni* dances and parades. As dummy battleships were towed through the streets of Mombasa, or marchers dressed in the full ceremonial uniform of the House of Lords paraded through Lamu, European observers could not make up their minds whether these shows were a tribute to white power or a mockery of it. They were, in fact, both. During the First World War, that climactic display of absurd but

massive European power, the *Beni* societies spread throughout East and
Central Africa, and remained active in towns, mining compounds and
'tribal' rural areas for many decades. They combined the wink with the
strut (Ranger 1975).[3]

These counter-versions of colonialism have been produced by scholars
who have not set out to use 'postcolonial' problematics and research
methodologies. One might well ask what sort of accounts of colonial
society will be produced by scholars who *do* make use of them. Of course,
'postcolonial' anthropologists cannot go back into the past and carry out
dialogic or participatory fieldwork, but anthropologists are increasingly
turning to historical reconstruction (Marcus 1992). In doing so they make
use in one way or another of 'postcolonial' theory.

Take, for example, recent anthropological work on Kenya. Carolyn
Martin Shaw's recent book represents one way of doing 'postcolonial'
anthropology on colonial society. Its first motto is 'Put History First'. Its
very title – *Colonial Inscriptions. Race, Sex and Class in Kenya* – is eloquent of
its approach (Shaw 1995). Much of the book is an ethnography of
ethnography, deconstructing the work of W. Scoresby and Katherine
Routledge, Louis Leakey and Jomo Kenyatta. Its illustrations feature the
dust-jackets of other authors' books and advertisements for Kenyan coffee,
rather than photographs of Kikuyu men and women.

Shaw's introduction invokes postmodernism, which 'leaves me secure
in my sense that the social is temporal, mutable, contingent, fragmentary,
localized, multi-vocal, the process and product of decentred selves'. And
this is what her version of colonial Kenya is like. It appeals to discourse
theory which confirms that 'in discourse, knowledge of self, other and
society are created in and through the exercise of and resistance to power'.
It appeals to interculturality, which is 'somewhat like the invention of
tradition that characterizes nation-states made up of diverse ethnic groups'.
This leads her to adumbrate a notion of colonial hybridity: 'The notion
of interculturality recognizes the power differential between the colonizer
and the colonized, but also recognizes that arrows of influence may be
drawn from the colonized to the colonizers, and also that interaction with
the African people and landscape reshaped European ideas, attitudes and
practices' (Shaw 1995: 1–27).

The second motto of the book is 'Examine Race, Class, Gender and
Sexuality as conditions of social practice, belief and discourse'. So its
direct ethnographic contribution is contained in chapters entitled 'The
Production of Women: Kikuyu Gender and Politics at the Beginning of
the Colonial Era' and 'Kikuyu Women and Sexuality'. It is, in short, a
thoroughly 'postcolonial' account of colonial Kenya. And it is tantalisingly
interactive, with recent accounts by historians of Kenya: with John Lonsdale and Bruce Berman's work on Leakey and Kenyatta, for example, or
with Luise White's work on gender (Berman and Lonsdale 1991; White

1990). Yet I think there are more directly historical ways of writing 'postcolonial' accounts of colonial societies. A striking example is J. A. Fadiman's book, *When We Began, There Were Witchmen. An Oral History from Mount Kenya* (Fadiman 1993).

Fadiman's oral material was collected as long ago as 1969 and 1970 and then written up with the perspective of twenty years, so that it belongs to two different moments of Kenya's postcoloniality. It was collected in splendidly dialogic and submissive fashion:

> My tactic was to gather together what in the old days would have been called a 'warrior band', in this instance allowed by tradition to seek wisdom instead of war. I selected my research assistants from men of what would have been warrior age had warriorhood survived. Among this group my foreign background was less conspicuous and intimidating. As long as I was nothing more than one member of a band, Meru elders could still feel that they were teaching Meru youth. (Fadiman 1993: 8)

What emerges from Fadiman's listening is an account of conquest and disruption very different from earlier narratives of the 'establishment of the colonial administration', and an account of the making of the Meru as a self-conscious entity very different from Kenyan cultural nationalist histories of ethnic units over centuries. Fadiman's early colonialism is like Vansina's: a time of violence, disruption, disease and famine. His Meru are made through a multitude of small cultural transactions and a host of in-migrations to Mount Kenya. Colonial conquest brought a traumatic inversion of roles:

> Meru warriorhood began to die as the road emerged within the forests. The transformation of war leaders into chiefs and enforcers and their rank and file into manual labourers did far more to kill the military ethic than mere surrender without battle. For the first time in their history warriors of an entire generation were forced to take a role reserved for women, working as equals beside them and sharing identical punishment. (Fadiman 1993: 140)

'Senior warriors', men in their late twenties, became chiefs and headmen, an idea which 'initially horrified those chosen, since subordination to the elders had formed the core of Meru communal thought' (Fadiman 1993: 142).

One response to the falling apart of traditional things was a Christian youth revolution, in which boys grasped at the pleasure and power of learning to read; followed Christian fashions of dress and hairstyle; rejected warriorhood. They were mocked, jostled, beaten by youth who still clung to warrior tradition. On one occasion in 1913 five Christian boys were burned to death when their hut was fired. These cleavages and tensions came to their climax in the First World War:

> The second generation of colonialism is remembered as the time of Urogi, or

'witchcraft', when growing numbers of the conquered turned to the supernatural to bring some sense of comfort to their lives ... World War I reached Meru in mid-1915 ... Long lines of newly disarmed warriors were roped together and marched off to war [to be used as carriers]. By 1916 they began to return, emaciated, stumbling skeletons ... With them came the dysentery they had contracted while on the campaign. [It] broke out in every Meru region and among those of every age ... administrators began to record scores, then hundreds, and finally thousands of deaths ... In 1917–18 the rising tide of illness was intensified by famine. (Fadiman 1993: 256–60)

There followed cattle disease and the flu epidemic. These disasters triggered strife between age-sets and profound economic depression. The Meru 'plunged into despair': 'What remained, among men of the younger age-sets was a raging sense of betrayal, joined to feelings of rising despair as intense and poignant as those felt by their elders. For perhaps the first time in Meru history, neither the present nor the future offered hope' (Fadiman 1993: 264). The 1920s are remembered as a time of witch-finding and of secret societies, a time recorded vividly by Fadiman in three long chapters.

Once again Fadiman's colonialism is very different from that in 'most history books'; his witchcraft is very different from the versions offered by functionalist anthropology. Fadiman himself argues that the 1930s represented a 'golden age' of stability and unity. Under administrators sympathetic to 'custom' a 'fragile alliance, colonial and Meru, came to life'. This decade is closer to the model of colonialism implied by the contrast with 'postcolonialism'. But as he notes, 'the new era would be brief'. The alliance was an alliance of elders which did not include the young. In years to come some of them formed independent churches and schools; some took Mau Mau oaths; 'finally the peoples of Mount Kenya would revolt, and the men of Meru – driven apart by what would become a Gikuyu civil war – would fight on both sides, their tribal unity destroyed' (Fadiman 1993: 346).

This is a new kind of colonial history. There is much similar work in other parts of Africa. A rather different kind of reinterpretation is offered for colonialism in Zambia, for example, by Henrietta Moore and Megan Vaughan's superb *Cutting Down Trees* (Moore and Vaughan 1994). This begins with two chapters on 'The Colonial Construction of Knowledge' and then proceeds to offer a counter-understanding. It emerges from this book too that any colonial 'golden age' of stability was very brief. In this case it was based on a temporary alliance with young 'progressives' around the modernisation of African agriculture. This broke down as the young progressives became leaders of the mass nationalist movement. Moore and Vaughan convey brilliantly the ways in which colonial dynamics continued into the postcolonial period: migrant labour, *citemene* cultivation, the state's modernising programme of agrarian reform.

The message of the new anthropology and history, therefore, is twofold. Colonial Africa was much more like postcolonial Africa than most of us have hitherto imagined. And its dynamics have continued to shape postcolonial society. It is only when this message has been digested that we can establish what the real peculiarities of postcolonial Africa are.

Notes

1. My own most recent account of pre-ethnic identities and the transition to ethnicity is 'The Nature of Ethnicity: Lessons from Africa', which is to appear in a book edited by Edward Mortimer based on the Warwick Debates on 'Ethnicity, Nationalism and Statehood', held in October, November and December 1995.

2. I contrast Vansina's approach with that of Steven Feierman in *Peasant Intellectuals. Anthropology and History in Tanzania* (Feierman 1990). I write: 'For Vansina the pluralism of twentieth-century Africa implies the end of the great tradition and the inevitable impotence of modern African thought. But, for Feierman, pluralism is the essence of creativity ... Whereas for Vansina colonial imposition rendered traditional creativity impossible, for Feierman it was possible for peasant intellectuals creatively to select even while colonialism was imposing its deadening classifications' (Ranger 1993).

3. There are many parallels elsewhere in colonial Africa, perhaps the most striking being *Les Belges* of Katanga and *Le Sape* of Brazzaville, 'whereby young men from the Congo and Zaire ... systematically accumulate designer clothing, moving up the ranks of finery ... with clearly defined age classes and competitive cat-walking' (Friedman, 1995: 29). The work of Phyllis Martin on fashion and recreation in colonial Brazzaville provides an indispensable background to postcolonial studies of *Le Sape*.

References

Arnfred, Signe (ed.). 1995. *Issues of Methodology and Epistemology in Postcolonial Studies.* Roskilde: IDS.

Berman, Bruce and Lonsdale, John. 199.'John Louis Leakey's Mau Mau: a Study in Politics and Knowledge', *History and Anthropology* 5 (2): 143–209.

Ekholm, Kajsa. 1991. *Catastrophe and Creation: the Transformation of an African Culture.* London: Harwood.

Ekholm-Friedman, Kajsa and Sundberg, Anne. 1995. 'Ethnic War and Ethnic Cleansing in Brazzaville', in Kaarsholm (ed.), *From Post-Traditional to Post-Modern?*

Fadiman, Jeffrey. 1993. *When We Began, There Were Witchman. An Oral History from Mount Kenya.* Berkeley: University of California Press.

Feierman, Steven. 1990. *Peasant Intellectuals. Anthropology and History in Tanzania.* Madison: University of Wisconsin Press.

Friedman, Jonathan. 1995. 'Global System, Globalization and the Parameters of Modernity: Is Modernity a Cultural System', in Kaarsholm (ed.), *From Post-Traditional to Post-Modern?*.

Hannerz, Ulf. 1987. 'The World in Creolization', *Africa* 57: 546–59.

— 1991. 'Scenarios for Peripheral Cultures', in A. D. King (ed.), *Culture, Globalization and the World System.* London: Macmillan.

— 1992. *Cultural Complexity*. New York: Columbia University Press.

— 1995. 'The Social Organization of Creolization', in Kaarsholm (ed.), *From Post-Traditional to Post-Modern?*.

Hansen, Thomas B. 1995. 'Inside the Romanticist Episteme', in Arnfred (ed.), *Issues of Methodology*.

Kaarsholm. P. (ed.). 1995. *From Post-Traditional to Post-Modern? Interpreting the Meaning of Modernity in Third World Urban Societies*. Roskilde: IDS.

Marcus, George. 1992. 'Past, Present and Emergent Identities: Requirements for Ethnographies of Late Twentieth-century Modernity Worldwide', in S. Lash and J. Friedman (eds), *Modernity and Identity*. Oxford: Blackwell.

Moore, Henrietta and Vaughan, Megan. 1994. *Cutting Down Trees. Gender, Nutrition and Agricultural Change in the Northern Province of Zambia, 1890–1990*. London: James Currey.

Prakash, Gyan. 1990. 'Writing Post-Orientalist Histories of the Third World: Perspectives from Indian Historiography', *Comparative Studies in Society and History* 32 (1).

Ranger, Terence. 1975. *Dance and Society in Eastern Africa, 1890–1970. The Beni Ngoma*. London: Heinemann.

— 1993. 'The Invention of Tradition Revisited: the Case of Colonial Africa', in T. Ranger and O. Vaughan (eds), *Legitimacy and the State in Twentieth-Century Africa*. London: Macmillan.

Shaw, Carolyn. 1995. *Colonial Inscriptions. Race, Sex and Class in Kenya*. Minneapolis: University of Minnesota Press.

Vansina, Jan. 1990. *Paths in the Rainforests. Towards a History of Political Tradition in Equatorial Africa*. London: James Currey.

White, Luise. 1990. 'Bodily Fluids and Usufruct: Controlling Property in Nairobi, 1917–1939', *Canadian Journal of African Studies* 24 (3): 418–38.

Index

above, trope of, 96
accumulation, new forms of, 195–210
Achebe, Chinua, 273
administration, modern, 139
aeroplanes, magical, 200, 202, 203
aesthetics of power, 148–50
Africa: conquest of, 275; crisis of, 29–54; marginalisation of, 29, 34–6; re-traditionalisation of, 32–4; seen as unevolved, 48; written off, 46
African National Congress (ANC), 31, 138, 150, 151, 152, 155
Africanisation, political, 14
Africanists, 23, 29, 32, 40, 45, 49, 273
Africanness, 30, 31, 47, 264
Afrikaner Weerstandbeweging (AWB), 11, 157
Afrikaners, 156
agency, problematised, 14
agriculture, 33; in South Africa, 153
Ahmad, Aijaz, 7, 8
aid, definition of projects, 46
AIDS, 3, 18, 167, 176, 178, 181, 183, 187; campaigns against, 183; education about, 184, 185; effect on Kampala women, 167; research on, 173; testing, 125
Algeria, 37, 42
Alliance for Democracy (Aford) (Malawi), 110, 127
aLuund people, 15, 76, 84, 85, 88, 89, 90, 93, 97
ambivalence, 16
Amin, Idi, 174
Amselle, J. L., 98
Anderson, Benedict, 153
Angola, 31, 35, 36, 75, 76, 77, 85
animalisation of the other, 233–4
animality of spirits, 233
animism, 229
anthropologist: as migrant, 264; as voyeur, 251; immunising of, 256; trust of, 252

anthropology, 45, 151, 248; colonial, 21; hegemony of, 247; historiography of, 265; objectivity of, 252; of religion, 246, 247
anti-colonialism, 4, 114
apartheid, 136, 138, 142, 148, 149, 151, 158; end of, 141; modernism of, 141
Appadurai, Arjun, 245
Appiah, Anthony, 136, 137, 139, 140
Appiah, Kwame, 7
Arewa village, 222; spread of Islam in, 224–6
Armstrong, Richard, 111
Arnfred, Signe, 271–2
l'arrangement, 95
arziki, 225
Association of Traditional Healers (Cameroon), 213
Associations Sportives et Communales (Senegal), 71
aural sense, 255
authenticity, 88–90; return to, 80
autochthony, 154, 155, 156; myths of, 155
Azimayi Achikatolika, 123
Al Azmed, A., 226

Baba, healer, 198, 201, 202
backwardness, notion of, 45
Baganda women, 172
Bagayogo, 59
Bakhtin, M., 2, 6
Ball, D. W., 186
bamalaaya, 172, 173
banality of power, 2
Banda, Aleke, 112
Banda, Hastings, 8, 9, 107–35; ambiguity of home origins, 107; artificial history of, 111; as trickster, 10; as white man, 112; biographies of, 9; burial arrangements for, 107; challenges to authority of, 109; disbelief in biography of, 113;